W9-CQN-119

2002

LLEWELLYN'S

MOON SIGN

BOOK

With Lunar Forecasts by Gloria Star

Editor/Designer: Sharon Leah
Cover Design: Kevin R. Brown
Cover Art: Giovannina Colalillo
Special thanks to Leslie Nielsen
for astrological proofreading.
ISBN 0-7387-0031-2

LLEWELLYN WORLDWIDE
P.O. Box 64383 Dept. 0031-2
St. Paul, MN 55164-0383 U.S.A.

AND GARDENING ALMANAC

TABLE OF CONTENTS

Leisure & Recreation Section: How to Choose the Best Dates for Leisure & Recreation Activities   155

Animals and Hunting; Arts; Fishing; Friends; Parties (Hosting or Attending); Sports; Travel; Writing

Business & Legal Section: How to Choose the Best Dates for Business & Legal Activities   231

Advertising (in Print); Advertising (Electronic); Business, Education; Business, Opening; Business, Starting; Buying; Buying Clothing; Buying Furniture; Buying Machinery, Appliances, or Tools; Buying Stocks; Collections; Consultants, Working With; Contracts, Bid On; Copyrights/Patents, Apply for; Electronics, Buying; Electronics, Repair; Legal Matters; Loans; Mailing; Mining; New Job, Beginning; Photography, Radio, TV, Film, and Video; Promotions; Selling or Canvassing; Signing Papers; Staff, Fire; Staff, Hire; Travel; and Writing

Farm, Garden, & Weather Section: How to Choose the Best Dates for Farm, Garden, & Weather Activities   287

Animals and Breeding; Cultivating; Cutting Timber; Fertilize and Composting; Grafting; Harvesting Crops; Irrigation; Lawn Mowing; Picking Mushrooms; Planting; Pruning; Spraying and Weeding; and Weather

Gloria Star's Personal Lunar Forecasts

Moon Sign Book Contributors

2002

JANUARY

S	M	T	W	T	F	S
		1	2	3	4	5
6	7	8	9	10	11	12
13	14	15	16	17	18	19
20	21	22	23	24	25	26
27	28	29	30	31		

FEBRUARY

S	M	T	W	T	F	S
					1	2
3	4	5	6	7	8	9
10	11	12	13	14	15	16
17	18	19	20	21	22	23
24	25	26	27	28		

MARCH

S	M	T	W	T	F	S
					1	2
3	4	5	6	7	8	9
10	11	12	13	14	15	16
17	18	19	20	21	22	23
24	25	26	27	28	29	30
31						

APRIL

S	M	T	W	T	F	S
	1	2	3	4	5	6
7	8	9	10	11	12	13
14	15	16	17	18	19	20
21	22	23	24	25	26	27
28	29	30				

MAY

S	M	T	W	T	F	S
			1	2	3	4
5	6	7	8	9	10	11
12	13	14	15	16	17	18
19	20	21	22	23	24	25
26	27	28	29	30	31	

JUNE

S	M	T	W	T	F	S
						1
2	3	4	5	6	7	8
9	10	11	12	13	14	15
16	17	18	19	20	21	22
23	24	25	26	27	28	29
30						

JULY

S	M	T	W	T	F	S
	1	2	3	4	5	6
7	8	9	10	11	12	13
14	15	16	17	18	19	20
21	22	23	24	25	26	27
28	29	30	31			

AUGUST

S	M	T	W	T	F	S
				1	2	3
4	5	6	7	8	9	10
11	12	13	14	15	16	17
18	19	20	21	22	23	24
25	26	27	28	29	30	31

SEPTEMBER

S	M	T	W	T	F	S
1	2	3	4	5	6	7
8	9	10	11	12	13	14
15	16	17	18	19	20	21
22	23	24	25	26	27	28
29	30					

OCTOBER

S	M	T	W	T	F	S
		1	2	3	4	5
6	7	8	9	10	11	12
13	14	15	16	17	18	19
20	21	22	23	24	25	26
27	28	29	30	31		

NOVEMBER

S	M	T	W	T	F	S
					1	2
3	4	5	6	7	8	9
10	11	12	13	14	15	16
17	18	19	20	21	22	23
24	25	26	27	28	29	30

DECEMBER

S	M	T	W	T	F	S
1	2	3	4	5	6	7
8	9	10	11	12	13	14
15	16	17	18	19	20	21
22	23	24	25	26	27	28
29	30	31				

To Readers

If you are among the rapidly increasing numbers who believe that the universe is operated upon a well-defined plan wherein each individual has a chance to advance and achieve success according to his or her degree of understanding and effort put forth toward that objective . . . this BIG little book may truly be for you a guide to victory.

Llewellyn George

Much has changed in our world since those words appeared in the *Moon Sign Book* in 1948, but we have the same basic needs, desires, and concerns today as that generation did. We want to realize success and advance as the result of our efforts, too. It is possible to achieve many of the things we want in our lives by using the knowledge of cycles within our universe that has been accumulated through the millenniums by men and women who have observed the correlation between events in the heavens and those on Earth. Their observations inform us about the best times to undertake important events, but it's up to us to understand and incorporate the knowledge of universal cycles into our daily lives. The *Moon Sign Book* provides you with essential tools that you can use to reap the benefits of timing events based on lunar cycles and the cycles of planets.

While the Sun is indeed the origin and sustainer of life on Earth, the exposure of the Sun's light and heat alone would not offer the stimulus to change and growth as do the tides that respond to lunar influences. Using astrological knowledge in our everyday lives will nurture and support us, just as the lunar cycle supports the growth of all living things on Earth.

From the very beginnings of life, Earth's two companions in the sky—the Sun and the Moon—established two separate rhythms that continue to this day: the Sun with its pattern of heat and light, and the setting of the seasons; the Moon raising and lowering the water in and with which life is nourished.

Twice each lunar day (a 24.8-hour period), the tides are high; and twice each lunar month (29.5 days) at Full and New Moons, there are higher tides. With each rise of the water, there is a new stirring of life in the waters, and with each retreat of the waters, life is left behind on the shores for other creatures to consume—thus setting the basic patterns of growth and harvest.

About Almanacs

If you wish to plan by the Moon, it is important to know how the *Moon Sign Book* differs from most almanacs. Most almanacs list the placement of the Moon by the constellation. For example, when the Moon is passing through the constellation of Capricorn, they list the Moon as being in Capricorn. The *Moon Sign Book*, however, lists the placement of the Moon in the zodiac by sign, not constellation.

The zodiac is a belt of space extending out from the Earth's equator. It is divided into twelve segments of thirty degrees each. Each segment represents one of the signs of the zodiac and bears the name of a constellation. However, the constellations are not in the same place in the sky as the segment of space named after them. In other words, the constellations and the signs don't "match up."

For astronomical calculations, the Moon's place is given as being in a constellation; but for astrological purposes the Moon's place should be figured in the zodiacal sign, which is its true place in the zodiac, and nearly one sign different from the astronomical constellation. The *Moon Sign Book* figures the Moon's placement for astrological purposes.

For example, if the common almanac gives the Moon's place in the constellation Taurus, its true place in the zodiac is in the zodiacal sign of Gemini. Thus it is readily seen that those who use the common almanac may be planting seeds when they think that the Moon is in a fruitful sign, while in reality it would be in one of the most barren signs of the zodiac. To obtain desired results, planning must be done according to sign.

Some common almanacs confuse the issue further by inserting at the head of their columns "Moon's Sign" when they really mean "Moon's Constellation." In the *Moon Sign Book*, however, "Moon's sign" means "Moon's sign."

Tools for Timing

The *Moon Sign Book* contains five tools that can be used separately or in combination to help you achieve optimal results for your efforts. The first tool is our easy-to-use Astro Almanac, found on pages 19–27, which lists the best dates each month to begin important activities.

The dates provided are determined from the sign and phase of the Moon and the aspects the Moon makes to other planets. For example, the best time to apply for a new job would be when the Moon is in one of the earth signs of Taurus, Virgo, or Capricorn, and making favorable aspects to Jupiter or the Sun. If your personal Sun sign is involved, that's even better. However, when the Moon is in Capricorn you would want to avoid asking for a raise because those in positions of authority would not be as sensitive to your desires. (Capricorn energy can be very somber, conservative,

and structured.) To further increase the likelihood of getting the raise you seek, select a time between a New and Full Moon, the waxing phase.

While the dates in the Astro Almanac are approximate, you can fine-tune the timing of events by also taking into consideration your own Sun and Moon sign.

The Moon Tables and the Lunar Aspectarian/Favorable and Unfavorable Days Tables found on pages 34–57, the Gardening Dates Tables found on pages 302–309, and the Best Dates to Destroy Weeds and Pests on pages 310–311, make up the second set of tools. The Moon Tables list the day, date, time, sign, phase, and element (air, earth, fire, or water) the Moon is in; the Lunar Aspectarian gives the aspects of the Moon to other planets, and the Favorable and Unfavorable Days Tables take your Sun sign into consideration; the Gardening Date Tables provide dates and times for various gardening activities; and the last named table is useful for any occasion that calls for ridding yourself of unwanted circumstances, including garden pests, a bad relationship, or a bad habit, for example. New tables are compiled each year.

Of course, every day is important and brings its opportunities for doing good work, but some days are special days. By knowing the dates of favorable and unfavorable influences you have the opportunity to think before it's time to act, and to set a day in advance for any affair that will be most in keeping with the good results you desire. If you're unable to affect the timing of something, at the very least you will be aware of the potential energies, which will in turn afford you the chance to determine your actions ahead of time.

The *Moon Sign Book* offers you a third tool for working with lunar energies. The Personal Lunar Forecasts written by renowned astrologer Gloria Star tell you what is in store for you based on your Moon sign. This approach is different from Llewellyn's *Sun Sign Book*, which makes forecasts based on the Sun sign. While the Sun in an astrological chart represents the basic essence, or personality, the Moon represents the internal, or private you—your feelings, emotions, and subconscious. Knowing what's in store for your Moon can give you great insight for personal growth. If you don't know your Moon sign, you can figure it out using the Grant Lewi system outlined on page 65.

The fourth tool is informative articles on using the energy that is unique to each Moon. In addition to using the Moon's sign and phase to help you plant and maintain your garden, you can use the information to your advantage in your relationships at home, work, or place of business. The articles are written by people who successfully use the Moon to enhance their daily lives. We hope that they will enhance your knowledge about what the Moon can do for you, too.

A Note About Astrologers

Today, astrologers rely on ancient texts and incorporate new findings and research into their practice. However, astrology is an art, not a science. It is therefore possible for astrologers to vary, one from another, in their views and in the emphasis they chose to place on astrological components.

Understanding Lunar Astrology

The Moon's cycles and their correlation with everyday life are the foundation of the *Moon Sign Book*. By providing explicit tables and articles on the Moon's influence, we hope to bring a part of this valuable astrological knowledge within reach of everyone. Let us begin by looking at some basic astrological principles.

Everyone has seen the Moon wax and wane through a period of approximately twenty-nine and a half days. This circuit from New Moon to Full Moon and back again is called the *lunation cycle*. The cycle is divided into parts, called quarters

quarter is the time of germination, emergence, beginnings, and outwardly directed activity.

Second Quarter

The second quarter begins halfway between the New Moon and the Full Moon, when the Sun and Moon are ninety degrees apart. This half Moon rises around noon and sets around midnight, so it can be seen in the western sky during the first half of the night. The second quarter is the time of growth, development, and articulation of things that already exist.

Third Quarter

The third quarter begins at the Full Moon, when the Sun is opposite the Moon and its full light can shine on the full sphere of the Moon. The round Moon can be seen rising in the east at sunset, and then rising a little later each evening. The Full Moon stands for illumination, fulfillment, completion, drawing inward, unrest, and emotional expressions. The third quarter is a time of maturity, fruition, and the assumption of the full form of expression.

Fourth Quarter

The fourth quarter begins about halfway between the Full Moon and New Moon, when the Sun and Moon are again at ninety degrees, or square. This decreasing Moon

or phases. The astrological system of naming the lunar phases does not always correspond to systems used in other almanacs and calendars. It is therefore important to follow only the *Moon Sign Book* or Llewellyn's *Astrological Calendar* for timing events.

First Quarter

The first quarter begins at the New Moon, when the Sun and Moon are conjunct. (The Sun and Moon are in the same degree of the same sign.) The Moon is not visible at first, since it rises at the same time as the Sun. The New Moon phase is a time for new beginnings that favor growth, the externalization of activities, and the expansion of ideas. The first rises at midnight, and can be seen in the east during the last half of the night, reaching the overhead position just about as the Sun rises. The fourth quarter is a time of disintegration, drawing back for reorganization, and for reflection.

Signs and Influences

Today, due to the movement of our solar system around the galaxy of stars, the signs and constellations no longer coincide. Except for a few fixed stars, astrology does not deal with the stars or constellations at all. We are only concerned with the planets, including the Sun and Moon, and their positions in the signs of the zodiac. These signs are divided into different categories to help us better understand their natures.

Elements or Triplicities

Each of the signs is classified as either fire, earth, air, or water. These are the four basic elements. The fire signs Aries, Sagittarius, and Leo are action oriented, outgoing, energetic, and spontaneous. The earth signs Taurus, Capricorn, and Virgo are more stable, conservative, practical, and oriented to the physical realm. While air signs Gemini, Aquarius, and Libra are sociable, critical, and tend to respond with intellect rather than feeling. The water signs Cancer, Scorpio, and Pisces are emotional, receptive, intuitive, and can be very sensitive.

Qualities

Each sign is also classified as being either cardinal, mutable, or fixed. There are four signs in each quadraplicity, one sign of each element. The cardinal signs of Aries, Cancer, Libra, and Capricorn initiate action. The fixed signs of Taurus, Leo, Scorpio, and Aquarius maintain through stubbornness and persistence. The mutable signs of Pisces, Sagittarius, Gemini, and Virgo adapt to and tolerate situations.

Rulerships

Each planet has one or two signs in which its nature is particularly enhanced. These planets are said to "rule" these signs. The Sun rules Leo, the Moon rules Cancer, Mercury rules Gemini and Virgo, Venus rules Taurus and Libra, Mars rules Aries, Jupiter rules Sagittarius, Saturn rules Capricorn, Uranus rules Aquarius, Neptune rules Pisces, and Pluto rules Scorpio.

Nature and Fertility

Each sign is classified as either fruitful, semi-fruitful, or barren. This classification is the most important for *Moon Sign Book* readers, for the timing of most events depends on the fertility of the sign occupied by the Moon. The water signs—Cancer, Scorpio, and Pisces—are the most fruitful. The semi-fruitful signs are the feminine earth signs Taurus and

Capricorn, and the masculine air sign Libra. The barren signs are the masculine fire signs Aries, Leo, and Sagittarius; the masculine air signs Gemini and Aquarius, and the feminine earth sign Virgo.

The Moon in the Signs

Aries Moon

An Aries Moon has a masculine, dry, barren, fiery energy. It is an excellent time for starting things, but Aries lacks staying power. Use this assertive, outgoing sign for making changes, and for doing work that requires skillful, but not necessarily patient, use of tools. Things occur rapidly but also quickly pass. Aries rules the head and face.

Taurus Moon

A Taurus Moon personifies placid patience. The accent is on things that are long lasting and tend to increase in value. This is not a good time to seek change—especially in financial matters. While it is a good time to obtain a loan, bankers and others in charge of money are slow to make decisions. Things begun now tend to become habitual and hard to alter. Taurus rules the neck and throat.

Gemini Moon

A Gemini Moon favors intellectual pursuits and mental games over practical concerns. People are generally more changeable than usual.

Because Gemini is a barren sign and primarily mental it is not favored for agricultural matters, although it is an excellent time to prepare for activities. Gemini rules the hands, arms, lungs, and nerves.

Cancer Moon

A Cancer Moon stimulates rapport between people and sharpens sensitivity. With it comes a strong drive toward self-indulgence, especially with food and drink. Because Cancer is traditionally the most fertile of the signs, it is associated with mothering. It can be a time of personal warmth and friendship, supporting growth and nurturance. Cancer rules the breasts and stomach.

Leo Moon

A Leo Moon has a masculine, hot, dry, fiery, barren energy. The accent here is on showmanship, playful activity, romance, and entertaining. Leo types can be domineering and confident. It's an excellent time for charitable activities. Leo rules the heart and back.

Virgo Moon

A Virgo Moon is favorable for anything that requires painstaking attention, and for intellectual matters—especially those requiring exactness rather than innovation. Virgo is the sign of bargain hunting; and it's friendly toward agricultural matters with the greatest emphasis on harvesting vegetables. It is an excellent time to care for animals, especially training and veterinarian work. Virgo rules the intestines.

Libra Moon

A Libra Moon benefits anything that tends to beautify. Artistic work, especially involving color, is greatly enhanced in this sign. This Moon enjoys starting things of an intellectual nature, and because Libra is the sign of partnership and union, this transit can be good for forming partnerships of any kind, agreements, and negotiations. A Libra Moon accentuates teamwork—particularly teams of two. Libra rules the lower back and kidneys.

Scorpio Moon

A Scorpio Moon increases awareness of psychic power. Scorpio's energy is cold, fixed, and fruitful. This is the most intense sign, and when the Moon is here everything feels deeper—sometimes bordering on obsession. Now is a good time to do research, and to end connections thoroughly. Scorpio rules the sex organs.

Sagittarius Moon

A Sagittarius Moon encourages flights of imagination and confidence in the flow of life. Fiery, dry, and mutable, Sagittarius is the most

philosophical of signs. Candor is enhanced at this time, as is honesty. This is an excellent time to "get things off your chest." Now is a time for dealing with institutions of higher learning, publishing companies, and the law. It's also a good time for sport and adventure. Sagittarius rules the hips and thighs.

Capricorn Moon

A Capricorn Moon increases awareness of the need for structure, discipline, and organization. Institutional activities are favored, but this Moon sign should be avoided if you're seeking favors as those in authority can be insensitive under this influence. This is a good time to set goals and plan for the future, tend to family business, taking care of details requiring patience or a businesslike manner. Capricorn rules the knees, bones, and skin.

Aquarius Moon

An Aquarius Moon favors activities that are unique and individualistic. It's concerned for humanitarian issues, society as a whole, and seeks to make improvements. It promotes the gathering of social groups for friendly exchanges. People tend to react and speak from an intellectual rather than emotional viewpoint. Aquarius rules the calves and ankles.

Pisces Moon

A Pisces Moon favors withdrawal into the self, making this is an excellent time for retreat, meditation, sleep, prayer, or making that dreamed-of escape on a fantasy vacation. However, things are often not what they seem to be with the Moon in Pisces. Personal boundaries tend to be fuzzy. Pisces rules the feet.

Some Final Notes

We get a number of letters and phone calls every year from readers asking how to find certain information in the *Moon Sign Book* and how to use this information.

The best advice we can give is to read the entire introduction to each section. We provide examples using the current Moon and aspect tables so that you can follow along and get familiar with the process. At first, using the tables may seem confusing because there are several factors to take into account, but if you read the directions carefully and practice a little bit, you'll be a Moon sign pro in no time.

RETROGRADES

When the planets cross the sky they occasionally appear to move backward as seen from Earth. When a planet turns "backward" it is said to be retrograde. When it turns forward again, it is said to "go direct." The point at which the movement changes from one direction to another is called a station.

When a planet is retrograde, its expression is delayed or out of kilter with the normal progression of events. Generally, it can be said that whatever is planned during this period will be delayed, but usually it will come to fruition when the retrograde is over. Of course this only applies to activities ruled by the planet that is retrograde. Mercury retrogrades are easy to follow.

Mercury Retrograde

Mercury rules informal communications—reading, writing, and speaking; short errands or trips; and computers, for example. Whenever Mercury is retrograde, things ruled by Mercury tend to get fouled up or misunderstood. The general rule is: if Mercury is retrograde, avoid informal means of communication, or double-check everything twice.

Table of Retrograde Periods for 2002
(Times are listed in Eastern Standard Time)

Saturn	09/26/01	7:04 pm	02/07/02	8:33 pm
Jupiter	11/02/01	10:35 am	03/01/02	10:16 am
Mercury	01/18/02	3:52 pm	02/08/02	12:28 pm
Pluto	03/20/02	9:55 am	08/26/02	6:01 am
Neptune	05/13/02	7:10 am	10/20/02	8:53 am
Mercury	05/15/02	1:51 pm	06/08/02	10:12 am
Uranus	06/02/02	7:11 pm	11/04/02	1:27 am
Mercury	09/14/02	2:39 pm	10/06/02	2:28 pm
Venus	10/10/02	1:35 pm	11/21/02	2:12 am
Saturn	10/11/02	8:01 am	02/22/03	2:41 am
Jupiter	12/14/02	7:22 am	04/03/03	10:04 pm
Mercury	01/02/03	10:21 pm	01/22/03	8:08 pm

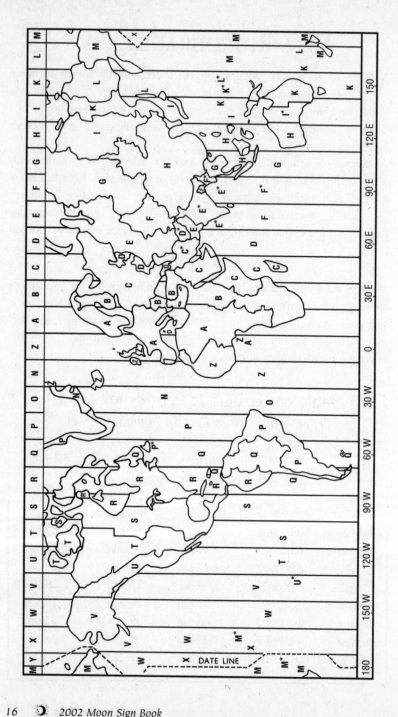

TIME ZONE CONVERSIONS
World Time Zones
(Compared to Eastern Standard Time)

(R)   EST—Used

(S)   CST—Subtract 1 hour

(T)   MST—Subtract 2 hours

(U)   PST—Subtract 3 hours

(V)   Subtract 4 hours

(V*) Subtract 4½ hours

(W)   Subtract 5 hours

(X)   Subtract 6 hours

(Y)   Subtract 7 hours

(Q)   Add 1 hour

(P)   Add 2 hours

(P*) Add 2½ hours

(O)   Add 3 hours

(N)   Add 4 hours

(Z)   Add 5 hours

(A)   Add 6 hours

(B)   Add 7 hours

(C)   Add 8 hours

(C*) Add 8½ hours

(D)   Add 9 hours

(D*) Add 9½ hours

(E)   Add 10 hours

(E*) Add 10½ hours

(F)   Add 11 hours

(F*) Add 11½ hours

(G)   Add 12 hours

(H)   Add 13 hours

(I)   Add 14 hours

(I*) Add 14½ hours

(K)   Add 15 hours

(K*) Add 15½ hours

(L)   Add 16 hours

(L*) Add 16½ hours

(M)   Add 17 hours

(M*) Add 17½ hours

Important!

All times given in the *Moon Sign Book* are set in Eastern Standard Time (EST). Use the time zone conversions chart and table to calculate the adjustment for your time zone. You must also adjust for Daylight Saving Time where applicable.

USING THE ASTRO ALMANAC

Llewellyn's Astro Almanac is a quick reference tool for finding the best dates for anything from asking for a raise to buying a car. The dates provided, which are approximate, are determined from the Moon's sign and phase, and the aspects to the Moon. We have removed dates that have long Moon void-of-course periods from the list. Although some of these dates may meet the criteria listed for your particular activity, the Moon void would nullify the positive influences of that day. We have not removed dates with short Moon voids, however, and we have not taken planetary retrogrades into account. To learn more about Moon void-of-course and planetary retrogrades, see pages 15 and 59–64.

We have also removed eclipse dates and days with lots of squares to the Moon. Like Moon voids, squares could nullify the "good" influences of a given day. Eclipses lend an unpredictable energy to a day. We have removed eclipse dates so that you may begin your activities on the strongest footing possible.

Another thing to bear in mind when using the Astro Almanac is that sometimes the dates given may not be favorable for your Sun sign, or for your particular interests. The Astro Almanac does not take personal factors into account, such as your Sun and Moon sign, your schedule, etc. That's why it is important for you to learn how to use the entire process to come up with the most beneficial dates for you. To do this, read the instructions under "Using the Moon Tables" (pages 28–33). That way, you can get the most out of the power of the Moon!

Astro Almanac

Activity	Jan.	Feb.	Mar.	Apr.	May	Jun.	Jul.	Aug.	Sep.	Oct.	Nov.	Dec.
Advertise in Print	11, 12	8, 9, 20	7, 9, 20	3, 4, 5, 15, 16, 17, 30	12, 13, 14	9, 10	6, 7, 8, 22, 23	3, 4, 18, 30, 31	15, 17	13, 23, 24, 25	8, 20, 21	5, 6, 17, 18
Advertise on TV, Radio, Internet	11, 12, 14, 15	8, 9, 10, 11, 20	7, 9, 10, 11, 19, 20	3, 4, 5, 6, 7, 16, 17, 30	2, 3, 4, 12, 13, 14	9, 10, 27, 28	6, 7, 8, 22, 23	3, 4, 18, 20, 30, 31	15, 17, 18, 19, 27	13, 14, 15	8, 10, 11, 20, 21	5, 6, 7, 8, 17, 18
Apply for Copyright or Patent	14, 15, 24, 25	10, 11, 20, 21	9, 10, 11, 20	6, 7, 16, 17, 18	3, 4, 13, 30, 31	1, 26, 27, 28	6, 24, 25	3, 4, 20, 21, 22, 30	1, 16, 17, 18, 26, 27, 28	14, 15, 24, 25	11, 20, 21	7, 8, 9, 17, 18, 19
Apply for Job or Promotion	21, 21, 23	17, 18	17, 18, 24, 25	3, 4, 22, 23	20, 21, 29, 30	16, 17, 24, 25, 26	4, 5, 13, 21, 22, 23	1, 2, 9, 10, 18, 19, 28, 29	7, 14, 15, 24, 25	3, 4, 11, 12, 13, 22, 31	8, 17, 27, 28	5, 6, 15, 16, 24, 25
Ask for Favors	21, 22	17, 18, 19, 24, 25	17, 18, 24, 25	13, 14, 15, 19, 20	17, 18, 19	13, 14, 15	11				17, 18, 19	14, 15, 16
Begin New Venture			15				21, 22, 23	18, 19, 20, 21	14, 15, 16	11, 12, 13, 14, 15	8, 10, 11	8, 9

Astro Almanac

Activity	Jan.	Feb.	Mar.	Apr.	May	Jun.	Jul.	Aug.	Sep.	Oct.	Nov.	Dec.
Bid on Contracts	24, 25	8, 9, 21, 22	7, 8, 20, 21	3, 4, 5, 15, 16, 17	1, 2, 12, 13, 28	10, 11, 25	21, 22	3, 4, 18, 19, 30, 31	1, 14, 15, 26, 27, 28	11, 12, 13 24, 25	7, 8, 9, 21, 22,	5, 17, 18, 19
Brewing	7, 8	3, 4	2, 3, 30, 31	9, 10, 27	5, 6	1, 2, 29, 30	8, 9, 26, 27, 28	5, 6, 23, 24	1, 2, 3, 30	26, 27	22, 23	1, 2, 20, 21
Buy Animals (sheep or smaller)	2, 3	26, 27	26, 27	22, 23	19, 20, 21	15, 16, 17	13, 14	9, 10	6, 7	3, 4, 30, 31	1, 27, 28	24, 25, 26
Buy Large Animals	10, 11, 16, 17, 18	5, 6, 12, 13	4, 5, 6, 12, 13	1, 2, 8, 9, 10, 28, 29, 30	5, 6, 7, 26	2, 8, 22, 23, 29, 30	19, 20, 21, 26, 27	16, 17, 23, 24	12, 13, 19, 20	9, 10, 16, 17, 18	5, 6, 7, 13, 14	4, 5, 10, 11, 31
Buy Antiques	24, 25	20, 21	19, 20, 21	15, 16, 17	12, 13, 14	9, 10	6, 7, 8	3, 4, 30	1, 2, 26, 27, 28	23, 24, 25	20, 21	17, 18, 19
Buy an Automobile	12, 24, 25	7, 8, 9, 20, 21, 22	7, 8, 19, 20, 21	3, 4, 15, 16, 17	12, 13, 14, 28, 29	9, 10, 11	6, 7, 8, 21, 22, 23	3, 4, 18, 19, 30, 31	14, 15, 26, 27, 28	11, 12, 23, 24, 25	8, 9, 20, 21	5, 6, 17, 18, 19

Astro Almanac

Activity	Jan.	Feb.	Mar.	Apr.	May	Jun.	Jul.	Aug.	Sep.	Oct.	Nov.	Dec.
Buy Permanent Home		17, 18, 19	17, 18	18, 19, 20, 21	15, 16, 17, 18	12, 13, 14, 15	10, 11, 12	5, 6, 7, 8, 9				
Buy Real Estate for Appreciation	18, 19, 20	15, 16, 17, 22, 23	14, 15, 16, 21, 22	18, 19, 24, 25	16, 22, 23	11, 12, 13, 18, 19	10, 11, 15, 16, 21, 22, 23	11, 12, 13, 17, 18, 19	14, 15	11, 12, 13	8, 9, 15, 16	5, 6, 13, 14
Buy Clothing	3, 4, 5, 6, 22, 23, 28, 30, 31	1, 2, 3, 17, 18, 19	1, 2, 17, 18, 26, 27, 28	14, 15, 23, 24, 25	10, 11, 12, 20, 21, 22, 23	7, 8, 16, 17, 18, 19	4, 5, 13, 14, 15, 16, 31	1, 10, 11, 12, 28, 29	6, 7, 8, 9, 24, 25, 26	3, 4, 5, 6, 21, 22, 31	1, 2, 3, 4, 18, 27, 28, 29, 30	15, 16, 24, 25, 26, 27
Cut Hair Decrease Growth	3, 4, 30, 31	11	9, 10, 11	5, 6, 7	3, 4, 30, 31	1, 9, 10, 26, 27, 28	6, 25, 29, 30	2, 3, 4, 30, 31	1	3, 4, 23, 24, 30, 31	1, 20, 21, 27, 28	24, 25
Cut Hair Increase Growth	18, 19	15, 16, 17	14, 15, 16	12	26	22, 23	19, 20, 21, 22, 23	15, 16, 17, 18, 19	12, 13, 14, 15	9, 10, 11, 12, 13, 18, 19, 20	5, 6, 7, 8, 9, 15, 16	4, 5, 6, 7, 12, 13, 14
Cut Timber	2, 3, 12, 13	7, 8, 9	7, 8	3, 4, 30	1, 2, 10, 11, 28, 29	6, 7, 8, 24, 25	4, 5, 6, 31	1, 2, 27, 28, 29, 30	24, 25, 26	3, 4, 5, 21, 22, 23, 31	1, 27, 28	24, 25

Astro Almanac

Activity	Jan.	Feb.	Mar.	Apr.	May	Jun.	Jul.	Aug.	Sep.	Oct.	Nov.	Dec.
Canning	7, 8	3, 4, 11, 12	2, 3, 12, 13, 30	8, 9, 10, 26, 27	5, 6	1, 2, 29, 30	9, 10, 26, 27	5, 6	1, 2, 3, 29, 30	26, 27	3, 4, 5, 22, 23, 24	1, 2, 3, 19, 20, 28, 29, 30
Collect Money	7, 8	3, 4, 5	30, 31	26, 27	24, 25, 26	20, 21	17, 18	13, 14, 15	10, 11	7, 8	4, 5	1, 2, 28, 29
Deal with Legal Matters	9, 10	5, 6	4, 5, 6	1, 2, 28, 29, 30	26, 27	22, 23	19, 20, 21	16, 17	12, 13	9, 10, 11	6, 7	3, 4, 30, 31
Dock, Dehorn Animals	14, 15	10, 11, 12	10, 11	6, 7, 13, 14, 16	11, 12, 13	7, 8, 9, 10, 11	5, 6, 7	2, 3, 4, 5, 31	1, 6	3, 4, 5, 6, 31	1, 2, 3, 4, 30	1, 2, 27, 28
End a Relation-ship	7, 8, 9, 10, 11, 12, 13	5, 6, 7, 8, 9, 10, 11	7, 8, 9, 10, 11	5, 6, 7, 11, 12	4, 5, 8, 9, 10, 11, 12	4, 5, 6, 7, 8, 9, 10	3, 4, 5, 6, 7, 8	2, 3, 4, 7, 8	4, 5, 6, 7	1, 2, 3, 4, 5, 6, 31	1, 2, 3, 4, 28, 29, 30	1, 2, 3, 4, 28, 29, 30, 31
Entertain	1, 23, 24, 25	1, 2, 21, 24, 25, 28	1, 19, 20, 24, 25, 28, 29	18, 20, 21, 24, 25	12, 13, 14, 17, 18, 19, 21, 22, 23	9, 10, 13, 14, 15, 18, 19	6, 7, 8, 11, 12, 15, 16	3, 4, 7, 8, 11, 12, 30, 31	4, 5, 8, 9, 26, 27, 28	1, 2, 5, 6, 7, 23, 24, 28, 29, 30	1, 2, 3, 20, 21, 25, 26, 29, 30	17, 18, 19, 23, 26, 27

Astro Almanac

Activity	Jan.	Feb.	Mar.	Apr.	May	Jun.	Jul.	Aug.	Sep.	Oct.	Nov.	Dec.
Extract Teeth	16, 17, 18, 24, 25	13, 14, 20, 21	19, 20, 21, 26	16, 17, 22, 23	13, 14, 20, 21	11, 12, 16, 17, 22, 23	13, 14, 19, 20	10, 11, 16, 17	12, 13, 19, 20	9, 10, 16, 17	6, 13	10, 11, 18
Fire Staff	7, 8, 9, 10, 11, 12, 13	5, 6, 7, 8, 9, 10, 11	7, 8, 9, 10, 11	5, 6, 7, 11, 12	4, 5, 8, 9, 10, 11, 12	4, 5, 6, 7, 8, 9, 10	3, 4, 5, 6, 7, 8	3, 4, 5, 6, 7, 8	4, 5, 6, 7	1, 2, 3, 4, 5, 6, 31	1, 2, 3, 4, 28, 29, 30	1, 2, 3, 4, 28, 29, 30, 31
Form Partnership	5, 6	1, 2, 28	1, 28, 29	24, 25	22, 23	18, 19	15, 16	11, 12	8, 9	5, 6	2, 3, 4, 29, 30	26, 27
Get Teeth Filled	1, 2, 7, 8, 29, 30	3, 4	3, 4, 12, 13, 30, 31	8, 9, 10, 27	6, 7	2, 3, 29, 30	26, 27, 28	23, 24, 28, 29, 30	4, 5, 24, 25	21, 22, 28, 29, 30	4, 5, 25, 26	1, 2, 23, 24, 28, 29, 30
Get Hair Perm	21	18, 19, 20	17, 18	14, 15	17, 18, 19		10, 11, 12	8, 9				
Hunt			4, 5, 6	1, 2, 3, 28, 29, 30	25, 26, 27, 28	22, 23, 24	1, 2, 3, 4, 19, 20, 21, 28, 29, 30, 31	15, 16, 17, 25, 26, 27	12, 13, 14, 21, 22, 23	9, 10, 11, 18, 19, 20, 21	5, 6, 7, 15, 16, 17	12, 13, 14

Astro Almanac

Activity	Jan.	Feb.	Mar.	Apr.	May	Jun.	Jul.	Aug.	Sep.	Oct.	Nov.	Dec.
Hire Staff	24, 25	20, 21, 26, 27, 28	19, 20, 21, 26, 27	16, 17, 22, 23	13, 14, 20, 21	11, 16, 17	14, 15	3, 4, 9, 10	6, 7	3, 4	1	17, 18
Join a Social Club	24, 25	20, 21	19, 20, 21, 28	15, 16, 17, 24, 25	12, 13, 21, 22, 23	19, 20	15, 16, 17	11, 12, 13, 20, 21	8, 9, 17, 18, 19	14, 15	11, 12	7, 8, 9, 17, 18
Move into a House		17, 18, 19	17, 18	18, 19, 20, 21	15, 16, 17, 18	12, 13, 14, 15	10, 11, 12	5, 6, 7, 8, 9				
Neuter or Spay Animals	9, 10, 11, 12, 16, 17, 18	6, 7, 8, 9, 13, 14	7, 8, 9, 12, 13	4, 8, 9, 10	5, 6, 7	3, 4						4, 31
Paint a Building	5, 6	1, 2, 28	1, 28, 29	24, 25	22, 23	18, 19	15, 16	11, 12	8, 9	5, 6	2, 3, 4, 29, 30	26, 27
Pour Concrete	1, 2, 28, 29	9, 10, 11	6, 7	3, 4, 30, 31	2, 3, 4, 30, 31	1, 7, 8, 27, 28	4, 5, 6, 24, 25, 26	1, 2, 28, 29	24, 25	1, 2, 21, 22, 28, 29, 30	25, 26, 27	22, 23

Astro Almanac

Activity	Jan.	Feb.	Mar.	Apr.	May	Jun.	Jul.	Aug.	Sep.	Oct.	Nov.	Dec.
Sell Items at a Garage Sale	11, 12, 13, 24, 25	8, 9, 10, 20, 21	7, 8, 19, 20, 21	3, 4, 15, 16, 17	1, 2, 12, 13, 14, 28, 29	9, 10, 24, 25	6, 7, 8, 22, 23	2, 3, 4, 18, 19, 20, 30, 31	1, 14, 15, 26, 27, 28	11, 12, 13, 23, 24, 25	8, 9, 20, 21, 22	5, 6, 7, 17, 18, 19
Sell Real Estate	12, 13, 26, 27	8, 9, 22, 23	7, 8, 22, 23	3, 4, 19, 30	1, 2, 15, 16, 28, 29	11, 12, 13, 24, 25, 26	9, 10, 22, 23	5, 6, 18, 19	1, 2, 3, 14, 15, 29, 30	11, 12, 13, 26, 27, 28	8, 9, 22, 23	5, 6, 20, 21
Set Fence Posts	1, 2, 29, 30	10, 11	9, 10, 11	5, 6, 7	3, 4, 5, 10, 11, 31	1, 7, 8, 27, 28	4, 5, 6, 25, 26, 27	1, 2, 28, 29	4, 5, 24, 25, 26	1, 2, 28, 29	25, 26	22, 23
Sign Contracts	4, 5	20, 21	1, 2, 19, 20, 21, 28, 29	16, 17, 24, 25	13, 14	10, 11, 18, 19	7, 8, 16, 17	3, 4, 11, 12, 13, 30, 31	1, 7, 8, 9	24, 25	2, 3, 20, 21, 29, 30	17, 18, 19, 26, 27
Start a Diet	4, 31	1, 28	28						5, 6	3, 4, 30, 31	1, 27, 28	5, 6, 25
Start Investing in Stocks	28, 29	24, 25, 26	24, 25	20, 21, 22	18, 19	14, 15	11, 12, 13		4, 5	1, 2, 28, 29, 30	25, 26	22, 23, 24

Astro Almanac

Activity	Jan.	Feb.	Mar.	Apr.	May	Jun.	Jul.	Aug.	Sep.	Oct.	Nov.	Dec.
Start Negotiations	5, 6	1, 2, 28	1, 2, 29	24, 25	22, 23	18, 19	15, 16	11, 12	8, 9	5, 6	2, 3, 4, 29, 30	26, 27
Start Remodeling a Building	18, 19, 26, 27	17, 18, 22, 23	14, 15, 16, 21, 22	18, 19	16, 22, 23	11, 12, 13, 18, 19	10, 11, 15, 16, 21, 22, 23	11, 12, 13, 17, 18, 19	14, 15	11, 12, 13	8, 9, 15, 16	5, 6, 13, 14
Start Roofing a Building			9, 10, 11	6, 7, 8	3, 4, 8, 9, 31	1, 4, 5, 6, 27, 28	1, 2, 3, 24, 25, 29, 30	26, 27 31	16, 17, 18, 22, 23, 27, 28			
Start a Savings Account	13, 21, 22, 23	17, 18, 19	17, 18	13, 14, 15	10, 11, 12	24	22, 23	18, 19	14, 15, 16	11, 12, 13	8, 9	5, 6, 7, 14, 15, 16
Stop a Bad Habit	1, 2, 3, 12, 13, 29, 30, 31	1, 6	4, 5, 6	10, 11, 12, 29	8, 9, 27, 28	4, 5, 6	1, 2, 4, 29, 30	3, 4, 7, 8, 25, 26, 30, 31	1, 4, 5, 6, 7, 21, 22, 26, 28	1, 2, 3, 4, 24, 25, 28, 29, 30, 31	1, 20, 21, 25, 26, 27, 28	4, 22, 23, 24, 25, 31
Train an Animal	3, 4, 24, 25, 31	20, 21	20, 27	16, 17	13, 14, 21	9, 10, 11, 15, 16, 17	6, 7, 8, 13, 14	3, 4, 10, 11, 31	1, 6, 7, 27, 28	3, 4, 24, 25, 31	1, 20, 21, 27, 28	17, 18, 24, 25

Astro Almanac

Activity	Jan.	Feb.	Mar.	Apr.	May	Jun.	Jul.	Aug.	Sep.	Oct.	Nov.	Dec.
Travel for Recre-ation/Fun	24, 25, 26	20, 21, 24, 25	19, 20, 24, 25	15, 16, 17, 20, 21	12, 13, 14, 17, 18, 19	13, 14, 15, 22, 23	11, 12, 19, 20	7, 8, 9, 15, 16, 17	12, 13	9, 10, 11	5, 6, 7	4, 5, 17, 18, 19
Travel Alone for Retreat	16, 17, 18	12, 13, 14	11, 12, 13	8, 9, 10	5, 6	1, 2, 3, 29, 30	26, 27	22, 23, 24	19, 20, 21	16, 17, 18	12, 13, 14	9, 10, 11
Visit Dentist	2, 3	26, 27	26, 27	22, 23	19, 20, 21	15, 16, 17	13, 14	9, 10	6, 7	3, 4, 30, 31	1, 27, 28	24, 25, 26
Visit Physician	2, 3	26, 27	26, 27	22, 23	19, 20, 21	15, 16, 17	13, 14	9, 10	6, 7	3, 4, 30, 31	1, 27, 28	24, 25, 26
Wean Children	11, 12, 13, 14, 15, 16, 17, 18	5, 6, 7, 8, 9, 10, 11, 12, 13, 14	5, 6, 7, 8, 9, 10, 11, 12, 13	1, 2, 3, 4, 5, 6, 7, 8, 9, 28, 29, 30	1, 2, 3, 4, 5, 6, 26, 27, 28, 29, 30, 31	1, 2, 3, 22, 23, 24, 25, 26, 27, 28, 29, 30	19, 20, 21, 22, 23, 24, 25, 26, 27, 28	16, 17, 18, 19, 20, 21, 22, 23, 24	12, 13, 14, 15, 16, 17, 18, 19, 20	9, 10, 11, 12, 13, 14, 15, 16, 17	6, 7, 8, 9, 10, 11, 12, 13, 14	3, 4, 5, 6, 7, 8, 9, 10,11
Work as a Volunteer	3, 4, 13, 14, 15, 30, 31	10, 11, 26, 27	9, 10, 11, 26, 27	5, 6, 7, 22, 23	3, 4, 19, 20, 21, 30, 31	1, 16, 17, 26, 27, 28	13, 14, 24, 25	9, 10, 20, 21, 22	6, 7, 8, 16, 17, 18	3, 4, 13, 14, 15, 30, 31	1, 10, 11, 27, 28, 29	7, 8, 9, 24, 25

USING THE MOON TABLES

Timing activities is one of the most important things you can do to ensure their success. In many Eastern countries, timing by the planets is so important that practically no event takes place without first setting up a chart for it. Weddings have occurred in the middle of the night because that was when the influences were best. You may not want to take it that far, but you can still make use of the influences of the Moon whenever possible. It's easy and it works!

In the *Moon Sign Book* you will find the information you need to plan just about any activity: weddings, fishing, making purchases, cutting your hair, traveling, and more. Not all of the things you do will fall on favorable days, but we provide the guidelines you need to pick the best day out of the several from which you have to choose. The primary method in the *Moon*

Sign Book for choosing your own dates is to use the Moon Tables that begin on page 34. Following are instructions, examples, and directions on how to read the Moon Tables; and more advanced information on using the Lunar Aspectarian and Favorable and Unfavorable Days Tables, Moon void-of-course, and retrograde information to choose the dates that are best for you personally.

To enhance your understanding of the directions given below, we highly recommend that you read the sections of this book called About Almanacs on page 7, Understanding Lunar Astrology on page 9, Retrogrades on page 15, and Moon Void-of-Course on page 58. It's not essential that you read these before you try the examples below, but reading them will deepen your understanding of the date-choosing process.

The Five Basic Steps

Step 1: Directions for Choosing Dates

Look up the directions for choosing dates for the activity that you wish to begin. The directions are listed at the beginning of the following sections of this book: Home, Health, & Beauty; Leisure & Recreation; Business & Legal; and Farm, Garden, & Weather. Check the Table of Contents to see in what section the directions for your specific activity are listed. The activities contained in each section are listed after the name of the section in the Table of Contents. For example, directions for choosing a good day for canning are listed in the Home, Health, & Beauty Section, and directions for choosing a good day to meet a new friend are in the Leisure Section. Read the directions for your activity, then go to step two.

Step 2: Check the Moon Tables

You'll find two tables for each month of the year beginning on page 34. The Moon Tables on the left-hand pages include the day and date, the sign the Moon is in, the element of that sign, the nature of the sign, the Moon's phase, and the times that it changes sign or phase. If there is a time listed after a date, that time is the time when the Moon moves into that zodiac sign. Until then, the Moon is considered to be in the sign for the previous day.

The abbreviation *Full* signifies Full Moon and *New* signifies New Moon. The times listed directly after the abbreviation are the times when the Moon changes sign. The times listed after the phase indicate when the Moon changes phase.

If you know the month you would like to begin your activity, turn directly to that month. You will be using the Moon's sign and phase information most often when you begin choosing your own dates. All times are listed in Eastern Standard Time (EST). Use the Time Zone Conversion chart and table on page 16–17 to convert time to your own time zone.

When you have found some dates that meet the criteria for the correct Moon phase and sign for your activity, you may have completed the process. For certain simple activities, such as getting a haircut, the phase and sign information is all that is needed. If the directions for your activity include information on certain lunar aspects, however, you should consult the Lunar Aspectarian. An example of this would be if the directions told you not to perform a certain activity when the Moon is square (Q) Jupiter.

Step 3: Check the Lunar Aspectarian

On the pages opposite the Moon Tables you will find the Lunar Aspectarian and the Favorable and Unfavorable Days Tables. The Lunar Aspectarian gives the aspects (or angles) of the Moon to the other planets. In a nutshell, it tells where the Moon is in relation to the other planets in the sky. Some placements of the Moon in relation to other planets are favorable, while others are not. To use the Lunar Aspectarian, which is the left half of this table, find the planet that the directions list as favorable for your activity, and run down the column to the date desired. For example, the Health & Beauty section says that you should avoid aspects to Mars if you are planning surgery. You would look for Mars across the top and then run down that column looking for days where there are no aspects to Mars (as signified by empty boxes). If you want to find a favorable aspect (sextile [X] or trine [T]) to Mercury, run your finger down the column under Mercury until you find an X or T. Adverse aspects to planets are squares [Q] or oppositions [O]. A conjunction [C] is sometimes beneficial, sometimes not, depending on the activity or planets involved.

Step 4: Favorable and Unfavorable Days Tables

The Favorable and Unfavorable Days Tables are helpful in choosing your personal best dates, because they consider your Sun sign. All Sun signs are listed on the right half of the Lunar Aspectarian Table. Once you have determined which days meet the criteria for phase, sign, and aspects for your activity, you can determine if those days are positive for you. To find out if a day is positive for you, find your Sun sign and then look down the column. If it is marked *F*, it is very favorable. If it is marked *f*, it is slightly favorable; *U* is very unfavorable; and *u* means slightly unfavorable. Once you have selected good dates for the activity you are about to begin, you can go straight to the examples section beginning on the next page. However, if you are up to the challenge and would like to learn how to fine-tune your selections even further, read on.

Step 5: Void-of-Course Moon and Retrogrades

This last step is perhaps the most advanced portion of the procedure. It is generally considered poor timing to make decisions, sign important papers, or start special activities during a Moon void-of-course period or during a Mercury retrograde. Once you have chosen the best date for your activity based on steps one through four, you can check the Void-of-Course Table, beginning on page 59, to find out if any of the dates you have chosen have void periods.

The Moon is said to be void-of-course after it has made its last aspect to a planet within a particular sign, but before it has moved into the next sign. Put simply, during the void-of-course period the Moon is "at rest," so activities initiated at this time generally don't come to fruition. You will notice that there are many void periods during the year, and it is nearly impossible to avoid all of them. Some people choose to ignore these altogether and do not take them into consideration when planning activities.

Next, you can check the Table of Retrograde Periods on page 15 to see what planets are retrograde during your chosen date(s).

A planet is said to be retrograde when it appears to move backward in the sky as viewed from the Earth. Generally, the farther a planet is away from the Sun, the longer it can stay retrograde. Some planets will retrograde for several months at a time. Avoiding retrogrades is not as important in lunar planning as avoiding the Moon void-of-course, with the exception of the planet Mercury.

Mercury rules thought and communication, so it is important not to sign papers, initiate important business or legal work, or make crucial decisions during these times. As with the Moon void-of-course, it is difficult to avoid all planetary retrogrades when beginning events, and you may choose to ignore this step of the process. Following are some examples using some or all of the steps outlined above.

Using What You've Learned

Let's say you need to make an appointment to have your hair cut. Your hair is thin and you would like it to look thicker. You look in the Table of Contents to find the section of the book with directions for hair care. You find that it is in the Home, Health, & Beauty section. Turning to that section you see that for thicker hair you should cut hair while the Moon is Full and in the sign of Taurus, Cancer, or Leo. You should avoid the Moon in Aries, Gemini, or Virgo. We'll say that it is the month of January. Look up January in the Moon Tables (page 34). The Full Moon falls on January 28 at 5:50 pm. The Moon moves into the sign of Leo January 28 at 3:31 am, and remains in Leo until January 30 at 3:40 am, so January 28 meets both the phase and sign criteria.

Let's move on to a more difficult example using the sign and phase of the Moon. You want to buy a permanent home. After checking the Table of Contents and finding the house purchasing instructions located in the Home, Health, & Beauty section under "House Purchasing," you'll read that it says you should buy a home when the Moon is in Taurus, Cancer, or Leo). You need to get a loan, so you should also look in the Business & Legal section under "Loans." Here it says that the third and fourth Moon quarters favor the borrower (you). You are going to buy the house in June. Look up June in the Moon Tables. The Moon is in the third quarter June 1, the fourth quarter June 2–9, and in the third quarter again June 25–30. The Moon is in Taurus from 7:07 EST on June 6 until 5:29 am June 9. The best days for obtaining a loan would be June 6–8, while the Moon is in Taurus.

Just match up the best signs and phases (quarters) to come up with the best dates. With all activities, be sure to check the Favorable and Unfavorable Days for your Sun sign in the table adjoining the Lunar Aspectarian. If there is a choice between several dates, pick the one most favorable for you (marked F under your Sun sign). Because buying a home is an important business decision, you may also wish to see if there are Moon voids or a Mercury retrograde during these dates.

Now let's look at an example that uses signs, phases, and aspects. Our example this time is starting new home construction. We will use February as the example month. Look in the Home, Health, & Beauty section under "Building." It says that the Moon should be in the first quarter of the fixed sign of Taurus or Leo. You should select a time when the Moon is not making unfavorable aspects to Saturn. (Good aspects are sextiles and trines, marked X and T. Conjunctions are usually considered good if they are not conjunctions to Mars, Saturn, or Neptune.) Look in the February Moon Table. You will see that the Moon is in the first quarter February 12–19. The Moon is in Taurus from 4:58 pm EST on February 17 through February 19. Now, look to the Lunar Aspectarian. We see that there are no squares or oppositions to Saturn during this time. In addition, there are no negative aspects to Mars on these dates. If you wanted to start building your house in February, the best dates would be February 18–19.

Use Common Sense!

Some activities depend on outside factors. Obviously, you can't go out and plant when there is a foot of snow on the ground. You should adjust to the conditions at hand. If the weather was bad during the first quarter, when it was best to plant crops, do it during the second quarter while the Moon is in a fruitful sign. If the Moon is not in a fruitful sign during the first or second quarter, choose a day when it is in a semi-fruitful sign. The best advice is to choose either the sign or phase that is most favorable when the two don't coincide.

To Summarize

In order to make the most of your activities, check with the *Moon Sign Book*. First, look up the activity under the proper heading, then look for the information given in the tables (the Moon Tables, Lunar Aspectarian, or Favorable and Unfavorable Days). Choose the best date considering the number of positive factors in effect. If most of the dates are favorable, there is no problem choosing the one that will fit your schedule. However, if there aren't any really good dates, pick the ones with the least number of negative influences.

January Moon Table

Date	Sign	Element	Nature	Phase
1 Tue.	Leo	Fire	Barren	3rd
2 Wed. 6:34 pm	Virgo	Earth	Barren	3rd
3 Thu.	Virgo	Earth	Barren	3rd
4 Fri. 8:23 pm	Libra	Air	Semi-fruitful	3rd
5 Sat.	Libra	Air	Semi-fruitful	4th 10:55 pm
6 Sun. 11:41 pm	Scorpio	Water	Fruitful	4th
7 Mon.	Scorpio	Water	Fruitful	4th
8 Tue.	Scorpio	Water	Fruitful	4th
9 Wed. 4:57 am	Sagittarius	Fire	Barren	4th
10 Thu.	Sagittarius	Fire	Barren	4th
11 Fri. 12:18 pm	Capricorn	Earth	Semi-fruitful	4th
12 Sat.	Capricorn	Earth	Semi-fruitful	4th
13 Sun. 9:41 pm	Aquarius	Air	Barren	New 8:29 am
14 Mon.	Aquarius	Air	Barren	1st
15 Tue.	Aquarius	Air	Barren	1st
16 Wed. 9:00 am	Pisces	Water	Fruitful	1st
17 Thu.	Pisces	Water	Fruitful	1st
18 Fri. 9:35 pm	Aries	Fire	Barren	1st
19 Sat.	Aries	Fire	Barren	1st
20 Sun.	Aries	Fire	Barren	1st
21 Mon. 9:47 am	Taurus	Earth	Semi-fruitful	2nd 12:47 pm
22 Tue.	Taurus	Earth	Semi-fruitful	2nd
23 Wed. 7:28 pm	Gemini	Air	Barren	2nd
24 Thu.	Gemini	Air	Barren	2nd
25 Fri.	Gemini	Air	Barren	2nd
26 Sat. 1:17 am	Cancer	Water	Fruitful	2nd
27 Sun.	Cancer	Water	Fruitful	2nd
28 Mon. 3:31 am	Leo	Fire	Barren	Full 5:50 pm
29 Tue.	Leo	Fire	Barren	3rd
30 Wed. 3:40 am	Virgo	Earth	Barren	3rd
31 Thu.	Virgo	Earth	Barren	3rd

January

Lunar Aspectarian | **Favorable and Unfavorable Days**

	Sun	Mercury	Venus	Mars	Jupiter	Saturn	Uranus	Neptune	Pluto	Aries	Taurus	Gemini	Cancer	Leo	Virgo	Libra	Scorpio	Sagittarius	Capricorn	Aquarius	Pisces
1						X		0	T	f	u	f		F		f	u	f		U	
2							0			f	u	f		F		f	u	f		U	
3	T		T		X	Q			Q		f	u	f		F		f	u	f		U
4		T		0							f	u	f		F		f	u	f		U
5	Q		Q		Q	T		T	X	U		f	u	f		F		f	u	f	
6							T			U		f	u	f		F		f	u	f	
7		Q				T		Q			U		f	u	f		F		f	u	f
8	X		X	T				Q			U		f	u	f		F		f	u	f
9		X				0		X		f		U		f	u	f		F		f	u
10							X		C	f		U		f	u	f		F		f	u
11				Q						f		U		f	u	f		F		f	u
12				0						u	f		U		f	u	f		F		f
13	C		C	X						u	f		U		f	u	f		F		f
14		C				T		C		f	u	f		U		f	u	f		F	
15							C		X	f	u	f		U		f	u	f		F	
16										f	u	f		U		f	u	f		F	
17					T	Q			Q		f	u	f		U		f	u	f		F
18	X		X	C							f	u	f		U		f	u	f		F
19				Q	X			X		F		f	u	f		U		f	u	f	
20		X					X		T	F		f	u	f		U		f	u	f	
21	Q		Q							F		f	u	f		U		f	u	f	
22		Q			X			Q			F		f	u	f		U		f	u	f
23						Q					F		f	u	f		U		f	u	f
24	T	T	T	X		C		T		f		F		f	u	f		U		f	u
25						T			0	f		F		f	u	f		U		f	u
26				Q	C					f		F		f	u	f		U		f	u
27										u	f		F		f	u	f		U		f
28	0	0	0	T			X	0		u	f		F		f	u	f		U		f
29								0	T	f	u	f		F		f	u	f		U	
30					X	Q				f	u	f		F		f	u	f		U	
31									Q		f	u	f		F		f	u	f		U

February Moon Table

Date	Sign	Element	Nature	Phase
1 Fri. 3:44 am	Libra	Air	Semi-fruitful	3rd
2 Sat.	Libra	Air	Semi-fruitful	3rd
3 Sun. 5:35 am	Scorpio	Water	Fruitful	3rd
4 Mon.	Scorpio	Water	Fruitful	4th 8:33 am
5 Tue. 10:21 am	Sagittarius	Fire	Barren	4th
6 Wed.	Sagittarius	Fire	Barren	4th
7 Thu. 6:08 pm	Capricorn	Earth	Semi-fruitful	4th
8 Fri.	Capricorn	Earth	Semi-fruitful	4th
9 Sat.	Capricorn	Earth	Semi-fruitful	4th
10 Sun. 4:15 am	Aquarius	Air	Barren	4th
11 Mon.	Aquarius	Air	Barren	4th
12 Tue. 3:53 pm	Pisces	Water	Fruitful	New 2:41 am
13 Wed.	Pisces	Water	Fruitful	1st
14 Thu.	Pisces	Water	Fruitful	1st
15 Fri. 4:26 am	Aries	Fire	Barren	1st
16 Sat.	Aries	Fire	Barren	1st
17 Sun. 4:58 pm	Taurus	Earth	Semi-fruitful	1st
18 Mon.	Taurus	Earth	Semi-fruitful	1st
19 Tue.	Taurus	Earth	Semi-fruitful	1st
20 Wed. 3:50 am	Gemini	Air	Barren	2nd 7:02 am
21 Thu.	Gemini	Air	Barren	2nd
22 Fri. 11:16 am	Cancer	Water	Fruitful	2nd
23 Sat.	Cancer	Water	Fruitful	2nd
24 Sun. 2:36 pm	Leo	Fire	Barren	2nd
25 Mon.	Leo	Fire	Barren	2nd
26 Tue. 2:47 pm	Virgo	Earth	Barren	2nd
27 Wed.	Virgo	Earth	Barren	Full 4:17 am
28 Thu. 1:47 pm	Libra	Air	Semi-fruitful	3rd

February

	Sun	Mercury	Venus	Mars	Jupiter	Saturn	Uranus	Neptune	Pluto	Aries	Taurus	Gemini	Cancer	Leo	Virgo	Libra	Scorpio	Sagittarius	Capricorn	Aquarius	Pisces
1		T		O	Q	T		T			f	u	f		F		f	u	f		U
2	T		T					T	X	U		f	u	f		F		f	u	f	
3		Q			T			Q		U		f	u	f		F		f	u	f	
4	Q		Q								U	f	u	f		F		f	u	f	f
5		X					Q				U	f	u	f		F		f	u	f	f
6	X			T		O		X	C	f		U	f	u	f		F		f	u	
7			X				X			f		U	f	u	f		F		f	u	
8				Q	O					u	f		U		f	u	f		F		f
9										u	f		U		f	u	f		F		f
10		C				T		C		u	f		U		f	u	f		F		f
11				X					X	f	u	f		U		f	u	f		F	
12	C		C					C		f	u	f		U		f	u	f		F	
13					T	Q					f	u	f		U		f	u	f		F
14									Q		f	u	f		U		f	u	f		F
15		X			Q	X		X			f	u	f		U		f	u	f		F
16				C					T	F		f	u	f		U		f	u	f	
17	X	Q					X			F		f	u	f		U		f	u	f	
18			X		X			Q			F		f	u	f		U		f	u	f
19								Q			F		f	u	f		U		f	u	f
20	Q	T				C		T			F		f	u	f		U		f	u	f
21			Q						O	f		F		f	u	f		U		f	u
22	T			X	C	T				f		F		f	u	f		U		f	u
23			T							u	f		F		f	u	f		U		f
24				Q						u	f		F		f	u	f		U		f
25		O					X	O	T	f	u	f		F		f	u	f		U	
26			T	X				O		f	u	f		F		f	u	f		U	
27	O		O		Q				Q	f	u	f		F		f	u	f			U
28				Q							f	u	f		F		f	u	f		U

March Moon Table

Date	Sign	Element	Nature	Phase
1 Fri.	Libra	Air	Semi-fruitful	3rd
2 Sat. 1:51 pm	Scorpio	Water	Fruitful	3rd
3 Sun.	Scorpio	Water	Fruitful	3rd
4 Mon. 4:55 pm	Sagittarius	Fire	Barren	3rd
5 Tue.	Sagittarius	Fire	Barren	4th 8:25 pm
6 Wed. 11:48 pm	Capricorn	Earth	Semi-fruitful	4th
7 Thu.	Capricorn	Earth	Semi-fruitful	4th
8 Fri.	Capricorn	Earth	Semi-fruitful	4th
9 Sat. 9:56 am	Aquarius	Air	Barren	4th
10 Sun.	Aquarius	Air	Barren	4th
11 Mon. 9:56 pm	Pisces	Water	Fruitful	4th
12 Tue.	Pisces	Water	Fruitful	4th
13 Wed.	Pisces	Water	Fruitful	New 9:03 pm
14 Thu. 10:34 am	Aries	Fire	Barren	1st
15 Fri.	Aries	Fire	Barren	1st
16 Sat. 11:01 pm	Taurus	Earth	Semi-fruitful	1st
17 Sun.	Taurus	Earth	Semi-fruitful	1st
18 Mon.	Taurus	Earth	Semi-fruitful	1st
19 Tue. 10:20 am	Gemini	Air	Barren	1st
20 Wed.	Gemini	Air	Barren	1st
21 Thu. 7:06 pm	Cancer	Water	Fruitful	2nd 9:28 pm
22 Fri.	Cancer	Water	Fruitful	2nd
23 Sat.	Cancer	Water	Fruitful	2nd
24 Sun. 12:12 am	Leo	Fire	Barren	2nd
25 Mon.	Leo	Fire	Barren	2nd
26 Tue. 1:44 am	Virgo	Earth	Barren	2nd
27 Wed.	Virgo	Earth	Barren	2nd
28 Thu. 1:04 am	Libra	Air	Semi-fruitful	Full 1:25 pm
29 Fri.	Libra	Air	Semi-fruitful	3rd
30 Sat. 12:21 am	Scorpio	Water	Fruitful	3rd
31 Sun.	Scorpio	Water	Fruitful	3rd

March

Lunar Aspectarian   Favorable and Unfavorable Days

	Sun	Mercury	Venus	Mars	Jupiter	Saturn	Uranus	Neptune	Pluto	Aries	Taurus	Gemini	Cancer	Leo	Virgo	Libra	Scorpio	Sagittarius	Capricorn	Aquarius	Pisces
1		T				T		T	X	U		f	u	f		F		f	u	f	
2				0	T		T			U		f	u	f		F		f	u	f	
3	T	Q						Q			U		f	u	f		F		f	u	f
4			T				Q				U		f	u	f		F		f	u	f
5	Q				0			X		f		U		f	u	f		F		f	u
6		X	Q				X		C	f		U		f	u	f		F		f	u
7				T	0					u	f		U		f	u	f		F		f
8	X									u	f		U		f	u	f		F		f
9			X	Q						u	f		U		f	u	f		F		f
10						T		C	X	f	u	f		U		f	u	f		F	
11		C					C			f	u	f		U		f	u	f		F	
12				X	T	Q					f	u	f		U		f	u	f		F
13	C								Q		f	u	f		U		f	u	f		F
14					Q						f	u	f		U		f	u	f		F
15			C			X		X	T	F		f	u	f		U		f	u	f	
16						X				F		f	u	f		U		f	u	f	
17		X		C	X			Q			F		f	u	f		U		f	u	f
18											F		f	u	f		U		f	u	f
19	X					Q					F		f	u	f		U		f	u	f
20		Q	X			C		T	0	f		F		f	u	f		U		f	u
21	Q					T				f		F		f	u	f		U		f	u
22			X	C						u	f		F		f	u	f		U		f
23		T	Q							u	f		F		f	u	f		U		f
24	T					X		0		f	u	f		F		f	u	f		U	
25			T	Q			0		T	f	u	f		F		f	u	f		U	
26				X	Q					f	u	f		F		f	u	f		U	
27		0		T					Q		f	u	f		F		f	u	f		U
28	0				Q	T		T				f	u	f		F		f	u	f	
29			0				T		X	U		f	u	f		F		f	u	f	
30					T			Q			U		f	u	f		F		f	u	f
31				0			Q				U		f	u	f		F		f	u	f

April Moon Table

Date	Sign	Element	Nature	Phase
1 Mon. 1:48 am	Sagittarius	Fire	Barren	3rd
2 Tue.	Sagittarius	Fire	Barren	3rd
3 Wed. 6:58 am	Capricorn	Earth	Semi-fruitful	3rd
4 Thu.	Capricorn	Earth	Semi-fruitful	4th 10:29 am
5 Fri. 4:07 pm	Aquarius	Air	Barren	4th
6 Sat.	Aquarius	Air	Barren	4th
7 Sun.	Aquarius	Air	Barren	4th
8 Mon. 3:57 am	Pisces	Water	Fruitful	4th
9 Tue.	Pisces	Water	Fruitful	4th
10 Wed. 4:40 pm	Aries	Fire	Barren	4th
11 Thu.	Aries	Fire	Barren	4th
12 Fri.	Aries	Fire	Barren	New 2:21 pm
13 Sat. 4:55 am	Taurus	Earth	Semi-fruitful	1st
14 Sun.	Taurus	Earth	Semi-fruitful	1st
15 Mon. 3:56 pm	Gemini	Air	Barren	1st
16 Tue.	Gemini	Air	Barren	1st
17 Wed.	Gemini	Air	Barren	1st
18 Thu. 1:01 am	Cancer	Water	Fruitful	1st
19 Fri.	Cancer	Water	Fruitful	1st
20 Sat. 7:20 am	Leo	Fire	Barren	2nd 7:48 am
21 Sun.	Leo	Fire	Barren	2nd
22 Mon. 10:35 am	Virgo	Earth	Barren	2nd
23 Tue.	Virgo	Earth	Barren	2nd
24 Wed. 11:22 am	Libra	Air	Semi-fruitful	2nd
25 Thu.	Libra	Air	Semi-fruitful	2nd
26 Fri. 11:15 am	Scorpio	Water	Fruitful	Full 10:00 pm
27 Sat.	Scorpio	Water	Fruitful	3rd
28 Sun. 12:13 pm	Sagittarius	Fire	Barren	3rd
29 Mon.	Sagittarius	Fire	Barren	3rd
30 Tue. 4:03 pm	Capricorn	Earth	Semi-fruitful	3rd

April

Lunar Aspectarian | **Favorable and Unfavorable Days**

	Sun	Mercury	Venus	Mars	Jupiter	Saturn	Uranus	Neptune	Pluto	Aries	Taurus	Gemini	Cancer	Leo	Virgo	Libra	Scorpio	Sagittarius	Capricorn	Aquarius	Pisces
1	T	T				0		X			U		f	u	f		F		f	u	f
2									C	f		U		f	u	f		F		f	u
3			T			0		X		u	f		U		f	u	f		F		f
4	Q	Q								u	f		U		f	u	f		F		f
5				T						f	u	f		U		f	u	f		F	
6			Q			T		C		f	u	f		U		f	u	f		F	
7	X	X		Q				C	X	f	u	f		U		f	u	f		F	
8			X		T						f	u	f		U		f	u	f		F
9						Q			Q		f	u	f		U		f	u	f		F
10				X							f	u	f		U		f	u	f		
11						Q	X	X		F		f	u	f		U		f	u	f	
12	C								T	F		f	u	f		U		f	u	f	
13		C			X		X				F		f	u	f		U		f	u	f
14			C					Q			F		f	u	f		U		f	u	f
15				C		Q				f		F		f	u	f		U		f	u
16						C		T		f		F		f	u	f		U		f	u
17	X							T	0	f		F		f	u	f		U		f	u
18		X			C					u	f		F		f	u	f		U		f
19			X							u	f		F		f	u	f		U		f
20	Q			X						f	u	f		F		f	u	f		U	
21		Q				X		0	T	f	u	f		F		f	u	f		U	
22	T		Q	Q		0					f	u	f		F		f	u	f		U
23		T			X	Q			Q		f	u	f		F		f	u	f		U
24			T	T							f	u	f		F		f	u	f		U
25					Q	T		T	X	U		f	u	f		F		f	u	f	
26	0							T			U		f	u	f		F		f	u	f
27						T		Q			U		f	u	f		F		f	u	f
28		0	0			Q				f		U		f	u	f		F		f	u
29				0		0		X	C	u	f	U		f	u	f		F		f	u
30								X		u	f		U		f	u	f		F		f

May Moon Table

Date	Sign	Element	Nature	Phase
1 Wed.	Capricorn	Earth	Semi-fruitful	3rd
2 Thu. 11:43 pm	Aquarius	Air	Barren	3rd
3 Fri.	Aquarius	Air	Barren	3rd
4 Sat.	Aquarius	Air	Barren	4th 2:16 am
5 Sun. 10:46 am	Pisces	Water	Fruitful	4th
6 Mon.	Pisces	Water	Fruitful	4th
7 Tue. 11:22 pm	Aries	Fire	Barren	4th
8 Wed.	Aries	Fire	Barren	4th
9 Thu.	Aries	Fire	Barren	4th
10 Fri. 11:32 am	Taurus	Earth	Semi-fruitful	4th
11 Sat.	Taurus	Earth	Semi-fruitful	4th
12 Sun. 10:04 pm	Gemini	Air	Barren	New 5:45 am
13 Mon.	Gemini	Air	Barren	1st
14 Tue.	Gemini	Air	Barren	1st
15 Wed. 6:33 am	Cancer	Water	Fruitful	1st
16 Thu.	Cancer	Water	Fruitful	1st
17 Fri. 12:52 pm	Leo	Fire	Barren	1st
18 Sat.	Leo	Fire	Barren	1st
19 Sun. 5:01 pm	Virgo	Earth	Barren	2nd 2:42 pm
20 Mon.	Virgo	Earth	Barren	2nd
21 Tue. 7:19 pm	Libra	Air	Semi-fruitful	2nd
22 Wed.	Libra	Air	Semi-fruitful	2nd
23 Thu. 8:38 pm	Scorpio	Water	Fruitful	2nd
24 Fri.	Scorpio	Water	Fruitful	2nd
25 Sat. 10:20 pm	Sagittarius	Fire	Barren	2nd
26 Sun.	Sagittarius	Fire	Barren	Full 6:51 am
27 Mon.	Sagittarius	Fire	Barren	3rd
28 Tue. 1:54 am	Capricorn	Earth	Semi-fruitful	3rd
29 Wed.	Capricorn	Earth	Semi-fruitful	3rd
30 Thu. 8:35 am	Aquarius	Air	Barren	3rd
31 Fri.	Aquarius	Air	Barren	3rd

May

Lunar Aspectarian **Favorable and Unfavorable Days**

Day	Sun	Mercury	Venus	Mars	Jupiter	Saturn	Uranus	Neptune	Pluto	Aries	Taurus	Gemini	Cancer	Leo	Virgo	Libra	Scorpio	Sagittarius	Capricorn	Aquarius	Pisces
1	T				O					u	f		U		f	u	f		F		f
2										u	f		U		f	u	f		F		f
3		T	T					C		f	u	f		U		f	u	f		F	
4	Q			T		T			X	f	u	f		U		f	u	f		F	
5		Q				C					f	u	f		U		f	u	f		F
6	X		Q	Q	T	Q			Q		f	u	f		U		f	u	f		F
7											f	u	f		U		f	u	f		F
8		X						X		F		f	u	f		U		f	u	f	
9			X	X	Q	X			T	F		f	u	f		U		f	u	f	
10							X			F		f	u	f		U		f	u	f	
11					X			Q			F		f	u	f		U		f	u	f
12	C					Q					F		f	u	f		U		f	u	f
13		C					T			f		F		f	u	f		U		f	u
14			C	C	C				O	f		F		f	u	f		U		f	u
15							T			u	f		F		f	u	f		U		f
16						C				u	f		F		f	u	f		U		f
17	X									u	f		F		f	u	f		U		f
18		X				X	X	O	T	f	u	f		F		f	u	f		U	
19	Q		X	X		O				f	u	f		F		f	u	f		U	
20		Q			X	Q			Q		f	u	f		F		f	u	f		U
21	T		Q	Q							f	u	f		F		f	u	f		U
22		T			Q	T		T	X	U		f	u	f		F		f	u	f	
23				T		T				U		f	u	f		F		f	u	f	
24			T		T			Q			U		f	u	f		F		f	u	f
25								Q			U		f	u	f		F		f	u	f
26	O	O						X		f		U		f	u	f		F		f	u
27					O	X			C	f		U		f	u	f		F		f	u
28			O	O						u	f		U		f	u	f		F		f
29					O					u	f		U		f	u	f		F		f
30		T								u	f		U		f	u	f		F		f
31	T					T		C	X	f	u	f		U		f	u	f		F	

June Moon Table

Date	Sign	Element	Nature	Phase
1 Sat. 6:37 pm	Pisces	Water	Fruitful	3rd
2 Sun.	Pisces	Water	Fruitful	4th 7:05 pm
3 Mon.	Pisces	Water	Fruitful	4th
4 Tue. 6:51 am	Aries	Fire	Barren	4th
5 Wed.	Aries	Fire	Barren	4th
6 Thu. 7:07 pm	Taurus	Earth	Semi-fruitful	4th
7 Fri.	Taurus	Earth	Semi-fruitful	4th
8 Sat.	Taurus	Earth	Semi-fruitful	4th
9 Sun. 5:29 am	Gemini	Air	Barren	4th
10 Mon.	Gemini	Air	Barren	New 6:46 pm
11 Tue. 1:15 pm	Cancer	Water	Fruitful	1st
12 Wed.	Cancer	Water	Fruitful	1st
13 Thu. 6:39 pm	Leo	Fire	Barren	1st
14 Fri.	Leo	Fire	Barren	1st
15 Sat. 10:23 pm	Virgo	Earth	Barren	1st
16 Sun.	Virgo	Earth	Barren	1st
17 Mon.	Virgo	Earth	Barren	2nd 7:29 pm
18 Tue. 1:11 am	Libra	Air	Semi-fruitful	2nd
19 Wed.	Libra	Air	Semi-fruitful	2nd
20 Thu. 3:42 am	Scorpio	Water	Fruitful	2nd
21 Fri.	Scorpio	Water	Fruitful	2nd
22 Sat. 6:42 am	Sagittarius	Fire	Barren	2nd
23 Sun.	Sagittarius	Fire	Barren	2nd
24 Mon. 11:01 am	Capricorn	Earth	Semi-fruitful	Full 4:42 pm
25 Tue.	Capricorn	Earth	Semi-fruitful	3rd
26 Wed. 5:36 pm	Aquarius	Air	Barren	3rd
27 Thu.	Aquarius	Air	Barren	3rd
28 Fri.	Aquarius	Air	Barren	3rd
29 Sat. 3:00 am	Pisces	Water	Fruitful	3rd
30 Sun.	Pisces	Water	Fruitful	3rd

June

Lunar Aspectarian   **Favorable and Unfavorable Days**

Day	Sun	Mercury	Venus	Mars	Jupiter	Saturn	Uranus	Neptune	Pluto	Aries	Taurus	Gemini	Cancer	Leo	Virgo	Libra	Scorpio	Sagittarius	Capricorn	Aquarius	Pisces
1							C			f	u	f		U		f	u	f		F	
2	Q	Q		T							f	u	f		U		f	u	f		F
3			T		T	Q			Q		f	u	f		U		f	u	f		F
4		X		Q							f	u	f		U		f	u	f		F
5	X		Q		Q	X		X	T	F		f	u	f		U		f	u	f	
6							X			F		f	u	f		U		f	u	f	
7				X				Q			F		f	u	f		U		f	u	f
8			X		X						F		f	u	f		U		f	u	f
9		C						Q			F		f	u	f		U		f	u	f
10	C					C		T	O	f		F		f	u	f		U		f	u
11							T			f		F		f	u	f		U		f	u
12				C	C					u	f		F		f	u	f		U		f
13		X	C							u	f		F		f	u	f		U		f
14								O	T	f	u	f		F		f	u	f		U	
15	X					X	O			f	u	f		F		f	u	f		U	
16		Q		X							f	u	f		F		f	u	f		U
17	Q				X	Q			Q		f	u	f		F		f	u	f		U
18		T	X					T		U		f	u	f		F		f	u	f	
19				Q	Q	T			X	U		f	u	f		F		f	u	f	
20	T		Q					T	Q		U		f	u	f		F		f	u	f
21				T	T						U		f	u	f		F		f	u	f
22		O	T			Q				f		U		f	u	f		F		f	u
23						O		X	C	f		U		f	u	f		F		f	u
24	O					X				u	f		U		f	u	f		F		f
25				O						u	f		U		f	u	f		F		f
26					O					f	u	f		U		f	u	f		F	
27		T	O					C	X	f	u	f		U		f	u	f		F	
28						T				f	u	f		U		f	u	f		F	
29	T					C					f	u	f		U		f	u	f		F
30		Q		T	Q				Q		f	u	f		U		f	u	f		F

July Moon Table

Date	Sign	Element	Nature	Phase
1 Mon. 2:49 pm	Aries	Fire	Barren	3rd
2 Tue.	Aries	Fire	Barren	4th 12:19 pm
3 Wed.	Aries	Fire	Barren	4th
4 Thu. 3:16 am	Taurus	Earth	Semi-fruitful	4th
5 Fri.	Taurus	Earth	Semi-fruitful	4th
6 Sat. 2:01 pm	Gemini	Air	Barren	4th
7 Sun.	Gemini	Air	Barren	4th
8 Mon. 9:36 pm	Cancer	Water	Fruitful	4th
9 Tue.	Cancer	Water	Fruitful	4th
10 Wed.	Cancer	Water	Fruitful	New 5:26 am
11 Thu. 2:08 am	Leo	Fire	Barren	1st
12 Fri.	Leo	Fire	Barren	1st
13 Sat. 4:41 am	Virgo	Earth	Barren	1st
14 Sun.	Virgo	Earth	Barren	1st
15 Mon. 6:39 am	Libra	Air	Semi-fruitful	1st
16 Tue.	Libra	Air	Semi-fruitful	2nd 11:47 pm
17 Wed. 9:13 am	Scorpio	Water	Fruitful	2nd
18 Thu.	Scorpio	Water	Fruitful	2nd
19 Fri. 1:02 pm	Sagittarius	Fire	Barren	2nd
20 Sat.	Sagittarius	Fire	Barren	2nd
21 Sun. 6:26 pm	Capricorn	Earth	Semi-fruitful	2nd
22 Mon.	Capricorn	Earth	Semi-fruitful	2nd
23 Tue.	Capricorn	Earth	Semi-fruitful	2nd
24 Wed. 1:40 am	Aquarius	Air	Barren	Full 4:07 am
25 Thu.	Aquarius	Air	Barren	3rd
26 Fri. 11:04 am	Pisces	Water	Fruitful	3rd
27 Sat.	Pisces	Water	Fruitful	3rd
28 Sun. 10:39 pm	Aries	Fire	Barren	3rd
29 Mon.	Aries	Fire	Barren	3rd
30 Tue.	Aries	Fire	Barren	3rd
31 Wed. 11:17 am	Taurus	Earth	Semi-fruitful	3rd

July

Lunar Aspectarian — **Favorable and Unfavorable Days**

	Sun	Mercury	Venus	Mars	Jupiter	Saturn	Uranus	Neptune	Pluto	Aries	Taurus	Gemini	Cancer	Leo	Virgo	Libra	Scorpio	Sagittarius	Capricorn	Aquarius	Pisces
1					T						f	u	f		U		f	u	f		F
2	Q							X	T	F		f	u	f		U		f	u	f	
3		X	T	Q	Q	X				F		f	u	f		U		f	u	f	
4							X	Q			F		f	u	f		U		f	u	f
5	X										F		f	u	f		U		f	u	f
6			Q	X	X			Q			F		f	u	f		U		f	u	f
7								T	0	f		F		f	u	f		U		f	u
8			X			C	T			f		F		f	u	f		U		f	u
9		C								u	f		F		f	u	f		U		f
10	C			C	C					u	f		F		f	u	f		U		f
11								0		f	u	f		F		f	u	f		U	
12						X			T	f	u	f		F		f	u	f		U	
13			C				0				f	u	f		F		f	u	f		U
14	X	X				Q			Q		f	u	f		F		f	u	f		U
15				X	X			T		U		f	u	f		F		f	u	f	
16	Q	Q				T			X	U		f	u	f		F		f	u	f	
17			X	Q	Q			T			U		f	u	f		F		f	u	f
18						Q					U		f	u	f		F		f	u	f
19	T	T		T	T			Q			U		f	u	f		F		f	u	f
20			Q					X	C	f		U		f	u	f		F		f	u
21						0	X			f		U		f	u	f		F		f	u
22			T							u	f		U		f	u	f		F		f
23						0				u	f		U		f	u	f		F		f
24	0	0		0				C		f	u	f		U		f	u	f		F	
25						T			X	f	u	f		U		f	u	f		F	
26							C			f	u	f		U		f	u	f		F	
27									Q		f	u	f		U		f	u	f		F
28			0		T	Q					f	u	f		U		f	u	f		F
29	T			T				X		F		f	u	f		U		f	u	f	
30		T							T	F		f	u	f		U		f	u	f	
31					Q	X	X			F		f	u	f		U		f	u	f	

August Moon Table

Date	Sign	Element	Nature	Phase
1 Thu.	Taurus	Earth	Semi-fruitful	4th 5:22 am
2 Fri. 10:46 pm	Gemini	Air	Barren	4th
3 Sat.	Gemini	Air	Barren	4th
4 Sun.	Gemini	Air	Barren	4th
5 Mon. 7:02 am	Cancer	Water	Fruitful	4th
6 Tue.	Cancer	Water	Fruitful	4th
7 Wed. 11:27 am	Leo	Fire	Barren	4th
8 Thu.	Leo	Fire	Barren	New 2:15 pm
9 Fri. 1:03 pm	Virgo	Earth	Barren	1st
10 Sat.	Virgo	Earth	Barren	1st
11 Sun. 1:38 pm	Libra	Air	Semi-fruitful	1st
12 Mon.	Libra	Air	Semi-fruitful	1st
13 Tue. 3:01 pm	Scorpio	Water	Fruitful	1st
14 Wed.	Scorpio	Water	Fruitful	1st
15 Thu. 6:25 pm	Sagittarius	Fire	Barren	2nd 5:12 am
16 Fri.	Sagittarius	Fire	Barren	2nd
17 Sat.	Sagittarius	Fire	Barren	2nd
18 Sun. 12:15 am	Capricorn	Earth	Semi-fruitful	2nd
19 Mon.	Capricorn	Earth	Semi-fruitful	2nd
20 Tue. 8:16 am	Aquarius	Air	Barren	2nd
21 Wed.	Aquarius	Air	Barren	2nd
22 Thu. 6:11 pm	Pisces	Water	Fruitful	Full 5:29 pm
23 Fri.	Pisces	Water	Fruitful	3rd
24 Sat.	Pisces	Water	Fruitful	3rd
25 Sun. 5:48 am	Aries	Fire	Barren	3rd
26 Mon.	Aries	Fire	Barren	3rd
27 Tue. 6:32 pm	Taurus	Earth	Semi-fruitful	3rd
28 Wed.	Taurus	Earth	Semi-fruitful	3rd
29 Thu.	Taurus	Earth	Semi-fruitful	3rd
30 Fri. 6:45 am	Gemini	Air	Barren	4th 9:31 pm
31 Sat.	Gemini	Air	Barren	4th

August

Lunar Aspectarian   **Favorable and Unfavorable Days**

Day	Sun	Mercury	Venus	Mars	Jupiter	Saturn	Uranus	Neptune	Pluto	Aries	Taurus	Gemini	Cancer	Leo	Virgo	Libra	Scorpio	Sagittarius	Capricorn	Aquarius	Pisces
1	Q			Q				Q			F		f	u	f		U		f	u	f
2		Q	T		X			Q			F		f	u	f		U		f	u	f
3	X							T		f		F		f	u	f		U		f	u
4				X		C			O	f		F		f	u	f		U		f	u
5		X	Q					T		u	f		F		f	u	f		U		f
6										u	f		F		f	u	f		U		f
7			X		C					u	f		F		f	u	f		U		f
8	C			C				O	T	f	u	f		F		f	u	f		U	
9		C				X	O			f	u	f		F		f	u	f		U	
10									Q		f	u	f		F		f	u	f		U
11			C		X	Q					f	u	f		F		f	u	f		U
12	X			X				T	X	U		f	u	f		F		f	u	f	
13				Q	T	T				U		f	u	f		F		f	u	f	
14		X						Q			U		f	u	f		F		f	u	f
15	Q			Q			Q				U		f	u	f		F		f	u	f
16			X		T			X	C	f		U		f	u	f		F		f	u
17	T	Q		T		O	X			f		U		f	u	f		F		f	u
18			Q							f		U		f	u	f		F		f	u
19		T								u	f		U		f	u	f		F		f
20					O					u	f		U		f	u	f		F		f
21			T					C	X	f	u	f		U		f	u	f		F	
22	O			O		T	C			f	u	f		U		f	u	f		F	
23									Q		f	u	f		U		f	u	f		F
24											f	u	f		U		f	u	f		F
25	O				T	Q		X			f	u	f		U		f	u	f		F
26			O					T		F		f	u	f		U		f	u	f	
27				T		X	X			F		f	u	f		U		f	u	f	
28	T				Q			Q			F		f	u	f		U		f	u	f
29							Q				F		f	u	f		U		f	u	f
30	Q	T		Q	X						F		f	u	f		U		f	u	f
31								T	O	f		F		f	u	f		U		f	u

September Moon Table

Date	Sign	Element	Nature	Phase
1 Sun.4:14 pm	Cancer	Water	Fruitful	4th
2 Mon.	Cancer	Water	Fruitful	4th
3 Tue. 9:36 pm	Leo	Fire	Barren	4th
4 Wed.	Leo	Fire	Barren	4th
5 Thu. 11:16 pm	Virgo	Earth	Barren	4th
6 Fri.	Virgo	Earth	Barren	New 10:10 pm
7 Sat. 10:57 pm	Libra	Air	Semi-fruitful	1st
8 Sun.	Libra	Air	Semi-fruitful	1st
9 Mon. 10:48 pm	Scorpio	Water	Fruitful	1st
10 Tue.	Scorpio	Water	Fruitful	1st
11 Wed.	Scorpio	Water	Fruitful	1st
12 Thu. 12:44 am	Sagittarius	Fire	Barren	1st
13 Fri.	Sagittarius	Fire	Barren	2nd 1:08 pm
14 Sat. 5:47 am	Capricorn	Earth	Semi-fruitful	2nd
15 Sun.	Capricorn	Earth	Semi-fruitful	2nd
16 Mon. 1:54 pm	Aquarius	Air	Barren	2nd
17 Tue.	Aquarius	Air	Barren	2nd
18 Wed.	Aquarius	Air	Barren	2nd
19 Thu. 12:18 am	Pisces	Water	Fruitful	2nd
20 Fri.	Pisces	Water	Fruitful	2nd
21 Sat. 12:11 pm	Aries	Fire	Barren	Full 8:59 am
22 Sun.	Aries	Fire	Barren	3rd
23 Mon.	Aries	Fire	Barren	3rd
24 Tue. 12:55 am	Taurus	Earth	Semi-fruitful	3rd
25 Wed.	Taurus	Earth	Semi-fruitful	3rd
26 Thu. 1:26 pm	Gemini	Air	Barren	3rd
27 Fri.	Gemini	Air	Barren	3rd
28 Sat.	Gemini	Air	Barren	3rd
29 Sun. 12:01 am	Cancer	Water	Fruitful	4th 12:03 pm
30 Mon.	Cancer	Water	Fruitful	4th

September

	Sun	Mercury	Venus	Mars	Jupiter	Saturn	Uranus	Neptune	Pluto	Aries	Taurus	Gemini	Cancer	Leo	Virgo	Libra	Scorpio	Sagittarius	Capricorn	Aquarius	Pisces
1			T	X		C	T			f		F		f	u	f		U		f	u
2	X	Q								u	f		F		f	u	f		U		f
3			Q							u	f		F		f	u	f		U		f
4		X			C			0	T	f	u	f		F		f	u	f		U	
5			X			X	0			f	u	f		F		f	u	f		U	
6	C			C					Q		f	u	f		F		f	u	f		U
7						Q					f	u	f		F		f	u	f		U
8		C			X			T	X	U		f	u	f		F		f	u	f	
9						T	T			U		f	u	f		F		f	u	f	
10			C	X	Q			Q			U		f	u	f		F		f	u	f
11	X						Q				U		f	u	f		F		f	u	f
12		X		Q	T			X				U		f	u	f		F		f	u
13	Q						X		C	f		U		f	u	f		F		f	u
14			X			0				f		U		f	u	f		F		f	u
15		Q		T						u	f		U		f	u	f		F		f
16	T									u	f		U		f	u	f		F		f
17		T	Q		0			C	X	f	u	f		U		f	u	f		F	
18						T	C			f	u	f		U		f	u	f		F	
19			T							f	u	f		U		f	u	f		F	
20				0					Q		f	u	f		U		f	u	f		F
21	0					Q					f	u	f		U		f	u	f		F
22		0			T			X	T	F		f	u	f		U		f	u	f	
23						X	X			F		f	u	f		U		f	u	f	
24					Q			Q		F		f	u	f		U		f	u	f	
25			0	T							F		f	u	f		U		f	u	f
26	T	T						Q			F		f	u	f		U		f	u	f
27					X			T	0	f		F		f	u	f		U		f	u
28				Q		C	T			f		F		f	u	f		U		f	u
29	Q	Q								f		F		f	u	f		U		f	u
30			T	X						u	f		F		f	u	f		U		f

October Moon Table

Date	Sign	Element	Nature	Phase
1 Tue. 6:58 am	Leo	Fire	Barren	4th
2 Wed.	Leo	Fire	Barren	4th
3 Thu. 9:52 am	Virgo	Earth	Barren	4th
4 Fri.	Virgo	Earth	Barren	4th
5 Sat. 9:51 am	Libra	Air	Semi-fruitful	4th
6 Sun.	Libra	Air	Semi-fruitful	New 6:18 am
7 Mon. 8:57 am	Scorpio	Water	Fruitful	1st
8 Tue.	Scorpio	Water	Fruitful	1st
9 Wed. 9:21 am	Sagittarius	Fire	Barren	1st
10 Thu.	Sagittarius	Fire	Barren	1st
11 Fri. 12:45 pm	Capricorn	Earth	Semi-fruitful	1st
12 Sat.	Capricorn	Earth	Semi-fruitful	1st
13 Sun. 7:51 pm	Aquarius	Air	Barren	2nd 12:33 am
14 Mon.	Aquarius	Air	Barren	2nd
15 Tue.	Aquarius	Air	Barren	2nd
16 Wed. 6:07 am	Pisces	Water	Fruitful	2nd
17 Thu.	Pisces	Water	Fruitful	2nd
18 Fri. 6:13 pm	Aries	Fire	Barren	2nd
19 Sat.	Aries	Fire	Barren	2nd
20 Sun.	Aries	Fire	Barren	2nd
21 Mon. 6:57 am	Taurus	Earth	Semi-fruitful	Full 2:20 am
22 Tue.	Taurus	Earth	Semi-fruitful	3rd
23 Wed. 7:17 pm	Gemini	Air	Barren	3rd
24 Thu.	Gemini	Air	Barren	3rd
25 Fri.	Gemini	Air	Barren	3rd
26 Sat. 6:10 am	Cancer	Water	Fruitful	3rd
27 Sun.	Cancer	Water	Fruitful	3rd
28 Mon. 2:20 pm	Leo	Fire	Barren	3rd
29 Tue.	Leo	Fire	Barren	4th 12:28 am
30 Wed. 6:59 pm	Virgo	Earth	Barren	4th
31 Thu.	Virgo	Earth	Barren	4th

October

Lunar Aspectarian   **Favorable and Unfavorable Days**

Day	Sun	Mercury	Venus	Mars	Jupiter	Saturn	Uranus	Neptune	Pluto	Aries	Taurus	Gemini	Cancer	Leo	Virgo	Libra	Scorpio	Sagittarius	Capricorn	Aquarius	Pisces
1	X	X						0		u	f		F		f	u	f		U		f
2			Q		C				T	f	u	f		F		f	u	f		U	
3							X	0		f	u	f		F		f	u	f		U	
4				X	C				Q		f	u	f		F		f	u	f		U
5		C				Q	T				f	u	f		F		f	u	f		U
6	C				X				X	U		f	u	f		F		f	u	f	
7						T	T	Q		U		f	u	f		F		f	u	f	
8			C		Q						U		f	u	f		F		f	u	f
9		X		X			Q	X			U		f	u	f		F		f	u	f
10	X				T				C	f		U		f	u	f		F		f	u
11		Q		Q		0	X			f		U		f	u	f		F		f	u
12			X							u	f		U		f	u	f		F		f
13	Q			T						u	f		U		f	u	f		F		f
14		T			0			C		f	u	f		U		f	u	f		F	
15	T		Q				C		X	f	u	f		U		f	u	f		F	
16						T				f	u	f		U		f	u	f		F	
17			T						Q		f	u	f		U		f	u	f		F
18				0		Q					f	u	f		U		f	u	f		F
19		0						X		F		f	u	f		U		f	u	f	
20					T		X		T	F		f	u	f		U		f	u	f	
21	0				X		Q			F		f	u	f		U		f	u	f	
22			0		Q						F		f	u	f		U		f	u	f
23						Q					F		f	u	f		U		f	u	f
24				T				T		f		F		f	u	f		U		f	u
25		T			X		T		0	f		F		f	u	f		U		f	u
26	T			Q	C					f		F		f	u	f		U		f	u
27			T							u	f		F		f	u	f		U		f
28		Q								u	f		F		f	u	f		U		f
29	Q			Q	X	C		0	T	f	u	f		F		f	u	f		U	
30		X					X	0		f	u	f		F		f	u	f		U	
31	X			X					Q	f	u	f		F		f	u	f		U	

November Moon Table

Date	Sign	Element	Nature	Phase
1 Fri. 8:28 pm	Libra	Air	Semi-fruitful	4th
2 Sat.	Libra	Air	Semi-fruitful	4th
3 Sun. 8:10 pm	Scorpio	Water	Fruitful	4th
4 Mon.	Scorpio	Water	Fruitful	New 3:34 pm
5 Tue. 8:01 pm	Sagittarius	Fire	Barren	1st
6 Wed.	Sagittarius	Fire	Barren	1st
7 Thu. 9:59 pm	Capricorn	Earth	Semi-fruitful	1st
8 Fri.	Capricorn	Earth	Semi-fruitful	1st
9 Sat.	Capricorn	Earth	Semi-fruitful	1st
10 Sun. 3:27 am	Aquarius	Air	Barren	1st
11 Mon.	Aquarius	Air	Barren	2nd 3:52 pm
12 Tue. 12:42 pm	Pisces	Water	Fruitful	2nd
13 Wed.	Pisces	Water	Fruitful	2nd
14 Thu.	Pisces	Water	Fruitful	2nd
15 Fri. 12:38 am	Aries	Fire	Barren	2nd
16 Sat.	Aries	Fire	Barren	2nd
17 Sun. 1:23 pm	Taurus	Earth	Semi-fruitful	2nd
18 Mon.	Taurus	Earth	Semi-fruitful	2nd
19 Tue.	Taurus	Earth	Semi-fruitful	Full 8:34 pm
20 Wed. 1:25 am	Gemini	Air	Barren	3rd
21 Thu.	Gemini	Air	Barren	3rd
22 Fri. 11:48 am	Cancer	Water	Fruitful	3rd
23 Sat.	Cancer	Water	Fruitful	3rd
24 Sun. 8:00 pm	Leo	Fire	Barren	3rd
25 Mon.	Leo	Fire	Barren	3rd
26 Tue.	Leo	Fire	Barren	3rd
27 Wed. 1:42 am	Virgo	Earth	Barren	4th 10:46 am
28 Thu.	Virgo	Earth	Barren	4th
29 Fri. 4:54 am	Libra	Air	Semi-fruitful	4th
30 Sat.	Libra	Air	Semi-fruitful	4th

November

Lunar Aspectarian

Favorable and Unfavorable Days

	Sun	Mercury	Venus	Mars	Jupiter	Saturn	Uranus	Neptune	Pluto	Aries	Taurus	Gemini	Cancer	Leo	Virgo	Libra	Scorpio	Sagittarius	Capricorn	Aquarius	Pisces
1						Q					f	u	f		F		f	u	f		U
2				C	X			T	X	U		f	u	f		F		f	u	f	
3						T	T			U		f	u	f		F		f	u	f	
4	C	C	C		Q			Q			U		f	u	f		F		f	u	f
5						Q					U		f	u	f		F		f	u	f
6				X	T			X	C	f		U		f	u	f		F		f	u
7						0	X			f		U		f	u	f		F		f	u
8		X	X							u	f		U		f	u	f		F		f
9	X			Q						u	f		U		f	u	f		F		f
10			Q					C		f	u	f		U		f	u	f		F	
11	Q	Q		T	0				X	f	u	f		U		f	u	f		F	
12			T			T	C			f	u	f		U		f	u	f		F	
13									Q		f	u	f		U		f	u	f		F
14	T	T				Q					f	u	f		U		f	u	f		F
15							X				f	u	f		U		f	u	f		F
16				0	T				T	F		f	u	f		U		f	u	f	
17			0			X	X			F		f	u	f		U		f	u	f	
18								Q			F		f	u	f		U		f	u	f
19	0				Q			Q			F		f	u	f		U		f	u	f
20		0						T			F		f	u	f		U		f	u	f
21					X				0	f		F		f	u	f		U		f	u
22			T	T		C	T			f		F		f	u	f		U		f	u
23										u	f		F		f	u	f		U		f
24			Q	Q						u	f		F		f	u	f		U		f
25	T	T						0		f	u	f		F		f	u	f		U	
26				X	C	X	0		T	f	u	f		F		f	u	f		U	
27	Q		X							f	u	f		F		f	u	f		U	
28		Q							Q		f	u	f		F		f	u	f		U
29	X					Q		T			f	u	f		F		f	u	f		U
30		X			X			T	X	U		f	u	f		F		f	u	f	

December Moon Table

Date	Sign	Element	Nature	Phase
1 Sun. 6:15 am	Scorpio	Water	Fruitful	4th
2 Mon.	Scorpio	Water	Fruitful	4th
3 Tue. 6:58 am	Sagittarius	Fire	Barren	4th
4 Wed.	Sagittarius	Fire	Barren	New 2:34 am
5 Thu. 8:39 am	Capricorn	Earth	Semi-fruitful	1st
6 Fri.	Capricorn	Earth	Semi-fruitful	1st
7 Sat. 12:54 pm	Aquarius	Air	Barren	1st
8 Sun.	Aquarius	Air	Barren	1st
9 Mon. 8:46 pm	Pisces	Water	Fruitful	1st
10 Tue.	Pisces	Water	Fruitful	1st
11 Wed.	Pisces	Water	Fruitful	2nd 10:49 am
12 Thu. 7:58 am	Aries	Fire	Barren	2nd
13 Fri.	Aries	Fire	Barren	2nd
14 Sat. 8:43 pm	Taurus	Earth	Semi-fruitful	2nd
15 Sun.	Taurus	Earth	Semi-fruitful	2nd
16 Mon.	Taurus	Earth	Semi-fruitful	2nd
17 Tue. 8:43 am	Gemini	Air	Barren	2nd
18 Wed.	Gemini	Air	Barren	2nd
19 Thu. 6:30 pm	Cancer	Water	Fruitful	Full 2:10 pm
20 Fri.	Cancer	Water	Fruitful	3rd
21 Sat.	Cancer	Water	Fruitful	3rd
22 Sun. 1:48 am	Leo	Fire	Barren	3rd
23 Mon.	Leo	Fire	Barren	3rd
24 Tue. 7:05 am	Virgo	Earth	Barren	3rd
25 Wed.	Virgo	Earth	Barren	3rd
26 Thu. 10:53 am	Libra	Air	Semi-fruitful	4th 7:31 pm
27 Fri.	Libra	Air	Semi-fruitful	4th
28 Sat. 1:41 pm	Scorpio	Water	Fruitful	4th
29 Sun.	Scorpio	Water	Fruitful	4th
30 Mon. 4:01 pm	Sagittarius	Fire	Barren	4th
31 Tue.	Sagittarius	Fire	Barren	4th

December

Day	Sun	Mercury	Venus	Mars	Jupiter	Saturn	Uranus	Neptune	Pluto	Aries	Taurus	Gemini	Cancer	Leo	Virgo	Libra	Scorpio	Sagittarius	Capricorn	Aquarius	Pisces
1			C	C		T		Q		U		f	u	f		F		f	u	f	
2					Q		Q				U		f	u	f		F		f	u	f
3								X			U		f	u	f		F		f	u	f
4	C	C			T				C	f		U		f	u	f		F		f	u
5			X	X		0	X			f		U		f	u	f		F		f	u
6										u	f		U		f	u	f		F		f
7			Q	Q						u	f		U		f	u	f		F		f
8	X				0			C	X	f	u	f		U		f	u	f		F	
9						T	C			f	u	f		U		f	u	f		F	
10		X	T	T							f	u	f		U		f	u	f		F
11	Q								Q		f	u	f		U		f	u	f		F
12		Q			Q						f	u	f		U		f	u	f		F
13					T			X	T	F		f	u	f		U		f	u	f	
14	T					X	X			F		f	u	f		U		f	u	f	
15		T	0	0				Q			F		f	u	f		U		f	u	f
16					Q						F		f	u	f		U		f	u	f
17								Q			F		f	u	f		U		f	u	f
18					X			T	0	f		F		f	u	f		U		f	u
19	0					C	T			f		F		f	u	f		U		f	u
20			T	T						u	f		F		f	u	f		U		f
21		0								u	f		F		f	u	f		U		f
22								0		u	f		F		f	u	f		U		f
23			Q	Q	C	X	0		T	f	u	f		F		f	u	f		U	
24	T									f	u	f		F		f	u	f		U	
25			X	X					Q		f	u	f		F		f	u	f		U
26	Q	T				Q					f	u	f		F		f	u	f		U
27					X			T	X	U		f	u	f		F		f	u	f	
28		Q				T	T			U		f	u	f		F		f	u	f	
29	X			C	Q			Q			U		f	u	f		F		f	u	f
30		X	C				Q				U		f	u	f		F		f	u	f
31					T			X	C	f		U		f	u	f		F		f	u

Moon Void-of-Course

By Kim Rogers-Gallagher

The Moon makes a loop around the Earth in about twenty-eight days, moving through each of the signs in two-and-a-half days (or so). As she passes through the thirty degrees of each sign, she "visits" with the planets in numerical order by forming angles or aspects with them. Because she moves one degree in just two to two-and-a-half hours, her influence on each planet lasts only a few hours, then she moves along. As she approaches the late degrees of the sign she's passing through, she eventually reaches the planet that's in the highest degree of any sign, and forms what will be her final aspect before leaving the sign. From this point until she actually enters the new sign, she is referred to as void-of-course, or void.

Think of it this way: the Moon is the emotional "tone" of the day, carrying feelings with her particular to the sign she's "wearing" at the moment. After she has contacted each of the planets, she symbolically "rests" before changing her costume, so her instinct is temporarily on hold. It's during this time that many people feel "fuzzy" or "vague"—scattered, even. Plans

or decisions we make now will usually not pan out. Without the instinctual "knowing" the Moon provides as she touches each planet, we tend to be unrealistic or exercise poor judgment. The traditional definition of the void Moon is that "nothing will come of this," and it seems to be true. Actions initiated under a void Moon are often wasted, irrelevant, or incorrect—usually because information is hidden, missing, or has been overlooked.

Although it's not a good time to initiate plans, routine tasks seem to go along just fine. However, this period is really ideal for what the Moon does best: reflection. It's at this time that we can assimilate what the world has tossed at us over the past few days.

On the lighter side, remember that there are other good uses for the void Moon. This is the time period when the universe seems to be most open to loopholes. It's a great time to make plans you don't want to fulfill or schedule things you don't want to do. See the table on pages 59–64 for a schedule of the 2002 Moon void-of-course times.

Moon Void-of-Course

Last Aspect		Moon Enters New Sign		
Date	Time	Date	Sign	Time
January				
2	6:16 am	2	Virgo	6:34 pm
4	2:30 am	4	Libra	8:23 pm
6	11:05 am	6	Scorpio	11:41 pm
8	4:03 pm	9	Sagittarius	4:57 am
11	1:49 am	11	Capricorn	12:18 pm
13	2:24 pm	13	Aquarius	9:41 pm
15	7:25 pm	16	Pisces	9:00 am
18	9:27 pm	18	Aries	9:35 pm
20	8:50 pm	21	Taurus	9:47 am
23	7:29 am	23	Gemini	7:28 pm
25	2:23 pm	26	Cancer	1:17 am
26	2:03 pm	28	Leo	3:31 am
29	6:04 pm	30	Virgo	3:40 am
31	6:46 am	1	Libra	3:44 am
February				
2	7:45 pm	3	Scorpio	5:35 am
5	9:02 am	5	Sagittarius	10:21 am
7	7:38 am	7	Capricorn	6:08 pm
10	1:50 am	10	Aquarius	4:15 am
12	5:21 am	12	Pisces	3:53 pm
14	2:44 am	15	Aries	4:26 am
17	2:55 pm	17	Taurus	4:58 pm
19	6:34 pm	20	Gemini	3:50 am
22	2:53 am	22	Cancer	11:16 am
24	8:39 am	24	Leo	2:36 pm
26	11:30 am	26	Virgo	2:47 pm
27	10:17 pm	28	Libra	1:47 pm
March				
2	6:57 am	2	Scorpio	1:51 pm

Moon Void-of-Course

Last Aspect		Moon Enters New Sign		
Date	**Time**	**Date**	**Sign**	**Time**
4	9:43 am	4	Sagittarius	4:55 pm
6	9:31 pm	6	Capricorn	11:48 pm
8	10:06 am	9	Aquarius	9:56 am
11	2:28 pm	11	Pisces	9:56 pm
13	9:03 pm	14	Aries	10:34 am
16	4:08 pm	16	Taurus	11:01 pm
19	7:53 am	19	Gemini	10:20 am
21	1:14 pm	21	Cancer	7:06 pm
23	5:19 am	24	Leo	12:12 am
25	8:57 pm	26	Virgo	1:44 am
27	8:31 pm	28	Libra	1:04 am
29	7:57 pm	30	Scorpio	12:21 am
31	9:13 pm	1	Sagittarius	1:48 am
		April		
3	2:13 am	3	Capricorn	6:58 am
5	4:59 am	5	Aquarius	4:07 pm
7	11:09 pm	8	Pisces	3:57 am
10	12:31 pm	10	Aries	4:40 pm
13	4:52 am	13	Taurus	4:55 am
15	11:53 am	15	Gemini	3:56 pm
17	9:17 pm	18	Cancer	1:01 am
19	6:55 pm	20	Leo	7:20 am
22	7:30 am	22	Virgo	10:35 am
24	9:06 am	24	Libra	11:22 am
26	8:29 am	26	Scorpio	11:15 am
28	9:25 am	28	Sagittarius	12:13 pm
30	1:10 pm	30	Capricorn	4:03 pm
		May		
1	12:17 pm	2	Aquarius	11:43 pm
5	7:46 am	5	Pisces	10:46 am

Moon Void-of-Course

| Last Aspect | | Moon Enters New Sign | | |
Date	Time	Date	Sign	Time
6	9:11 pm	7	Aries	11:22 pm
10	8:47 am	10	Taurus	11:32 am
12	7:29 pm	12	Gemini	10:04 pm
15	4:08 am	15	Cancer	6:33 am
17	6:27 am	17	Leo	12:52 pm
19	3:34 pm	19	Virgo	5:01 pm
21	11:53 am	21	Libra	7:19 pm
23	6:39 pm	23	Scorpio	8:38 pm
25	8:20 pm	25	Sagittarius	10:20 pm
28	1:40 am	28	Capricorn	1:54 am
29	6:46 am	30	Aquarius	8:35 am
June				
1	4:19 pm	1	Pisces	6:37 pm
3	5:58 am	4	Aries	6:51 am
6	4:47 pm	6	Taurus	7:07 pm
9	3:14 am	9	Gemini	5:29 am
11	11:05 am	11	Cancer	1:15 pm
13	4:44 pm	13	Leo	6:39 pm
15	8:17 pm	15	Virgo	10:23 pm
17	7:29 pm	18	Libra	1:11 am
20	1:38 am	20	Scorpio	3:42 am
22	4:27 am	22	Sagittarius	6:42 am
24	8:38 am	24	Capricorn	11:01 am
26	2:37 am	26	Aquarius	5:36 pm
29	12:12 am	29	Pisces	3:00 am
July				
1	12:43 am	1	Aries	2:49 pm
4	12:11 am	4	Taurus	3:16 am
6	10:57 am	6	Gemini	2:01 pm
8	6:37 pm	8	Cancer	9:36 pm

Moon Void-of-Course

Last Aspect		Moon Enters New Sign		
Date	Time	Date	Sign	Time
10	11:25 pm	11	Leo	2:08 am
13	1:42 am	13	Virgo	4:41 am
15	12:08 am	15	Libra	6:39 am
17	5:58 am	17	Scorpio	9:13 am
19	9:35 am	19	Sagittarius	1:02 pm
21	2:44 pm	21	Capricorn	6:26 pm
23	10:05 pm	24	Aquarius	1:40 am
26	6:47 am	26	Pisces	11:04 am
28	9:01 pm	28	Aries	10:39 pm
31	10:48 am	31	Taurus	11:17 am
August				
2	5:58 pm	2	Gemini	10:46 pm
5	3:42 am	5	Cancer	7:02 am
7	11:27 am	8	Leo	2:15 pm
9	8:36 am	9	Virgo	1:03 pm
11	7:01 am	11	Libra	1:38 pm
13	10:11 am	13	Scorpio	3:01 pm
15	1:13 pm	15	Sagittarius	6:25 pm
17	6:39 pm	18	Capricorn	12:15 am
19	3:13 pm	20	Aquarius	8:16 am
22	5:29 pm	22	Pisces	6:11 pm
25	1:58 am	25	Aries	5:48 am
27	4:18 pm	27	Taurus	6:32 pm
29	11:44 pm	30	Gemini	6:45 am
September				
1	11:55 am	1	Cancer	4:14 pm
3	3:31 pm	3	Leo	9:36 pm
5	8:33 pm	5	Virgo	11:16 pm
7	7:54 pm	7	Libra	10:57 pm
9	7:52 pm	9	Scorpio	10:48 pm

Moon Void-of-Course

Last Aspect		Moon Enters New Sign		
Date	**Time**	**Date**	**Sign**	**Time**
11	5:52 pm	12	Sagittarius	12:44 am
14	2:54 am	14	Capricorn	5:47 am
16	12:58 am	16	Aquarius	1:54 pm
18	9:35 pm	19	Pisces	12:18 am
21	9:36 am	21	Aries	12:11 pm
23	10:29 pm	24	Taurus	12:55 am
26	4:27 am	26	Gemini	1:26 pm
28	10:01 pm	29	Cancer	12:01 am
30	1:59 pm	1	Leo	6:58 am
		October		
3	8:16 am	3	Virgo	9:52 am
5	8:22 am	5	Libra	9:51 am
7	7:29 am	7	Scorpio	8:57 am
9	7:38 am	9	Sagittarius	9:21 am
11	11:08 am	11	Capricorn	12:45 pm
13	5:42 pm	13	Aquarius	7:51 pm
16	4:15 am	16	Pisces	6:07 am
18	4:17 pm	18	Aries	6:13 pm
21	4:55 am	21	Taurus	6:57 am
23	9:14 am	23	Gemini	7:17 pm
26	4:01 am	26	Cancer	6:10 am
28	3:22 am	28	Leo	2:20 pm
30	4:51 pm	30	Virgo	6:59 pm
		November		
1	6:19 pm	1	Libra	8:28 pm
3	5:56 pm	3	Scorpio	8:10 pm
5	11:48 am	5	Sagittarius	8:01 pm
7	7:14 pm	7	Capricorn	9:59 pm
9	3:22 am	10	Aquarius	3:27 am
12	9:06 am	12	Pisces	12:42 pm

Moon Void-of-Course

Last Aspect		Moon Enters New Sign		
Date	**Time**	**Date**	**Sign**	**Time**
14	8:38 pm	15	Aries	12:38 am
17	9:06 am	17	Taurus	1:23 pm
19	8:34 pm	20	Gemini	1:25 am
22	7:07 am	22	Cancer	11:48 am
24	11:51 am	24	Leo	8:00 pm
26	8:51 pm	27	Virgo	1:42 am
29	12:01 am	29	Libra	4:54 am
		December		
1	6:06 am	1	Scorpio	6:15 am
2	11:15 pm	3	Sagittarius	6:58 am
5	2:55 am	5	Capricorn	8:39 am
5	3:20 pm	7	Aquarius	12:54 pm
9	1:35 pm	9	Pisces	8:46 pm
12	12:02 am	12	Aries	7:58 am
14	12:18 pm	14	Taurus	8:43 pm
17	12:11 am	17	Gemini	8:43 am
19	2:10 pm	19	Cancer	6:30 pm
21	4:31 am	22	Leo	1:48 am
23	11:58 pm	24	Virgo	7:05 am
26	2:10 am	26	Libra	10:53 am
28	7:15 am	28	Scorpio	1:41 pm
30	12:04 pm	30	Sagittarius	4:01 pm

FIND YOUR MOON SIGN

Every year we give tables for the position of the Moon during that year, but it is more complicated to provide tables for the Moon's position in any given year because of its continuous movement. However, the problem was solved by Grant Lewi in *Astrology for the Millions* (available from Llewellyn Worldwide).

Grant Lewi's System

Step 1:

Find your birth year in the Natal Moon Tables located on pages 68–77.

Step 2:

Run down the left-hand column and see if your birth date is there.

Step 3:

If your birth date is in the left-hand column, run over this line until you come to the column under your birth year. Here you will find a number. This is your base number. Write it down, and go directly to the direc-tion under the heading "What to Do with Your Base Number" on page 66.

Step 4:

If your birth date is not in the left-hand column, get a pencil and paper. Your birth date falls between two numbers in the left-hand column. Look at the date closest after your birth date; run across this line to your birth year. Write down the number you find there, and label it "top number." Directly beneath it on your piece of paper write the number printed just above it in the table. Label this "bottom number." Subtract the bottom number from the top number. If the top number is smaller, add 360 and subtract. The result is your difference.

Step 5:

Go back to the left-hand column and find the date before your birth date. Determine the number of days between this date and your birth date. Write this down and label it "intervening days."

Step 6:

Note which group your difference (found at step 4) falls in.

Difference	Daily Motion
80–87	22 degrees
88–94	13 degrees
95–101	14 degrees
102–106	15 degrees

Note: If you were born in a leap year and use the difference between February 26 and March 5, then the daily motion is slightly different. If you fall into this category and your difference use the figures below.

Difference	Daily Motion
94–99	12 degrees
100–108	13 degrees
109–115	14 degrees
115–122	15 degrees

Step 7:

Write down the "daily motion" corresponding to your place in the proper table of difference above. Multiply daily motion by the number labeled "intervening days" (found at step 5).

Step 8:

Add the result of step 7 to your bottom number (under step 4). This is your base number. If it is more than 360, subtract 360 from it and call the result your base number.

What to Do with Your Base Number

Turn to the Table of Base Numbers on page 67 and locate your base number in it. At the top of the column you will find the sign your Moon was in. In the far left-hand column you will find the degree the Moon occupied at 7:00 am of your birth date if you were born under Eastern Standard Time (EST). Refer to the Time Zone Conversions chart and table on pages 16–17 to adjust information for your time zone.

If you don't know the hour of your birth, accept this as your Moon's sign and degree. If you do know the hour of your birth, get the exact degree as follows:

If you were born after 7:00 am EST, determine the number of hours after the time that you were born. Divide this by two, rounding up if necessary. Add this to your base number, and the result in the table will be the exact degree and sign of the Moon on the year, month, date, and hour of your birth.

If you were born before 7:00 am EST, determine the number of hours before the time that you were born. Divide this by two. Subtract this from your base number, and the result in the table will be the exact degree and sign of the Moon on the year, month, date, and hour of your birth.

Table of Base Numbers

	♈ (13)	♉ (14)	♊ (15)	♋ (16)	♌ (17)	♍ (18)	♎ (19)	♏ (20)	♐ (21)	♑ (22)	♒ (23)	♓ (24)
0°	0	30	60	90	120	150	180	210	240	270	300	330
1°	1	31	61	91	121	151	181	211	241	271	301	331
2°	2	32	62	92	122	152	182	212	242	272	302	332
3°	3	33	63	93	123	153	183	213	243	273	303	333
4°	4	34	64	94	124	154	184	214	244	274	304	334
5°	5	35	65	95	125	155	185	215	245	275	305	335
6°	6	36	66	96	126	156	186	216	246	276	306	336
7°	7	37	67	97	127	157	187	217	247	277	307	337
8°	8	38	68	98	128	158	188	218	248	278	308	338
9°	9	39	69	99	129	159	189	219	249	279	309	339
10°	10	40	70	100	130	160	190	220	250	280	310	340
11°	11	41	71	101	131	161	191	221	251	281	311	341
12°	12	42	72	102	132	162	192	222	252	282	312	342
13°	13	43	73	103	133	163	193	223	253	283	313	343
14°	14	44	74	104	134	164	194	224	254	284	314	344
15°	15	45	75	105	135	165	195	225	255	285	315	345
16°	16	46	76	106	136	166	196	226	256	286	316	346
17°	17	47	77	107	137	167	197	227	257	287	317	347
18°	18	48	78	108	138	168	198	228	258	288	318	248
19°	19	49	79	109	139	169	199	229	259	289	319	349
20°	20	50	80	110	140	170	200	230	260	290	320	350
21°	21	51	81	111	141	171	201	231	261	291	321	351
22°	22	52	82	112	142	172	202	232	262	292	322	352
23°	23	53	83	113	143	173	203	233	263	293	323	353
24°	24	54	84	114	144	174	204	234	264	294	324	354
25°	25	55	85	115	145	175	205	235	265	295	325	355
26°	26	56	86	116	146	176	206	236	266	296	326	356
27°	27	57	87	117	147	177	207	237	267	297	327	357
28°	28	58	88	118	148	178	208	238	268	298	328	358
29°	29	59	89	119	149	179	209	239	269	299	329	359

Month	Date	1911	1912	1913	1914	1915	1916	1917	1918	1919	1920
Jan.	1	289	57	211	337	100	228	23	147	270	39
Jan.	8	20	162	299	61	192	332	110	231	5	143
Jan.	15	122	251	23	158	293	61	193	329	103	231
Jan.	22	214	335	120	256	23	145	290	68	193	316
Jan.	29	298	66	221	345	108	237	32	155	278	49
Feb.	5	31	170	308	69	203	340	118	239	16	150
Feb.	12	130	260	32	167	302	70	203	338	113	239
Feb.	19	222	344	128	266	31	154	298	78	201	325
Feb.	26	306	75	231	353	116	248	41	164	286	60
Mar.	5	42	192	317	77	214	2	127	248	26	172
Mar.	12	140	280	41	176	311	89	212	346	123	259
Mar.	19	230	5	136	276	39	176	308	87	209	346
Mar.	26	314	100	239	2	124	273	49	173	294	85
Apr.	2	52	200	326	86	223	10	135	257	35	181
Apr.	9	150	288	51	184	321	97	222	355	133	267
Apr.	16	238	14	146	286	48	184	318	96	218	355
Apr.	23	322	111	247	11	132	284	57	181	303	96
Apr.	30	61	208	334	96	232	19	143	267	43	190
May	7	160	296	60	192	331	105	231	4	142	275
May	14	246	22	156	294	56	192	329	104	227	3
May	21	331	122	255	20	141	294	66	190	312	105
May	28	69	218	342	106	240	29	151	277	51	200
Jun.	4	170	304	69	202	341	114	240	14	151	284
Jun.	11	255	30	167	302	65	200	340	112	235	11
Jun.	18	340	132	264	28	151	304	74	198	322	114
Jun.	25	78	228	350	115	249	39	159	286	60	209
Jul.	2	179	312	78	212	349	122	248	25	159	293
Jul.	9	264	39	178	310	74	209	350	120	244	20
Jul.	16	349	141	273	36	161	312	84	206	332	123
Jul.	23	87	237	358	125	258	48	168	295	70	218
Jul.	30	187	321	86	223	357	131	256	36	167	302
Aug.	6	272	48	188	319	82	219	360	129	252	31
Aug.	13	359	150	282	44	171	320	93	214	342	131
Aug.	20	96	246	6	133	268	57	177	303	81	226
Aug.	27	195	330	94	234	5	140	265	46	175	310
Sep.	3	281	57	198	328	90	229	9	138	260	41
Sep.	10	9	158	292	52	180	329	102	222	351	140
Sep.	17	107	255	15	141	279	65	186	312	91	234
Sep.	24	203	339	103	244	13	149	274	56	184	319
Oct.	1	288	68	206	337	98	240	17	148	268	52
Oct.	8	18	167	301	61	189	338	111	231	360	150
Oct.	15	118	263	24	149	290	73.	195	320	102	242
Oct.	22	212	347	113	254	22	157	284	65	193	326
Oct.	29	296	78	214	346	106	250	25	157	276	61
Nov.	5	26	177	309	70	197	348	119	240	7	161
Nov.	12	129	271	33	158	300	81	203	329	112	250
Nov.	19	221	355	123	262	31	164	295	73	202	334
Nov.	26	305	88	223	355	115	259	34	165	285	70
Dec.	3	34	187	317	79	205	359	127	249	16	171
Dec.	10	138	279	41	168	310	89	211	340	120	259
Dec.	17	230	3	134	270	40	172	305	81	211	343
Dec.	24	313	97	232	3	124	267	44	173	294	78
Dec.	31	42	198	325	87	214	9	135	257	25	181

Month	Date	1921	1922	1923	1924	1925	1926	1927	1928	1929	1930
Jan.	1	194	317	80	211	5	127	250	23	176	297
Jan.	8	280	41	177	313	90	211	349	123	260	22
Jan.	15	4	141	275	41	175	312	86	211	346	123
Jan.	22	101	239	3	127	272	51	172	297	83	222
Jan.	29	203	325	88	222	13	135	258	34	184	306
Feb.	5	289	49	188	321	99	220	359	131	269	31
Feb.	12	14	149	284	49	185	320	95	219	356	131
Feb.	19	110	249	11	135	281	60	181	305	93	230
Feb.	26	211	334	96	233	21	144	266	45	191	314
Mar.	5	297	58	197	343	107	230	8	153	276	41
Mar.	12	23	157	294	69	194	328	105	238	6	140
Mar.	19	119	258	19	157	292	68	190	327	104	238
Mar.	26	219	343	104	258	29	153	275	70	200	323
Apr.	2	305	68	205	352	115	240	16	163	284	51
Apr.	9	33	166	304	77	204	337	114	247	14	149
Apr.	16	130	266	28	164	303	76	198	335	115	246
Apr.	23	227	351	114	268	38	161	285	79	208	331
Apr.	30	313	78	214	1	123	250	25	172	292	61
May	7	42	176	313	85	212	348	123	256	23	160
May	14	141	274	37	173	314	84	207	344	125	254
May	21	236	359	123	277	47	169	295	88	217	339
May	28	321	88	222	11	131	259	34	181	301	70
Jun.	4	50	186	321	94	220	358	131	264	31	171
Jun.	11	152	282	45	182	324	93	215	354	135	263
Jun.	18	245	7	134	285	56	177	305	96	226	347
Jun.	25	330	97	232	20	139	268	44	190	310	78
Jul.	2	58	197	329	103	229	9	139	273	40	181
Jul.	9	162	291	54	192	333	101	223	4	144	272
Jul.	16	254	15	144	294	65	185	315	104	236	355
Jul.	23	338	106	242	28	148	276	54	198	319	87
Jul.	30	67	208	337	112	238	20	147	282	49	191
Aug.	6	171	300	62	202	341	110	231	15	152	281
Aug.	13	264	24	153	302	74	194	324	114	244	4
Aug.	20	347	114	253	36	157	285	65	206	328	95
Aug.	27	76	218	346	120	248	29	156	290	59	200
Sep.	3	179	309	70	213	350	119	239	25	161	290
Sep.	10	273	32	162	312	83	203	332	124	252	13
Sep.	17	356	122	264	44	166	293	75	214	337	105
Sep.	24	86	227	354	128	258	38	165	298	70	208
Oct.	1	187	318	78	223	358	128	248	35	169	298
Oct.	8	281	41	170	322	91	212	340	134	260	23
Oct.	15	5	132	274	52	175	303	85	222	345	115
Oct.	22	97	235	3	136	269	46	174	306	81	216
Oct.	29	196	327	87	232	7	137	257	44	179	307
Nov.	5	289	50	178	332	99	221	349	144	268	31
Nov.	12	13	142	283	61	183	313	93	231	353	126
Nov.	19	107	243	12	144	279	54	183	315	91	225
Nov.	26	206	335	96	241	17	145	266	52	189	314
Dec.	3	297	59	187	343	107	230	359	154	276	39
Dec.	10	21	152	291	70	191	324	101	240	1	137
Dec.	17	117	252	21	153	289	63	191	324	99	234
Dec.	24	216	343	105	249	28	152	275	60	199	322
Dec.	31	305	67	197	352	115	237	9	162	285	47

Month	Date	1931	1932	1933	1934	1935	1936	1937	1938	1939	1940
Jan.	1	60	196	346	107	231	8	156	277	41	181
Jan.	8	162	294	70	193	333	104	240	4	144	275
Jan.	15	257	20	158	294	68	190	329	104	239	360
Jan.	22	342	108	255	32	152	278	67	202	323	88
Jan.	29	68	207	353	116	239	19	163	286	49	191
Feb.	5	171	302	78	203	342	113	248	14	153	284
Feb.	12	267	28	168	302	78	198	339	113	248	8
Feb.	19	351	116	266	40	161	286	78	210	332	96
Feb.	26	77	217	1	124	248	29	171	294	59	200
Mar.	5	179	324	86	213	350	135	256	25	161	306
Mar.	12	276	48	176	311	86	218	347	123	256	29
Mar.	19	360	137	277	48	170	308	89	218	340	119
Mar.	26	86	241	10	132	258	52	180	302	69	223
Apr.	2	187	334	94	223	358	144	264	34	169	315
Apr.	9	285	57	185	321	95	227	355	133	264	38
Apr.	16	9	146	287	56	178	317	99	226	349	128
Apr.	23	96	250	18	140	268	61	189	310	80	231
Apr.	30	196	343	102	232	7	153	273	43	179	323
May	7	293	66	193	332	103	237	4	144	272	47
May	14	17	155	297	64	187	327	108	235	357	139
May	21	107	258	28	148	278	69	198	318	90	239
May	28	205	351	111	241	17	161	282	51	189	331
Jun.	4	301	75	201	343	111	245	13	154	280	55
Jun.	11	25	165	306	73	195	337	117	244	5	150
Jun.	18	117	267	37	157	288	78	207	327	99	248
Jun.	25	215	360	120	249	28	169	291	60	200	339
Jul.	2	309	84	211	353	119	254	23	164	289	64
Jul.	9	33	176	315	82	203	348	125	253	13	160
Jul.	16	126	276	46	165	297	87	216	336	108	258
Jul.	23	226	8	130	258	38	177	300	69	210	347
Jul.	30	317	92	221	2	128	262	33	173	298	72
Aug.	6	41	187	323	91	211	359	133	261	21	170
Aug.	13	135	285	54	175	305	97	224	346	116	268
Aug.	20	237	16	138	267	49	185	308	78	220	355
Aug.	27	326	100	232	10	136	270	44	181	307	80
Sep.	3	49	197	331	100	220	8	142	270	31	179
Sep.	10	143	295	62	184	314	107	232	355	125	278
Sep.	17	247	24	147	277	58	194	317	89	228	4
Sep.	24	335	108	243	18	145	278	55	189	316	88
Oct.	1	58	206	341	108	229	17	152	278	40	188
Oct.	8	151	306	70	193	322	117	240	4	134	288
Oct.	15	256	32	155	287	66	203	324	100	236	13
Oct.	22	344	116	253	27	154	287	64	198	324	98
Oct.	29	68	214	350	116	239	25	162	286	49	196
Nov.	5	161	316	78	201	332	126	248	12	145	297
Nov.	12	264	41	162	298	74	212	333	111	244	22
Nov.	19	353	125	262	36	162	296	73	207	332	108
Nov.	26	77	222	0	124	248	33	172	294	58	205
Dec.	3	171	325	87	209	343	135	257	19	156	305
Dec.	10	272	50	171	309	82	220	341	120	253	30
Dec.	17	1	135	271	45	170	306	81	217	340	118
Dec.	24	86	231	10	132	256	43	181	302	66	214
Dec.	31	182	333	95	217	354	142	265	27	167	313

Month	Date	1941	1942	1943	1944	1945	1946	1947	1948	1949	1950
Jan.	1	325	88	211	353	135	258	22	165	305	68
Jan.	8	50	176	315	85	219	348	126	256	29	160
Jan.	15	141	276	50	169	312	87	220	340	123	258
Jan.	22	239	12	133	258	52	182	303	69	224	352
Jan.	29	333	96	221	2	143	266	32	174	314	75
Feb.	5	57	186	323	95	227	358	134	265	37	170
Feb.	12	150	285	58	178	320	96	228	349	131	268
Feb.	19	250	20	142	267	62	190	312	78	234	359
Feb.	26	342	104	231	11	152	274	43	182	323	83
Mar.	5	65	196	331	116	236	8	142	286	46	179
Mar.	12	158	295	66	199	328	107	236	10	139	279
Mar.	19	261	28	150	290	72	198	320	102	243	8
Mar.	26	351	112	242	34	161	281	53	204	332	91
Apr.	2	74	205	340	125	244	16	152	294	55	187
Apr.	9	166	306	74	208	337	117	244	19	148	289
Apr.	16	270	36	158	300	81	206	328	112	252	17
Apr.	23	360	120	252	42	170	290	63	212	340	100
Apr.	30	83	214	350	133	254	25	162	302	64	195
May	7	174	316	82	217	346	127	252	27	158	299
May	14	279	45	166	311	90	215	336	123	260	26
May	21	9	128	261	50	179	299	72	221	349	110
May	28	92	222	1	141	263	33	173	310	73	204
Jun.	4	184	326	91	226	356	137	261	36	168	307
Jun.	11	287	54	174	322	98	224	344	134	268	34
Jun.	18	17	137	270	60	187	308	81	231	357	119
Jun.	25	102	231	11	149	272	42	183	318	82	213
Jul.	2	194	335	99	234	7	145	269	44	179	316
Jul.	9	296	63	183	332	106	233	353	144	277	43
Jul.	16	25	147	279	70	195	318	89	241	5	129
Jul.	23	110	240	21	157	280	52	192	327	91	224
Jul.	30	205	343	108	242	18	153	278	52	190	324
Aug.	6	304	71	192	341	115	241	3	153	286	51
Aug.	13	33	156	287	80	203	327	98	251	13	138
Aug.	20	119	250	30	165	289	63	201	336	99	235
Aug.	27	216	351	117	250	28	162	287	61	200	332
Sep.	3	314	80	201	350	125	249	13	161	296	59
Sep.	10	41	165	296	90	211	336	108	260	21	146
Sep.	17	127	261	39	174	297	74	209	345	107	246
Sep.	24	226	359	126	259	38	170	295	70	209	341
Oct.	1	323	88	211	358	135	257	22	170	306	67
Oct.	8	49	174	306	99	220	344	118	269	30	154
Oct.	15	135	272	47	183	305	84	217	353	116	256
Oct.	22	236	8	134	269	47	180	303	80	217	351
Oct.	29	333	95	220	7	144	265	31	179	315	75
Nov.	5	58	181	317	107	229	352	129	277	39	162
Nov.	12	143	283	55	192	314	94	225	1	125	265
Nov.	19	244	18	141	279	55	189	311	90	225	0
Nov.	26	343	104	229	16	153	274	39	189	323	84
Dec.	3	67	189	328	115	237	360	140	284	47	171
Dec.	10	153	292	64	200	324	103	234	9	136	274
Dec.	17	252	28	149	289	63	199	319	100	234	9
Dec.	24	351	112	237	27	161	282	47	199	331	93
Dec.	31	76	198	338	123	246	9	150	293	55	180

Month	Date	1951	1952	1953	1954	1955	1956	1957	1958	1959	1960
Jan.	1	194	336	115	238	6	147	285	47	178	317
Jan.	8	297	67	199	331	107	237	9	143	278	47
Jan.	15	30	150	294	70	200	320	104	242	9	131
Jan.	22	114	240	35	161	284	51	207	331	94	223
Jan.	29	204	344	124	245	17	155	294	55	189	325
Feb.	5	305	76	207	341	116	246	18	152	287	56
Feb.	12	38	159	302	80	208	330	112	252	17	140
Feb.	19	122	249	45	169	292	61	216	340	102	233
Feb.	26	215	352	133	253	27	163	303	63	199	333
Mar.	5	314	96	216	350	125	266	27	161	297	75
Mar.	12	46	180	310	91	216	351	121	262	25	161
Mar.	19	130	274	54	178	300	86	224	349	110	259
Mar.	26	225	14	142	262	37	185	312	72	208	356
Apr.	2	324	104	226	358	135	274	37	169	307	83
Apr.	9	54	189	319	100	224	360	131	271	34	170
Apr.	16	138	285	62	187	308	97	232	357	118	269
Apr.	23	235	23	150	271	46	194	320	82	217	5
Apr.	30	334	112	235	6	146	282	48	177	317	91
May	7	62	197	330	109	232	8	142	279	42	177
May	14	146	296	70	196	316	107	240	6	127	279
May	21	243	32	158	280	54	204	328	91	225	15
May	28	344	120	244	15	155	290	55	187	326	100
Jun.	4	71	205	341	117	241	16	153	288	51	186
Jun.	11	155	306	79	204	325	117	249	14	137	288
Jun.	18	252	42	166	290	63	214	336	101	234	25
Jun.	25	354	128	253	26	164	298	63	198	335	109
Jul.	2	80	214	351	125	250	24	164	296	60	195
Jul.	9	164	315	88	212	335	126	259	22	147	297
Jul.	16	260	52	174	299	72	223	344	110	243	34
Jul.	23	3	137	261	37	173	307	71	209	343	118
Jul.	30	89	222	2	134	258	33	174	304	68	205
Aug.	6	174	324	97	220	345	134	268	30	156	305
Aug.	13	270	62	182	308	82	232	353	118	254	42
Aug.	20	11	146	269	48	181	316	79	220	351	126
Aug.	27	97	232	11	143	267	43	183	314	76	215
Sep.	3	184	332	107	228	355	143	278	38	166	314
Sep.	10	280	71	191	316	92	241	2	127	265	50
Sep.	17	19	155	278	58	189	325	88	230	359	135
Sep.	24	105	242	20	152	274	54	191	323	84	225
Oct.	1	193	341	116	237	4	152	287	47	174	324
Oct.	8	291	79	200	324	103	249	11	135	276	58
Oct.	15	27	163	287	68	198	333	98	239	8	143
Oct.	22	113	252	28	162	282	64	199	332	92	235
Oct.	29	201	350	125	245	12	162	295	56	182	334
Nov.	5	302	87	209	333	114	256	19	144	286	66
Nov.	12	36	171	297	76	207	341	109	247	17	150
Nov.	19	121	262	37	171	291	73	208	341	101	244
Nov.	26	209	0	133	254	20	173	303	65	190	345
Dec.	3	312	95	217	342	124	265	27	154	295	75
Dec.	10	45	179	307	84	216	348	119	255	27	158
Dec.	17	129	271	46	180	299	82	218	350	110	252
Dec.	24	217	11	141	263	28	184	311	73	199	355
Dec.	31	321	103	225	352	132	273	35	164	303	84

Month	Date	1961	1962	1963	1964	1965	1966	1967	1968	1969	1970
Jan.	1	96	217	350	128	266	27	163	298	76	197
Jan.	8	179	315	89	217	350	126	260	27	161	297
Jan.	15	275	54	179	302	86	225	349	112	257	36
Jan.	22	18	141	264	35	189	311	74	207	359	122
Jan.	29	105	225	1	136	275	35	173	306	85	206
Feb.	5	188	323	99	225	360	134	270	35	171	305
Feb.	12	284	64	187	310	95	235	357	121	267	45
Feb.	19	26	150	272	46	197	320	81	218	7	130
Feb.	26	113	234	11	144	283	45	182	315	93	216
Mar.	5	198	331	109	245	9	142	280	54	180	313
Mar.	12	293	73	195	332	105	244	5	142	277	54
Mar.	19	34	159	280	71	205	329	90	243	15	139
Mar.	26	122	243	19	167	291	54	190	338	101	226
Apr.	2	208	340	119	253	18	151	290	63	189	323
Apr.	9	303	82	204	340	116	252	14	150	288	62
Apr.	16	42	167	288	81	213	337	99	253	23	147
Apr.	23	130	253	28	176	299	64	198	347	109	235
Apr.	30	216	349	128	261	27	161	298	71	197	333
May	7	314	90	213	348	127	260	23	158	299	70
May	14	51	176	298	91	222	345	109	262	32	155
May	21	137	263	36	186	307	74	207	357	117	245
May	28	225	359	137	270	35	172	307	80	205	344
Jun.	4	325	98	222	357	137	268	31	168	309	78
Jun.	11	60	184	308	99	231	353	119	270	42	163
Jun.	18	146	272	45	195	315	82	217	6	126	253
Jun.	25	233	10	145	279	43	183	315	89	214	355
Jul.	2	336	106	230	6	147	276	40	178	318	87
Jul.	9	70	191	318	108	241	1	129	279	51	171
Jul.	16	154	281	56	204	324	91	227	14	135	261
Jul.	23	241	21	153	288	52	193	323	98	223	5
Jul.	30	345	115	238	16	156	286	47	188	327	97
Aug.	6	79	200	327	116	250	10	138	288	60	180
Aug.	13	163	289	66	212	333	99	238	22	144	270
Aug.	20	250	32	161	296	61	203	331	106	233	14
Aug.	27	353	124	246	27	164	295	55	199	335	106
Sep.	3	88	208	336	126	259	19	147	297	68	189
Sep.	10	172	297	77	220	342	108	249	30	152	279
Sep.	17	260	41	170	304	72	212	340	114	244	23
Sep.	24	1	134	254	37	172	304	64	208	344	115
Oct.	1	97	217	344	136	267	28	155	308	76	198
Oct.	8	180	306	88	228	351	117	259	38	161	289
Oct.	15	270	50	179	312	82	220	350	122	254	31
Oct.	22	10	143	262	47	182	313	73	217	353	123
Oct.	29	105	226	352	146	275	37	163	318	84	207
Nov.	5	189	315	97	237	359	127	268	47	168	299
Nov.	12	281	58	188	320	93	228	359	130	264	39
Nov.	19	19	151	271	55	191	321	82	225	3	131
Nov.	26	113	235	1	157	282	45	172	328	92	215
Dec.	3	197	326	105	245	7	138	276	55	176	310
Dec.	10	291	66	197	328	102	237	7	139	273	48
Dec.	17	30	159	280	63	202	329	91	234	13	139
Dec.	24	121	243	11	167	291	53	183	337	101	223
Dec.	31	204	336	113	254	14	149	284	64	184	320

Month	Date	1971	1972	1973	1974	1975	1976	1977	1978	1979	1980
Jan.	1	335	109	246	8	147	279	56	179	318	90
Jan.	8	71	197	332	108	243	6	144	278	54	176
Jan.	15	158	283	69	207	328	93	240	18	139	263
Jan.	22	244	20	169	292	54	192	339	102	224	4
Jan.	29	344	117	255	17	156	288	64	188	327	99
Feb.	5	81	204	342	116	253	14	153	287	63	184
Feb.	12	167	291	79	216	337	101	251	26	147	271
Feb.	19	252	31	177	300	62	203	347	110	233	14
Feb.	26	353	126	263	27	164	297	72	199	334	109
Mar.	5	91	224	351	124	262	34	162	296	72	204
Mar.	12	176	312	90	224	346	122	262	34	156	203
Mar.	19	261	55	185	309	72	226	356	118	243	37
Mar.	26	1	149	270	37	172	320	80	208	343	130
Apr.	2	100	233	360	134	270	43	170	307	80	213
Apr.	9	184	320	101	232	355	131	273	42	164	302
Apr.	16	271	64	194	317	82	235	5	126	254	46
Apr.	23	9	158	278	47	181	329	88	217	352	139
Apr.	30	109	242	8	145	278	52	178	318	88	222
May	7	193	329	111	240	3	141	282	50	173	312
May	14	281	73	203	324	92	243	14	134	264	54
May	21	19	167	287	55	191	337	97	226	3	147
May	28	117	251	16	156	286	61	187	328	96	231
Jun.	4	201	339	120	249	11	151	291	59	180	323
Jun.	11	291	81	213	333	102	252	23	143	273	63
Jun.	18	29	176	296	64	201	346	106	234	13	155
Jun.	25	125	260	25	167	295	69	196	338	105	239
Jul.	2	209	349	129	258	19	162	299	68	188	334
Jul.	9	300	90	222	341	111	261	32	152	282	72
Jul.	16	40	184	305	72	212	354	115	243	24	163
Jul.	23	133	268	35	176	303	78	206	347	114	248
Jul.	30	217	0	137	267	27	172	308	77	197	344
Aug.	6	309	99	230	350	120	271	40	161	290	83
Aug.	13	51	192	314	81	223	2	124	252	34	171
Aug.	20	142	276	45	185	312	86	217	356	123	256
Aug.	27	225	10	146	276	36	182	317	86	206	353
Sep.	3	317	109	238	360	128	281	48	170	299	93
Sep.	10	61	200	322	90	232	10	132	262	43	180
Sep.	17	151	284	56	193	321	94	228	4	132	264
Sep.	24	234	20	155	284	45	191	326	94	215	2
Oct.	1	325	120	246	9	136	291	56	179	308	103
Oct.	8	70	208	330	101	241	19	140	273	51	189
Oct.	15	160	292	66	202	330	102	238	12	140	273
Oct.	22	243	28	165	292	54	199	336	102	225	10
Oct.	29	334	130	254	17	146	301	64	187	318	112
Nov.	5	79	217	338	112	249	27	148	284	59	197
Nov.	12	169	300	76	210	339	111	247	21	148	282
Nov.	19	253	36	175	300	63	207	347	110	234	18
Nov.	26	344	139	262	25	156	310	73	195	329	120
Dec.	3	87	226	346	122	257	36	157	294	67	206
Dec.	10	177	310	84	220	347	121	255	31	156	292
Dec.	17	261	45	185	308	72	216	356	118	242	28
Dec.	24	355	148	271	33	167	318	81	203	340	128
Dec.	31	95	235	355	132	265	44	166	303	76	214

Month	Date	1981	1982	1983	1984	1985	1986	1987	1988	1989	1990
Jan.	1	226	350	129	260	36	162	300	71	205	333
Jan.	8	315	89	225	346	126	260	36	156	297	72
Jan.	15	53	188	309	73	225	358	119	243	37	168
Jan.	22	149	272	35	176	319	82	206	348	129	252
Jan.	29	234	0	137	270	43	172	308	81	213	343
Feb.	5	324	98	234	354	135	270	44	164	306	82
Feb.	12	64	196	317	81	236	6	128	252	48	175
Feb.	19	157	280	45	185	328	90	217	356	138	260
Feb.	26	242	10	145	279	51	182	316	90	222	353
Mar.	5	332	108	242	15	143	280	52	185	313	93
Mar.	12	74	204	326	104	246	14	136	275	57	184
Mar.	19	166	288	55	208	337	97	227	19	147	268
Mar.	26	250	20	154	300	60	191	326	111	230	1
Apr.	2	340	119	250	24	151	291	60	194	322	103
Apr.	9	84	212	334	114	255	22	144	286	66	192
Apr.	16	175	296	66	216	346	106	237	27	156	276
Apr.	23	259	28	164	309	69	199	336	119	240	9
Apr.	30	349	130	258	33	160	302	68	203	331	113
May	7	93	221	342	124	264	31	152	297	75	201
May	14	184	304	75	225	355	114	246	36	165	285
May	21	268	36	175	317	78	207	347	127	249	18
May	28	358	140	266	41	170	311	76	211	341	122
Jun.	4	102	230	350	135	272	40	160	307	83	210
Jun.	11	193	313	84	234	3	123	255	45	173	294
Jun.	18	277	45	185	325	87	216	357	135	258	27
Jun.	25	8	149	275	49	180	320	85	219	352	130
Jul.	2	110	239	359	146	281	49	169	317	92	219
Jul.	9	201	322	93	244	11	133	263	55	181	304
Jul.	16	286	54	196	333	96	225	7	143	266	37
Jul.	23	19	158	284	57	191	328	94	227	3	138
Jul.	30	119	248	7	155	290	57	178	327	101	227
Aug.	6	210	331	101	254	19	142	272	66	189	313
Aug.	13	294	64	205	341	104	236	16	152	274	48
Aug.	20	30	166	293	66	202	337	103	236	13	147
Aug.	27	128	256	17	164	299	65	187	335	111	235
Sep.	3	218	340	110	264	27	151	281	75	197	321
Sep.	10	302	75	214	350	112	247	24	160	282	59
Sep.	17	40	174	302	74	212	345	112	245	23	156
Sep.	24	138	264	26	172	309	73	197	343	121	243
Oct.	1	226	349	119	274	36	159	292	84	206	329
Oct.	8	310	86	222	359	120	258	32	169	291	70
Oct.	15	50	183	310	84	220	354	120	255	31	165
Oct.	22	148	272	35	181	319	81	206	352	130	251
Oct.	29	234	357	130	282	44	167	303	92	214	337
Nov.	5	318	96	230	8	129	268	40	178	300	79
Nov.	12	58	193	318	93	229	4	128	265	39	175
Nov.	19	158	280	44	190	329	90	214	2	139	260
Nov.	26	243	5	141	290	53	175	314	100	223	345
Dec.	3	327	106	238	16	139	277	49	185	310	88
Dec.	10	66	203	326	103	237	14	136	274	48	185
Dec.	17	167	288	52	200	337	98	222	12	147	269
Dec.	24	252	13	152	298	62	184	324	108	232	355
Dec.	31	337	114	248	24	149	285	59	193	320	96

Month	Date	1991	1992	1993	1994	1995	1996	1997	1998	1999	2000
Jan.	1	111	242	15	145	281	53	185	317	92	223
Jan.	8	206	326	108	244	16	136	279	56	186	307
Jan.	15	289	54	210	337	99	225	21	147	270	37
Jan.	22	18	158	299	61	190	329	110	231	2	140
Jan.	29	119	252	23	155	290	62	193	326	101	232
Feb.	5	214	335	116	254	24	145	287	66	193	315
Feb.	12	298	63	220	345	108	235	31	155	278	47
Feb.	19	29	166	308	69	201	337	119	239	12	148
Feb.	26	128	260	32	164	299	70	202	335	111	240
Mar.	5	222	356	124	265	32	166	295	76	201	337
Mar.	12	306	87	229	354	116	259	39	164	285	72
Mar.	19	39	189	317	77	211	360	128	248	22	170
Mar.	26	138	280	41	172	310	90	212	343	121	260
Apr.	2	230	5	133	275	40	175	305	86	210	345
Apr.	9	314	98	237	3	123	270	47	173	294	83
Apr.	16	49	198	326	86	220	9	136	257	31	180
Apr.	23	148	288	50	180	320	98	221	351	132	268
Apr.	30	238	13	143	284	48	183	315	95	218	353
May	7	322	109	245	12	132	281	55	182	302	93
May	14	57	207	335	95	228	18	144	267	39	190
May	21	158	296	59	189	330	106	230	1	141	276
May	28	247	21	154	292	57	191	326	103	227	1
Jun.	4	330	119	253	21	141	291	64	190	311	102
Jun.	11	66	217	343	105	236	28	152	276	48	199
Jun.	18	168	304	68	199	340	114	238	11	150	285
Jun.	25	256	29	165	300	66	199	337	111	236	10
Jul.	2	339	129	262	29	150	300	73	198	321	111
Jul.	9	74	227	351	114	245	38	160	285	57	209
Jul.	16	177	313	76	210	348	123	246	22	158	293
Jul.	23	265	38	175	309	75	208	347	120	245	19
Jul.	30	349	137	272	37	160	308	83	206	331	119
Aug.	6	83	237	359	123	255	48	169	293	67	218
Aug.	13	186	322	84	221	356	132	254	33	166	302
Aug.	20	273	47	185	318	83	218	356	129	253	29
Aug.	27	358	146	282	45	169	317	93	214	340	128
Sep.	3	93	246	7	131	265	56	177	301	78	226
Sep.	10	194	331	92	231	4	141	263	43	174	311
Sep.	17	281	56	194	327	91	228	5	138	261	39
Sep.	24	8	154	292	53	178	326	102	223	349	137
Oct.	1	104	254	16	139	276	64	186	310	89	234
Oct.	8	202	339	101	241	13	149	273	53	183	319
Oct.	15	289	66	202	337	99	238	13	148	269	49
Oct.	22	16	164	301	61	187	336	111	231	357	148
Oct.	29	115	262	25	148	287	72	195	318	100	242
Nov.	5	211	347	111	250	22	157	283	61	193	326
Nov.	12	297	76	211	346	107	247	22	157	277	58
Nov.	19	24	174	309	70	194	346	119	240	5	159
Nov.	26	126	270	33	156	297	80	203	328	109	251
Dec.	3	220	355	121	258	31	165	293	69	202	334
Dec.	10	305	85	220	355	115	256	31	165	286	67
Dec.	17	32	185	317	79	203	357	127	249	13	169
Dec.	24	135	278	41	166	306	89	211	338	117	260
Dec.	31	230	3	131	266	41	173	303	78	211	343

Month	Year	2001	2002	2003	2004	2005	2006	2007	2008	2009	2010
Jan.	1	355	128	263	33	165	300	74	203	336	111
Jan.	8	89	228	355	117	260	39	165	288	71	211
Jan.	15	193	317	79	209	4	127	249	20	174	297
Jan.	22	280	41	174	310	91	211	346	121	261	21
Jan.	29	4	137	273	42	175	308	84	211	345	119
Feb.	5	97	238	3	126	268	49	173	296	80	221
Feb.	12	202	326	87	219	12	136	257	31	182	306
Feb.	19	289	49	184	319	99	220	356	130	269	31
Feb.	26	13	145	283	49	184	316	94	219	355	127
Mar.	5	106	248	11	147	278	59	181	317	90	229
Mar.	12	210	334	95	244	20	145	265	56	190	315
Mar.	19	298	58	193	342	107	229	4	153	277	40
Mar.	26	23	153	293	69	193	325	104	239	4	136
Apr.	2	116	257	20	155	289	67	190	325	101	237
Apr.	9	218	343	104	255	28	154	274	67	198	323
Apr.	16	306	68	202	351	115	239	12	162	285	50
Apr.	23	32	162	303	77	202	334	114	247	12	146
Apr.	30	127	265	29	163	300	75	199	333	112	245
May	7	226	352	113	264	37	162	284	76	207	331
May	14	314	77	210	1	123	248	21	172	293	59
May	21	40	173	312	86	210	345	122	256	20	157
May	28	138	273	38	171	311	83	207	342	123	254
Jun.	4	235	0	122	273	46	170	294	84	217	339
Jun.	11	322	87	219	11	132	257	30	181	302	68
Jun.	18	48	183	320	95	218	356	130	265	29	168
Jun.	25	149	281	46	181	321	92	216	352	132	262
Jul.	2	245	8	132	281	56	178	304	93	227	347
Jul.	9	330	95	229	20	140	266	41	190	310	76
Jul.	16	56	195	328	104	227	7	138	274	38	179
Jul.	23	158	290	54	191	330	101	224	2	140	272
Jul.	30	254	16	142	290	65	186	313	101	236	356
Aug.	6	339	103	239	28	149	274	52	198	319	84
Aug.	13	65	205	336	112	236	17	147	282	47	188
Aug.	20	167	299	62	201	338	110	232	12	149	281
Aug.	27	264	24	151	299	74	194	321	111	245	5
Sep.	3	348	112	250	36	158	282	63	206	328	93
Sep.	10	74	215	345	120	246	26	156	290	58	197
Sep.	17	176	309	70	211	347	120	240	22	157	290
Sep.	24	273	33	159	309	83	203	330	122	253	14
Oct.	1	356	120	261	44	167	291	73	214	336	103
Oct.	8	84	224	354	128	256	34	165	298	68	205
Oct.	15	184	318	78	220	355	129	248	31	167	299
Oct.	22	281	42	167	320	91	212	338	132	261	23
Oct.	29	5	129	271	52	175	301	82	222	344	113
Nov.	5	95	232	4	136	266	42	174	306	78	213
Nov.	12	193	327	87	229	5	137	257	40	177	307
Nov.	19	289	51	176	331	99	221	346	143	268	31
Nov.	26	13	139	280	61	183	312	91	231	352	123
Dec.	3	105	240	13	144	276	51	183	315	87	223
Dec.	10	203	335	96	237	15	145	267	48	188	315
Dec.	17	297	59	185	341	107	229	356	152	277	39
Dec.	24	21	150	288	70	190	322	98	240	0	134
Dec.	31	114	249	22	153	285	60	191	324	96	232

Home, Health,

& Beauty

Section

How To Choose the Best Dates for Home, Health, & Beauty Activities

Automobiles

When buying an automobile, select a time when the Moon is conjunct, sextile, or trine to Mercury, Saturn, or Uranus; and in the sign Gemini or Capricorn.

Brewing

It is best to brew between the Full Moon and in the third or fourth quarter. Plan to start the process when the Moon is in Cancer, Scorpio, or Pisces.

Building

Turning the first sod for the foundation marks the beginning of the building. For best results excavate the site when the Moon is in the first quarter of the fixed sign Taurus or Leo, and making favorable aspects to Saturn.

Canning

Can fruits and vegetables when the Moon is in either the third or fourth quarter and in the water sign of Cancer or Pisces. Preserves and jellies use the same quarters and the signs Cancer, Pisces, or Taurus.

Concrete

Pour concrete when the Moon is in the third quarter of the fixed signs: Taurus, Leo, or Aquarius.

Dental Work

Visit the dentist when the Moon is in Virgo, or pick a day marked favorable for your Sun sign. Mars should be marked X, T, or C; Saturn, Uranus, and Jupiter should not be marked Q or O. Teeth are best removed when the Moon is in Gemini, Virgo, Sagittarius, or Pisces, and during the first or second quarter. Avoid the Full Moon! The day should be favorable for your lunar cycle, and Mars and Saturn should be marked C, T, or X. Fillings should be done in the third or fourth quarters in the signs of Taurus, Leo, Scorpio, or Pisces. The same applies for plates.

Dressmaking

William Lilly wrote in 1676: "Make no new clothes, or first put them on when the Moon is in Scorpio or afflicted by Mars, for they will be apt to be torn and quickly worn out." Design, repair, or sew clothes in the first and second quarters of Taurus, Leo, or Libra on a day marked favorable for your Sun sign. Venus, Jupiter, and Mercury should be aspected, but avoid hard aspects to Mars or Saturn.

Eyes and Eyeglasses

Have your eyes tested and glasses fitted on a day marked favorable for your Sun sign, and on a day that falls during your favorable lunar cycle (check Moon Tables starting on page 34). Mars should not be in aspect with the Moon. The same applies for any treatment of the eyes, which

should also be started during the Moon's first or second quarter.

Fence Posts

Set the posts when the Moon is in the third or fourth quarter of the fixed sign Taurus or Leo.

Habits

To end any undesirable habit, including smoking, start on a day when the Moon is in the third or fourth quarter and in the barren sign of Gemini, Leo, or Aquarius. Aries, Virgo and Capricorn may be suitable as well. Make sure your lunar cycle is favorable. Avoid lunar aspects to Mars or Jupiter. However, favorable aspects to Pluto are helpful.

Hair Care

Haircuts are best when the Moon is in the mutable Gemini, Sagittarius, or Pisces; or earthy Taurus or Capricorn, but not in barren Virgo. Look for favorable aspects to Venus. For faster growth, hair should be cut when the Moon is in Cancer or Pisces in the first or second quarter. To make hair grow thicker, cut it when the Moon is Full or in opposition to the Sun (marked O in the Lunar Aspectarian) in the signs of Taurus, Cancer, or Leo up to and at, but not after, the Full Moon. However, if you want your hair to grow more slowly, the Moon should be in Aries, Gemini, or Virgo in the

third or fourth quarter, with Saturn square or opposing the Moon.

Permanents, straightening, and hair coloring will take well if the Moon is in Taurus or Leo and Venus is marked T or X. You should avoid hair treatments if Mars is marked Q or O, especially if heat is to be used. For permanents, a trine to Jupiter is helpful. The Moon also should be in the first quarter, and check the lunar cycle for a favorable day in relation to your Sun sign.

Health

A diagnosis is more likely to be successful when the Moon is in the cardinal signs: Aries, Cancer, Libra, or Capricorn; and less so when in air signs: Gemini, Sagittarius, Pisces, or Virgo. Begin a recuperation program when the Moon is in a cardinal or fixed sign and the day is favorable to your sign. Enter hospitals at these times. For surgery, see "Surgical Procedures." Buy medicines when the Moon is in Virgo or Scorpio.

Home Furnishings

Saturn days (Saturday) are good for buying, and Jupiter days (Thursday) are good for selling. Items bought on days when Saturn is well aspected tend to wear longer and purchases tend to a more conservative.

House Purchasing

If you desire a permanent home, buy when the New Moon is in Taurus, Cancer, or Leo. Each sign will affect choice in a different way. For example, a home bought when the Moon is in Taurus is likely to be more practical and have a country look—right down to the split rail fence—while a house purchased when the Moon is in Leo is more likely to be a showplace.

If you're buying for speculation and a quick turnover, be certain that the Moon is in a cardinal sign: Aries, Cancer, Libra, or Capricorn. Avoid buying in a fixed sign.

Lost Articles

Search for lost articles during the first quarter and when your Sun sign is marked favorable. Also check to see that the planet ruling the lost item is trine, sextile, or conjunct the Moon. The Moon governs household utensils; Mercury letters and books; and Venus clothing, jewelry, and money.

Marriage

The best time for marriage to take place is during the time when the Moon is increasing; just after it has past the first quarter, but is not yet a Full Moon. Good signs for the Moon to be in are Taurus, Cancer, Leo, and Libra.

The Moon in Taurus produces the most steadfast marriages, but if the partners later want to separate they may have a difficult time. Make sure that the Moon is well aspected (X or T), especially to Venus or Jupiter. Avoid aspects to Mars, Uranus, or Pluto. Avoid Aries, Gemini, Virgo, Scorpio, and Aquarius Moons.

Moving

Make sure that Mars is not aspecting to the Moon. Move on a day favorable to your Sun sign, or when the Moon is conjunct, sextile, or trine the Sun.

Mowing the Lawn

Mow the lawn in the first or second quarter to increase growth. If you wish to retard growth, mow in the third or fourth quarter.

Painting

The best time to paint buildings is during the waning phase of the Moon, and in the sign Libra. If the weather is hot, do the painting while the Moon is in Taurus; if the weather is cold, paint while the Moon is in Leo. Another good sign for painting is Aquarius. Schedule the painting for the fourth quarter as the wood is drier and the paint will penetrate. Around the New Moon the wood is likely to be damp, and the paint is subject to scalding when hot weather hits it. It is not advisable to paint while the Moon is in Cancer, Scorpio, or Pisces if the temperature is below 70° F, as it is apt to creep, check, or run.

Pets

Take home new pets when the day is favorable to your Sun sign or the Moon is trine, sextile, or conjunct Mercury, Venus, or Jupiter, or in the sign of Virgo or Pisces. However, avoid days when the Moon is either square or opposing the Sun, Mars, Saturn, Uranus, Neptune, or Pluto. When selecting a pet, have the Moon well aspected by the planet that rules the animal. Cats are ruled by the Sun, dogs by Mercury, birds by Venus, horses by Jupiter, and fish by Neptune.

Train pets when the Moon is in Virgo, or when the Moon trines Mercury.

Neuter or spay animals when the Moon is in Sagittarius, Capricorn, or Pisces—when it has passed beyond the body part affected (Scorpio). Avoid the week before and after the Full Moon. Declaw cats in the dark of the Moon. Avoid the week before and after the Full Moon and the sign of Pisces.

Romance

The same principles hold true for starting a relationship as for marriage. However, since there is less control of when a romance starts, it is sometimes necessary to study it after the fact. Romances begun under an increasing Moon are more likely to be permanent or satisfying, while those begun during the decreasing Moon will tend to transform the participants. The tone of the relationship can be guessed from the sign the Moon is in. Romances begun with the Moon in Aries may be impulsive. Those begun in Capricorn will take greater effort to bring to a desirable conclusion, but they may be very rewarding. Good aspects between the Moon and Venus are good influences. Avoid unfavorable apsects to Mars, Uranus, and Pluto. Ending relationships is facilitated by a decreasing Moon, particularly in the fourth quarter. This causes the least pain and attachment.

Sauerkraut

The best tasting sauerkraut is made just after the Full Moon in the fruitful signs of Cancer, Scorpio, or Pisces.

Selecting A Child's Sex

Count from the last day of menstruation to the day of its next beginning, and divide the interval between the two dates into halves. Pregnancy in the first half produces females, but copulation should take place with the Moon in a feminine sign. Pregnancy in the latter half, up to three days of the beginning of menstruation, produces males, but copulation should take place with the Moon in a masculine sign. The three-day period before the next period again produces females.

Shingling

Begin roofing a building in the decrease of the Moon (third or fourth quarter), when the Moon is in Aries or Aquarius. However, shingles laid during the New Moon have a tendency to curl at the edges.

Surgical Procedures

The flow of blood, like ocean tides, appears to be related to Moon phases. To reduce hemorrhage after a surgery, schedule it within one week before or after a New Moon.

Schedule surgery to occur during the increase of the Moon if possible, as wounds heal better and vitality is greater than during the decrease of the Moon. Avoid surgery within one week before or after the Full Moon. Select a date when the Moon is past the sign governing the part of the body involved in the operation. For example, abdominal operations should be done when the Moon is in Sagittarius, Capricorn, or Aquarius. To find the signs and the body parts they rule, turn to the chart on page 86. The further removed the Moon sign is from the sign ruling the afflicted part of the body, the better.

For successful operations, avoid lunar aspects to Mars, and look for favorable aspects to Venus and Jupiter. Do not operate when the Moon is applying to any aspect of Mars (this tends to promote inflammation and complications). See the Lunar Aspectarian (pages 34–57) to determine days with negative Mars aspects and positive Venus and Jupiter aspects. Never operate with the Moon in the same sign as a person's Sun sign or Ascendant. Let the Moon be in a fixed sign and avoid square or opposing aspects. The Moon should not be void-of-course. Avoid amputations when the Moon is conjunct or opposed the Sun (C or O) or opposed by Mars.

Cosmetic surgery should be done in the increase of the Moon, when the Moon is not square or in opposition to Mars. Avoid days when the Moon is square or opposing Saturn or the Sun.

Weaning Children

To wean a child successfully, do so when the Moon is in Sagittarius, Capricorn, Aquarius, or Pisces— signs that do not rule vital human organs. By observing this astrological rule, much trouble for parents and child may be avoided.

Weight, Losing

If you want to lose weight, the best time to get started is when the Moon is in the third or fourth quarter, and the barren sign of Virgo. Review the section on "Using the Moon Tables" beginning on page 28 to help you select a date that is favorable to begin your weight loss program.

Wine and Drinks Other Than Beer

It is best to start brewing when the Moon is in Pisces or Taurus. Sextiles or trines to Venus are favorable, but avoid aspects to Mars or Saturn.

Zodiac Signs & Their Corresponding Body Parts

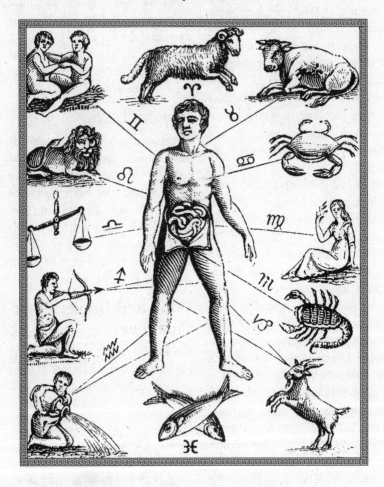

♈	= Aries	♎	= Libra
♉	= Taurus	♏	= Scorpio
♊	= Gemini	♐	= Sagittarius
♋	= Cancer	♑	= Capricorn
♌	= Leo	♒	= Aquarius
♍	= Virgo	♓	= Pisces

Moon Sign Excellence

By Phyllis Firak-Mitz, M.A.

Our Moon sign—the sign the Moon was in when we were born—is a blueprint that describes how and what we most want to give and receive to feel nourished, comfortable, and safe; and what type of dynamics we want in our relationships to feel valued and intimate. If we choose lifestyles and relationships that support our Moon sign's needs, and take responsibility for our emotional health, we set the stage for creating success in all areas of our lives. We can learn to recognize when we've gone off track emotionally, and we can learn how to bring ourselves back to emotional health. For that to happen, though, we much first become personally aware. Sometimes the simplest shifts in attitude can make the most profound differences in the quality of life.

This article will help you to recognize when your emotions are off course, as well as help you to develop the qualities and positive attributes that will support your emotional needs. Just as a parent guides their child to discern between useful and destructive emotional expressions, we need to parent our lunar (emotional) energies to develop what in our nature serves us, and step away from tendencies that can hold us back. As we gain emotional maturity, we learn to nurture ourselves so we can accomplish our destiny, as well as interact successfully and lovingly with others. If we

fail to evolve our lunar energies, we'll confuse self-nurturing with self-indulgence. We'll be needy in relationships, or perhaps become self-destructive.

Aries Moon

The fiery emotional energy lies within the hero who willingly stands for
what is right, even if that puts him at odds with others. The emotional
need is to be self-reliant and to do things in his or her own way

If you have an Aries Moon, using your considerable courage to be true
to yourself can bring your dynamic emotions to maturity. Self-knowledge
is important to ensure that it's your higher nature that you champion, and
not your ego position that wants to dominate or conquer at any cost. If you
have a me-against-them attitude most of the time, you're emotionally off
track. Feeling alone in the world is often the result of your own actions
and not the fault of others. You might be approaching things in an overly
competitive or combative way. Or you may act so independently that
others don't think you need anything, even love, from them. Sometimes
your path will call you to be selfish, but other times it's a cue that you need
to include others in your actions and decisions.

Your conquering, competitive spirit can be used to vanquish fears and
exalt your own personal best. Part of nurturing yourself is letting others be
there for you. Recognize the power of vulnerability (the one emotion you
hate to express) as it might be the very thing that opens the door to
allowing others to know and love you more.

Taurus Moon

Strong, steady, calm emotions that can't be rushed, and feelings gathered
and revealed over time are this Moon's legacy. Security, loyalty, and a committed nature that provides an oasis of safety are its gifts.

If you have a Taurus Moon, your gift of loyal determination is useful in
cultivating those things within that offer true and lasting value and security. Self-esteem, loyalty to your heart, and recognizing that everything you
are (and have) is already enough will go a long way toward cultivating
inward emotional security. If you attempt to get security from the world—
investing most of your time collecting material things—you'll find comfort
but not true security, and you might feel that others don't value you.
Check to see if you are valuing yourself, or resisting other's attempts to
give to you.

It's important to evaluate your commitments periodically to make sure you are not remaining loyal to relationships or situations that no longer serve you. When hurt, remember that holding on to resentment, or withholding from others, delays the healing process. If you get feedback that you're acting stubborn or making your own needs more important than those around you, you might want to assess if you have made some thing more important than being loving.

Gratitude is one of the simplest yet most profound ways you can tap into the sense of security and value you crave. Being grateful for who you are and what you have will open your eyes to the abundance already in your life, setting the stage for even more of what you want to flow to you. Physical touch does a world of good for you.

Gemini Moon

Freedom to learn, travel, and talk with interesting people, and an intellectual approach with emotional distance are this Moons signature. Deep, probing, intense feelings are uncomfortable here. There is a need to understand rather than feel overwhelmed by emotions.

If your Moon is in clever Gemini, you benefit most by participating 100 percent with whatever circumstance you find yourself in instead of thinking the grass is greener elsewhere. If you don't take dominion over your lunar energies, you'll frequently feel you are missing something from your current situations, and convince yourself that you need to go find new ones in order to be satisfied. You'll hop from situation to situation and relationship to relationship without realizing fulfillment. You'll tell yourself you're keeping your options open, but in reality you're withholding your involvement, robbing yourself of real learning or transformation. You'll fear people are confining you, when it's actually your lack of involvement that keeps you trapped. If you get feedback that you're acting superficial or unreliable, which might reflect that you have not committed to being true to yourself, you'll be unable to be committed to others either.

One way to corral your restless nature is to approach each relationship and circumstance with curiosity. Seek to learn something new about yourself and your abilities that you can express each day.

Cancer Moon

A comfy home, a family (of any sort), and money tucked away fulfill the Cancer Moon's need to nurture someone or something. Sharing deep feelings and sensitivity with others makes those with a Cancer Moon feel truly connected and loved.

You can develop your Cancer Moon into maturity by using your powerful nurturing skills to stay centered and strong physically, emotionally, mentally, and spiritually. In doing so, you build an inner bounty that can be used to nurture yourself and others.

If you neglect your emotional development, feelings of need and hurt may lead you to believe that others aren't supporting or caring for you. If you feel like a martyr, or feel drained by your giving, check to see if you are overdoing, or giving for the wrong reasons.

Interestingly, along with having remarkable parenting skills, you have a very developed childlike nature as well. Whereas others struggle to get in touch with their inner child, you are always in touch with yours. Being comfortable with your innocence awakens the tenderness within others.

Leo Moon

A Leo Moon stimulates showmanship, generosity, and creativity, creating a sense of grandness that seeks to dramatize feelings for the entire world to see. Applause and admiration feed the soul of those born during this sign.

You can develop your Leo Moon's brilliance by using your natural courage to express heartfelt emotions. No one can resist your charm and magnificent spirit when you are expressing from your heart. You'll let go of negativity in order to keep your dignity intact, as well as stay on top of matters. However, if you're driven by your ego's need to feel superior to others, you'll expect special treatment, and huff and puff if you don't get the admiration that you think you deserve, confusing admiration with self-esteem. In truth, you're demanding from the world what you need to cultivate within yourself: love, honor, and self-respect. If you get the feedback that you're being a control freak, evaluate whether you have forgotten the magic and romance in life that spontaneity can bring.

You can bring yourself back to your personal best by remembering it's love that moves mountains, not your image or your demands. Sometimes, having a good laugh at yourself can be a great lift, too.

Virgo Moon

A Virgo Moon quickens the instinctive knowledge of how things can work most naturally and gracefully. It enjoys analyzing and sorting things out. Natural healers, those with a Virgo Moon are lifted up emotionally by serving others, and creating order. Work may be the source of great emotional satisfaction for these pragmatic and reasonable people. Unlike dramatic Leo, Virgo appreciates subtle, discreet expressions and affections.

You can cultivate the gifts of your mature Virgo Moon by directing your radarlike insights to recognizing how life's situations—no matter how dysfunctional they seem—are perfect vignettes for learning and growth. Doing so helps you to avoid becoming negative, and reminds you that the perfect order you seek already exists.

You can tell if you're off track emotionally if you continually feel frustrated by things not going right. If your focus is usually on what is wrong, you've probably moved into perfectionism—your biggest trap. If you're stifled with self-criticism, try focusing on what's right, and then evaluate what happens. If your criticism extends to others, check to see if you have exchanged being part of the solution for being part of the problem.

You can tap into your innate emotional intelligence by keeping a neutral, even curious, attitude about how things should work. Instead of envisioning a perfect order, envision yourself being in acceptance and cooperation with the order present order.

Libra Moon

Creating beauty and harmony with people and things is a Libra Moon's second nature. Tremendous sensitivity to balance is the motivation for creating as much graciousness in the environment as is possible. Preferring to be even-tempered, those with a Libra Moon dislike unattractive demonstrations of feelings, or feelings that separate them from others. They work to diffuse difficult feelings, often at their own expense.

You can bring out the mature elegance of your Libra Moon by holding to peace and harmony within yourself, regardless of what is going on around you. Instead of expecting the world to be fair and harmonious, or waiting for circumstances to be perfect before you are at peace, recognize that inner peace and harmony are present and available at all times.

You can tell if you are out of balance emotionally if the upsets and the injustices of those around you throw you off emotionally. Being passive-aggressive, and not directly claiming what you want (instead manipulating others into doing your bidding while you try to appear neutral) is another sign of unbalanced emotions.

You can bring yourself back into balance by remembering that it is an excellent relationship with yourself that you are striving to master. When you choose alignment within yourself, you will achieve the balance you seek.

Scorpio Moon

Uncovering the mysteries of life nurture those with a Scorpio Moon. Designed to deeply experience the gamut of emotions from joy to jealousy, from hatred to transcendent love, they are motivated to bring light into the darkness, exposing unaddressed issues and feelings in the self and others.

If your Moon is in Scorpio, you're private about your feelings (except anger) trusting them only to those with whom you enjoy deep intimacy. You can guide your Scorpio Moon to powerful maturity by using your penetrating insight to discover how loving and forgiving transforms negative feelings into positive avenues of growth and health. Your ability to recognize the presence of light, even in the darkest places, allows you to be a safe space for others to express and then heal their pain.

If you don't take conscious direction over your emotions, you become entrenched in problems and risk becoming addicted to the power of the negative. If hurt, you'll use resentment to create a wall of protection. But resisting others holds you back from a dynamic transformation that leads to the deep levels of intimacy you crave. You are a gifted strategist, but if you use your abilities to manipulate or seduce others, you violate their will, and they'll mistrust or fear you. If you get feedback you are acting in a controlling manner, check if you are being impatient with others' way of dealing with issues and insisting they work them out your way and in your timing. Intending to be a force of loving service puts you in touch with a frequency of healing and lifts you up.

Sagittarius Moon

Exploring philosophies and activities that expand your understanding of self and of life, travel, learning, and seeking spiritual and moral truth sustains those with a Sagittarius Moon. Gregarious and optimistic, they choose to approach life in a way that makes them happy. Painful feelings, like sadness or jealousy, feel awkward and embarrassing and are avoided.

You are uncomfortable when others express negativity, you may disappear until things feel better if your Moon is in Sagittarius. Your natural enthusiasm and joy awakens when you recognize the universal source of all things, even things that appear negative or confining.

Fear of confinement and the dread of limiting situations or relationships will knock you off track, and you'll bug-out long before you're able to receive the gifts the situation has to offer. You'll falsely project on to others the loss of freedom, but it might be your unwillingness to fully invest yourself with anyone that is really holding you back. Although you seek illumination you might avoid the challenges out of fear that your vulnerability will be exposed, but forgetting they can open you to greater awareness. If you get feedback that you're acting superficial, check to see if you are trying to live up to an ideal instead of living authentically.

You can bring yourself back into balance by remembering that a spiritual teacher of any discipline points to the inner life, not the outer life, as the place true freedom exists. Instead of thinking that fulfillment is over the next hill, you are truly free when you recognize the illumination you seek can be attained by participating fully wherever you are.

Capricorn Moon

Ambitious and capable, those with a Capricorn Moon often decide early in life to rely on themselves, overcoming any obstacle that gets in their way. Their cautious nature dictates that emotions be kept minimal, even stoic, thereby avoiding mushy displays that could leave them vulnerable or humiliated. This concern, combined with the tendency to be way too hard on themselves, can result in depression or melancholy.

If you were born with a Capricorn Moon, it takes a while, but once you do let someone become close to you, you are loyal, kind, and helpful to them. You have the emotional nature of a father figure, and it lifts you to help others help themselves.

You mature your Capricorn Moon by learning to accept and harness your feelings. As you become emotionally available, you can connect with other's inspiration and become a wise and beloved leader. If you don't mature your emotions, you'll become stilted, depressed, and unavailable to others. You'll make accomplishing tasks so important that all the joy of life or companionship is forgotten. You'll project that others can't nurture you adequately. But it's more likely that you put conditions on how you're will receive nurturing, rejecting any giving from others that doesn't come in the manner you expect or desire. And you'll believe others value you only for your achievements, underestimating your true worth. If you get feedback that you're acting harsh, check to see if your ambitions to achieve have gotten in the way of your love and respect for others, or yourself. Part of your lesson in life involves being a caring and responsible caretaker of both yourself and others. You stand a better chance of getting what you want emotionally if you let others know what it is.

Aquarius Moon

All the world is family to those with an Aquarius Moon. A social purpose or mission will sustain their well-being, but their concern for humanity isn't particularly emotional. They avoid letting feelings become too intense, preferring logic instead, and detachment from feelings until they can understand them in a factual manner. As visionaries, they feel compelled to awaken people to ways of becoming a better society.

If your Moon is in Aquarius, you have little need for passionate scenes, possessive relationships, or baring your darkest issues. You'll bring your emotions to maturity by directing your evolutionary drive to develop and maintain unconditional positive regard for yourself and others. As you demonstrate your ability to love your own uniqueness as well as appreciate others', you teach by example how to be a healthy community member.

If you don't evolve your emotional nature, logic becomes valued above all else, and instead of detaching from your feelings in order to understand them, you detach from them altogether. That makes you seem cold and unavailable emotionally, and discourages relationships. You might feel alienated from your community, thinking they don't understand or tolerate you. But it might actually be that they have not lived up to your ideals or standards of behavior and you have withdrawn your participation and tolerance from them. If you get feedback that you're acting distant or aloof, check to see if you have made your ideals about humanity more important than the humans themselves.

You can bring yourself back on track by listening to the wisdom of your heart. The power of loving can lead you out of the alienation and isolation that comes from of objectifying your own or others' feelings, and help you to understand the value of them. You can then connect with your self and others in a most genuine and profound way.

Pisces Moon

Music, art, fantasy, and acts of compassionate service help those with a Pisces Moon connect with the higher dimensions of the self. Their compassionate emotional nature motivates them to connect with others in a profound way.

If your Moon is in Pisces, you need to consciously develop emotional boundaries, or risk getting confused about who you are. You are universally sympathetic and compassionate—sometimes suffering, not for yourself, but for others. If you don't tend to your emotions, however, you'll be overwhelmed by painful feelings and consider yourself and others powerless, tragic victims of this harsh world. You'll forget that you are designed to transform negativity into something beneficial. Your urge to surrender to something higher, like selfless service or artistic flow, is seduced to surrendering to things like drugs, alcohol, or meaningless sex. If you forget that others are capable of finding solutions to their own problems, you might feel you have to save them, becoming codependent, and feeling drained and used. You may also mistakenly believe it's better to deceive others about your truth rather them hurt them with your honesty. If you get feedback that you're acting spacey, check to see if you have gone unconscious instead of facing something that's bothering you.

You can bring your emotions to maturity by surrendering negative feelings, then lift yourself with forgiveness and loving. When you stand in the strength of your compassionate understanding you become a powerful healer in the world. Be sure not to confuse martyrdom, which has a self-victimization tendency, with self-sacrifice, which can be self-empowering love to give to others, but you need to fill yourself up first—then give from your overflow.

A famous spiritual teacher once said the sign of emotional maturity is being kind to oneself. If we can manage that, plus bring ourselves back to emotional balance each time we go out of balance, we are well on the road to cultivating all the happiness and fulfillment our Moon sign has to offer!

The Sacred Art of Feeling

By Lisa Finander

What happens when a flood of emotions overwhelms us? Often, we respond by hating our emotions, repressing them, disowning them, and cursing them. Yet, we longingly search for happiness, fulfillment, and our life's purpose. As we conduct this search, we act without engaging those troublesome emotions. We ask our Moon to always wear a happy face, especially for us. We don't want to face the unhappy, stressed parts of ourselves. Why is that? Perhaps it is because our emotions have the power to drastically and completely change our lives in a moment's notice—much quicker and more convincingly than our minds and even our bodies can create change. On the other hand, maybe it is because we are alienated from our emotional selves and don't have a clue about where to begin.

Oftentimes we attempt to give our emotions power in the outer world by trying to make them like our mind. We think that it makes sense to fall in love with a person, we convince ourselves that we were right to feel a particular way, we believe that we can make ourselves love someone, or we think that we can learn to feel differently than we really do. While this attempt to synchronize the mind and feelings might seem reasonable, the mind can't make you feel anything, especially if you don't know where your feelings lie or how they operate. If we could force our feelings to be reasonable, we would be more successful in our attempts to avoid and repress our most unpleasant of emotions.

In astrology, Mercury (the mind) is a much different archetype from the Moon (our emotions). Mercury is the messenger of the gods. It's the planet closest to the Sun (our consciousness). The Moon, on the other hand, is the Great Mother, the triple goddess, the giver of life and death that is both feared and cherished. To commune with this feminine archetype takes courage, patience, gentleness, and compassion.

In a natal chart, the Moon represents nurturing, mothering, femininity, habits, fears, and unconscious behaviors and motivations. Our Moon sign characterizes the way we are instinctively, and how we react to changes in our environment. It is what we feel we need to do. Even before we are born, we are reacting in the womb to things in our environment. Since many of our behaviors and attitudes concerning stress are formed while we are preverbal, our reactions to stress become more unconscious when we are adults.

Think of your childhood experiences. Your mother may have been compassionate, but if you ignored her messages, disrespected her, and avoided contact with her, what was likely to be her reaction? If your mother was like most mothers, she reacted in a negative way to the above mentioned behaviors or attitudes. Whether or not your physical mother lived up to your ideal is beside the point. Her responses to you helped to form your feelings. You have an inner nurturer that wreaks havoc in your life when disregarded, snubbed, or abandoned—just like your mother did.

Learning to understand and respect your emotions requires a commitment to unite the emotional and intellectual parts of yourself in an inner marriage where you agree to be there for yourself in good times and in bad. The union between your unconscious emotional self and your conscious intellectual self has the same needs and struggles as the relationships in your outer life. For example, you can't force your emotions to change any more than you can force a person to change. You must trust the integrity of your emotions and be willing to confront the issues they bring up just like in your relationships. If you judge your emotions, the process, or yourself, you will miss out on an opportunity to appreciate yourself and your life on a deeper level.

Once you have made a commitment to yourself to explore your emotions, there are a few things to keep in mind as you go through the process. First, you can't cultivate one emotion without cultivating them all (i.e. happiness without sadness). Second, it is easier to start the process of observing your emotions on a day when you are feeling positive. Give yourself a few minutes to quiet down and clear your mind before starting. If you feel blocked, notice what you do when you are blocked. Then go back one more step and ask yourself what happens right before you notice you are blocked? This will help you to get underneath your daily consciousness and in contact with your lunar energies. Finally, remember that the sacred art of feeling is a humbling experience that will challenge your conscious illusions of control.

Your Moon sign represents what kinds of things make you feel better, and how barriers to the natural flow of this energy will cause stress. The release of the energy of your Moon can be positive or negative. When we fill ourselves emotionally with fears, hurts, worries, doubt, anger, jealousy, and negativity, that is what we use to fill others. Learning to become aware of how you respond to stress emotionally by Moon sign can help you find the language and ideas to make choices about how you want to express yourself in the future. Your Moon is your inner guiding wisdom.

In the following descriptions of the Moon signs, when I describe emotional ease, I'm describing positive expressions of the Moon's sign; and when I describe emotional stress and repression in each sign, I'm describing the negative, or shadow, side of the Moon's expression. The light image and dark image are archetypes (or mental images) that we can identify and use to help us understand where we might be in the spectrum.

Moon in Aries

Light image: Emotional hero
Emotional ease: You are emotionally aware of your feelings as they arise, emotionally intuitive in your environment, courageous, confident during crises, enthusiastic, able to make quick emotional decisions, living in the moment emotionally, able to forgive and forget, and emotionally independent. Your emotions are a source of creativity, and a connection to spirit. You take beneficial emotional risks, encourage personal development in self and others, and value feminine strength, emotional honesty, and independence in self and others.

Shadow image: Smothered spirit
Emotional stress and repression: You overpower others emotionally and/or feel overpowered by emotional outbursts. You have aggressive behaviors, quickly lose interest in something or someone after the initial conquest,

exhibit competitive behavior in relationships, and have self-imposed creative blocks. You tend to attract and thrive on emotional crisis in relationships as a means to overcome fear, disrespect femininity in self and in others, view compromise in relationships as weakness and as oppression of personal freedom and desires, and have a general lack of energy.

Moon in Taurus

Light image: Emotional riches
Emotional ease: You are loyal, dependable, determined, sensual, and respectful and honoring of the physical body. You provide material security for self and loved ones; are intuitive to the needs of the physical body, remember physical details, and soothe self and others with your voice.
Shadow image: Buried pleasure
Emotional stress and repression: You have buried emotional pleasure and emotional stress. Unable to move forward, you feel emotionally stuck in a rut. You control self and others through stubbornness and financial intimidation, spend money foolishly and/or have unrealistic fears around money. You overindulge in food, drink, sex, money, possessions, and work. You feel deprived and unappreciated. You displace emotional attachments onto material objects. You can be selfish and insensitive toward self and others, be bigoted, and have an explosive temper.

Moon in Gemini

Light image: Emotional language
Emotional ease: You have emotional intelligence, know intuitively how to cheer self and others through humor, willingly seek a variety of emotional opportunities and experiences, fluently express emotions through reading, writing, and talking, form intellectual bonds with others, feel optimistic, and generally like people and their ideas. You seek partners who understand you emotionally.
Shadow image: Emotional mute
Emotional stress and repression: You tend to gossip, but are unable to talk about feelings, and express only superficial emotions. Emotions cloud your ability to think. You may feel cut off from emotional self, and use cutting humor and words to isolate and distance others. You have trouble bonding with others, and tend to be two-faced.

Moon in Cancer

Light image: Emotional home

Emotional ease: You are sensitive and nurturing to self and others, easily form enduring emotional bonds with others, treat others as family, and have an excellent memory—remembering special occasions and the feelings connected with those occasions. You are emotionally devoted to family, heritage, home, and especially to your mother. You intuitively know the needs of others, are protective of self and loved ones, and value women and their role as mothers.

Shadow image: Wet wool blanket

Emotional stress and repression: You are often consumed by worry and fear, are emotionally manipulative, display childish behaviors when confronted—whining, dependency, clinging, passive-aggressive, etc. You form parent-child relationships with peers, and focus only on negative experiences of the past. You get stuck in the past, are possessive of people and belongings, abuses drugs and chemicals to escape feelings, and tend to be moody.

Moon in Leo

Light image: Emotional playmate

Emotional ease: You are emotionally demonstrative, fun-loving, entertaining, create from the heart, act loving and proud of self and loved ones. You are generous, respect self and others, value children and own inner child.

Shadow image: Uninvited sovereign

Emotional stress and repression: You tend to create obsessively, need constant attention and emotional reassurance from others—even if it is insincere or negative. You act vain and dominating, and have to win. You tend to have power struggles with men, authority or father figures. You are unable to relate to others as equals, see yourself either as master or slave, are narcissistic, and play instead of work.

Moon in Virgo

Light image: Emotional health

Emotional ease: You are able to detach from emotions to gain perspective, feel concerned for the well-being of others, and are helpful to loved ones.

You are sensitive to mood changes in self and in others. You are kind, gentle, able to spend time alone, and have an innate healing ability.

Shadow Image: Snowstorm

Emotional stress and repression: You tend to feel guilty when doing things for self, try to fix emotions of self and others through rational means, analyze instead of feel, and devalue emotions of self and others. You have self-deprecating behavior, self-denying behaviors and habits, and feel alienated from self and others.

Moon in Libra

Light image: Emotional beauty

Emotional ease: You have a romantic, harmonious, peaceful, compromising nature. You tend to soothe self through artistic pleasures and to surround self with beautiful things. You have an intuitive sense of balance, emotional good manners, values relationships with others, act graciously, and can bring people together.

Shadow image: *The Picture of Dorian Gray* (running at off-Broadway Irish Repertory Theatre)

Emotional stress and repression: You have a tendency to be interested in superficial appearances, have difficulty expressing personal needs and unpleasant emotions, are prone to angry outbursts, and only able to experience self as a part of "we" instead of "I." You generally move quickly from one relationship to another once the romance wears off, act lazy, get lost in fantasies and daydreams instead of facing problems, are afraid of being alone, unable to share authentic self with others, and can't emotionally commit to anything.

Moon in Scorpio

Light image: Emotional alchemy

Emotional ease: You are passionate, have deep emotions, are devoted, enjoy different cultures and out of the mainstream experiences, have strong intuition and occult abilities, and a healthy sexuality. You are emotionally transformative of self and others, able to support others through troubled times, can handle anything life throws your way, and are resourceful with others money.

Shadow image: Funeral pyre

Emotional stress and repression: You can be vengeful, bitter, controlling, punishing, and unable to move beyond the negative experiences of the past. Out of control emotions, obsessive-compulsive behaviors and habits, and superstitious are common. You can justify malicious behavior as provoked by others. You use others, and you use sex for power and control.

Moon in Sagittarius

Light image: Emotional truth

Emotional ease: You are generally optimistic, have strong religious and/or spiritual beliefs, honesty, humor, and independence. The outdoors, travel, and adventure foster your emotional well-being. You feel lucky, are adaptable, ethical, and moral. You tend to form relationships with others based on equality.

Shadow image: Snake-oil salesperson

Emotional stress and repression: You tend to feel stupid and/or like an intellectual snob. You act disrespectful of others' beliefs, philosophies, religions, and thought processes, change residence and travel to avoid problems, use personal belief system as excuse for negative behaviors, try to coerce others to own way of thinking, and are often unable to make a commitment to others. You look for ways to leave emotionally in relationships. You tend to escape obsessively into sports, hunting, gambling, travel, and dangerous adventures. You sell an inauthentic belief system, discount the suffering of others, and don't like to be touched.

Moon in Capricorn

Light image: Emotional achiever

Emotional ease: You have a strong sense of responsibility—especially to family, a dry humor, tend to offer guidance and wisdom to others, are hard-working, learn from mistakes, and are acutely aware of and sensitive to the obligations others carry—especially parents. You are patient, have follow-through, and a strong sense of destiny. You strive for positive recognition and achievement.

Shadow image: Empty hourglass

Emotional stress and repression: Your parental expectations stifle personal growth. You are afraid to break or challenge society's rules. You are unable to feel and/or express emotions, vulnerabilities, and weaknesses, and can't let down professional persona. You may have irrational goals and expectations of self, be oversensitive, and fear failure. You are trapped in parent-child relationships, discipline self and others for emotional disobedience, have difficulty forming relationships with women, and a tendency to form dependent relationships.

Moon in Aquarius

Light image: Emotional prodigy

Emotional ease: You enjoy connecting to others through humor, act unselfishly, are motivated by humanitarian causes, have quirky behaviors, like to be part of group activities, attract unusual partners, are able to channel inspirations and inventions from personal dreams, and have an immediate emotional reaction to people, places, and things. You need freedom in relationships, and an individual means of expression.

Shadow image: Electrical fire

Emotional stress and repression: Your personal life may be wrought with erratic, sudden, and upsetting upheavals. You are unable to express emotions directly, tend to use humor to mask feelings, possess little or no self-understanding, experience neurotic nervous energy, and are insensitive to personal needs and feelings of others. You tend to feel alienated from the world, and have trouble dealing with emotional pain—projecting it out onto others. You are unreachable, unable to form or maintain intimate relationships, have unsettling emotional habits and behaviors, and unconsciously sabotage the efforts of self and others.

Moon in Pisces

Light image: Emotional savior

Emotional ease: You tend to see the good in everybody and everything. You are compassionate, tender, an imaginative lover, a champion for those disadvantaged and in need, see the interconnectedness of all life, and have faith in the universe. You are able to materialize the ideas and images found in dreams and fantasies. You value the dreams of self and others, have strong intuitive and psychic abilities, and easily empathize with the feelings of others.

Shadow image: Blinding fog

Emotional stress and repression: You tend to attract parasitic people, feel chronically exhausted, have a false sense of self, are faithless, can't see people as they really are—instead, focusing on what they could be. You are delusional, oversensitive, easily dejected, impressionable, gullible and dependent.

Astrology and Weight Goals

By Nina Lee Braden

Have you ever eaten when you were worried about money? Or when you had feelings of low self-worth? Or when you felt insecure? Welcome to the club. As we know, eating isn't the answer to financial problems, low self-worth, or insecurity. But astrologically, because how we feel about food and how we use food are influenced by the Second House—the same house that also covers money, security, and feelings of self-worth—it is easy for us to confuse food with other Second House issues. Many of us have food, money, security, and self-worth all tangled together in our minds and in our subconscious.

In this article, we'll look at how Moon phases and transits can affect your eating and your weight. While both the Sun and Moon signs are important factors to consider, we'll concentrate mainly on the Moon's influence because of its connection with our emotions. All you need to know is your Moon sign right now, but if you want a better understanding of how your Sun, Moon, and Ascendant influence your eating and health, I recommend that you have an astrologer interpret your astrological natal chart. Information found in your astrological natal chart can help you can begin to achieve you weight goals. You can find your Moon sign by referring to the Find Your Moon Sign on pages 65–77, or by obtaining an astrological birth chart online, from an astrologer, or from Llewellyn's Chart Services.

We'll also look at ways to use the energy of Moon phases, and the changing energy of the Moon transiting through the signs, to help you along. Concentrating on your natal Moon sign, or the transiting Moon, can yield good results in working on your weight issues.

Often, the Moon's sign will show how and where we are most vulnerable. It can also show our dreams, desires, and ideals. In fact, if you want to know where someone's heart is, know his or her Moon sign. The Moon represents nurturing—how we nurture others and ourselves. We all need nurturing, but we need to be nurtured in individual ways.

The Moon in Your Life

The sign and placement of the Moon in the natal chart can provide clues as to the best ways to nurture on an individual level. When we feel in need of nurturing, it is all too easy to turn to food. If we know what our nurturing needs are, and we've prepared a list of how to meet those needs, we can turn to something other than food. When your basic emotional, safety, and security needs are not met, as represented by your Moon, you'll struggle all the more with your weight. To know what nurtures you, look at the sign and house location of your Moon in your natal chart.

If your Moon is in Aries, for example, you need to be first in at least one very important part of your life. You need to be very clear about how you are and what your personal boundaries are.

If your Moon is in Taurus, you need simplicity at the core of your life. You can have intrigues and complications all around you, but at your core, you need serenity and simplicity. A teddy bear will make some people feel safe and secure, but a good self-defense class is necessary for others.

If your Moon is in Gemini, you need mental variety and stimulation, and a lot of high-quality communication (both listening and talking) with someone who sees you as an equal and whom you see as an equal.

If your Moon is in Cancer, you need strong emotional connections, privacy, a strong inner life, and a place that you can call home.

If your Moon is in Leo, you need honest applause for sharing intimately of yourself, and you need joy experienced through creative self-expression.

If your Moon is in Virgo, you need a clean, orderly space in at least one key part of your life. This need for order is not frivolous or superficial. It is an essential component of who you are. You also need to have daily activity where you feel needed and helpful.

If your Moon is in Libra, you need harmony and balance; you need your one-on-one relationships to be positive and supportive, and peace is very important to you.

If your Moon is in Scorpio, you need intensity in your life. You need to examine areas of life that many people find difficult or uncomfortable: death, disease, sex, and the occult.

If your Moon is in Sagittarius, you need freedom, and to travel and explore. Travel can be mental or physical, but in some way you need to venture boldly into uncharted territory.

If your Moon is in Capricorn, you need tradition, structure, and organization. You need to express your ambition in healthy ways; you may also need to be in the public eye a great deal and to have a high profile in the community.

If your Moon is in Aquarius, you need to march to a different drummer. Boredom and routine are deadly and should be avoided. You need to look toward the future, to have long-term goals, and to be active in groups that try to make the world a better place.

If your Moon is in Pisces, you need to dream—to let your visions and imagination soar. You need to retreat periodically from the world in order to quietly look within yourself. You need to learn to transcend the daily details of life.

Utilizing the Moon's Phase and Sign

The Full Moon and the New Moon provide wonderful times that we can use to help us in our weight loss. On the Full Moon, we can release bad habits, grudges, fears, anger, or whatever else we want to release. Although releasing work is best done at the Full Moon, anytime from the Full Moon until just before the New Moon will work. The New Moon is also a wonderful time for starting new eating or exercise habits. Again, the New Moon is best for beginnings, but anytime from the New Moon until just before the Full Moon will work.

Each sign that the Moon passes through during the month provides its own special energy that we can utilize for weight issues, or any other concern. Although the transiting Moon affects all of us, it doesn't affect us all in quite the same way. For details on using the transits of your Moon with your individual chart, please consult your local astrologer.

The Moon in Aries is a time for new beginnings. It is an excellent time to start a new eating plan or any new program dealing with the body. If you are normally a couch potato who hates exercise, you may find it easier to propel yourself into movement each month when the Moon is in Aries.

When the Moon is in Taurus, plan to enjoy the physical world through your senses. It's not a time for vigorous exercise, but rather for becoming one with your body through the movements of yoga or tai chi. Serve and eat sensual, appealing foods. If you are trying to lose weight, find or pre-pare special low-calorie treats. Avoid feeling deprived. There are ways to treat yourself without eating a lot of high-fat foods.

Restlessness may be a problem when the Moon transits Gemini. Use this energy to do a variety of brief exercises, or to try out new and inter-esting foods. Gemini is a social sign, therefore, this is a good time to eat or exercise with a friend who supports you in your weight goals.

When the Moon transits through Cancer, you may find yourself feeling more emotional than usual. If you want to eat more when your emotions are heightened, or if you can't stand the sight of food when your emotions are strong, take preventative measures to have healthy comfort foods around. That way you won't be tempted to eat unhealthy foods, or to skip meals.

Eat out so that you can be seen when the Moon is in Leo. Go to the most popular restaurant in town, even if you only order a beverage and an appe-tizer. If you cook while the Moon is in Leo, make sure that the food looks and tastes good. Be creative with your exercise and make it personal.

You may find that you can analyze freely when the Moon is in Virgo, even if you normally hate counting calories or fat grams.
This is a good time to be practical, to re-eval-uate your food and exercise activities. Are you eating healthy? How healthy are you moving (or not moving)? Use your dis-crimination.

Plan time to beautify, balance, and reconnect with people when the Moon enters Libra (another social sign). This is a wonderful time to dance, or to do any form of beautiful movement. Make sure

that eating is harmonious. The mood for eating now is more important than what you eat.

When the Moon is in Scorpio, it is the perfect time to psychoanalyze yourself. Discover why you prefer certain foods under certain circumstances, why you can exercise healthily at some times but not at others, or what makes you tick in regards to weight issues. This is the time to explore all of the secrets of your weight problems and to find the hidden answers.

When the Moon enters Sagittarius, it is time to move and explore. This is the time to expand your fitness experience, try new exercises, or experiment with ethnic foods. It is also a wonderful time to visit the zoo or frolic outdoors with pets, particularly horses and large dogs.

In Capricorn, the Moon encourages us to work hard. Buckle down and discipline yourself. Push yourself to your limits. Traditional forms of exercise are best at this time. Pick a food role model and eat like your role model for the next few days.

There's a scent of something new in the air—something radical and unique—when the Moon is transiting through Aquarius. While the Moon is in Aquarius then, stand up for a cause you support, become a vegan, abandon your automobile, or enter a walkathon. Many a confirmed meat-eater finds that a vegetarian menu a few days a month adds fervor to life.

When the Moon travels through Pisces, reality becomes a bit vague and hard to grasp so take a break. You may find that it's difficult to stick to your normal routines of eating or exercising. Pamper yourself. Take a much-needed rest, but be on guard against excessive alcohol intake. In just a few days, the Moon will be back in Aries, and you'll be fired up and ready to begin a new cycle of experiences.

And so we see how the transiting Moon can affect our weight issues each month. If you study and use the transits of the Moon, you'll begin to feel like you have a secret advantage over your friends who are astrologically challenged.

As you work with your needs, as expressed by your Moon's sign and house, your weight issues should become easier to manage. You'll find that food and exercise become a part of the natural rhythm of life, and not things to be hated or feared.

Between Dark and Light

By Terry Lamb

Joan (not her real name) is a twenty-five-year-old woman whose child-hood family problems have made it difficult for her to select a definite career path for herself. She was born to a young mother and a military father who was away too much to be a support. Her mother was so over-whelmed that she gave Joan up to foster care when she was preschool age. Her parents divorced soon after. Although she and her biological family stayed in close contact, her mother never resumed care for her and they have had minimal contact. She has had difficulties following through on her desire to complete college, but she is currently enrolled in a commu-nity college, where she is enjoying some success.

Marcus is a forty-eight-year-old writer who, although his life has had some ups and downs, feels content with where he is now. He is deeply sat-isfied with his work, even though finances could be a little better. He enjoys a good and active relationship with his family and considers them an important part of his life. His parents have enjoyed a stable, happy mar-riage throughout his life, and his own marriage mirrors their experience. His relationships with his children are very close as well. He describes his life as "fulfilling" and "sometimes challenging, but basically stable."

The difference between the stories of these two people can be described in part by the relationship between the Sun and Moon in each one's birth chart. The Sun and Moon are the two most important astrological factors in our identity. When we describe ourselves, or others describe what they see in us, the Sun and Moon will almost certainly figure prominently in the description.

The Sun represents your basic self, often displayed through your directed actions. It is the part of you that decides what's most important for you, where your path with heart is. You are likely to identify with goals and display many personality traits that are in harmony with your Sun sign. (When you tell someone your sign, you are telling them the sign that the Sun was in at your birth.) The Sun is also the brave, exploring part of yourself—the part that accepts challenges and takes on the task of fulfilling your big goals.

The Moon represents the inner you that you share with close friends and family, but which others may not know at all. It is a conglomerate of all the things you have experienced in the past (whether in this or past lives)—your childhood or family experiences, memories, habits, and the things you've become conditioned to do by your daily environment. The Moon is expressed through our feelings and through the actions we take based on our habits and expectations from past experiences.

The Sun and Moon can be looked at as a pair to see how the outer and inner parts of us mesh with each other. It shows whether our inner and outer selves cooperate or conflict with each other. In our examples, Joan has a high level of inner conflict, while Marcus is at relative peace with himself.

The Sun/Moon relationship can also tell us about the world we were born into—our family and their circumstances, and the social and political world around them. It can tell us something about our purpose for being on the planet—the way we approach life and how we will seek to have an impact on it. It may also be able to tell us about the karma we have to fulfill with family and world, in the sense of what lessons we are working on from the past. Although karma seen through the chart can't be proven and is not meant to replace our awareness gained from the here and now, people tend to relate to the descriptions below with a feeling of resonance.

Because the Sun and Moon move at different speeds through the heavens, their relationship to each other varies from day to day. This gives us the lunar cycle, which is actually the cycle of the Sun/Moon relationship to each other. The first part of the cycle, from New to Full Moon, is called the waxing Moon, when its light grows. The second half is called the waning Moon, when its light is lessening. As the Moon grows, it represents an increase in conscious awareness, which peaks at the time of the Full Moon. After that, we integrate the Full Moon awareness into our unconscious, synthesizing it into our intuitive-instinctual side, as the Moon grows dark. For this reason, during the first half of the cycle awareness moves from instinct and insight to full consciousness, while in the second half we move from full consciousness to instinct and insight.

Your Place in the Sun/Moon Cycle

To find out more about your Sun/Moon type, you have to figure out where the Sun and Moon were relative to each other when you were born. The easiest thing, if you have your chart, is to measure the angle between the two planets. To measure the angle in an astrological chart, use the Sun as your starting point. Then find the shortest way to your Moon and trace your finger to it. If you went counterclockwise, you were born in the waxing half of the cycle. If you went clockwise, you were born in the waning half of the cycle. Count the degrees between them. (There are thirty degrees per sign.)

If you do not have your chart, you can still find out what relationship your Sun and Moon have if you count the days and hours between your birthday and the New or Full Moon that came before it. You can find out the date and time of the New or Full Moon for your birth location at any library, on the web, or through an ephemeris (tables of planetary positions), astronomy or astrology software, or an astrologer. Make sure to note whether you were born after the New Moon (in the waxing half of the cycle) or after the Full Moon (in the waning half of the cycle). If you are close to the boundary between types, the next type will fit you better than the earlier one.

The Trailblazer: The New Moon Type

0 to 3 days 15 hours after the New Moon (The Moon is 0–45 degrees ahead of the Sun)

If you are a Trailblazer, you may feel like you have always been sure of who you are. You place a higher value on what you think, feel, and know inside than on what others think and feel about you. Although you may be shy, you probably find that others are naturally drawn to you, regardless of their age. They may remark on your drive and sense of purpose, and consider

your goals extraordinary or idealistic. Your parents probably supported you in whatever path you wanted to pursue, offering whatever support they could so that you could gain the skills you needed to succeed.

You may tend to lack perspective on yourself, not knowing how you come across to others. You may feel emotionally exposed at times or have difficulty expressing your feelings. Generally, you move through life on instinct and intuition, without knowing why you want what you want or have chosen the path you're on. If you are not attuned to your inner self, you may feel as though your life has no plan; yet you are pulled along in a direction which you learn about as you fulfill it.

Family is very important to you, for good or ill. You may derive your sense of direction from your family, seeing your parents as role models for your own path. If your Sun and Moon are in the same sign, you blend well with your family—you are probably very comfortable there in many ways. You likely have the "family temperament"—like the same foods, enjoy the same pastimes. You may pursue the family business. Otherwise, your blending with the family will be less complete, and you will need to develop a more unique personality.

Your task in life is to break new ground in the world around you by focusing your inner forces externally. This gives you the clarity to maintain an internal locus of control, to place your own self-value above the value that others place on you. Karmically, you are meant to be who you are without modification by the external world, but you must learn to be receptive to it, because we all need to change and grow. You will most likely maintain a strong relationship with your family throughout your life. Once you have your own family, you will be very devoted to it.

Your partner will have to accept the large role that family plays in your life, whether yours or theirs. It may be difficult for you to shift loyalties from your family of origin to your partnership. Doing so does not mean that your love for your family is diminished, only that your relationship has grown. It may seem to your partner at times that you don't listen or understand their point of view. This may be something that you need to work on to succeed in relationships.

The Butterfly: The Crescent Moon Type

From 3 days 15 hours to 7 days 6 hours after the New Moon (Moon is 45–90 degrees from the Sun)

If you are a Butterfly, you were born when the Moon was a crescent in the sky at sunset. You are dependable; a good worker who has faith in the future in spite of the fact that sometimes life seems to be a struggle. You may often feel like you are reaching for something you can't quite see; but you know it's out there, so you trudge along, one foot in front of the other. It's like living in a chrysalis, but just like the butterfly you are incubating, growing quietly and invisibly until you are ready to break out of the darkness of the old form into the light.

You feel like this because you're caught between the past and the future. You're in the ambiguous place between the candle and the star. You have the patterns that your family taught you, but they don't seem quite right for you. You would like to see your parents as role models, but you can't make the stretch. You need to spring from your internal patterns of birthright and tradition to become your own person. When you do this, you become the butterfly, able to live in the ambiguous place in life and make it work for you. The secret of that place is that it is the fountain of creativity, and you become an expression of that fountain once you discover how you are different from what your family taught you to be.

You may have an on-again, off-again relationship with your family. Their ideals of what they want you to become don't really fit your true nature; an awareness that could stay submerged until you reach adulthood. When you peel off the teachings that aren't right for you, layer by layer, you completely liberate yourself.

Your task in life is to use your personal revelations as a source of creativity to share and set an example for others. You are also here to learn and teach faith. Karmically, you are meant to shed familial and past-life concepts that do not fit who you are. This may mean a break with your family, at least for a time, until you get in touch with your true self and can maintain it in the face of their often-unwitting pressure to wear the old mask.

In relationships, you need a partner you can talk to in order to sort things out, someone you can trust not to insert their own thoughts in place of your own developing awareness. It may take you time to figure out what you think and feel. If you let your partner know about your needs, whatever they are, your relationship will go more smoothly. Once you know yourself well, you can apply your inner fountain of creativity and insight to any relationship issue that arises.

The Mobilizer: The First Quarter Type

From 7 days 6 hours to 10 days 21 hours after the New Moon (90–135 degrees from the Sun)

If you are a Mobilizer, you can see a stark contrast between the past, present, and future. The past is soaked in traditions and behaviors that may seem superfluous and outmoded, even corrupt. You see life as a challenge to clear out what is outdated, less than perfect for the future. So a feeling of urgency and sense of purpose draw you into action about the changes you feel are necessary in order for the present to become a successful future.

Your life may be busy, filled with the tasks and projects you feel are essential to your goals. Even if you're not too sure what the goal is, you feel a need to keep moving, because there's so much to be done! Something pulls you along, no matter what. You're not big on plans—you're too busy taking action for that, but you are good at motivating others. Others usually see you as strong, active, and captivating. They will appreciate your energy and support if you're on their side, but they'll fear your command of the opposition's perspective if you're not. Your enthusiasm and energy are infectious, and you may find yourself in leadership roles. Even if you are in harmony with your family (which is true for some in this type), you're still busy making changes, and they've had to get used to it. There's much to admire in your parents, but you could never do things the way they do. What they did was right for them, but you have to find your own way.

You may always have known that you were not quite like the rest of your family. Sure, some things fit, but you've always known that you would strike out on your own when the time came. This doesn't mean that you can't and don't have a very good relationship with those you knew from the earliest days of your life, but there have probably been a few ups and downs along the way as you've sorted things out and they have adjusted to the person you needed to become. You may not always have been exactly sure of where you were headed, but the need for change was paramount.

Your task is to turn the past into the future. You are a processing unit, turning old ideas into new ones, preparing the way for what you can't quite grasp. Yet you know it's there, so you keep on going. Karmically, you are here to change—yourself and others. It delights you when you can find new ways to facilitate shifts in consciousness or form. Chances are good that change fascinates you, and you try to find ways to understand it.

In relationships, you run the risk of not giving your partner enough of your precious time in all your efforts to make the world a better place. It's important not to neglect your personal life and its pleasures (or pain). A well-balanced life is essential to fulfilling your own nature.

The Bloomer: The Gibbous Type

From 10 days 21 hours to 14 days after the New Moon (135–180 degrees from the Sun)

Just before something big happens, the Bloomer often feels it coming. If you are a Bloomer, you are full of expectation, straining toward the new awareness. You burgeon with freshness and innocence—free from the care that experience brings—yet you periodically slip into anxiety in the face of the wait. You yearn to be part of the future but are caught in the moment-that-has-yet-to-be.

You often make yourself busy with preparations to stave off your anticipation and get ready for the nameless thing is to come. This constant state of being in-between fills you with the longing to know the unknowable, but it can leave you feeling frustrated and incomplete. Yet, once you learn to master incompleteness, you find the great potential in it, because unspent energy holds great power. If you turn your longing into a quest, you can become expert at bringing something to its peak, to its blossom. This is a matter of technique and skill at harnessing energies. Others often see you as a technical expert because you put so much effort into understanding the fine points of your pursuits. Sometimes they may even protest their boredom when you launch into what you know are those absolutely essential intricacies of how things work.

In your family, you may have felt like the black sheep. You may have stood in the background and watched the others in amazement at times, and you may have even wondered if you were adopted, the differences seem so deep. There may be awkwardness in communication or understanding, but that doesn't mean that you didn't love each other. As an adult, you may continue to feel as though you were cut of a different cloth, but as you gain in self-knowledge, you will find that any feelings of alienation dissipate. You probably feel that your parents are better models of what not to be like—or at least what you could never emulate, because your orientation to life is so different.

Your task in this lifetime is to bring things to fruition, to prepare the way for new awareness. It is a fine art, one that is vital to the entire process. You will probably be drawn to some particular set of skills or techniques in order to fulfill this part of your nature. Karmically, your lesson is to master the moment of incompleteness. There is often a lesson about patience and being willingness to work in the background.

In relationships, you may fear being imperfect and struggle to better yourself to be ready for a partner, or to compensate for your partner's weaknesses. Remember to allow your partner their flaws so that they can grow; this allows you to take your own risks, make mistakes, and be forgiven. It is important not to take responsibility for what is not truly ours.

The Illuminator: The Full Type

0 to 3 days 15 hours after the Full Moon (Moon is 180–135 degrees before the Sun)

If you are an Illuminator, you cast light wherever you go. However, this can be tiring—sometimes it would be nice just to rest in the background for a while. When you bring light to the circumstances around you, it means that things change. You change right along with them—so much so that you may feel unstable at times. Others may see your life as glamorous or exciting, but sometimes life on the edge is a lot to bear.

What makes it so difficult is that you are in a constant state of deciding: should you follow the tried and true, or should you venture into the unknown? The choice is engendered by the insight you receive whenever you find yourself in a new situation. You naturally cut to the quick and know what's going on, much to your discomfort at times. That awareness brings on the choice of staying with the way things were or going with your new insight. The question is, do you trust yourself? Have you given your insights a chance, or do you play it safe? More than any other type, you are aware of the Full Moon when it occurs. Although it influences everyone, you are most acutely sensitive.

Your family life was probably somewhat checkered, even difficult. You may have gotten used to conflict as a daily occurrence. You may have found yourself in the middle of the fracas time and again, without knowing how you got there or how to stop. You may have come from a family, which did not stay together, and so you got used to splitting your loyalties and yourself into two separate beings, one for each household.

Your task in this life is to fulfill yourself and to empower the fulfillment of others. Karmically, you seek for the reconciliation of the two halves of yourself, and a way to calm the inner conflict you feel. The world is not black and white, but blendable into shades of gray. To mend the divide, it is important to listen to both sides of your nature and try out those new and untried concepts and principles to see if they work. Only then can you learn how the world works and trust your own inner process.

Relationships are important to you, and sometimes you may feel it necessary to set yourself aside in order to maintain peace. However, it usually isn't long before your true feelings come out, and the relationship is challenged again. You secretly long for the "relationship," the one person who will end all of your dilemmas (even if you already have a partner). When you are looking for a partner in this way, you are really looking for the lost parts of yourself. Only when you recover them can you have a whole, healthy partnership.

The Disperser: The Disseminating Type

From 3 days 15 hours to 7 days 6 hours after the Full Moon (The Moon is 135–90 degrees before the Sun)

In the wake of the Full Moon comes a release of energy suppressed until the moment of illumination. If you are a Disperser, you ride this energy wave and direct its flow. The moment of illumination is expansive—there is so much to share, so much to do! You are full of new ideas and the excitement they bring. You want to share them with everyone. This can be a joy ride, but not without its pitfalls. The largest danger is mistaking the energy for your own to use as you will. As you burn inside with the desire to let others know what you know, it is tempting to think that your way is the only way, because it is so crystal clear to you.

The aftermath of the Full Moon may leave you feeling imbued with the truth. You want to share your joy, your enthusiasm for how well your perspective can make everything work, so you take your message everywhere you go. You are a mover and a shaker; feeling as though you have your finger on the pulse of life. You love to surrender to the message, to the energy of light as it disperses through consciousness. To spread the essence of your message effectively, you must temper your own sense of what's true with the reality that there are many ways to understand and interpret it. If you don't, others may see you as "preachy." Once you learn to accommodate others' viewpoints, they are more likely to see your insightfulness and leadership qualities.

You probably came from an adventurous family, or one that had strong beliefs and principles. You may have engaged in lively discussions, and discipline was likely to have been based on your understanding of and adherence to those beliefs. As a group, you may have considered yourselves avant-garde, on the cutting edge of change. You may even have traveled frequently, or had a journalist in your midst. You may have idealized one or both of your parents, even if you never felt you could live up to their example.

Your life task is to spread the news, to be an agent of dispersion, to share your insights with others. Your karmic lesson in this is to learn to recognize the value of others' point of view and to be receptive to them. This will help others be open to your constantly evolving awareness.

Learning to listen to others is an essential skill to forming successful partnerships. Until you have learned this, your partner could be drowned out in the din of your own insights. Having a series of short-term partnerships is a sign that this may be a process in your relationships. Relationships work for you if you can allow yourself to take the time for them.

The Sage: The Last Quarter Type

From 7 days 6 hours to 10 days 21 hours after the Full Moon (The Moon is 90–45 degrees before of the Sun)

If you are a Sage, you participate in the involution of the Full Moon's energy. With the next New Moon right around the corner, it is time to integrate illumination and experience to derive wisdom. So, much of your growth is internalized, turned toward deep thought and strategy. You plan, plot, and devise. You listen to the voices of the past and weigh them against the insights of the present. Your challenge is to move toward a goal by choice, not habit. For you, the past is more distant, and you must choose whether and how much to rely on it. Yours is a path of synthesis. After you have finished integrating past and present, the insights that were new at the Full Moon have been absorbed into intuition and instinct. You can no longer differentiate them as distinct lessons—they are just a part of your overall wisdom, ready to be applied to the next stimulus that arises.

People often see you as quiet and unchanging, but deep inside you know that you are working on the next change. You may already have gone through at least one major transformation in your life, shocking those around you with the suddenness of it; but it wasn't sudden to you. Sometimes you may feel like a walking contradiction, feeling one way and behaving another. You may feel alienated and alone in your truth, finding it difficult to share what you feel is not yet "ready for prime time."

You may have felt like the parent in your family when growing up, perhaps because a parent was missing, or because you had the natural maturity to assume the role. You may have been acutely aware of the structures in your home—the rules, how much food or money there was—and you may worried about them or managed them. Even in a healthy family, you may have been a proponent of structure and held yourself to rules and boundaries that others may not have felt bound to uphold. This self-discipline may have given you the ability to achieve a high level of success in your youth.

Your task in life is to manifest the Full Moon awareness into responsible form. You are here to bring new ideas and philosophies into the organized system of society, culture, or government on however large or small a scale. Karmically, you need to learn to balance past and present in a way that fulfills the highest ideals of the structure or agency you serve. This means listening to the voices outside you, as well as those within.

In relationship, you may run the risk of isolating yourself from your partner. When we partner with someone, it is to include him or her in our life, and we can't do that without telling them how life is for us. Developing trust, and then sharing our real self, creates the support system you need to make those wise decisions.

The Visionary: The Balsamic Type

From 10 days 21 hours after the Full Moon to the New Moon (The Moon is 45–0 degrees before of the Sun)

If you are a Visionary, you were born right before the New Moon. Although you are part of an old, ending cycle, you can feel the new one coming. Your life is about feeling the future in the present and learning to live with it. You may feel out of step with the times. You can see something coming, or you know what needs to be done, but you may feel alone in your knowledge. Later—often years later—what you saw comes to fruition, and you realize that you were right. The truth is, you are closely in touch with an instinctive-intuitive world that others rarely sense, let alone live in. Because you have this contact with the inner world, you have a clear vision of the future. Like so many other visionaries, your ideas come before others can accept them, and so they are rejected, or commandeered by someone else when society is ready for them.

You rarely grow up to be what others expect. Over your life, you've encountered situations that make it apparent to you the past did not prepare you well enough to live in the future. So you to break away, often without fanfare or explanation. Others may find you hard to understand because they can't see what you do. They may view you as a prophet or martyr, or feel that you take unacceptably high risks.

In your family, you may have been the black sheep. You may have felt distinctly different from the rest of those you grew up with. You may have been called upon to make sacrifices or suffer for your family because of your personal ideals, or just because someone had to do it. Even if they accepted your visionary qualities, or had some of their own, theirs were different, and you may have often felt alone in your perceptions. You may not have felt that your parents were valid role models for you.

Your life task is to carry the seed of the next cycle, seeing into the future and adhering to its truth. It is your function to dream and be different. The biggest karmic lesson you face is to develop true clarity, without the taint of your own fears and expectations. This is a huge task, which requires constant vigilance, and it requires "alone time" to sort things out. It is also important to maintain a toehold in the world that others call reality while dreaming the future into existence.

In relationship, you may have trouble expressing your vision to your partner, either out of fear of rejection or simply because it just doesn't translate into words. Even if your partner can't see the future you see, it's good to share your vision, your feelings. Your partner can be your anchor to reality.

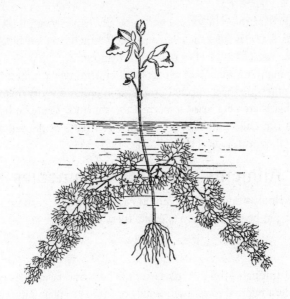

Medicinal Astrology

By *Sheri Ann Richerson*

Medicinal astrology, the use of herbs to treat physical and emotional symptoms, is one of the oldest medical traditions in our Western culture. While the exploration of herbs and astrology is ancient, with all the new information we have on herbs and their uses that our forefathers didn't, we can certainly make the most out of this information. Remember that herbal medicine is not meant to replace traditional medical care, but rather to be used as a supplement. A licensed physician should treat any condition that persists.

The three signs that are the foundation of your horoscope are the Sun, or life force; the Moon, or personality; and the Ascendant, or physical body. From the examination of the planetary combinations and placements in a natal or progressed chart, a medicinal astrologer can find likely physical or psychological ailments that may cause an individual a problem. It is known that certain herbs resonate with the energetic and health patterns identified in each astrological sign. A knowledgeable medicinal astrologer can determine from the individual's chart potential health problems. For example, people with the zodiacal sign Aries prominent in their astrological birth chart typically experience problems with their sinuses. (Aries rules the head and face.) A medicinal astrologer might suggest the use of basil leaf to relieve the symptoms.

While many medicinal astrologers recommend using more traditional methods of testing the suspected problems in order to verify them, proper diet and herbs are often used to correct the ailments. Using herbs medicinally, you can choose to support any or all of parts of the self as represented by their astrological sign.

Ailments and Herbal Remedies

Let's take a look at some of the common ailments within each sign and the herbs that can be used to help alleviate these problems.

Aries

(March 21 through April 20) rules over the head and face. Aries personalities are often referred to as "hotheaded" or "headstrong and impulsive." A health practitioner might suggest treatments for their head, sinuses, and skin, as well as something to calm them down. Elder flower is a cooling herb commonly used to support the overall health of the head. Hops flower is a nervine that induces calm and promotes good sleep, and vervain is used to fortify the nervous system and induce a calm state. Leaves from violets are used to nourish the mucus membranes. Basil leaf is a perfect choice to support the sinuses and nourish the mind. Marshmallow root is used to cool the emotions as well as calm the spirit. Dandelion root makes a supreme digestive tonic.

Taurus

(April 21 through May 21) rules the neck and throat. Taurus personalities, well-known for their slow, plodding manner, must learn how to maintain a healthy metabolism of fats, and they have the most need to nourish the throat and thyroid. Thyme is known to make a wonderful tonic for the throat together with helping to keep the immune system functioning properly. This is one herb that individuals with the Sun, Moon, or Ascendant in Taurus should keep a supply of, and regularly use. Red raspberry leaves make an excellent tonic for hormonal balance. Marshmallow is commonly used for the immune system and tissues, while plantain leaf is a terrific soothing herb for overall health. Sage is an anti-oxidant used to promote mental alertness burdock root makes a great tonic that is commonly used to aid in the digestion of fats and maintain a proper liver function, and kelp is generally used to promote a healthy thyroid gland and metabolism.

Gemini

Vervain

(May 22 through June 21) rules the shoulders, arms, hands, lungs, and nervous system. Gemini personalities, like butterflies, often flit from one interest or topic to another quite rapidly. They often need to fortify an active nervous system and lungs. Vervain is an excellent choice to help fortify the nervous system, induce calmness, and soothe the emotions. Other helpful herbs that support this endeavor are the flowers of elder, honeysuckle, and lavender. Mullein leaf is an optimal herb to use to help cool and moisten the throat and lungs. Fennel seed is a warm digestive herb that is soothing to the spirit, while fenugreek seed is utilized in nourishing the lungs. Other healthful herbs for Geminis include skullcap, which makes a wonderful cerebral tonic for the mind; parsley leaf, which is used to promote the body's balance and utilization of oxygen; and peppermint, which is a good digestive herb that also helps to calm.

Cancer

(June 22 through July 23) rules the stomach and breasts. Known for their nurturing qualities as well as for their mood swings, Cancer personalities must provide balance for both the stomach and digestion, as well as promote serenity. Caraway seed is a warming herb that is often used to promote healthy digestion. It also works well in conjunction with Irish moss, which is known to cool and smooth the gastrointestinal tract. Peppermint is also used by Cancers to promote calm feelings, as well as to aid digestion. Catnip can help the moody Cancer person to express their true feelings, while hyssop is a nervine that helps to support their serenity.

Leo

(July 24 through August 23) rules the heart, chest, upper back, and spine. Leo personalities have a need to tone the circulatory system, along with uplifting the spirit. Hawthorn leaves and flowers aid in supporting a healthy cardiovascular system. Other excellent herbs for a Leo include ginger root and calendula flower, which promote healthy blood circulation. Calendula flowers are usually made into a tonic and used that way. Orange peel is used to cool heat in the body, making it a perfect remedy for such Sun-loving people. Motherwort is a cardiac tonic and nervine for the heart and nerves.

Calendula Officinalis

Virgo

(August 24 through September 23) rules the lower intestine. A Virgo's attention to detail often leads to hypersensitivity or feelings of anxiety. It is important for Virgo personalities to maintain healthy digestion and intestinal function, in addition to maintaining a healthy nervous system. Dill seed is a digestive herb that is used to support the nervous system. Other herbs that will help induce a calm state are fennel seed, lavender flowers, peppermint, and rosemary. Skullcap is a great cerebral tonic as well as being a nerve nutrient. Caraway seed is a warming herb that is excellent for healthy digestion. Another herb that works well as a supreme digestive tonic is cinnamon bark. Parsley leaf helps to promote the body's balance and utilization of oxygen. Licorice root makes an excellent energizing and soothing tonic

Libra

(September 24 through October 23) rules the lower back and kidneys. Libra personalities need herbs that will help to cleanse their kidneys, tone the lower back, and nourish the mind. Libras like their life to be perfectly balanced, and marshmallow root is a perfect herb to help them in this feat. Marshmallow root can also be used to cool the emotions as well as the body. Parsley is used to promote the body's balance and utilization of oxygen, while dandelion leaves make an excellent cleansing herb for the body. Bilberry leaf is a natural strengthening herb, and burdock root makes a wonderful tonic for healthy kidneys. Plantain leaf is a great herb for overall health. Vervain and violet leaves are also excellent choices to help fortify the nervous system, induce calmness, and soothe the emotions.

Scorpio

(October 24 through November 22) rules over the reproductive organs and bowels. Scorpio's often find that they need to tone the reproductive system and enhance sensuality, in addition to learning to balance their intensity. Coriander seed is a good choice in herbs for Scorpios because it brings about a positive mood, as does blessed thistle, which also promotes overall health. Nettle leaves are another exceptional choice in herbs to nurture the overall health of Scorpios. Ginkgo biloba is excellent for nourishing the mind. Blackberry leaf makes a tonic that benefits both the reproductive organs and the blood. Another problem area for Scorpios is their nervous stomach. Some herbs to help alleviate this problem include peppermint, bee pollen, and St. John's wort. Basil is often used to nourish the mind. Herbs such as sarsaparilla, damiana, and oatstraw enhance the sensual side of Scorpios. Oatstraw also builds libido, and saw palmetto is a reproductive tonic.

Sagittarius

(November 23 through December 21) rules the hips and thighs. Well-known for their love of adventure, Sagittarians often need a remedy to calm and cool them down. Fennel seed is a warm digestive herb useful to many signs to promote a calm state. Burdock root, another multi-sign herb, is used to make a tonic that cools and purifies the blood, and a tonic made from agrimony is often used to cool the body. Red clover blossom is a great tonic to help promote overall health and cleansing of a Sagittarian's body. Centaury root is an excellent digestive tonic said to be named after the centaur, a symbol of Sagittarius.

Capricorn

(December 22 through January 20) rules the skeleton and knees. Capricorns, well-known for their leadership qualities and their desire to "climb" the ladder of success, need to use herbs that support their body structure, as well as to promote relaxation and balance. Ho shou wu root is a warming herb for the body, mind, and spirit of a Capricorn. Kava-kava root helps to nourish the mind, and peppermint is used to induce calmness. Horsetail and nettle leaves make a supreme tonic that benefits a Capricorn's body structure. Mullein leaves help to cool and moisten irritated body tissues.

Aquarius

(January 21 through February 19) rules the ankles and circulatory system. Those born with Aquarius prominent in the astrological birth chart frequently find that they have a need to alleviate stress, as well as enhance their circulation. Recommended herbs for alleviating stress include peppermint and ho shou wu root. Clove bud promotes healthy circulation; and gentian root, a bitter herb, is customarily useful for promoting a healthy nutrient assimilation. Another helpful herb for an Aquarius is cinnamon bark, which makes a wonderful digestive and warming tonic.

Pisces

(February 20 through March 20) rules the feet. For Pisces personalities who need to feel more grounded and focused, yellow dock is recommended. The use of white willow bark, often taken to improve the health of Pisces joints, is thought to be in direct relation to the fact that willow is flexible in water. Lemon balm is beneficial in helping to brighten a Pisces mood.

Other Uses for Herbs

In addition to taking herbs in capsules, or tonics, many healing properties of herbs can be taken advantage of in other ways. For example, many of the above herbs can be grown in your garden. Herbs are excellent container plants if you do not have traditional garden space available. Other excellent ways to enjoy the healing properties of herbs are in your culinary dishes, as well as using aromatherapy. Baths are known for their healing and calming effects; you can always add a few drops of essential oil, or toss in a handful of fresh herbs for a delightful and healing experience.

Editor's note: The contents of this article are not meant to diagnose, treat, prescribe, or substitute for consultation with a licensed health care professional. Herbs, whether used internally or externally, should be introduced in small amounts to allow the body to adjust and to detect possible allergies. Llewellyn Worldwide does not participate in, endorse, or have any authority or responsibility concerning private business transactions between its authors and the public. All related advisories were taken from the *American Herbal Products Association's Botanical Safety Handbook* (CRC Press, 1997).

Sage is not recommended for long-term use. Do not exceed recommended dosage.

Fenugreek is not recommended for use during pregnancy unless otherwise directed by a qualified expert. A number of common herbs fall into this category; it is therefore advised that you consult a qualified expert before using any herb for medicinal purposes if you are pregnant.

Catnip (or catmint) is a uterine stimulant and not recommended for use during pregnancy.

There is some concern that doses in excess of 3.0 grams of powdered motherwort extract may cause diarrhea, uterine, bleeding, and stomach irritation.

Prolonged use or high doses of licorice are not recommended except under supervision of a qualified health practitioner. Contraindicated for diabetics, and in hypertension, liver disorders, severe kidney insufficiency, and hypokalemia. May cause reversible potassium depletion and sodium retention.

Ho shou wu (Chinese knotweed) should not be used if you are suffering from diarrhea. The root is cathartic, and may cause gastric distress.

It is recommended that you consult a physician regularly when using saw palmetto for treatment of enlarged prostrate.

Gentian (*Gentiana lutea L.*), commonly known as yellow gentian or wild gentian, is not recommended for use if you have gastric and duodenal ulcers, or when gastric irritation or inflammation is present. Large-leaf gentian (*Gentiana macrophylla Bge.*) may cause nausea in high doses.

Individuals with a history of kidney stones should use yellow dock (also known as broad-leaved dock and curled dock) with caution.

Menus by Moonlight

By Kathleen Spitzer

As the Moon moves through all the signs of the zodiac (in approximately thirty days) it picks up the flavor of each sign, which in turn influences daily life. People around the world have long used the Moon as a guide in choosing the best days to bottle fruits, and make jams, bread, sauerkraut, pickles, and beer. Each sign has its own energy that contributes to the overall mood of the Moon.

If you know in which sign the Moon resides in your natal birth chart, consider that to be the New Moon of your own personal Moon cycle. The Moon's influence on you will be even stronger during those two or three days. Keep track of grocery shopping, meal preparation, and meals for a couple months to see how strongly you feel influenced by the Moon. If you have a Cancer Sun, Moon, or Ascendant, then look out! The Moon is definitely influencing your taste buds.

In general, the foods you are drawn to when the Moon is in a certain sign are not the foods of that sign, but the foods of their polar opposites. When the Moon is in Aries and thus dominated by fiery Mars, the foods that whet your taste buds are the delectable Venus-ruled fruits and vegetables of Libra. Consult Nicholas Culpeper's *The Complete Herbal* for more details of this theory.

How you eat and what you eat may change from day to day as you try to juggle work, kids, cooking, your beloved, and housekeeping. Take a look at the Moon to measure how you're doing.

The Moon in the Air Signs of Gemini, Libra, and Aquarius

When the Moon is in an air sign, you may be tempted to graze and nibble instead of sitting down to dine. You are more than likely eating on the run, and that demands food that can be carried by hand. You certainly don't feel like grocery shopping on these days unless you're off to enjoy an open-air farmers' market or a food shop that's a little out of the ordinary. These are the best days to get your family to try something new to them and different—a great vegetarian dish, or some unusual cuisine from another country, for example. You want to eat light and cook light.

When the Moon is in Gemini, Libra, or Aquarius, thinking about food has a greater appeal than actually preparing it. The Moon in Gemini, especially, could motivate you to opt for dinner at your favorite fast-food restaurant. Serve a special sandwich that you have grilled on these days. Work out a standard version to add to your repertoire so that you have the ingredients on hand so preparation and cooking are simple and fast.

Find a good boutique bread—maybe a sourdough with green and black olives. Stack a good ham or smoked turkey (have it sliced very thin for best flavor) and slices of sharp provolone cheese on bread slices; add caramelized onions, roasted red peppers, or eggplant. Top each sandwich with another bread slice, and grill the sandwich in olive oil seasoned with a dab of butter. Serve hot with an interesting deli potato salad you've always wanted to try. Garnish with a sour garlic pickle half for a punch of vitamin C.

You'll have the best luck interesting your family in food during an Aquarius Moon if you find something unusual to serve. Dig out your recipe for chocolate cake made with tomato soup or the one with mayonnaise. These are also the days to serve something with air beaten into it: cheese omelets, puff pastry covering a potpie, meringues with fruit for dessert. Get take-out hot-and-sour soup from your favorite Chinese restaurant and add some steamed brown rice to make it a little more rib sticking. Sweet and sour combinations seem more delectable when the Moon is in an air sign. Use your microwave to prepare these meals.

The Moon in Libra can really get your sweet tooth tingling. Of all the air signs, this is the one that lends itself to a gourmet interest in food. You can be particularly adept at food shopping today, choosing the best produce and finding the best quality for your money. Spend some time at a good deli and try something different and unusual. If your town has a restaurant with a really good buffet, this is the night to go out for dinner. Everybody wants a "little of this" and a "little of that" on these nights. To prepare food at home, think simple and prepare a "sweet" meal of airy waffles served with mixed berry sauce, real maple syrup, and whipped cream. Add some homemade, lean, breakfast sausage. On days when the Moon is in Libra, presentation is all, so be sure to garnish the plates with attractive and appealing tidbits. This is the perfect night to serve a romantic dinner to your beloved. Be sure and set the stage with starched linens, gleaming dishes, silver, and crystal. Don't forget the scented candles. Vanilla is an aphrodisiac! And so is asparagus; serve the following as an appetizer.

Marinated Asparagus

1 pound fresh asparagus (pencil slim is best)
Marinade:
1 shallot, minced
1 tablespoon red wine or balsamic vinegar
1 teaspoon lemon juice
½ teaspoon Dijon mustard
3 tablespoons olive oil
Salt and pepper to taste

Clean asparagus, trimming scales if they are large or filled with dirt. Cook in an asparagus steamer, or lay flat in a skillet. Add a pinch of salt to the water and cook until almost tender. Do not overcook! Drain and place in a flat dish to marinate. Mix the remaining ingredients and pour over the warm asparagus. Let cool and then refrigerate until almost ready to serve. They are best at room temperature. Divide into four servings and garnish with the marinade and long strips of lemon zest. Please Venus by adding violet blossoms, pansies, or chive blossoms for a colorful counterpoint.

The Moon in the Fire Signs of Aries, Leo, and Sagittarius

These are the days when you're thinking food is fuel. You want it fast, filling, and hearty. You are willing to eat it on the run and you don't want to spend a lot of time preparing it. A casserole out of the freezer is good; any one-pot meal is better. These are the days to drag out the Crock-Pot and throw in some veggies and meat. The packages of salad greens at the market shorten prep time. If you opt for the salad bar, you can produce a meal with very little trouble.

When the Moon is in Aries, you're feeling more impulsive than usual. Cheese is definitely on your mind, and either a deep-dish pizza or lasagna is easy choices to satisfy all the tides of this Moon. Care needs to be taken to avoid the high fat and calories offered in fast-food eateries. You would think that with the Mars connection that hot, spicy foods would tempt your taste buds, but soothing foods are actually more appealing. It may be a balance thing, using subtle spices in a simple pasta to counter the passions encouraged by the fiery Moon.

When the Moon is in Leo, simple meals hold the most appeal, but they must be made with best quality ingredients and be presented in a beautiful manner. These are the days for barbecue (make your own sauce). There is something about the flavor of charcoal that is very satisfying under a Leo Moon's influence. Try a mixed grill—small portions of a variety of meats and vegetables. Keep a spicy, infused olive oil to brush on the veggies. Rosemary, garlic, bay, and juniper are the strong spices to use on these days. A whiff of cinnamon can set off your taste buds, and the splash of color from a saffron-infused risotto is equally appealing. Don't overeat though, and be sure and work off the extra calories you consume.

You may feel the urge to track down a special ingredient when the Moon slides into Sagittarius. Exploring is definitely more fun than the cooking or eating. Eating is just for keeping up your strength for the next adventure. You want a square meal that's filling (think complex carbohydrates here) and if there are leftovers, then all the better. If it has a slightly foreign flair, then you've hit the culinary jackpot. Stuff a curried chicken salad in a pita pocket (or two) or try out the following recipe on your family. Even the peanut butter crowd may love it. You can serve it at room temperature if you're still yakking on the phone when it's done.

Asian Sesame Chicken Pasta

Sauce:

3 cloves garlic, minced

1 tablespoon red wine or balsamic vinegar

1 tablespoon brown sugar

⅓ cup chunky peanut butter

¼ cup soy sauce

⅓ cup toasted sesame oil

Hot chili oil to taste

Put everything but oils in the blender (or food processor) and blend for a minute. Then slowly drizzle in the oils while the blender is whirring.

Topping:

2 chicken breast halves—skinless, boneless, julienne-sliced, and cooked

4 tablespoons toasted sesame seeds

1 cup blanched pea pods—drain well

3 scallions—trim bulb and ends and chop well

1 tablespoon toasted sesame seeds

½ pound linguine—cooked al dente

Add chicken pieces, pea pods, and 4 tablespoons of toasted sesame seeds to linguine and toss with sauce. Place in serving dish and sprinkle with scallions and garnish with remaining sesame seeds.

Serves 6.

The Moon in the Earth Signs of Taurus, Virgo, and Capricorn

These are the days to take pleasure in your meals. You can bring a very practical turn of mind to shopping, choosing quality ingredients, knowing what to buy in bulk, and what to examine carefully before purchasing. Your needs may be simple, and you may feel picky, but you are looking for the best. You are more alert to the nutritive needs of your body and more willing to take the time to satisfy them. There will be little waste in food preparation, and you can probably throw together an appealing meal with supplies from the pantry.

If you are planning a dinner party and it's important that the meal consists of excellent quality, classic dishes (that are satisfying to all the senses) do it when the Moon is in Taurus. It will be a solid success. (If this is a career move, take advantage of the Moon in Capricorn!) Taurus energy lends itself to second helpings. Fresh fruit salads (think Venus) are very appealing now. Live a little now and toss those pansies or chive blossoms into the green salads. Take the time to make a special sauce, or fresh chutney, for the entrée, and gravy for the mashed potatoes.

Health issues will be at the back of your mind when the Moon is in Virgo, and that means that you're feeling discriminating about your meals. You want good, well-prepared food that is honestly presented. You'll probably use fresh produce rather than frozen or canned. Stir-fries are the best choice, punctuated with breads made with whole grains. Bean dishes can be calming, along with anything made with yogurt if you're feeling a little jumpy. You probably think your own cooking is better than any restaurant's on these days. You may even give some attention to cleaning the kitchen!

Simple foods like good breads, oatmeal, or barley are appealing under a Capricorn Moon. So are classic dishes such as a rib roast. You'll want your meals perfectly cooked and presented. If you are feeling a little gloomy, then lighten the mood with fun, but filling foods—asparagus tips on toast can take advantage of the spring harvest, or a corn roast is perfect for a summer's evening. This is a good time to entertain, and when the Moon is here you may want to do it at a restaurant that suits the needs of the occasion. If you really feel like spending some time in the kitchen, then make bread. Skip the bread machine though, and do it yourself.

Start this bread while you're cleaning up the kitchen on Saturday night and it will be ready for Sunday brunch in the morning. It's a traditional New England recipe.

Oatmeal Molasses Batter Bread

1 cup old fashioned oats
2 cups boiling water
1 packet yeast
3 tablespoons warm water
Pinch of sugar
½ cup unsulfured molasses
1 tablespoon salt
1 cup whole wheat flour
3 cups unbleached white flour

Soak the oatmeal for one half-hour in the boiling water. Dissolve yeast in the warm water and add a good pinch of sugar. Let bubble and proof for about 10 minutes. Add the molasses, salt, and oatmeal mixture. Stir in all the flour. Cover with plastic wrap and a clean dish towel and let rise overnight.

In the morning, stir down the dough and pour into two greased loaf pans. Let rise 1 hour and bake in a preheated 350° oven 1 hour.

Always start cooking with cold water (water that has been sitting around in the hot water heater isn't as fresh). You can speed up this recipe by adding a second packet of yeast, but then you can't leave it overnight.

The Moon in the Water Signs of Cancer, Scorpio, and Pisces

These are days when you really feel like a domestic god or goddess. You love food! You want to cook! You want to eat, and you want to do it at home. Fluid retention can be a problem when the Moon lingers here so you should probably limit salt and caffeine intake. Drinking lots of water or a cup of dandelion tea can help with this. Also it would be wise to avoid eating if you are bored, angry, or inclined to stuff your feelings.

The Moon is so happy when it is in its natural home of Cancer, and you may be lured by comfort foods from your childhood. Just picture a white, fluffy, baked potato set adrift with melting butter and clouds of sour cream. Think cheeses, yogurt, creamy soups, cucumbers, and seafood. Maybe ice cream with a gooey topping for dessert. You may also crave Chinese or French cuisine, and will punctuate your cooking with hot and spicy foods like garlic, onions, and chili peppers. If you shop now, you may find yourself stocking your pantry for a rainy day. When the Moon moves into Scorpio, you will know what you want to eat and probably can't be dissuaded. You might be happy with a fresh-made pesto-sauced pasta accompanied by garlic bread, but that will be as spicy as it gets. This Mars-influenced Moon often brings with it, not a taste for hot and spicy, but for the cool and creamy. Whichever your taste buds are set for, it must be superb and well prepared. You will easily stick to your diet on these days. Drink lots of water and eat plenty of fruits and vegetables.

Don't shop with the Moon in Pisces or you may wake up a couple days later (when the Moon is in Aries) and wonder why you purchased Dutch Indonesian vegetable pickle! This is another seafood sign with a taste that is easily satisfied. Just select from the beautifully laid-out seafood available in the grocery stores nowadays. Foods with sharp flavor won't be appealing (no Brussels sprouts today). The family probably won't be too fussy and will eat what you set out, which will undoubtedly be a fairly simple meal because that's about all you'll want to prepare. This is the day you will want to serve dessert, though.

This chowder is comforting, creamy, white, and made with seafood. It is also quick and simple to make, satisfying to eat, and best of all, low in fats and calories.

Fish Chowder

1½ pounds haddock, cod, or swordfish
2 cups bottle clam broth or substitute cold water
1 small carrot cut into ¼ inch slices
1 stalk celery in a fine dice
Bay leaf
Pinch of thyme
4 springs flat leaf parsley
1 tablespoon olive oil
1 medium chopped onion
2 medium potatoes, diced
4 cups skim milk
1 egg yolk, beaten

Dash of cayenne or hot paprika

Salt, pepper, and chopped fresh parsley

Bring fish, bay, thyme, and parsley to a boil in a saucepan. Cover and reduce heat. Let simmer for about 15 minutes. Do not overcook or fish will toughen.

In a soup pot, cook onions in olive oil until translucent. Strain broth into the kettle. Add the potatoes and milk; cover and let simmer about 20 minutes. Stir a little broth to the beaten egg yolk, and then add back into the broth. Add fish and vegetables, discarding bay leaf and parsley sprigs. Season with salt and pepper. Keep hot, without boiling. Ladle into bowls and serve garnished with a dash of paprika and a pinch of minced parsley.

Serves 4.

A Full Palette of Lunar Colors

By Lisa Finander

I like to think of the twelve signs of the zodiac as twelve different paint colors on an artist's palette. We are all born with certain colors (astrological signs) on our palette (natal chart). We use these colors to paint on our canvases (create our lives). As time goes by, we develop patterns of how we paint our world based on the colors we were born with. Say, for example, that the color red is the sign of Aries. A person born with a prevalent amount of Aries in his or her chart would then use the color red to handle most of his or her life situations. While the Aries person is becoming astute at using red, the problem lies in how many red paintings does one person need over his or her lifetime? The challenge is then how to become an expert at using your colors while acquiring new colors along the way to enhance the masterpiece that is you. One way to add more color into your life is to follow the monthly cycle of the Moon.

The Moon moves through all twelve signs of the zodiac in about twenty-eight days. It spends approximately two-and-one-half days in each sign. If you have purchased a lunar almanac before, you are probably familiar with the guides that tell you the best days to plant, cut your hair, start a diet, etc. In this article, I am suggesting another way of linking to the daily placement of the Moon by making an emotional connection. There is an innate gentleness to the flow of the Moon as it passes through the signs. When you tap into its rhythm, you have the chance to experience these monthly changes naturally. Just like inhaling and exhaling, certain signs support our need to expand in the world while other signs encourage us to pull back and release.

In my own life, I have tracked the daily placement of the Moon and found that certain days were better for certain activities because I had the emotional energy to do them. Something that felt impossible when the Moon was in one sign became doable a few days or a week later. It was not only doable; it was enjoyable. When I stopped trying to force myself to produce results that were not in alignment the placement of the Moon, life became less hectic.

The information I propose in this article is not a rigid kind of planning that dogmatizes doing certain things during certain signs. Instead, I am suggesting that you take a moment to reflect on where the Moon is and incorporate some of the qualities of the sign into your daily activities. For example, the Moon might be in the dreamy, sympathetic sign of Pisces on a day when you have an important meeting to direct. Instead of being frustrated that your meeting wasn't scheduled during a more assertive Moon sign, connect to the uniting and compassionate qualities of the sign by using them when appropriate during your meeting. This might be a time when you can see the good in everyone, and everyone can sacrifice a little of himself or herself to help out. Remember when the Moon is in Pisces, it is not in Pisces just for you, everyone will be experiencing the influence of the Moon whether they are conscious of it or not. It is also helpful to remember that what you are feeling right now is most likely going to change in a few days along with the Moon sign, so take advantage of the easy times and know that the difficult ones won't last forever.

I like to take note of the placement of the Moon because it helps me keep track of what I am doing and where I am going. Instead of days, weeks, months, and years of my life going by without much conscious thought or intention, I get an opportunity each month to focus my attention on up to twelve different areas of my life.

There are many ways to use the information compiled under each sign. You might begin by spending a few months writing your daily thoughts and feelings into a journal, and then compare your notes to the placement of the Moon. You could begin by focusing on the signs that relate to what you want in your life. For example, every month when the Moon is in the sign of Capricorn, you could spend some or all of the time in that two-and-one-half day period concentrating on activities that would enhance your career, social status, and/or destiny. Approximately two weeks later when the moon is in Cancer, you could spend those days creating a nurturing and supportive home environment. You could also take the information literally, and focus on the color connected to the sign, adding something of that color into your life. Whatever way you choose to incorporate the information, remember and believe that you are a talented artist, and that your life is a beautiful work of art.

I have associated colors whose meanings and visual responses incorporate some of the main qualities of each sign. This is not an exhaustive list of the colors that can be used for each sign, therefore, I encourage you to explore and compile your own correlations for each sign.

Adding Complementary Colors

Moon in Aries: Time to Add Red

Try something new. Take a risk. Make or sit by a fire. Exercise. Get enthusiastic about your life. Create something. Go on an adventure. Test your courage. Express anger openly and honestly. Release emotions as they occur. Forgive and forget. Find out who you are. Put your ideas into action. Use your energy to get things done. Get excited about something or someone. Explore an uncharted idea or environment. Develop your identity. Do something freeing. Be independent. Begin something.

Moon in Taurus: Time to Add Orange

Cultivate a plant, garden, or your yard. Take care of an outstanding money issue. Invest in your future. Use your determination. Fight for what you want. Start or make progress on a long-range goal. Get a massage. Try aromatherapy. Enjoy a good meal. Indulge your senses. Take a walk in nature. Create something using your hands with dough, clay, or earth. Take an art class. Teach something to someone else. Sing, use your voice, or take a voice lesson. Purchase some land. Develop or strengthen a positive body image.

Moon in Gemini: Time to Add Yellow

Make a phone call. Write a letter to someone whose ideas you admire. Start a conversation with a neighbor. Share ideas with friends. Expose yourself to new information and ideas. Apply a new way of thinking to an old situation. Tell a joke. Use your hands to do something mechanical. Learn a craft. Read. Introduce yourself to someone you would like to get to know. Study something scientific. See your life from a different perspective. Use your rational abilities. Disengage from melodramatic relationships. Take a mental vacation. Go for a short drive.

Moon in Cancer: Time to Add Silver

Spend some time making your home more comfortable and beautiful. Put something of value in a safe place. Spend time with family. Create close nurturing bonds with others. Communicate with your mother. Express emotions. Do something loving for you. Spend sometime around or in water. Take positive steps to feel more secure and stable. Visit people and places from your past. Be loyal to who you are. Remember your past. Recreate or enjoy something enjoyable from your past—a meal, a feeling, a movie, or a memory. Take time to reflect on your life.

Moon in Leo: Time to Add Gold

Have some fun. Go out in the sunshine. Play with your inner child. Do something romantic for your beloved. Start a romance. Write a love letter. Do something that boosts your self-confidence. Do something with or for children. Exercise your authority. Do something just for you. Do something creative. Let others know about your talents. Buy a lottery ticket. Take an acting class. Change your hairstyle. Be generous with yourself and others. Add some drama to your life. Express the love in your heart. Take pride in yourself and your accomplishments.

Moon in Virgo: Time to Add Navy

Take care of details. Analyze something. Make a healthy change in your life. Respect your emotions. Become more sensitive and intuitive to your surroundings. Do a kind act for a pet, animal, and/or nature. Use your mind to come up with practical answers. Purify something. Perfect something. Take some time to be alone. Find your inner voice. Learn ways to foster a healthy body. Fix something. Use discrimination in making decisions. Use your healing abilities. Focus on your work. Detach from an emotional situation to gain a clearer perspective. Use your humor to gain perspective. Make order out of chaos.

Moon in Libra: Time to Add Green

Propose marriage. Form a legal partnership. Make something in your life more beautiful. Get a makeover. Go to the library. See a movie or play. Attend the opera. Go museum hopping. Take an art appreciation class. Find a way to strike a compromise in important relationships. Relax in peaceful surroundings. Help mediate an intense situation. Show good manners. Be polite. Do something social. Pay attention to outward appearances. Give yourself permission to be lazy. Entertain. Buy some art. Handle legal issues diplomatically. Maintain equality in relationships.

Moon in Scorpio: Time to Add Black

Investigate something further. Solve a mystery. Have sex. Explore psychic avenues. Have an astrology, tarot, or psychic reading. Transform an inert relationship. Feel intensely about something. Make a commitment to stick with something through good times and bad. Ponder the meaning of life and death. Transform the taboo into the sacred. Spend some time reinventing yourself. Look beneath the surface of situations in your life. Study psychology. Let a circumstance that you feel angry, resentful, jealous, or resentful about be released. Learn the basis behind some societal ideal, or someone's behavior. Divest yourself of a bad habit.

Moon in Sagittarius: Time to Add Purple

Tell the truth. Plan or take a vacation to a faraway place. Learn about a different culture, philosophy, religion, and/or spirituality. Help someone understand a complex theory. Do something to strengthen your beliefs. Be humorous and optimistic. Tell your story. Sign up for higher education classes. Further your knowledge in something you only have superficial knowledge in. Expand your mind. Play a game. Go to the races. Spend time with friends. Go to the theater. Spend sometime outdoors. Get some exercise. Enjoy some sports. Learn a foreign language. Perform or take part in a ritual.

Moon in Capricorn: Time to Add Brown

Finish something. Take steps to strengthen your career. Work towards your goals, your destiny. List and recognize your past achievements. Take responsibility for something or someone. Mentor someone. Learn from someone older or more advanced than yourself. Take your time. Invest in your retirement, Do something practical with money. Develop your sense of timing. Be professional. Don't be afraid to fail. Develop self-reliance. Release burdens. Be respectful of yourself and others. Structure your life in a positive manner. Recognize, value, and accept the weakness and vulnerabilities in self and others.

Moon in Aquarius: Time to Add White

Do something out of this world. Join a group. Invent something. Entertain a group. Express your eccentricity. Shake up the status quo. Challenge old stagnant bureaucracies. Spend sometime with someone who is very different then yourself. Be accepting of the different views of others. Do something for the good of humanity. Focus on something for the future. Explore alternative treatments. Be unpredictable. Enjoy your freedom. Spend some time thinking outside the box. Share one of your unique viewpoints with others. Put the needs of the many above the needs of the one.

Moon in Pisces: Time to Add Teal

Imagine something. Show compassion. Be empathetic to yourself and others. Let free-floating emotions arise and dissipate. Have faith. Revere your sensitivity. Become one with the universe. See the good in yourself and others. Listen to your dreams. Follow psychic impressions. Challenge reality. Fantasize. Sleep. Create something from your imagination. Do a guided visualization. Help someone in need. Express your kindness and gentleness. See the "gray" areas of life. Stop *doing* and start *being*. Sacrifice yourself to a worthy cause.

Your Moon's Effect on Eating and Exercise

By Carole LaVoie

Ancient astrologers understood how the Moon effects the body and assigned the Moon rulership of the stomach, breasts, and body fluids. In accordance with this line of reasoning, the Moon also represents our appetite, food selection, motivations for eating, and the actual ingestion process.

It is the actual zodiac sign of the Moon at the time of birth (the sign your Moon was in when you were born) that reflects how we each meet personal health, diet, and fitness needs. We tend to express personal needs in positive ways when the Moon is well aspected to other planets in our astrological birth chart. If the Moon is not favorably aspected, though, more of the negative characteristics of the Moon's sign are likely to be expressed.

This article will explain how the twelve Moon signs are expressed through diet and exercise, and how you can know if you're expressing positive or negative qualities of your natal Moon. If you find that you're expressing more negative qualities, you can elect to take the steps necessary to get your life back in balance. You can find your Moon sign by referring to Find Your Moon Sign on pages 65–77 in this book. You can also have a complete horoscope cast for yourself by a professional astrologer, or use the chart service provided by Llewellyn Worldwide. With a chart, you would also know your Sun sign and Ascendant (or rising sign), which also reflect on your personal health. If you know your Sun sign and Ascendant, then read the delineations for those zodiac signs, too.

Aries

We begin with the first fire sign, Aries. People with this Moon sign usually have very high energy—the kind that runs until its exhausted and then collapses. This high level of activity requires adequate amounts of water to cool the body, and the nutrients found in meat dishes supplemented with enough carbohydrates and fruits to provide stamina. It's advisable, however, for an Aries to avoid excessive quantities of hot, spicy, or salty foods. Hunger tends to strike an Aries quickly and food is usually eaten fast, which can interfere with the body's ability to assimilate it properly. They have contagious enthusiasm and a quick temper, which can result in getting "hot under the collar." Their anger can motivate them to grab junk foods.

Movement is a must for an Aries, but they're not the best team players. Individual sports, such as running, walking, skating, skiing, or biking, can provide a real challenge and good exercise. Their stamina comes in spurts, so exercises that are fast and strenuous offer good benefits. They'll need to take a break to reenergize, though.

Optimal health is achieved and maintained by alternating high activity with rest and relaxation. When an Aries is expressing emotional needs in a positive manner, the challenge will be to improve speed and endurance. When they are emotionally out of balance, they'll risk physical injury to prove superiority to or over others. Drinking adequate amounts of water to cool the body during and after exercise is important. Aries rules the head, and it is common for people with Aries prominent in their natal chart to experience headaches, migraines, heatstroke, or acne.

Herbs that can be helpful for an Aries are: alfalfa, a blood purifier; molasses, for energy; and nettles, the leaves of which are a good source of iron.

Taurus

From the rapid, fiery quality of Aries, we move to the sensuous, earthiness of Taurus. Taurus Moon people eat for the dining experience, preferring tasty, high-quality foods that please the physical senses. Each bite is savored for its flavor, texture, and aroma. However, actual nutrition may take a back seat to sweet, creamy indulgences in order to satisfy their gourmet palate. (Chocolate and creamy foods are their nemesis.) Those little indulgences add up to larger garment sizes and lower self-esteem, which can throw the Taurus person into binging on rich, expensive foods that are high in calories but empty of nutrition. While a Taurus may have a slower metabolism by nature, his or her increasing size can promote an even more sedentary lifestyle.

A scheduled, balanced diet with abundant greens and limited snacks, which includes iodine and fiber, will help them to maintain good health. A well-balanced Taurus will be determined to eat healthy and stay fit, but when self-worth drops, or feelings of deprivation surface (feelings that can be derived from the idea that someone else has more resources, safety, or security), their sense of balance is gone.

Exercise must be pleasurable (not hard work) for a Taurus. Free weights, moderate aerobics, dancing, golfing, gentle cycling, and yoga stretches to music are very suitable. Making the commitment to be physically fit, setting a routine, wearing glamorous workout clothes, and holding a positive self-image will help provide the motivation to exercise. Finally, a Taurus needs to take frequent short breaks.

Taurus rules the throat and neck, and problems with the thyroid, tonsils, and adenoids, in addition to a tendency toward easy weight gain are common complaints of those with this Moon sign. Feeling positive self-worth is the key to success for a Taurus. But feelings of denial, jealousy, or possessiveness, as well as the need to hoard items, should be resolved. Optimum health is achieved when a Taurus feels valued and confident.

Herbs that are helpful to a Taurus are licorice, which is good for sore throat and hoarseness; nasturtium leaves, for strengthening the throat area; and fenugreek tea (made from ground seeds), which is excellent for sore throats and fevers.

Gemini

People born with a Gemini Moon are an adaptable group with strong thinking, reasoning, and communicating traits. Their strong orientation to the mental realm can make it difficult for them to distinguish between feelings and thoughts, though. Their attitude toward health, therefore, may be inconsistent, fluctuating between a fastidious or careless attitude toward exercise and diet. Eating may be regarded as an annoyance that breaks up boredom and stimulation—what they like best—and be taken to such excess that it becomes exhausting. Instead of thinking about or doing five other things at once, Gemini people need to focus on eating during meals. Three to five daily servings of fresh fruit along with calming foods such as leafy, green vegetables are recommended. A balanced diet supplemented with fish oils, B-complex vitamins, and substantial doses of dolomite will help keep a Gemini emotionally balanced. Skipping meals, opting instead for junk food is a good indicator of emotional imbalance. Maintaining healthy variety is important for a Gemini's peace of mind, and managing nervous stress is the key to their good health.

Gemini rules the two arms, hands, shoulders, and lungs, as well as the nervous system, which makes movement of these body parts essential to their good health. Tennis, volleyball, basketball, darts, horseshoes, croquette, aerobics, swimming, and deep breathing exercises are all excellent activities for a Gemini, while checkers and video games can promote mental agility and provide relaxation.

Helpful herbs for Gemini people are parsley, which is high in magnesium, and useful for treating nervous problems; fenugreek for treating mucus conditions of the lungs; and kava-kava, which is a good remedy for insomnia and nervousness.

Cancer

Individuals born with this Moon sign are extremely sensitive to the Moon's cycles. They are emotional by nature—okay, let's face it—they're moody. Their challenge is to learn how to be self-nurturing because their natural tendency is to nurture everyone else. Listening to the body and intuitively choosing the right foods in correct portions can do this. Nourishing soups and juices are fantastic for Cancers. Emotional insecurity usually throws them off balance and into overindulgent behaviors. Eating excessive carbohydrates and dairy, or turning to comfort foods— snacks, starches, or ice cream, for example—in an attempt to increase feelings of security will only add to their problems, though. Weight gain happens easily enough and fluid retention will vacillate with the Moon's phases. Emotional stress will also create an imbalance in the potassium/sodium ratio, reinforcing the tendency to keep weight on. Their remedy is to let go of old feelings and patterns, a difficult challenge, but one that will help them to stabilize emotionally.

Cancer rules over the breasts, the stomach, and all body fluids. Consequently, anemia, eating disorders, stomach upsets, ulcers, and problems with the duodenum can occur if they body systems get out of balance. For optimum health, it's important to release old feelings and learned behavior pat-

terns. Exercise can be an aid in letting go of the past, as well as providing emotionally support in the present. People who have a Cancer Moon enjoy exercise best when it can be done with good friends in a cozy environment. Workouts at home with friends may provide just the right motivation. Water-based exercises, toning and stretching with calisthenics, yoga, tai chi, or qigong are all good alternatives. Soothing music and creative visualization are also beneficial.

Herbs that are helpful for Cancers include fennel, which increases the flow of urine, menstrual blood, and mother's milk; papaya leaf tea to aid digestion and comfort the stomach and intestines; and saffron to aid digestion.

Leo

Individuals born with a Leo Moon, the second fire sign, love to shine. They usually believe that showing off a glamorous body is fun. A Leo's food choices can be lavish and sumptuous, centering on meat products with lots of fats (choose wisely, though, and trim the fat). When Leos are emotionally out of balance—feeling heartsick, heartbroken, neglected, or otherwise in need of attention—they can easily overindulge on food and alcoholic beverages. Heavy, creamy, fatty foods that act as sedatives are often chosen by Leo people feeling out of sorts. Their blood cholesterol levels need to be monitored, though, and foods eaten that will revitalize the body. When Leos are expressing their needs in a positive manner—enjoying life and being creative—they will choose healthy foods that are low in fats and taste delicious. Spicy hot foods, especially those made with extra-hot peppers, help to keep the heart healthy, as do CoQ10, shark cartilage, flaxseed oil, and fiber.

As the Sun is the heart of the solar system, Leo rules the heart and circulatory system, and these areas of the body that will become stressed if emotional and physical balance is not maintained. Leo people need a variety of cardiovascular exercises. These may include running, jogging, trampoline, skiing, skating, swing dancing—anything that gets the heart pumping strong. Working out with a group is the best motivation for Leos, who prefer an audience to show off their progress and rippling muscles, too. The focus should be on upper body toning. For optimum health, Leos need to have a creative outlet that will provide a sense of well-being, self-approval, and personal satisfaction.

Healthy herbs for Leos are cayenne powder added to liquids or food, which stimulates the heart and circulatory system; horseradish for detoxification; and borage leaf tea for strengthening the heart.

Virgo

Earthy Virgos abandon the Leo's love for flair in favor of making discriminating choices where food is concerned. Food selections will usually be made with meticulous care. A vegetarian lifestyle, vitamin and mineral supplements, making breads from scratch, and foods grown through organic methods are great options for health conscious Virgos. Freshness, nutrition, and variety will help keep them from getting stuck in a rut. Rice and whole grains will keep the digestive tract functioning properly, and drinking adequate amounts of water will flush the body's system. An emotionally balanced Virgo will prefer being informed about what they put into their body; and they'll rarely overeat.

Virgo rules the intestinal tract, in particular, the small intestine, and people with a strong Virgo emphasis in their natal chart will tend to have problems with digestion and assimilating food. Digestive ailments include constipation, loose bowels, colitis, and food allergies. Virgos are also prone to emotional stress that can also lead to constipation, digestive problems, and loose bowel.

Demanding exercises can strain and even frustrate a Virgo, so walking, hiking, fencing, free weights, and stepping are more appropriate.For optimum health Virgos need to schedule daily time to exercise as well as to rest and relax.

Herbs that are helpful for a Virgo are blackberry, which taken in tea form is a remedy for mild diarrhea and sore throats; chamomile to calm restlessness, anxiety, nervous stomach, and insomnia; and lavender to soothe nervous conditions.

Libra

Balance is vital to people with a Libra Moon—especially in the relationships that they must be in. Relationship demands can and do create emotional imbalance in Libra people, as will hormone and chemical changes. Their food plan should include a balance of protein, carbohydrates, liquids, and fiber. Special care should be taken to keep blood sugars in balance. An emotionally balanced Libra will follow a sensible eating program and maintain an ideal weight. When out of balance, however, they run the risk of overindulging in sweets—their nemesis. Once the craving for sugar set in, it's downhill from there. Dried fruits instead of white sugars for that sweet tooth, or sugar-free pies and desserts in moderation will help to maintain balance. Social drinking and caffeine may also be taken to in excess.

Exercise done with a partner, which could include a personal trainer, is best for Libras. Partner sports, such as tennis, bicycling (especially a bicycle built for two), badminton, ballroom dancing, wrestling, sparring, or gymnastics (where turns are take to spot) are also good choices.

Libra rules the lower back and kidneys. When relationships become problems, trouble can develop in these areas. For optimum health, balance must be maintained in all of life's activities. Relationships can be a great source of comfort and security but some independence should be maintained, too.

Helpful herbs for Libras include cleavers, a powerful diuretic used for all kidney and bladder problems; corn silk leaves that made into a tea is useful for bladder and kidney conditions; and parsley leaves, which will help alleviate bladder infections.

Scorpio

A Scorpio Moon contains the energy of great focus, passion, intensity, and enormous self-control. When a food pleases a Scorpio, they can eat just that until sick of it and then never eat it again! Emotionally balanced Scorpios will select meaty, nourishing food that often includes leeks, onions, and garlic, and they'll avoid junk foods. However, feelings of insecurity, jealousy, or being cheated will throw them into binge eating. A sensible, balanced food plan is important because of a Scorpio's tendency to go to extremes. Very hot foods are comforting, and wine can help digestion.

Scorpio rules the reproductive organs and colon. Individuals who hold back their emotions and don't eliminate old patterns tend to have problems

in these areas. A daily portion of roughage and adequate water are recommended to maintain a healthy colon. But laxatives, which can be habit forming, should not be used with regularity. Be flexible. Learn to forgive, and let life surprise you. For optimum health, choose a good source of protein and fluids, and avoid getting into ruts that can cause imbalances.

Scorpio people adapt well to intense exercise, and are great at making the commitment to regular workouts—until their routine is broken. It's important to get back on track, and remembering how sexy vigorous exercise can make one feel is often just the motivation that's needed. Riding bike or rowing with the team provide excellent workouts for those with a Scorpio Moon.

Herbs that are helpful for Scorpios are dong quai, a Chinese herb used for most female ailments; aloe vera, that when taken internally regulates the bowels and has a laxative affect; and saw palmetto berries can be used in treating diseases of the reproductive organs, testes, and prostrate.

Sagittarius

The Sagittarius Moon is energized with enthusiasm. Those with this Moon sign are often drawn to worldwide ethnic cultures, providing great opportunities to experience various culinary delights. When a Sagittarius person is emotionally balanced, food choices will be rather exotic, maybe macrobiotic, as they need to believe in a dietary plan and life philosophy before adopting it. Experimenting with various herbs and spices, particularly from the Far and Middle East can provide delightful surprises. Meats, vegetables, fruits, sprouts, oatmeal, bulgar wheat, rices, and eggs will support the body nicely, but fatty foods should be avoided. Supplements of vitamin B-12, iron, biotin, and panothetic acid are also good to promote strong nerves. When a Sagittarius is out of balance, which can occur when hope and faith are lost, they have a tendency to overindulge in fats and sweets and drink excessive amounts of alcohol.

Exercise for total body toning, but emphasis should be on the hips, thighs, and buttocks, which are ruled by Sagittarius. Exhaled breath is important to completely cleanse your body of carbon dioxide. Specific yoga breathing techniques can help with that. Outdoor sports such as hiking, hunting, rafting, spelunking, climbing, horseback riding, walking, and hang gliding are suggested activities to keep Sagittarians healthy and breathing deeply. For optimum health, a smoke-free environment, which would promote deep breathing, is preferable.

Herbs that are helpful for Sagittarians are wild yams, which is used in small quantities to alleviate cramping and muscle spasms; dandelion root and leaves are a strong liver and blood detoxifier; and wheat germ is good for extra energy.

Capricorn

A Capricorn Moon is one of great ambition and achievement. When Capricorns are feeling emotionally balanced, they are likely to eat three well-balanced meals a day, preferring meat and potatoes to trying new dishes. Adding some fish and plenty of calcium, along with magnesium, boron, phosphorous and vitamins C and D will result in better nutrition though. A good source is yogurt with active cultures. Flaxseed oil is wonderful along with glucosamine and chondroiton supplements, MSM (an organic form of sulfur that is easily absorbed into the system), and green tea. Overachievers by nature, and worrisome about their reputation, Capricorns have a strong tendency to work too much. Eating and meetings often go hand in hand so nutrition may be sacrificed in order to close that contract. The drive to succeed and the stress surrounding achievements can knock a Capricorn off balance emotionally. The remedy is to be less self-critical and acknowledge what is already done instead of what hasn't yet been accomplished. Sitting down to dinner without doing business is helpful, too.

Staying flexible and keep joints mobile should be a high priority for Capricorns, as Capricorn rules the knees. Nutritional, emotional, or physical imbalances will likely result in knee problems and joint stiffness. Runners need to be sure their shoes are cushioned and supportive so their knees don't get jolted. Getting exercise at the golf course while talking shop, or on the dance floor, squash or tennis court, gym, or dojo are all good ways for Capricorn individuals to get and stay healthy. For optimum health, Capricorn's need to slow down and lighten up about life. Laugh more and be less self-critical.

Herbs that are helpful for Capricorns are silica and horsetail, which is extremely rich in minerals and useful to maintain strong bones and to help heal broken bones; and wintergreen that when rubbed on the body or used in a bath is extremely helpful for muscle or joint pain.

Aquarius

People born with an Aquarius Moon love things that are new, inventive, and unusual. Eating at new restaurants and experimenting with food—though so many ingredients may be substituted that the result is nothing like the original— for colors and taste are right up their alley. (It was probably a person with Moon in Aquarius who invented s'mores.) It's best for those with Aquarius prominent in their natal chart to keep the evening meals light, and taking a larger meal at midday. Limiting starches that deplete energy is also advisable. An Aquarian who is emotionally out of balance tends to skip meals, eat on the run, and snack all day. Another hazard to balanced health is their attraction to fad diets or unsubstantiated gimmicky potions that can disrupt body chemistry.

For optimum health, Aquarians need to have a creative outlet, and to find out where personal identity and freedom can be accessed. They should avoid getting stuck behind a desk or computer, and develop an active social life instead. There is a natural resistance to commitment and routine so the best exercise plan will allow "drop-ins." Varying the routine, exercising with friends, and trying new things to help avoid boredom are important considerations for Aquarians. Since Aquarius rules the ankles, it is important to keep them strong and healthy by taking the time to stretch before exercising. Gymnastics, skating, martial arts, high diving, hockey, soccer, luge, snowmobiling, or belly dancing are good exercise choices.

Herbs that are helpful for Aquarians are the bark of prickly ash, which is an excellent stimulant that increases warmth in the extremities, and is used to obtain relief from arthritis and rheumatism; catnip, a mild sedative useful for children; and lady slipper, which is used as a tonic for exhausted nervous systems, and also for improving circulation.

Pisces

The Pisces Moon is that of the dreamer, whose loving, sensitive nature needs foods that are gentle and nurturing. Fish is a wonderful food choice for born during a Pisces Moon, as are greens, seaweed, healthy juices, nourishing vegetable soups, broth, or pureed soup; miso; beans (and sprouted alfalfa, mung, or garbanzo beans), tahini, honey, and tea. When Pisces people are feeling emotionally balanced, they will eat intuitively, selecting the right foods in the right amounts. But when emotionally upset or hurt they tend to eat the wrong foods unconsciously, and weight gain occurs very quickly. Caffeine should be limited, and dairy should be avoided, as it produces more mucus than the body can handle, which can lead to colds, sniffles, and fatigue. Alcohol is another thing that needs to be limited for optimum health. Food allergies and reactions to certain ingredients such as MSG can be a problem. Saunas and jacuzzi baths can be wonderfully cleansing and reinvigorating. So is spending time at the seashore.

For optimum health it's important for those with a Pisces Moon to understand that while their constitution is strong, it's also sensitive. Their sensitivity to negative energy means that is very important for them to be surrounded with positive people and situations. Negative energies are draining and will weaken the body over time. Exercise needs to be a gentle and soothing escape. Exercise accompanied by music or that has a video to follow is even better. Yoga, tai chi, qigong, water sports, ballet, croquet, gymnastics with ribbons, dance, walking, and jazzercise are all suitable to a Pisces' nature. Cold extremities and foot injuries or sprains are common complaints from those with a Pisces Moon. Pisces rules the feet. It's important for Pisces people to wear comfortable, supportive shoes to protect the feet from cold or injury.

Herbs that may be helpful for Pisces are echinacea, to fight colds and infections; mugwort, used in dream pillows to promote dreams and inner psychic states; and kava-kava, which is known to promote deep sleep and clear dreams.

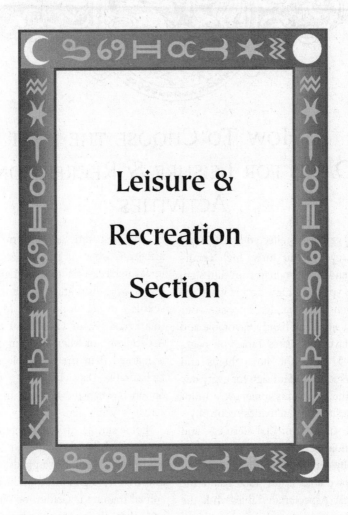

Leisure &

Recreation

Section

How To Choose the Best Dates for Leisure & Recreation Activities

Everyone is affected by the lunar cycle. Your lunar high occurs when the Moon is in your Sun sign, and your lunar low occurs when the Moon is in the sign opposite your Sun sign. The handy Favorable and Unfavorable Dates Tables on pages 34–57 give the lunar highs and lows for each Sun sign for every day of the year. This lunar cycle influences all your activities: your physical strength, mental alertness, and manual dexterity are all affected.

By combining the Favorable and Unfavorable Dates Tables and the Lunar Aspectarian Tables with the information given in the list of astrological rulerships, you can choose the best time to begin many activities.

The best time to perform an activity is when its ruling planet is in favorable aspect to the Moon— that is, when its ruling planet is trine, sextile, or conjunct the Moon (marked T, X, or C in the Lunar Aspectarian), or when its ruling sign is marked *F* in the Favorable and Unfavorable Days Tables. Another option is when the Moon is in the activity's ruling sign.

For example, if you wanted to find a good day to train your dog, you would look under animals, and find that the sign corresponding to animal training is Gemini or Virgo, and that their ruling planet is Mercury. Then, you would consult the Favorable and Unfavorable Days Tables to find a day when Mercury (the ruling planet) is trine, sextile, or conjunct (T, X, or C) the Moon; or when Gemini or Virgo (the ruling signs) are marked F in the Favorable and Unfavorable Days Table; or when the Moon is in Gemini or Virgo.

Animals and Hunting

Animals: Virgo and Pisces; Mercury and Jupiter.

Animal training: Virgo, Gemini; Mercury

Cats: Leo and Virgo; Venus

Dogs: Virgo; Mercury

Fish: Cancer and Pisces; Neptune or the Moon,

Birds: Gemini; Mercury, Venus

Game animals: Sagittarius

Horses, trainers, riders: Sagittarius; Jupiter

Hunters: Sagittarius; Jupiter,

Arts

Acting, actors: Leo or Pisces; the Sun or Neptune

Art in general: Libra; Venus

Ballet: Neptune or Venus

Ceramics: Saturn

Crafts: Mercury or Venus

Dancing: Taurus or Pisces; Venus or Neptune

Drama: Venus or Neptune

Embroidery: Venus

Etching: Mars

Films, filmmaking: Leo or Aquarius; Neptune or Uranus,

Literature: Mercury, Gemini

Music: Taurus or Libra; Venus or Neptune

Painting: Libra; Venus

Photography: Aquarius or Pisces; Neptune or Uranus

Printing: Gemini; Mercury

Theaters: Leo; the Sun or Venus

Fishing

During the summer months the best time of the day to fish is from sunrise to three hours after, and from two hours before sunset till one hour after. Fish do not bite in cooler months until the air is warm, from noon to 3 pm. Warm, cloudy days are good. The most favorable winds are from the south and southwest. Easterly winds are unfavorable. The best days of the month for fishing are when the Moon changes quarters, especially if the change occurs on a day when the Moon is in a water sign (Cancer, Scorpio, Pisces). The best period in any month is the day after the Full Moon.

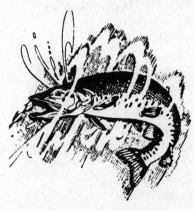

Friends

The need for friendship is greater when the Moon is in Aquarius or when Uranus aspects the Moon. Friendship prospers when Venus or Uranus is trine, sextile, or conjunct the Moon. The chance meeting of acquaintances and friends is facilitated by the Moon in Gemini.

Parties (Hosting or Attending)

The best time for parties is when the Moon is in Gemini, Leo, Libra, or Sagittarius with good aspects to Venus and Jupiter. There should be no aspects to Mars or Saturn.

Barbecues: Moon or Mars
Casinos: Venus, Sun, or Jupiter
Festivals: Venus
Parades: Jupiter or Venus

Sports

Acrobatics: Aries; Mars
Archery: Sagittarius; Jupiter,
Ball games in general: Venus
Baseball: Mars
Bicycling: Gemini; Mercury or Uranus
Boxing: Mars
Calisthenics: Mars, Neptune
Chess: Mercury, Mars
Competitive sports: Mars
Coordination: Mars
Deep-sea diving: Pisces; Neptune
Exercising: Sun
Football: Mars

Golf: Sagittarius, Aries, Libra; Mars or Jupiter
Horse racing: Sagittarius; Jupiter
Jogging: Gemini; Mercury
Physical vitality: Sun
Polo: Venus, Uranus, Jupiter, or Saturn
Racing (other than horse): Sun, Uranus
Ice skating: Neptune
Roller skating: Mercury
Sporting equipment: Sagittarius; Jupiter
Sports in general: Leo; Sun
Strategy: Saturn
Swimming: Pisces, Cancer; Neptune
Tennis: Mercury, Venus, Mars, or Uranus
Wrestling: Mars

Travel

Long trips which threaten to exhaust the traveler are best begun when the

Sun is well aspected to the Moon and the date is favorable for the traveler. If traveling with others, good aspects from Venus are desirable. For enjoyment, aspects to Jupiter are preferable; for visiting, aspects to Mercury. To prevent accidents, avoid squares or oppositions to Mars, Saturn, Uranus, or Pluto.

For air travel, choose a day when the Moon is in Sagittarius or Gemini and well aspected to Mercury, Jupiter, or Uranus. Avoid adverse aspects of Mars, Saturn, or Uranus.

For automobile travels, chose a day when the Moon is in Gemini and making good aspects to Mercury.

For boating, the Moon should be in the water sign Cancer or making easy aspects to Neptune.

Eat in restaurants when the Moon is in Cancer or Virgo, and making favorable aspects to Venus and Jupiter.

Hotels: Cancer, Venus
Motorcycle travel: Favorable aspects to Uranus
Parks: Leo; Sun
Picnics: Leo; Venus,
Rail: Gemini; Mercury or Uranus

Writing

Write for pleasure or publication when the Moon is in Gemini. Mercury should be direct and making favorable (T, X, or C) aspects to Mercury, Uranus, and Neptune to promote ingenuity.

Hunting & Fishing Dates

From/To	Quarter	Sign
January 6, 11:41 pm - January 9, 4:57 am	4th	Scorpio
January 16, 9:00 am - January 18, 9:35 pm	1st	Pisces
January 26, 1:17 am - January 28, 3:31 am	2nd	Cancer
February 3, 5:35 am - February 5, 8:33 am	3rd	Scorpio
February 12, 3:53 pm - February 15, 4:26 am	1st	Pisces
February 22, 11:16 am - February 24, 2:36 pm	2nd	Cancer
March 2, 1:51 pm - March 4, 4:55 pm	3rd	Scorpio
March 4, 4:55 pm - March 6, 8:25 pm	3rd	Sagittarius
March 11, 9:56 pm - March 13, 10:34 am	4th	Pisces
March 21, 7:06 pm - March 21, 9:28 pm	2nd	Cancer
April 30, 12:21 am - April 1, 1:48 am	3rd	Scorpio
April 1, 1:48 am - April 3, 6:58 am	3rd	Sagittarius
April 8, 3:57 am - April 10, 4:40 pm	4th	Pisces
April 18, 1:01 am - April 20, 7:20 am	1st	Cancer
April 26, 10:00 pm - April 28, 12:13 pm	3rd	Scorpio
April 28, 12:13 pm - April 30, 4:03 pm	3rd	Sagittarius
May 5, 10:46 am - May 7, 11:22 pm	4th	Pisces
May 15, 6:33 am - May 17, 12:52 pm	1st	Cancer
May 23, 8:38 pm - May 25, 10:20 pm	2nd	Scorpio
May 25, 10:20 pm - May 28, 1:54 am	2nd	Sagittarius
June 1, 6:37 pm - June 4, 7:05 pm	3rd	Pisces
June 11, 1:15 pm - June 13, 6:39 pm	1st	Cancer
June 20, 3:42 am - June 22, 6:42 am	2nd	Scorpio
June 22, 6:42 am - June 24, 11:01 am	2nd	Sagittarius
June 29, 3:00 am - July 1, 2:49 pm	3rd	Pisces
July 1, 2:49 pm - July 4, 2:12 pm	3rd	Aries
July 8, 9:36 pm - July 11, 5:26 am	4th	Cancer
July 17, 9:13 am - July 19, 1:02 pm	2nd	Scorpio
July 19, 1:02 pm - July 21, 6:26 pm	2nd	Sagittarius
July 26, 11:04 am - July 28, 10:39 pm	3rd	Pisces

Hunting & Fishing Dates

July 28, 10:39 pm - July 31, 11:17 am	3rd	Aries
August 5, 7:02 am - August 7, 11:27 am	4th	Cancer
August 13, 3:01 pm - August 15, 6:25 pm	1st	Scorpio
August 15, 6:25 pm - August 18, 12:15 am	2nd	Sagittarius
August 22, 6:11 pm - August 25, 5:48 am	3rd	Pisces
August 25, 5:48 am - August 27, 6:32 pm	3rd	Aries
September 1, 4:14 pm - September 3, 9:36 pm	4th	Cancer
September 9, 10:48 pm - September 12, 12:44 am	1st	Scorpio
September 12, 12:45 pm – September 14, 2:54 am	1st	Sagittarius
September 19, 12:18 am - September 21, 8:59 pm	2nd	Pisces
September 21, 12:11 pm - September 24, 12:55 am	3rd	Aries
September 29, 12:01 am - October 1, 6:58 am	3rd	Cancer
October 7, 8:57 am - October 9, 9:21 am	1st	Scorpio
October 9, 9:21 am – October 11, 11:08 am	1st	Sagittarius
October 16, 6:07 am - October 18, 6:13 pm	2nd	Pisces
October 18, 6:13 pm - October 21, 6:57 am	2nd	Aries
October 26, 6:10 am - October 28, 2:20 pm	3rd	Cancer
November 3, 8:10 pm - November 4, 3:34 pm	4th	Scorpio
November 5, 8:01 pm – November 7, 8:00 pm	1st	Sagittarius
November 12, 12:42 pm - November 15, 12:38 am	2nd	Pisces
November 15, 12:38 am - November 17, 1:23 pm	2nd	Aries
November 22, 11:48 am - November 24, 8:00 pm	3rd	Cancer
December 1, 6:15 am - December 3, 6:58 am	4th	Scorpio
December 9, 8:46 pm - December 11, 10:49 am	1st	Pisces
December 12, 7:58 am - December 14, 8:43 pm	2nd	Aries
December 19, 6:30 pm - December 22, 1:48 am	3rd	Cancer
December 28, 1:41 pm - December 30, 4:01 pm	4th	Scorpio

Legends and Lore of the Moon

By Kenneth Johnson

Shakespeare called it "the inconstant Moon, that monthly changes in her circled orb." A great deal of lunar folklore focuses on that inconstancy. In China, for example, it is said that there once lived a brave archer who traveled beyond the sunrise and the sunset to the ends of the world. There, after a long quest, he discovered the elixir of eternal life. He brought it back home with him, intent on making himself immortal. But his wife beat him to the punch, so to speak, and downed the elixir when her husband wasn't looking. She was immortal now, but somewhat in disgrace for her bad manners.

The lady was banished to the Moon, and there she remains. Some say the angry immortals actually transformed her into a toad. (The contours of the lunar landscape did in fact appear to the ancient Chinese to be shaped like a toad.) Others, however, say that it is a rabbit in the Moon rather than a toad in the Moon. The rabbit, companion of the banished lady, still assists her with her immortal theft, churning and preparing that magical elixir.

China isn't the only place where the Moon is associated with an elixir of life. The same is true in India, where the Moon is perceived as a frolicsome bad-boy god.

Chandra, the Moon king, keeper of the elixir of immortality, had twenty-seven wives (these were the astrological Mansions of the Moon, the constellations along the lunar ecliptic). Since they were all goddesses in their own right, it was mere godly courtesy that the Moon king should honor the goddess in all her aspects by spending equal time (one night of his motion) with each wife. But being the bad boy that he was, he became fascinated with the erotic goddess Rohini (the star Aldebaran in Taurus), and he wouldn't leave her mansion. The other wives became ferociously angry, and begged their father, the great world maker, to curse their faithless husband unto death. He gladly did so, and Chandra began to waste away from sickness. But then the ladies repented (apparently the bad-boy Moon King had a certain charm).

But the world maker sadly informed his daughters that the curses of the gods can never be entirely undone, they can only be modified. So Chandra must still grow sickly every month, even though he will be made well again. And that's why the Moon waxes and wanes.

But even this punishment didn't teach Chandra his lesson. He later gained notoriety by abducting Tara, the wife of the planet Jupiter. Since Jupiter was the high priest of the gods, this was a fairly serious issue. In fact, it caused a war in heaven, with the various planetary gods lining up on either side for Jupiter or for the Moon. Since such a conflict threatened to overturn the universe as a whole, Brahma the Creator stepped in and forced Chandra to return Tara to her husband. It was already too late, though. Tara was pregnant by Chandra. Their child is the charming, clever, and occasionally untrustworthy planet Mercury.

The Moon king, however, was not only tolerated but revered and worshiped because he kept the elixir of immortality. Without it, even the gods must die. And for us mortals, it is our own little portion of that eternal nectar that is responsible for keeping us happy, contented, and joyful.

Let us not imagine that King Chandra got off too easy. After all, there's yet another story about his run-in with a demon in the shape of a dragon that tried to steal the elixir. Chandra raised a holler, and the god Vishnu sliced the dragon in two. Unfortunately for Chandra, the dragon had already gleaned a sip of nectar, and was now immortal—and immortally angry with the Moon king for causing him to get cut in two. He chases the Sun and Moon through the sky, and occasionally succeeds in swallowing them—at least temporarily. This, of course, is an eclipse, and this is why the medieval astrologers referred to the Moon's North Node, or eclipse marker, as the Dragon's Head.

The eclipse demon was known to many cultures. Among the Vikings, for example, the Sun and Moon were sister and brother respectively, and they drove their chariots through the sky on a daily basis. However, each

of them was pursued by a wild, hungry wolf, which occasionally caught them in his jaws, only to be forced by the gods to release them.

Although the Viking Moon god, like Chandra, is pursued by an eclipse demon, he is different from his Hindu counterpart in many ways. He seems to be a good fellow rather than a bad boy. The story goes that Mani the Moon god rescued two children who were being abused by an evil stepfather. Their names were Biuki and Bili, and they were forced to draw water from the stepfather's well continually. Mani took them with him up to the sky and set them to work tending his own divine well that was filled with (you guessed it) the nectar of immortality. Mani, by the way, is the original man in the Moon. If the Chinese perceived a toad or a rabbit amongst the lunar formations, the Vikings perceived the face of old Mani. And what about Biuki and Bili, you may ask? Change the *b*'s into *j*'s and you will recognize two old nursery rhyme friends—Jack and Jill with their pail of water.

If pre-Christian Scandinavians thought the Moon was a good fellow, the ancient Egyptians thought the Moon was downright divine. They had no less than three separate deities associated with the Moon. First, there was Thoth the Moon god. He had the head of a crane and always carried a stylus, thus symbolizing that he was the god of writing and the intellectual mind. His symbolism later became merged with that of the Greek god Hermes, and he became known as Hermes-Thoth, god of wisdom and magic.

Then there was Hathor, the Egyptian love goddess, who is also associated with the Moon. Her sacred animal was the bull, and she was often depicted with bull's horns. The bull's horns are, of course, a symbol of the crescent Moon. They also remind us that the Moon is exalted in the constellation of Taurus. In fact, the god Mithras, associated with the constellation of Orion, reaches forth his celestial hand to grasp the horns of Taurus, the bull as cosmic sacrifice. And what about the horns of the Taurus bull? We meet the red star Aldebaran (found in the middle of

Taurus, and called the "bull's eye") once again. We met her earlier as Rohini, the erotic nymph in the tale of the Hindu Moon God.

But back to Egypt. There is, of course, one more lunar figure in the Egyptian pantheon, and this is Isis. She was the principal goddess of Egypt—the queen of the gods. It was she who gathered up the scattered pieces of her slain husband Osiris and put them back together again. She also spoke the mystic charms that brought him back to life so that he could become the Lord of the otherworld. Isis wears the horns of the lunar crescent, too.

Perhaps the most charming (and certainly the most romantic) story about the Moon comes from ancient Greece, though. Many people have heard Artemis and/or Diana named as the Greek or Roman Moon goddess, but this is only partly true. Because she carried a bow and arrows, her bow was associated with the crescent Moon during later antiquity. But more often than not, the Moon goddesses of Greek times were Hecate (the dark Moon) and Selene. Our last story concerns Selene.

There was a handsome young man named Endymion; one night in his wanderings he feel asleep in a cave. The goddess Selene rose in the night sky, cast her light down upon the world, and saw Endymion sleeping there in his cave. Gently, she descended to Earth, kissed him on the eyelids, and then lay down beside him. She was a shy goddess who longed to be near Endymion but who feared the intensity of his mortal passions. So she placed him under an enchantment; he later returned to that very same cave, fell asleep, and never awoke. But he never died either. He sleeps there still, immortal. Each night when she leaves her station in the sky, Selene slips into the cave, kisses her lover on the eyelids once more, and lies beside him in the blissful sleep of the gods.

The Moon in Electional Astrology

By Kevin Burk

The goal of electional astrology is to choose a time for an important event to start so that the outcome of the event might be favorable. Essentially, when we use electional astrology, we're attempting to align our intentions and desires harmoniously with the universal planetary cycles. Before going further, there are some basic truths, or facts, about electional astrology that we should address.

First, not every event is important enough to make an election. We need to recognize that electional astrology is generally reserved for events of some importance to us. It's not necessary to elect a chart for when you mail your utility bill; you may, on the other hand, wish to elect a chart on when to mail your taxes (more on this later when we cover ways of making yourself invisible in the electional chart).

Second, there is no such thing as a perfect chart. A bad chart does not mean a bad or unfavorable outcome—and a good chart does not necessarily ensure success. Weddings are one of the more traditional events for electional astrology, but when considering weddings, we also need to remember there is no perfect day for your marriage. Ultimately, the success of your marriage is more dependent on you and your spouse than on whether the ceremony started at 4:25 or 4:30 pm. A bad chart isn't going to doom your endeavor to failure, and a good chart isn't going to ensure success.

And finally, even with the most important events, you can't always elect a chart, and this is perfectly acceptable. Surgeries are events that are often important enough to elect, but sometimes we don't have the luxury of choosing when we need surgery; or you may be forced to take a final exam on a day with unfavorable aspects. If you know the material, you're going to pass the exam.

With electional astrology, you can make a wish-list of what you'd like to see for a given event, with the understanding that you're going to be lucky to get one or two of the things on that list in the final outcome. Even when working with simple Moon phases and aspects, it's not always easy, or necessary, to find a time that includes everything on our wish list. Likewise, finding the luckiest day in the world, with the Moon trine Jupiter and conjunct the fixed star Spica, isn't going to make that lottery ticket you bought a winner.

Electional astrology is designed to take some of the anxiety out of life, so don't let yourself become more anxious because you're not able to use it every time you want to. Its function is simply to help us to relieve some anxiety about important events, and to perhaps smooth out some of the inevitable bumps in the road.

The Moon's Role in Electional Astrology

The Moon is the fastest-moving body in the heavens, and because of this the Moon is perhaps the most important planet to consider in electional astrology. The most basic use of the Moon in choosing dates and times to do things involves working with the phases of the Moon. The Moon's phases are determined by the Moon's relationship to the Sun at any given time. Each month, the New Moon occurs when the Moon and Sun are conjunct each other (at the same degree by sign), and there is no Moon visible in the night sky. Since the Moon moves much faster than the Sun, the Moon steadily moves ahead of the Sun each day, and more of the Moon is visible each night. The Full Moon occurs when the Sun and Moon are in opposition—180 degrees apart; the Moon rises at sunset and sets at sunrise. At the full phase, the Moon is as far from the Sun as it can get.

Now, rather than moving away from the Sun, the Moon begins to catch up to the Sun, and each night, less and less of the Moon is visible until the Moon catches up to the Sun again and we reach the next New Moon.

Although there are actually eight phases of the Moon (new, crescent, first quarter, gibbous, full, disseminating, last quarter, and balsamic), the most basic elections are only concerned with whether the Moon is waxing (growing—from the New Moon to the Full Moon) or waning (shrinking—from the Full Moon to the next New Moon). If you want something to grow, build, expand, or evolve, try and begin during the waxing or growing cycle of the Moon. If, on the other hand, you want something to shrink, be torn down, or otherwise disappear, try and begin the project on the waning, or shrinking cycle of the Moon. If you're starting a new business, for example, you will probably want to begin with a waxing Moon because you want your business to grow. If you're starting a new diet, on the other hand, it's probably better to wait until after the Full Moon and begin on a waning Moon, since your objective is to lose weight.

The New Moon phase needs a little more explanation. The Moon's phase is considered to be New when the Moon is between 0 degrees and 45 degrees in front of the Sun. The period of time immediately after the New Moon is called "the dark of the Moon." This is the two or three day period when no Moon visible in the sky. The dark of the Moon can not be considered part of the waxing or the waning phase of the Moon, as the Moon is not visible in the sky at all. The ancients didn't consider the waxing period of the cycle to begin until the Moon was actually visible. If you are trying to pick a time when you will have a very low profile, or when your actions are not meant to be noticed or to have a definite outcome, the dark of the Moon is an excellent time to choose. This, for example, might be a good time to mail your income tax returns, as it encourages them to simply slide through the system, helping you to avoid any undue hassles. Don't, however, begin something during the dark of the Moon that you want to see grow and flourish—wait at least a day or two until the Moon is once again visible.

The Moon in Medical Electional Astrology

The waxing and waning rules certainly apply when electing for a medical procedure. For example, if you're having a tumor removed, it's advantageous to do so under a waning Moon to discourage it from growing back. More importantly than this, however, is the rule that you should always avoid having surgery performed when the Moon is in the sign that rules that part of your body. For example, Aries rules the head and face; Taurus the throat and neck; Gemini the lungs, arms, shoulders, and hands; Cancer the breasts and stomach; Leo the heart and back; Virgo the intestines; Libra the kidneys, prostate, ovaries, and uterus; Scorpio the genitals, lower abdomen, appendix, and bladder; Sagittarius the thighs, hips, and liver; Capricorn the bones, knees, and pancreas; Aquarius the calves, blood vessels and lymphatic system; and Pisces the feet and skin.

If the procedure is surgical, try and avoid the Full Moon because this phase of the Moon tends to increase bleeding. Also, if possible, avoid hard aspects between the Moon and Mars, which can both increase bleeding and the chance of fever, infection, and complications from the procedure. Finally, a good, harmonious relationship between the Sun and Moon can help to support a speedy recovery.

It's important to remember that you're not always going to have the luxury of choosing when you can have a medical procedure performed. If you do have a choice, however, you can take a quick look at the Moon's location on the dates in question, and choose the most beneficial time.

Lunar Aspects and Events in Electional Astrology

Because the Moon moves so quickly through the signs, it also forms the greatest number of aspects to the other planets, often in rapid succession. In electional astrology, each aspect that the Moon forms while in a given sign represents an important event. The order of the aspects formed by the Moon represents a sequence of events, and the last aspect formed before it enters the next sign shows the outcome of the event. Before we can look at this in greater detail, however, we need to define a few concepts relating to aspects in classical electional astrology.

Aspects Used in Electional Astrology

When working with electional astrology, the only aspects that matter are the so-called Ptolemaic aspects. These are the conjunction (0 degrees, planets in the same sign), the opposition (180 degrees, planets in opposing signs), the trine (120 degrees, planets in the same element), the square (90 degrees, planets in the same modality), and the sextile (60 degrees, planets in the same polarity but different elements).

When is an Aspect an Aspect?

The central question is how to determine when two planets are close enough together for an aspect to actually be considered to be in effect. The term orb describes a sphere of influence surrounding a physical body. While astrologers may elect to use different orbs in their work, generally, the following degrees of orb are acceptable in electional astrology (the Sun is more influential in the birth chart, therefore, it has the widest orb): Sun, up to 15 degrees; Moon, up to 12 degrees; Mercury, Venus, and Mars, up to 7 degrees; and Jupiter and Saturn, up to 9 degrees.

A fundamental rule when working with aspects is: applying aspects are more powerful than separating aspects because applying aspects represent events that are going to happen, while separating aspects represent events that have already happened. The closer to exact an aspect is, the stronger it is.

The Void-of-Course Moon

The last concept we have to introduce is that of the void-of-course Moon. From the point where the Moon makes it's last aspect in a sign to the point where the Moon enters the next sign, the Moon is considered to be void-of-course. The Moon shows what things are happening in the day; the aspects that the Moon makes indicate events. When the Moon has no more aspects to make before it changes signs, this is an indication that nothing else is going to happen until there is a significant change in the underlying situation. The Moon goes void-of-course at the moment that the last aspect becomes exact. Once an aspect begins to separate, it represents an event in the past, something that has already happened, and that we can't change.

In the classical literature, we are told time and again to avoid the void-of-course Moon. This is not necessarily a hard-and-fast rule, however. The

thing to remember about the void-of-course Moon is that it represents a time when you are not going to be able to have much of an influence on the outcome of the events. All of the major decisions have been made, and what's left is to simply let the events play out their natural course.

This is not necessarily a bad thing—in fact, sometimes, this is exactly the outcome that you are looking for!

Working with a void-of-course Moon is like operating "under the radar." For example, when filing your taxes, mailing the tax forms under a void-of-course Moon is one way to encourage your taxes to slide through the system without incurring any undue attention or hassle from the Internal Revenue Service. I should point out that while the void-of-course Moon may be an advantageous time to file your taxes, I wouldn't recommend actually doing your taxes under a void-of-course Moon. When you fill out the forms you want to pick a time conducive to focus, attention to detail, and sharp minds. One more disclaimer: if you are in a hurry to receive your refund check, you probably want to avoid the void-of-course Moon or the dark of the Moon when filing your taxes. A low profile can also mean that your return and your refund check will take longer to process.

The void-of-course Moon has some caveats, naturally. William Lilly said in *Christian Astrology* (originally published in 1647) that the Moon could not be considered to be truly void when it is in Cancer, Taurus, Sagittarius, or Pisces. Astrologer J. Lee Lehman has worked with these void Moons, and in her experience, while events didn't unfold in the way that she would have expected them, the outcomes were consistently very favorable. In many of her business dealings, she has taken to electing times to meet with new business clients during these void Moons.

Understanding when the Moon goes void-of-course is very important to selecting a successful date and time for an event because the last aspect that the Moon makes before going void represents the outcome of the matter. Do not underestimate the importance of this! You may find a chart with wonderful lunar aspects—say the Moon moves from a trine to Venus to a conjunction with Jupiter—and under most circumstances, this would be a very favorable chart. But if the Moon's last aspect before going void is, say a square to Saturn, you can count on your parade being rained on. No matter how much help, support, and luck you receive from Venus and Jupiter, the last thing that you're going to experience is Saturn coming along (usually in the form of some external authority figure) and telling you that you can't get what you want.

Easy Lunar Aspects: Jim Shawvan's Opportunity Periods

The easiest way to work with the Moon's aspects in electional astrology is to look for an "opportunity period." This is a technique developed by a colleague of mine in San Diego, Jim Shawvan, and it can be used quite effectively for simple elections.

To find an opportunity period, look at the aspect when the Moon goes void-of-course in a sign. Opportunity periods exist when the Moon goes void on an easy aspect, which Jim defines as any trine or sextile to the Sun, Mercury, Venus, or Jupiter. If the Moon's last aspect is a square, conjunction, or opposition to Mars, Saturn, Uranus, Neptune, or Pluto, there is no opportunity period in that sign.

Assuming that the Moon's last aspect is an easy aspect as defined above, work backward through the sign looking at the previous aspects of the Moon until you come to a difficult aspect of the Moon. The opportunity period begins as soon as the Moon has completed its last difficult aspect in a sign, and continues until it goes void-of-course. If the Moon makes no difficult aspects in a sign, the opportunity period begins as soon as the Moon enters the sign.

Opportunity periods are excellent times to begin events that are important to you, but not necessarily important enough to require a specifically timed and tuned election time. Because they represent periods of time when the Moon is only making easy and harmonious aspects, they represent a flowing, direct, and easy progression of events.

As noted when we discussed the void-of-course Moon, events under these void Moons may not unfold quite as you would expect. They often result in favorable outcomes because the Moon is either dignified enough in her own right (by rulership in Cancer and exaltation in Taurus) or ruled by Jupiter (in Pisces and Sagittarius). Therefore, when the Moon is void-of-course in these signs, it can also be looked on as an opportunity period.

The next exception has to do with the Moon conjunct the Sun. Even though the Moon conjunct the Sun is considered to be an "easy" aspect and, therefore, can help to define an opportunity period, the timing of this opportunity period is very important. Planets that are within seventeen degrees of the Sun are "under the Sun's beams" and are quite debilitated. These planets are effectively made invisible because the Sun outshines them and we can no longer see them in the sky. When the Moon is under the Sun's beams, it is not an opportunity period. More to the point, it is the "dark of the Moon," when there is no Moon visible in the sky, so it's generally not a good time to be starting any projects (at least not any projects where you want things to grow and develop).

Of course, this exception also has an exception. While it's true that planets under the Sun's beams are very debilitated, when a planet gets to be within seventeen minutes of arc of the Sun, it becomes strongly dignified. This is a condition called *cazimi*, which means "in the heart of the Sun." The Moon is *cazimi* for about a half-hour before and a half-hour after the exact moment of the New Moon, and this can be considered an opportunity period.

Eclipses

Eclipses are another important factor to consider when working with the Moon in electional astrology. Eclipses occur twice a year, always come in groups of at least two (one solar at the New Moon and one lunar at the Full Moon), and occasionally, they come in groups of three (solar, lunar, solar or lunar, solar, lunar). The most important thing to recognize about eclipses is that they represent an interruption in the normal lunar cycles. Under normal circumstances, the Full Moon represents a release of all of the energies that the Moon has collected during the previous lunar cycle. During an eclipse cycle, however, and particularly during a lunar eclipse, the Earth's shadow comes between the Sun and the Moon, interrupting and interfering with the release of the energies. In the context of electional astrology and events, what happens during a lunar eclipse is that everything proceeds exactly as we would expect it to, and then at the last moment, something entirely unforeseen and unexpected occurs which interferes with the expected outcome of the events.

A solar eclipse occurs during a New Moon, and this time the Moon's shadow gets in the way, representing unexpected and hidden (and, as we're dealing with the Moon, here, unconscious and emotional) energies that are going to play very important parts in the events of the following lunar cycle. Again, from a strictly electional standpoint, we're dealing with unknown and unpredictable factors in the equation.

It's not always possible to avoid electing times that occur during an eclipse cycle; after all, eclipse cycles can last for up to six weeks. If you do find that you need to consider a date or time that occurs in an eclipse cycle, be aware that you may be confronted with unexpected obstacles and hidden motivations, and be absolutely certain that you have enough other positive and encouraging factors to justify your choice.

Putting it All Together

We've covered a number of Moon-based techniques that you can use to make simple elections. Let's review some of the most important concepts.

Before you decide to elect a date and time for an event, you must decide if the event is actually significant enough to you to merit the effort. Consider what it is that you want to accomplish.

The simplest elections involve making sure that you're beginning your event on an appropriate phase of the Moon. If you want something to grow, choose the waxing phase; but if you want something to shrink or diminish, choose the waning phase. And if you want something to go unnoticed, or to not produce much of a result, choose the dark of the Moon or a void-of-course Moon. If you're not able to find an acceptable time during the waxing phase of the Moon, another option is to choose a time that is based around the closing trine between the Moon and the Sun. Even though this is a waning Moon, the Moon-Sun trine is an extremely fortunate aspect, and can be used quite effectively for events that are meant to grow and flourish.

Use the tables in this book to find Moon phases and aspects, and make a note of opportunity periods during the year. Mark them on your calendar. These time periods are also excellent to choose for simple elections.

The Water Goddesses

By Dorothy Oja

Τ he water signs Cancer, Scorpio, and Pisces exemplify the feminine qualities of nurturance, family, community, sensitivity, adaptation, and other virtues of water energy. In astrology, water represents the ability to feel, connect with, sense, remember, recall, and protect all that is or ever was. We might say that the water signs contain the archives of the development of humanity. After all, it absorbs into its self whatever enters its realm. Water dissolves and unifies. All the water signs share a deep, subtle, and often, painful sensitivity—or even vulnerability—which can at times overwhelm them. At other times water signs are like a balm—their compassionate tending soothes the emotions of others. Water soothes and inspires with a unifying presence and mirrors the soul essence beneath the structures of everyday life. The Moon, Pluto, and Neptune, respectively, rule the water signs Cancer, Scorpio, and Pisces. When you read and reflect on the following goddess myths, you will hopefully see the interconnections between the three signs and the selected goddesses because the water signs have the common denominators as described above.

The goddesses are universal. They speak to us in endless complex and intricate symbols. All goddesses serve to remind us of the deep roots of the past that, although often hidden from view in modern times, can never be destroyed. We see the goddesses everywhere if we choose to open our sensibilities to their handiwork. Characteristics of many of the goddesses relate to any number of astrological signs. It is this very fact that makes the goddesses more universal in their meaning. Following are some goddesses that relate to the water signs Cancer, Scorpio, and Pisces.

Cancer Water Goddesses

Cancer is the first water sign in the natural order of the zodiac. It is a cardinal water sign, which means that it takes initiative in the arena and environment of the family and community and in the vast realm of our emotional nature. It speaks to us of foundation, security, and mothering. In Cancer we are always longing for home. "There's no place like home," says Dorothy in the *Wizard of Oz*, and Cancer firmly believes this. More than believing this, Cancer embraces and embodies home and mother with an indescribably comforting sensibility. Home is a haven—an inner world/womb, far from the harsh realities on the outside. Cancer is the full knowledge of feminine nature that is both constant and changing, like the tides. And like the ocean tide, it has a point in its cycle where it pauses and takes sensations within, digests them, and then brings forth a newly synthesized understanding.

Hera (Roman Juno)

Hera was the celebrated queen of heaven long before the patriarchal tribes came along and brought their king Zeus. Wanting to form an alliance, they wished to match Zeus with Hera. Hera was not, in fact, interested but Zeus changed himself into her favorite bird, the cuckoo, and fell into her lap injured and bedraggled. Hera's compassion was aroused and she tried to save the little bird. Suddenly, Zeus transformed himself again and proceeded to rape Hera. Horrified and shamed, Hera chose to marry Zeus to save her dignity. She then became her more familiar manifestation as the celebrated wife of Zeus, king of the gods. Hera retained her status as queen of heaven. It is said that Hera's hopes and desires for marital and conjugal happiness were dashed by Zeus's many indiscretions. She became a fury to be contended with, the archetype of the jealous and unhappy wife.

The myth of Hera concerns woman primarily acting in a marriage relationship and details some of the issues encountered in the sign of Cancer. Cancer, in fact, has a high tolerance for forgiving and making allowances—

an attitude that, taken to the extreme, creates many problems and much unhappiness. Cancer is one of the signs of the zodiac that finds it hard to say no. Hera showed her nurturing instinct in her response to the bedraggled cuckoo disguised as Zeus. She remained the wife of Zeus despite his mistreatment of her. This is not a judgment of her for right or wrong. The decision to stay or to go rests deeply in the heart of the woman. You might say Hera was in a political pickle. With the cultural climate at the time, in order to retain her power and protect her people, she most likely felt she had to stay married to Zeus. Unfortunately, due to the vagaries of her unhappy marriage, Hera is most widely known as the vindictive and jealous wife. But knowing the full story, we can see there's so much more to Hera. Before Zeus, Hera was the patron goddess of all women and personified and celebrated the three stages of womanhood—maiden, lover, crone.

What message does Hera have for Cancer? Hera hoped to find fulfillment in her relationship with Zeus. The message we can take is that the responsibility for fulfillment and happiness always rests only within oneself. This is particularly a female issue through the centuries, and in modern times the sexes are struggling to shift and change precisely this concept of fulfillment.

Demeter (Roman Ceres)

Demeter is the great mother and represents all things and all process that have to do with women's issues and women's bodies. The myth of Demeter is linked to her daughter Persephone, who was taken from her by Hades, lord of the underworld and transformed into his queen. Demeter is forced to find her own life beyond her daughter, as all devoted mothers must let their children go to follow their fate. The mourning, which Demeter undergoes at the loss of her daughter, is natural but eventually becomes excessive and she allows all the crops to die. This speaks to the over-identification that some women make with their children at the expense of developing themselves and their personal selves and other talents.

Demeter portrays woman as mother and child-rearer, which is an essential aspect of the Cancer archetype. It is the devoted, selfless aspect of Cancer, which seeks to provide a harmonious environment for growth and development. The withholding aspect of Demeter and Cancer, when she discovered that Hades, lord of the underworld, abducted Persephone and made her his queen, must be resolved in order for both mother and child to find a wholesome peace. In fact, when Persephone is finally restored to her mother, there is much cause for celebration. But it quickly becomes clear that things will never be the same. Evidently, Persephone has eaten some pomegranate seeds, which now bind her for a portion of each year to the realm of the underworld and her husband, Hades. This portion of the myth describes what the archetype of Cancer experiences, in terms of the cycles of a woman's life, as she moves among her various roles of maiden, wife, mother, and crone.

Demeter has to do with all things and activities that nurture and promote life. Demeter represents abundance and that characteristic in Cancer, which allows and gives encouragement to life and growth. Remember, Demeter was the grain goddess of all food that grows to sustain life. The Cancer archetype, the eternal archetype of mother, is the cohesive component in the family, which sustains our emotional nature. It is that element of unconditional love and unlimited nurturance that we all yearn to return to and experience again.

Scorpio Water Goddesses

Scorpio is a sign of the deepest mysteries of all humankind ones like death, birth, or sexuality that we must come to terms with whether we fully understand them or not. Those born under Scorpio are almost constantly in a state of flux, chaos, analysis, or renewal, and have a rich inner life often possessing an inscrutability that others cannot penetrate. Scorpio's fixity of purpose and concentration of energy can make them appear to be threatening to others. These natives undergo loss and death more so than others, and they are here to show us how to survive and reinvent ourselves over and over gain. Scorpios realize early that life is one of tradeoffs. You attain one goal with the simultaneous need to sacrifice something else in order to reach that goal. Scorpio's relationship with power is immense.

Each Scorpio native makes his or her own peace with empowerment. Overcoming one's weaknesses is one path to power or at the very least acknowledging flaws and working with them.

Persephone (Roman Kore)

What message does Persephone have for Scorpio? Transformation comes quickly to mind. In fact, she is known as the queen of the dead. In the case of Persephone, she was transformed by her experience in the underworld, never to be the same again, never to be the innocent child of her mother. She was transformed by the powerful experience of sexuality. She became the wife of Hades, god of the underworld and in the Roman version, Pluto, the ruler of the sign of Scorpio. The red seeds of the pomegranate portray the sensuous sexuality in the myth of Persephone and certainly also the violence in her initial abduction. Persephone also portrays the inevitable need to separate from the mother and become a woman in her own right. The transmutation in the underworld, the initiation into her sexuality, makes that passage and that transition in the cycle of woman irreversible.

Yet, there is a greater complexity to Persephone, as she was initially a victim and then became the queen of the underworld. She stands at the boundary of the worlds, the one above and the one below. She has passed between the veils and has acquired through this process transcendence and a strong mystical sensibility. She seems innocent and hard to figure out but she, in fact, is always bridging the known world and the unknown world. She is a true psychic for modern times and her interests gravitate to metaphysical consciousness. She is intensely intuitive, and that intuition can often keep her silent and unknowable to those around her. There is an aura of magic that she casts, and some, of course, will be uncomfortable with that. This aspect of Persephone describes a deep part of the Scorpio character, although this doesn't mean that it is always acknowledged or even developed. (Indeed, there are many different facets to each and every sign, as to each and every individual.)

Persephone's position at the threshold can alienate her and make her feel uncertain around her more practical and logically oriented peers, as well as in the presence of society's endorsement of scientific materialism. And the archetype of Persephone (as well as Scorpio) appears to require death or trauma on some level as a means of transformation. Early experiences with transformative events and situations create in Persephone a rich inner life and world, which she may not readily share with others. The struggle for Persephone (as for Scorpio) is to transform fully and develop inherent, latent potential. In other words, to bring back the gifts and riches from the underworld, the vast unconscious, and take one's place as a powerful being. After all, this is the myth of Persephone—she began as the maiden and she must eventually transform into the queen, the mistress of her power and her possibility.

Artemis (Roman Diana)

She was called Moon goddess and goddess of the wilds. She is most likely the oldest representation of the Great Mother Goddess. Her realm is nature and she enjoys a natural physical ruggedness and fitness. In the old myth, she traveled with a band of women—the nymphs—and she honored and nurtured the tribe and clan of women. She loved the hunt and the strategies of pursuit, very much like the strategic Scorpio nature that analyzes and plans based on information and a deep instinctual knowing. Artemis is natural and therefore enjoys natural expression in communication as well as in dress. She dislikes the false armor of pretense and affectation and avoids often-elaborate social conventions and dress codes. Artemis prefers being casual and comfortable. She has a wild and freedom-loving side to her nature that is unwilling to tolerate restraint in any form. She is her own woman, and she is in touch with her own unbridled power. (Scorpio energy equally holds that silent determination that will not be deterred. It has focus, a deep understanding, and willingness to explore the mysteries of life and death.)

Artemis was also known as the protector of the animals. She loved them but also realized that some must be sacrificed as food for humans. Hunting in the woods meant Artemis had to become knowledgeable about the cycles and rhythms of the animals she hunted. Hers is a kind of consciousness called mystical participation, to become one with nature and animals. So, there is an unsociable side to Artemis—the aspect who loved the quiet contemplation of nature (just as Scorpio has a strong inward energy that says I am complete in myself and that wants the chance to work with inner landscapes). In addition, Artemis is deeply concerned with the dual processes of life and death. In some versions of the myth, she is also described as a midwife being in the position of witnessing and participating in the process of birth and the simultaneous death of the maiden as the female become mother and nurturer. In this way, Artemis is a transformative goddess and suits the archetype of Scorpio well. Scorpio is intimately concerned with all processes that change and transmute existing situations into something else and includes a necessary incubation stage that must happen before the final transformation can be complete. Artemis describes the eternal life/death cycle that can be applied to anything. Indeed, these cycles need not always be huge or pivotal but can refer also to the daily ending and new beginnings that we take for granted.

Artemis combines the emotional, watery expression of the Moon's energy with the strategic and independent, determined expression of the fixed sign Scorpio. Artemis shows her independence and self-realization by playing the part of the huntress, and traveling and adventuring in the dark and complex forests. The name Diana links back to the Greek word *diania*, meaning "intelligence." Artemis/Diana possesses the emotional intelligence of Scorpio, which is also known as gut instinct. It's that part which allows women and men to know what to choose and what matches, what is congruent with or even what resonates with their present emotional understanding of a situation or their feelings and impressions about a person. Lastly, Artemis was a virgin goddess, which means to be one or complete in oneself. There are elements of the Scorpion nature that require and desire withdrawing into oneself to resolve and contemplate the complexities of one's nature or of one's life. The Scorpion nature that needs to experience this aspect is living out an aspect of Artemis.

Pisces Water Goddesses

Pisces is one of the most complex of all the zodiac signs. Its mutability or flexibility enacted through the element of water gives it more easily permeable boundaries. This condition can be both positive and negative in its manifestation. On the one hand, it allows Pisces to draw from its immediate environment and the ethers—or multiple dimensions—the magical messages and symbols that give meaning to life. On the other hand, it can mean that the Piscean nature falls prey to illusion or deception from excessive stimuli, or is overwhelmed from its receptivity to the emotional conditions of others and environmental conditions. Pisces can live on the edge of life, never quite certain what is real and what is imaginary. A Piscean that takes care to respect their own and others boundaries can learn to channel their special gift of illumination, compassion, and visionary manifestation. More than anything, the Pisces nature needs to reflect back, or to express, what it has absorbed, They often excels in the arts or music.

Ariadne

Ariadne means "very holy." Initially, she was worshiped only by women. Her myth is caught in the political, cultural, and religious shifts that took place in Greece, and that sought to suppress strong feminine cults and worship. Consequently, there are many versions of her myth. One myth of Ariadne is told like this—Ariadne helped the Athenian hero Theseus escape and find his way trough the Minoan labyrinth. Ariadne gave Theseus a spool of thread, and by holding on to the thread Theseus was able to find his way through. In another version of the myth, she herself threaded her way through the labyrinth, and by holding onto the thread Theseus was able to find his way through as well. Then, Ariadne and Theseus fled together on his ship across the seas. However, shortly after setting sail the next morning, they landed on the island of Naxos to rest and sleep on land. The following morning, when Ariadne awakened, the ship and Theseus were gone. Ariadne was abandoned. Later, Dionysus found her and Ariadne married this god of wine. Dionysus and Ariadne joined forces and had many children together. She became the leader of the Dionysian women but eventually died in childbirth.

Pisces, the sign of altered consciousness and altered states of perception, is often prey to addictions and so the connection to the Dionysian is strongly present. In fact, the unification of Pisces and the blurring of boundaries are also represented by the reported androgyny of Dionysus. Thus, Ariadne's encounter with Theseus seems less important than her marriage to Dionysus, a very complex god. Because she becomes his counterpart, she shares some of his characteristics of ecstasy, madness, vitality, chaos, and confusion. Dionysus, it is said, was the only one of the gods who was faithful and did not exploit women, and his attendants were always women. He was a woman's kind of god. This thread of androgyny points to an aspect of Pisces that can shift and change, understand and experience many personalities and fully experience many states of emotion and being

Ariadne knew the secrets of the labyrinth. In fact, she is called the mistress of the labyrinth. Now doesn't that sound like Pisces? The sign of Pisces holds all manner of secrets both for others and for itself. Pisces is the sign of self-discovery, inner discovery, the discovery of meaning, of how one fits into the scheme of things, and of how one's gifts can contribute to the whole. Pisces is also a feeling of connectedness, and the labyrinth of Ariadne is both connectedness and potential confusion of connection, which is a central issue of Pisces. Many who entered the famed labyrinth never returned. The high degree of sensitivity and sometimes the feeling of inferiority cause doubt and confusion to the point that Pisces questions its own feelings, which then can easily lead to despair and depression. This brings us to one of the prime task of Pisces, that is, to make sure that one does not get lost in the labyrinth but rather to find one's way through—to find meaning.

Hokhma

Hokhma is a Hebrew goddess whose name means "wisdom." Pisces has many facets and many expressions—one of them an extraordinary capacity for wisdom arising from its subtle sensitivities and the capacity to understand and recognize omens and portends. The story of Hokhma dates to 900 BC, but was excluded from the Bible (possibly due to patriarchal influence and the unwillingness to attribute wisdom to woman). In the *Apocrypha*, meaning "hidden," are many stories excluded from the main text of the Bible, including Hokhma's. It is told that Hokhma knows the structure of the world of life, and of its continual shifts and changes, including all the seasons of life. Hokhma is an example of the many-in-one. Just as Pisces shimmers and changes, like a shape-shifter, Hokhma takes on aspects and facets of numerous personalities. Hokhma, like Pisces, is light and ethereal as the mists that swirl mysteriously and the dance that is always willing to reveal itself in the Pisces nature.

Pisces, too, has a hidden side. Sometimes out of necessity in order not to be ridiculed but often to beguile or to seduce and to bring others into a magical world of discovery and sensual pleasures of many kinds. At the same time, to those who seek, Hokhma and Pisces will reveal the mysteries and will impart eternal wisdom. To follow the principle of Hokhma, it is said; you must first rid yourself of envy. There is no place for envy, which easily becomes spite and thus leads away from the clear light of divinity that Hokhma offers. Pisces energy operates best when free from strong negative attachments and when its energy can flow freely between other souls and offer a unifying presence that inspires and calms.

There is a magical inner quality in Hokhma that is said to shine from the eternal light. Some of that same quality shines in Pisces in its romanticism, dreaminess, and wistfulness, as well as in its compassion, concern, and caring for anyone (or anything) that suffers and needs solace. Hokhma also represents (as Pisces reflects) the inner knowing—the voices of intuition that, if we listen, will guide us because they stem from a deep well that is connected ultimately to the divine that knows all things. Hokhma operates primarily through the realm of the spirit, guiding through subtle messaging and delight. Her strength and temperance are inner qualities and her wisdom is available if we but take the time to be still and listen. The myth of Hokhma is an important one for the archetype of Pisces, for it is well-known that another side of Pisces is the sensation seeker and the one who blocks the more subtle messages of the spirit. When the messages of Hokhma cannot get through, the spirit can fall prey to melancholy or depression because it is cut off from the eternal guiding principle of wisdom and, ultimately, love.

Marriage and Other Traditional Astrological Elections

By Christopher Warnock, Esq.

Many of us have an awareness that the events in our lives are not random, but follow definite patterns and cycles, and that what Carl Jung termed *synchronicity* (connections based not on material causality, but meaningful coincidence) is truly meaningful in our everyday lives. As we pay closer attention to synchronicities in our lives we become aware that we are part of a greater pattern, traditionally termed *destiny* or *fate*. People interested in directing their future destiny can best benefit from astrology if they understand how astrology works and what information can be derived from it.

I am a practitioner of Renaissance (traditional) astrology. One area that Renaissance astrology is particularly suited to is answering questions concerning love and marriage. Since the stars rule passions and emotions, by asking a question regarding the future of a relationship and casting a horoscope for the time of the question, we can see clearly the future of the relationship. Renaissance astrology even gives us the tools to see if the person desired is enamored of the person asking the question or whether they are already involved with someone else.

Basically, astrology analogizes the cycles of the heavenly bodies with events below on Earth. These techniques provide a way to synthesize separate astrological factors and provide pinpoint, to the minute accuracy, for the best times to take action or start an activity.

What is Traditional Astrology?

The word "astrology" comes from the Greek *aster*, meaning "star," and *logos*, which has a wide variety of meanings including speech, ratio, and reason. Astrology is therefore the *speech* or *reason of the stars*.

The influence of heavenly bodies on the Earth is clear. The Sun and Earth's daily rotation produces day and night; the Sun and the Earth's annual orbit around it produces the seasons. The Moon's monthly orbit produces the tides.

But before the eighteenth century, philosophers, particularly of the Neoplatonic and Hermetic schools, saw much deeper connections. They viewed the cosmos as one great, interconnected whole, filled with material and spiritual sympathies and interconnections. The stars and planets were seen as the essential connection between the divine and the terrestrial.

Traditional astrologers believed that the stars and planets controlled the generation and corruption of all things on Earth. "As above, so below" says the *Emerald Tablet*, a famous Hermetic work. Thus traditional astrologers used the changing cycles and interactions of the planets to understand and predict almost any event here on Earth.

How Does Traditional Astrology Differ From Modern Astrology?

Astrology first emerged almost 4,000 years ago in Egypt, Babylonia, and Chaldea as an integral part of religious doctrines and practices. It then passed to the Greeks and Romans and died out in Europe during the Dark Ages with the loss of the necessary texts and mathematical skills.

But astrology was preserved by the advanced Middle Eastern Islamic civilization and passed to the West in the twelfth and thirteenth centuries. Astrology reached its greatest height in Europe in the medieval, Renaissance, and early modern periods from 1200 to 1700. With the subsequent rise of materialism and a purely mechanical explanation of reality, astrology went out of fashion during the eighteenth century of Enlightenment.

Astrology was revived in the late nineteenth and early twentieth centuries, but with many of the old teachings lost and the remaining techniques greatly simplified. In addition, modern astrology is predominately psychological in orientation. Thus, while modern astrology is excellent for counseling and self-discovery, it cannot make concrete predictions of events with the astounding accuracy of pre-1700s traditional astrology.

Tools of Traditional Astrology

Signs & Other Essential Dignities

One of the major tools of traditional astrology is the system of essential dignities. Using this system, traditional astrologers were able to gauge precisely the strength or weakness of any planet given its position in the zodiac. Each of the twelve signs consists of thirty degrees and is ruled by one planet. When a planet is in a sign that it rules, it is considered to be strong. One major difference between modern and traditional astrology is that traditional astrology does not make use of the modern planets—Uranus, Neptune, and Pluto—in the system of essential dignities. So for traditional astrology, Saturn, not Uranus, rules Aquarius; Jupiter, not Neptune, rules Pisces; and Mars, not Pluto, rules Scorpio.

Traditional astrologers used many more subdivisions of the zodiac, and each was given a certain number of positive or negative points ranging from +5 to −5. For example, if a planet is in the sign it rules (Moon in Cancer, or Venus in Libra) it has a value of +5. However, if the Moon is in Capricorn its value is −5, and Venus in Aries also has a value of −5. The system of essential dignities provides traditional astrologers with much more precise information about planetary strength or weakness than modern astrology, which uses only the rulerships and occasionally the exaltations of the planets.

The Houses

Another method used by astrologers is the system of houses, which are subdivisions based on the circle of the horizon and the circle of the meridian, which passes through a point directly overhead. This produces four basic points, the Ascendant and Descendant, and the Medium Coeli or Midheaven, and the Imum Coeli. These four points are further subdivided to produce a total of twelve houses. Each house represents a different area of life.

Here's an example of the use of the houses. If we had a question

Chart 1

concerning money we would look to the Second House, which signifies the possessions and wealth of the querent (person asking the question). We then look to see what sign is on the cusp (or beginning of the house in question). In this case, it is the Second House. If, for example, 1 degree of Aries was on the cusp of the Second, the Second House would be ruled by Mars, the planet that rules Aries. Knowing how strong or weak Mars is, we can gain valuable information about the corresponding strength or weakness of the querent's money.

Aspects

Among the tools used by both traditional and modern astrologers are aspects, which show the interactions and interrelationships between the planets. As we noted earlier, the zodiac is a 360-degree circle. Ancient astrologers subdivided the circle in half, producing the 180-degree opposition aspect, by thirds for the 120-degree trine aspect, in quarters for the 90-degree square aspect, and by sixths for the 60-degree sextile aspect. Thus, when planets are 60 degrees apart (for example, the Sun at 1 degree Aries and Mars at 1 degree of Gemini) they are said to be in sextile. The final aspect, which is the conjunction, occurs when planets are in the same degree of the zodiac. These five aspects are known as the Ptolemaic aspects, and they are the only aspects used by traditional astrologers.

Each of the aspects has a different meaning. The opposition, not surprisingly, is the strongest aspect, and signifies opposition. They do not encourage any action. The trine is the strongest aspect of friendship, love, and assistance. They do not motivate us to actually get out and do something though. A trine is more of a "go with the flow" energy. The square is an aspect of difficulty and challenges, but not as intense as the opposition. The sextile is an aspect of friendship and help, but not as powerful as the trine. The nature of the conjunction is neutral; its influence—positive or negative—depends on the character of the planets involved.

There are a number of differences between modern and traditional astrology and their use of aspects. In traditional astrology each planet has a zone of effectiveness before and after it is exactly in aspect known as an orb. In modern astrology the aspects, not the planets, are used to determine the orb. In addition, traditional astrology distinguishes between applying and separating aspects. An applying aspect shows what will happen and a separating aspect shows what has happened. I should note that this distinction is used more in traditional horary astrology, which answers questions based on a horoscope of the question, than in traditional natal astrology, which examines birth charts.

Let's look at an example. If the Sun is at 1 degree of Aries and Mars is at 5 degrees of Gemini then they are moving towards a sextile, but the aspect is not yet exact, as it will be when the Sun reaches 5 degrees of Aries. However, the Sun and Mars are close enough to perfection of the sextile that they are considered to be in orb and the effects of the sextile will be felt. If the Sun is ruler of the Second House, for example, and Mars is ruling the First House, and thus is the significator (the planet ruling the sign on the Ascendant) of the querent, we would judge that money (the Sun) was coming to (applying sextile) the querent (Mars).

Synthesis

Not only does traditional astrology employ many techniques to obtain detailed and useful information; it seeks a synthesis of these various techniques in order to answer the question presented. When I look at a chart, I see it as a script to a drama played out in the heavens. The planets are the actors and their strengths and weaknesses, loves and hates, future and past, are clearly delineated. Since the cycles of the heavens foretell the cycles of events here in Earth, by reading one we can predict the other.

While some philosophers, particularly those of the Stoic school, denied the existence of free will, believing instead that events were predetermined, most astrologers, by the Middle Ages, believed that the stars controlled only the body and the emotions. The soul (or divine spirit) was free if it could escape the control of the passions.

Electional astrology is based on this insight. By carefully examining the heavens we can align our free will with the celestial cycles and select the best times for taking action or beginning an activity here on Earth.

The Elections

I have provided a horoscope, or chart, showing the position of the planets as well as a specific date and time for two of the elections. Because these dates and times are based on house positions they are reasonably accurate if you are in the continental United States or Canada. For a higher degree of precision, if you have access to astrological software, adjust the time to the same degree of rising sign as given in each election, or consult a traditional astrologer.

Readers who wish to obtain the very best results from traditional elections should consult a traditional astrologer who can compare their birth chart with the chart of the election.

Now, what should be done at the time and date of the election? When you select a date for an action to happen, you are choosing a time for it to be born. If the date and time are convenient, the marriage elections provided here can be used to time the actual marriage ceremony. If the astrologically appropriate time and date are inconvenient for the ceremony, one option would be to use this election time to send out announcements or invitations, or to propose. The time and date chosen for marriage or love affair elections would be an excellent time for a love spell or astrological love talisman, too. They would also be appropriate for forming other types of partnerships.

Finally, readers should not despair if they cannot arrange their activity on one of the times provided. By consulting a traditional astrologer, they can obtain an election suited to their situation, and within the time and date needed.

The Marriage Elections

Rules for traditional marriage elections are provided by William Ramesey in his book *Astrologie Restored*, which was published in London in 1653. Generally, in elections the First House represents the elector (the person who has sought the election) and will be acting based upon it. In marriage elections, the Seventh House represents the elector's husband or bride-to-be. The Seventh House also represents the other party in any situation involving a permanent love relationship. When the situation involves a love affair or temporary relationship, the Fifth House, which relates to pleasure and games, signifies the other party. This is an important distinction to make and electors should be careful not to confuse a truly permanent relationship with a temporary infatuation. We will also look to the Tenth House to see if the marriage or relationship will work well and the Fourth House to see the final outcome.

The planets also have what are termed natural rulership (not dependent on houses or house rulerships) of various facets of the relationship or marriage. Mercury, for example, signifies children in a marriage election. Finally, particular Ascendants (or Rising signs) are considered to be favorable or unfavorable for marriage.

One of the difficulties with elections is that it is almost impossible to have every planet and house in favorable condition. The real skill in electional astrology comes in minimizing the inevitable negative factors and choosing the most favorable time and date given the constraints of the situation and the requirements of the elector.

February 18, 2002, at 9:34 am EST

2 degrees Taurus rising

In this chart Taurus, a fixed sign, is rising. Fixed signs are good for things we wish to last a long time, like marriage. It is the planetary hour

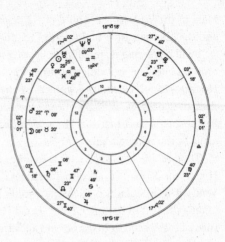

Chart for February 18, 2002, marriage election.

of Jupiter, which is considered a good hour for marriage. With Taurus rising, Venus is the ruler of the First House and signifies the elector (person seeking the information). Venus is strong in Pisces and in the Eleventh House of hopes, dreams, and friendship. Two degrees of Scorpio is on the Seventh House cusp, making Mars the significator of the spouse to be. Mars is in Aries, which he rules, and in the Twelfth, but close enough to the Ascendant to be moved into the First. The Moon is making a sextile to Venus, which is separating, but still in the same degree (indicating that the event is not yet past). As the Moon is exalted in Taurus, which Venus rules, the sextile strengthens it. Mercury has triplicity (meaning it is quite fortunate) showing good prospects of children in the marriage. Saturn, ruler of the Tenth House, is in triplicity, indicating a positive outlook for the marriage. Cancer is on the Fourth House cusp, and as the Moon is strong and well placed, this indicates a positive outlook for the marriage.

Negative indications: If we put Mars in the First, it moves Venus into the Twelfth. However, Venus in the Eleventh puts Mars in the Twelfth. Ideally, we would like a positive aspect between Mars and Venus, but the placement of Seventh House ruler, Mars in the First, helps make the connection, as does the very nice sextile of Venus to the Moon. By adjusting the Ascendant and the house rulers, we can use these strong significators for other purposes and activities. Venus is somewhat afflicted. Moving

Mars in the First House would put 2 degrees of Pisces on the Ascendant, and the alternate time of 7:06 am EST on February 18, 2002.

I will be pairing many of the following marriage elections with elections on the same date, but different times for love affairs (signified by the Fifth House) and job elections (signified by the Sixth House). Using an ascendant of 2 degrees of Pisces means that Cancer is on the Fifth and Sixth House cusps, and that the Moon signifies the significant other in a love affair or the potential job.

Thus, at 7:06 am EST Venus is exalted (very strong) in Pisces in the First House; the Moon is exalted in Taurus and is making an applying sextile to Venus. This election is particularly useful for a job as the Moon is also conjoining the Part of Fortune in the Second House (elector's money) and Mars, ruler of the Second, is in the Second and strong in his own sign of Aries. This emphasis on the Second House is very positive for financial gain.

February 23, 2002, at 9:20 am EST

4 degrees Taurus rising

In this chart, we have Taurus again—good for marriage, and a fixed sign for long duration. We have Venus as the ruler of the First and Mars as ruler of the Seventh, both strong and either one or the other well placed. Here the Moon is in Cancer and making a trine to Venus with only reception by triplicity. Saturn and Mercury are still strong, and the Moon rules the Fourth.

Negative indications: We see the same placement problems with Venus and Mars, and no aspect between them. Here the election is during the planetary hour of Mars, not considered to be a good time for marriage.

February 23, 2002, at 6:54 am EST

Job and love affair variation: 4 degrees Pisces rising

Here, again, we are using our Pisces Ascendant variation, so the Moon rules the Fifth and Sixth Houses. The Moon is strong in Cancer, and in an applying trine of Venus in the Pisces First House. Again this is a favorable election for financial gain as the result of a job as the Moon is conjunct the Part of Fortune. Love affairs should also be positive as the Moon, ruler of the Fifth House of pleasure, is in the Fifth House.

April 14, 2002, at 10:36 am EDT

4 degrees Cancer rising

This is a very nice chart. With Cancer rising, the Moon is ruling the First

House. It is the planetary hour of the Moon. The Moon is exalted in Taurus and is applying to a conjunction of Venus. Venus rules Taurus so the Moon and Venus have strong mutual reception as the Moon is in Venus' sign and Venus is in the Moon's exaltation. The conjunction takes place in the benefic Eleventh House of hopes, dreams, and friendship. The ruler of the Tenth is the Jupiter, exalted in Cancer and in the benefic First House, indicating a very positive relationship for the marriage. Mercury, the natural ruler of children in a marriage, and the Fourth House, in this chart, is at least dignified by face and in the benefic Tenth House. (Very nice election.)

Negative indications: Cancer is not a good rising sign for marriage, and the Seventh ruler, Saturn, is in the Twelfth House (you might be unaware of something important).

April 14, 2002 4:35 am EDT (3:35 am EST)

Job & Love Affair Variation: 4 degrees Pisces rising

The Moon, exalted in Taurus, conjoins Venus, in her sign Taurus, in the Second House of money. The Moon is again ruler of the Fifth of love affairs and pleasure and the Sixth of jobs.

April 19, 2002, at 10:13 am EDT

4 degrees Cancer rising

This is a variation on the April 14, 2002, election. The Moon, ruler of the First, applies to a trine to Venus. Once again Jupiter, ruler of the Tenth is in the First, an excellent indication for the success of the marriage. Mercury, significator of children, is again dignified by face, but now in the Eleventh House of hopes and friendship. One interesting thing about this chart is that Venus is the ruler of the Fifth, so this would also be a good time to have, or arrange for, a love affair or a date.

Negative indications: Again, Cancer rising, and it is the planetary hour of Saturn, which is negative. However, the strength of the significators and their positive aspects potentially overcomes the negative influence of Saturn.

April 19, 2002, at 4:15am EDT

Job and love affair variation: 4 degrees Pisces rising

This time the Moon in Cancer is applying to a sextile of Venus in Taurus. The Moon and Jupiter in the Fifth assist with love and pleasure.

June 13, 2002, at 11:42 am EDT

6 degrees Virgo rising

As Virgo rises, Mercury is the significator of the elector and strong in Gemini, which he rules. Mercury is conjunct the Midheaven (cusp of the Tenth House) and ruler of the Tenth, providing a very positive indication of a harmonious and successful marriage. In addition, as Mercury (the natural significator of children in marriage elections) is very positive for children in this chart. Jupiter, exalted in the Eleventh, is the ruler of the Seventh representing the potential spouse. The Moon, strong in Cancer, has separated from Jupiter and then applies to a conjunction of Venus then a sextile to Mercury, tying all the significators together. Jupiter is also the ruler of the Fourth, and, by his strength, placement, and natural benefic quality, indicates a very positive outcome for the marriage.

Negative indications: Virgo is not recommend as a rising sign, and it is believed that the Mercury hour is not a good hour for marriage.

August 11, 2002, at 7:12 pm EDT

2 degrees Aquarius rising

As Aquarius rises, Saturn in the Fifth House, represents the elector. The Sun, in Leo, which he rules, is in the Seventh House, signifies the potential spouse.

The Sun makes a sextile to Saturn. The Moon is making an applying sextile to Jupiter, and then a conjunction to Venus. Venus is the ruler of the Fourth, promising a good outcome to the marriage. Mercury is strong in Virgo, which he rules and in the benefic Seventh House, providing a positive indication for children.

Negative indications: Neither Aquarius as a rising sign or the planetary hour of Saturn is recommended for marriage by our sources. The Moon is somewhat weak, though this is compensated for by the fact that she is in Libra, ruled by Venus and conjoining Venus. In addition, the Moon is separating from a strong Jupiter and going to a strong Venus.

Career and Job Elections

As in marriage elections the elector (the person who has sought the election and will be acting based upon it) is represented by the First House and its ruler. Just as we must distinguish between Seventh House (permanent relationship) and Fifth House (temporary relationship) in marriage elections, we must also be careful in career and job elections. The Tenth House is often overused, and represents management and high-level employees only, the Sixth House is the true significator of most jobs and employees.

May 11, 2002, at 6:41 am EDT

5 degrees Gemini rising

Because this election is for early Saturday morning, it is unlikely that a job interview could be scheduled for that time. Electors can use this time to fax, mail or e-mail a resume, or otherwise apply for the desired position.

In this chart the elector is represented by Mercury, strong in his sign Gemini and conjunct the Ascendant. The Tenth House ruler is Saturn in the First House, and conjunct the beneficial North Node. The placement of Saturn, Tenth House ruler, in the First, and its conjunction with the First House ruler, according to William Lilly, the famous astrologer in his 1647 *Christian Astrology*, indicates that the position will be obtained with ease and without much labor on the part of the elector.

The Moon is exalted in Taurus. The Moon is also the Second House ruler, representing the elector's finances. The strength of the Moon and the fact that she is making an applying sextile to beneficial Jupiter, the natural ruler of wealth, who is exalted in Cancer and in the Second House, means that the elector should do very well financially from the position.

Negative indications: It is Saturn's hour, which is not a particularly good time. The Moon is under the Sun's beams in the Twelfth House, but greatly assisted by the sextile to Jupiter.

May 11, 2002, at 1:58 pm EDT

Job variation: 7 degrees Virgo rising

This is a variation on the previous chart for a regular job rather than management position. Here again, as Virgo rises, Mercury is the significator of the elector. Mercury is in the Tenth, which means more work is necessary on the part of the elector to get the position. Mercury is still conjoining Saturn, now Sixth House ruler and significator of a regular job. The position of Saturn in the Tenth House of company management also bodes well for obtaining a job. The Moon is still applying to Jupiter, also indicating a positive outcome to the job hunt.

Election to Settle a Lawsuit

March 12, 2002, at 5:39 am EST

1 degree Pisces rising

As an attorney I am always interested in the use of astrology in conjunction with the law. In this election the First House represents the elector and the Seventh House represents the opponent. As Pisces rises, Jupiter is the significator of the elector and is strong in Cancer. Mercury is the ruler of Virgo, the sign on the cusp of the Seventh and represents the opponent. In lawsuit questions we look to see which significator is stronger, as that usually indicates who will win the case. Here Jupiter strong with a score of +4 and Mercury is very weak with a score of −14.

Mercury is also weak because it is in the elector's house, the First, and in Pisces, which he rules, showing the domination of the elector over the opponent. Mercury applies to a trine of Jupiter. In a civil lawsuit a sextile or trine between the First and Seventh House rulers indicates that the case will be settled.

Jupiter trines the Ascendant—a good indication in a lawsuit. Finally, the Moon is separating from Mercury and applying to a trine of Jupiter, further tying together the main significators.

In lawsuits, the Tenth House represents the judge, and since Sagittarius is on the Tenth House cusp, Jupiter also rules the judge meaning that he will favor the elector. Finally, it is a Jupiter hour, which is favorable for legal matters. As this election is fairly early in the morning it can be used it to fax, e-mail, or mail a settlement offer to your opponent.

Traditional astrology provides us with a glimpse of the order and coherence of the cosmos and the interconnections of Earth and the heavens. By using the full range of traditional techniques, amazing accuracy in prediction and control of elections is possible.

Chart for March 12, 2002

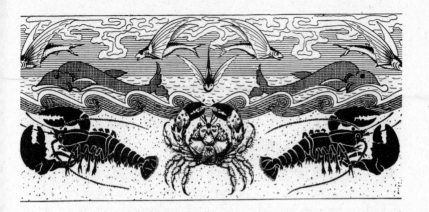

The Biological Moon

By Bruce Scofield

One of the most incredible sights I've ever seen occurred on a New Jersey beach when the Moon was full. Here's what happened. My band and I had played for a graduation party at Glassboro State College on a Saturday night in May, finishing up around 1:00 in the morning. After breaking down the equipment and loading our cars, we went to a late-night bar for a drink, and after that a diner for breakfast. Before we knew it, it was 5:00 in the morning. One of us suggested that we drive to Delaware Bay to watch the sunrise and take a swim. We arrived there just before dawn and just as the Moon was setting in the west over the water. We bolted from the cars and ran toward the water, only to be stopped short by an amazing sight. The beach was covered with thousands of crawling horseshoe crabs. It was the most primal scene I'd ever witnessed, and to top it off, the backdrop was a giant Full Moon. We chose not to go swimming that morning and stood there stunned by the spectacle.

What we had witnessed that morning on Delaware Bay was a massive sexual event. Horseshoe crabs, which are not really crabs but more closely related to insects, mate at the Full Moon. They are ancient survivors, and there they were, doing what they've been doing for 400 million years— moving to the Moon. It's called *lunar periodicity*.

The realization that the Moon is a regulator of the cyclic functions of marine organisms goes back to the ancient Greeks and Romans. In the fourth century, Aristotle noted that the gonads of sea urchins are largest at the Full Moon. This was good to know, as those gonads were the part of the urchin that was eaten. Cicero and Pliny also noted that oysters and shellfish grow according the cycle of the Moon, becoming fullest at the Full Moon. They spawn at both Full and New Moon. Many other marine organisms reach a sexual peak at the Full Moon because that's when their mating activities occur. When sexual fertilization in a species takes place outside of the body, as it does with these marine organisms, survival is enhanced if the population comes together at a specific time. And the timer for this group mating ritual is, of course, the Moon.

All sorts of things under the sea happen according to the cycle of the Moon. Even today fish vendors in Mediterranean markets will know that crabs are biggest when caught at the Full Moon. Crabs molt at the Full Moon because that's when they've grown so big that they can no longer fit into their shell. Eels begin the long migration from the rivers of Europe to their home in the Sargasso Sea right after a Full Moon. In California, a small fish called the grunion has a bizarre mating ritual that occurs two to four days after Full and New Moons. The females come ashore and dig themselves into the sand, where they lay eggs. Males land and cover the females with sperm, which drips down to the eggs. All of these are examples of monthly rhythms—lunar cycles used to time biological events.

Perhaps one of the strangest examples of lunar periodicity in marine organisms is that of the palolo worm that lives among the coral reefs near Fiji and Samoa. These worms, which live in cracks and holes in the coral, grow segments on the end of their bodies that store, depending on their sex, either sperm or eggs. At dawn on the first day of the last quarter of the Moon in October or November, the ends of the worms break off and swim to the surface, in a process known as swarming. (Swarming is directly linked to the lunar cycle.) There they encounter all the other worm-endings, which together create a bath of sperm and eggs. But, as it turns out the worms are considered a delicacy and the natives long ago figured out how to time this event by the Moon. The islanders' board canoes at dawn on the critical day, paddle out to the reefs, and scoop up the delicious worms.

The first day of the last quarter of the Moon in October and November may be the trigger for the palolo worm orgy, but it's not what gets the coral going in the Gulf of Mexico. There, on the ocean floor, at the Flower Garden Banks National Marine Sanctuary, several species of brain and star corals release eggs and sperm in August—on the eighth night after the Full Moon of that month. These huge fifteen-foot corals know just when their annual reproductivefest must occur, and like the palolo worms, the timing is absolutely critical. The only way these organisms can ensure their sperm and eggs meet and perpetuate their species is to simultaneously let go of millions of eggs and sperms. A lack of synchronization would mean that these reproductive cells would probably never join because they would be widely dispersed by the ocean currents.

Mass coral spawning was only recently recognized by science. It was first observed on the Great Barrier Reef in Australia during the 1980s. Then, in 1990, some recreational divers witnessed a mass spawning on a raised section of the ocean floor some 123 miles south of the Louisiana-Texas border. This led to the area becoming a designated marine sanctuary. These pristine reefs, called the Flower Garden Banks, are believed to be an example of what coral reefs were like before modern times—massive colonies of organisms all swooning to the Moon. Although marine biologists study other coral reefs throughout the world, many suffer from pollution and human disturbances and are no longer able to spawn on such a massive scale.

Fish and Other Crawly Things

The 29.53-day cycle of the Moon—from new to full and back to new—is but one lunar cycle that marine organisms have attuned themselves to. Every day the Moon rises and sets. If one counts the time from one moonrise to another, it amounts to 24.8 hours, just

over a solar day. Richard Alden Knight, who wrote books on fishing, found that fish bite more frequently during the times that the Moon rises and sets. He even created what are called solunar tables that fishermen have used for years to time their fishing trips. In his book *Moon Up–Moon Down* he tells of his informal studies of the behavior of fish and the Moon's rising and settings. His conclusion is that it's more than just the fish that get active as the Moon rises or sets, it's the entire aquatic environment—and especially the worms and other smaller creatures that the larger fish feed on. His insight is probably right. Scientific studies have shown that crayfish and crab feeding activity increases according to the lunar day.

We know that the Moon, with a little help from the Sun, causes the tides. One question that arises is whether the organisms are responding to the Moon itself, or simply to the tide. In the 1950s this question was addressed by biologist Frank A. Brown, Jr. In a famous experiment, Brown took oysters from Long Island Sound near Connecticut and transported them to Evanston, Illinois. He had already established that oysters actively feed twice a day at 12.5-hour intervals, half of the lunar day. In Illinois he wired the oysters shells in such a way that each time they opened their shells it would be recorded. He kept them in a saltwater tray and under low lighting, the best that could be done to simulate their natural environment. For two weeks the oysters opened up and fed as they had done in Long Island Sound at the same time of day. But then they shifted their schedule. They had tuned themselves into the cycle of the tides—if there were tides in Illinois. It seemed clear to Brown that the oysters were responding somehow to the Moon itself.

Brown's findings were not all that favorably received within the scientific community. Many other researchers had invested much time and money on a search for an internal biological clock. The notion that the Moon might be an external timer was difficult for them to accept and they attacked Brown's studies. One professor of zoology even went so far as to publish a paper called "Biological Clock in the Unicorn" in which he claimed to have proven that Brown's methods created false conclusions. For some years thereafter Brown's studies became a joke in the field of biology, and he even had difficulty getting funding for further research (a condition the entire astrological community has faced for centuries). Eventually a young expert in mathematics entered the picture and showed that Brown's critic had himself created an argument full of flaws. Brown was thus relieved of the disrespect tossed on him by an exceptionally clever, but ultimately wrong, critic.

More Creepy Crawlies

It's more than the marine world that moves with the Moon. I learned this one evening camping on the Kittatinny Ridge in New Jersey, again in May. After years of coaxing, I had finally convinced my wife to go backpacking with me. One late afternoon we, and another couple who had also never backpacked, hiked south on the Appalachian Trail to a grassy, almost perfect, campsite that presented a 180-degree view to the east. We put up our tents and I made a small campfire. As we sat there by the fire, a gigantic Full Moon rose up in the east. Just then, the other couple noticed a few five-inch long millipedes climbing up the side of their tent. A few minutes later, there were a dozen slowly making their way up the ripstop nylon. Within fifteen minutes our tents were covered with large millipedes and a panic broke out among my companions. My wife and the other couple dove into their tents, zipped them up, and refused to come out. I found the situation hilarious and walked around the campsite noting that the throngs of millipedes were climbing trees and rocks as well. While I had seen these insects before, I had never seen them in such large numbers. When morning came, they were gone, but needless to say, the camping trip was ruined.

Like marine organisms, the millipedes were probably engaged in some kind of mating ritual timed by the Full Moon. Many other land animals do the same. It's been shown that lemurs, distant cousins of humans, come into heat about five to six days before the Full Moon. One study reported that lemur orgies take place every other Full Moon. Studies of Indian buffalo cows noted that the females come into heat more often at Full Moon and New Moon than at any other time. African rats tend to mate on the midnight before the Full Moon, but this is less true for domesticated rats. And there's also the case of the human female whose natural menstrual cycle (menstrual actually means month or moon) is not twenty-eight days; it's been shown to be 29.5 days, exactly the lunar month.

Gerbils and Hamsters Over the Moon

My son had a gerbil named Boffer who would go bonkers for three to four days around the Full Moon. During those periods, she'd run on her wheel and scurry around her cage, waking us up in the middle of the night. It didn't seem to matter whether or not she could actually see the light of the Moon because she did the same thing when we kept her in a room with the blinds drawn. Biologist Frank Brown did some studies with hamsters and found that their activity periods, which he timed by a gauge on their running wheels, corresponded to the lunar day of twenty-five hours, as well as at Full and New Moon.

Brown's studies show that organisms respond to more than just one lunar rhythm. Biologist John D. Palmer's circalunidian clock hypothesis goes further and recognizes the existence of two separate lunar clocks, each linked to a tidal peak. Since tidal peaks occur at intervals of 12.4 hours, the two clocks combine to create the 24.8-hour lunar day cycle. Other organisms, including humans, have independent biological clocks operating all the time—some timed by the Sun, others by the Moon. For example, the circadian rhythms (recurring twenty-four hour cycles), driven by (depending on how you look at it) the Sun or the rotation of the Earth, are about and regulate, among other things, sleep and wakefulness cycles. There are many circadian cycles that don't necessarily run together, however. Lunar cycles exist separately from the many circadian cycles and they regulate other biological functions. It's not just a single clock that keeps an organism's system operating; it's far more complex than that.

The existence of lunar rhythms in organisms has long been known, but explanations for it are a different matter. Several have been proposed though none appear to explain all the phenomena observed. One explanation for lunar periodicity is that moonlight, the actual sensing of light, triggers a biological rhythm. It's been shown that human females with inconsistent menstrual cycles could regularize their periods to a twenty-nine-day rhythm by sleeping with a light shined on the walls and ceiling of the bedroom for several days in the middle of their cycle. Lemurs also seem to be affected by light. When there is none, they don't have orgies. Other studies on worms have shown that exposure to light can cause them to mature sexually well before they should. Even the palolo worms fail to swarm without lights to cue them, and if they are exposed to lights too early, they mate prematurely.

In their exploration of how light can possible trigger sexual responses, scientists have examined the pineal gland, and a small gland located deep in the brain. This gland appears to have a kind of control over other glands, which, in turn, produce hormones that affect the body. It appears that the pineal gland is light sensitive and that it has a direct effect on the pituitary gland that makes sex hormones. Although the pineal gland is deep inside the brain, there are direct links with the eyes, which, like fiber optics, bring light to it.

Another explanation for lunar periodicity has to do with what are called biological tides. We know the Moon moves the ocean, but does it also move the water in our bodies? There is indeed plenty of water in the human body. It's been suggested that, as the water in the body of an organism is pulled by the gravity of the Moon, however slight, the change upsets the electrolyte balance and consequently causes hormonal shifts and triggers nervous irritability. It's well-known that manic-depressive persons have wide mood swings and may go "over the top" during a Full Moon.

The ionization of the Earth's atmosphere is yet another possible explanation for the lunar effect. Ions are molecules of gas that have been altered by either gaining or losing an electron. If a molecule gains an electron, which has a negative charge, it becomes a negative ion. Negative ions, which are found at the seashore or near a waterfall, are said to bring calm and tranquility. If a molecule loses an electron, it becomes positively charged, a condition that is not so good for the body and mind. There is also the daily fluctuation of the geomagnetic index. This index peaks when the Moon is directly overhead and directly below us, which are near the points at which the ocean tides peak. Why should organisms be affected by magnetic changes? Why not, nervous systems are all basically electrical in nature.

It's in the Genes

Some recent research on the actual mechanisms for biological rhythms has produced fascinating results. In one study all sorts of chemicals were forced on organisms to see if any would affect their biological clocks. None were found. It was then found that the clocks would change, either losing or gaining time, only when the genetic material itself was altered chemically. The clock was deep in the genes, which was assumed all along since lunar periodicity is not a learned behavior. But exactly where the clock was located was found to depend on the species. In humans it's at the base of the brain; in birds, at the top in the pineal gland. Some marine organisms appear to have the seat of their biological clock located in their optic nerves. When the optical system is studied in detail, it appears that the clock can continue to operate even when most of the nerves are removed. In fact, it appears that the location of the clock is very widely distributed and can function in a single cell even with the nucleus removed. This suggests that the mechanism for timing and regulating an organism is something deep within the cell, and yet not concentrated in any one place.

Today, a large body of scientific data has been gathered that suggests many organisms, particularly those of a marine nature, time their reproductive or feeding cycles with the movements of the Moon. Still, in spite of meticulous record-keeping and scientific analysis, the influence of the Moon on life on Earth remains controversial. For example, scientists argue over whether the Moon is the external trigger, which Frank Brown showed to be the case with his oysters, or whether organisms make their own time internally. If a biological clock appears to be driven from the outside (i.e., the Moon) it is called exogenous. If an internal circuit drives it, it is called endogenous.

The study of lunar periodicity in organisms might reasonably be considered a branch of astrology. The greatest astrologer of the ancient world, Ptolemy, wrote that astrology has two main branches, natal astrology and universal astrology, the later dealing with the effects of the planets on nature. During the Renaissance, this latter branch came to be known as natural astrology. Because most modern astrologers have concerned themselves with natal astrology, which they must do to make a living, work in the field of natural astrology has been carried on by biologists. With scientists, who lack any real knowledge of astrology, conducting nearly all the research on this subject, we shouldn't expect them to validate the astrological hypothesis, as we understand it. What we have seen, and will continue to see, is essentially an appropriation of the territory that once belonged to astrology.

China: A Crisis of Nurturing

By Robin Antepara

In the early hours of June 4, 1989, Chinese armed troops moved into Beijing's Tiananmen Square and killed hundreds of students who were staging peaceful demonstrations. Thirteen years later, I still remember the cry of a friend who watched this tragedy on television: "The government is murdering its own children! How can they do such a thing?"

For a time after the massacre, it seemed as if the cycle of protests and crackdowns prompted by the 1989 incident had subsided. But then in July 1999, the government banned the religious sect Falun Gong after the group mounted a massive (but peaceful) sit-in in the capital. Since then, tens of thousands of followers have been jailed and, as of September 2000, thirty people have died in custody.

Indeed, the reigning Communist regime has become known for its draconian policies and murderous upheavals: actions that have profoundly affected the nation's young people. At the dawn of the new millennium there are still thousands of political prisoners in China, including teenaged Tibetan monks and student protesters from Tiananmen Square. In its apparent contempt for the nation's young, the Communist regime is not unlike Father Sky, the first ruler of the universe in Greek mythology.

Parent of the Titans and the Cyclops, he feared his children would rebel against him so he imprisoned them.

And yet this same regime that tortures and imprisons so many of its children was founded and built on principles of profound care giving. For years before the Communist revolution in 1949, Mao Zedong and countless others in the party lived in caves and mud huts with the nation's peasants, fighting the injustices that for so long had made their lives miserable. This dedication was in sharp contrast to the rank corruption and callousness of prior governments. The Communists, through their relentless grassroots work and unflinching integrity, were the only ones able to unify this immense, sprawling nation.

How can these two gaping contradictions—selfless dedication on the one hand, campaigns of terror on the other—possibly be explained? How can we begin to fathom the rationale behind ordering tanks to kill peaceful protesters, let alone the mindless barbarity of the Cultural Revolution? To address these and other questions we need to examine the birth chart of the People's Republic of China: October 1, 1949, at 10 am in Beijing.

An Astrological Profile of the People's Republic of China

At first glance, it's difficult to understand the astrological correlation for the world's largest remaining dictatorship—one that continues to enforce brutal occupations in Tibet and East Turkistan. In the October 1949 chart, the Sun is in peace-loving Libra. Ruled by Venus and symbolized by the scales, Libra people traditionally value harmony, beauty, and balance; not qualities associated with a ruthless authoritarian regime. The placement of the Moon in Aquarius (another air sign and a champion of freedom and human rights) doesn't exactly help explain this picture either.

However, the Sun and Moon do not tell the whole story. Of nearly equal importance is the Ascendant (or rising sign) that is derived from the point on the eastern horizon where the Sun rises. The Ascendant (ASC) is symbolic of one's persona. Persona, though, not only in the limited sense of facade, but rather one's orientation—the tools we use to navigate our way through life.

In the People's Republic of China (PRC) chart, Scorpio is on the Ascendant. Ruled by Pluto, a planet associated with sometimes wrenching transformation and change, Scorpio is interested in power and, in its shadow manifestation, with revenge and maintaining control at all costs. In this chart, the planet Venus (one's conscious capacity for relationship) is also in Scorpio, closely conjunct the Ascendant. The plot thickens when we see that Venus is squaring a Pluto-Mars conjunction in Leo, giving a double dose of the Scorpio urge for power and control.

Thus, we see a picture in which the placid Sun-Moon air trine is shadowed by darker Pluto energies. This is not to say that Scorpio always signifies a thirst for power and revenge. But here, with the square between two fixed signs, it's safe to assume there will be some frustration in the expression of the essential Scorpio energy. If nothing else, it helps explain the engine driving some of China's more extreme policies, particularly when seen in relation to Chinese history, which we'll be looking at in a moment.

But what else is going on here? The Midheaven of a chart signifies career and life path. In the PRC chart, mutable earth sign Virgo—known for precision, discrimination, and hard work—is on the Midheaven. This Midheaven well describes the discipline needed by the Communist leaders to unify their vast country back in the earlier half of the twentieth century.

Let's take a deeper look at the Midheaven. Virgo is ruled by Mercury, which here is retrograde, meaning that it appeared to be moving backward at the moment the PRC came into existence. This would indicate potential confusion about the overarching goals and objectives of the Communist order. And as we'll see shortly, this is borne out by recent Chinese history in which the leadership has lurched between socialist and capitalist policies. Compounding the situation is the fact that Mercury is closely conjunct Neptune, a planet associated with mysticism and transcendence, in its positive manifestations, and delusion and escapism in its shadow manifestation.

To fully understand the significance of these astrological measurements, we need to take a moment to consider modern Chinese history in more detail.

A Short History of Modern China

Ever since the fall of the Ming dynasty in the seventeenth century, China has been beset by enormous problems. The disintegration of the Ming was due to many complex factors, primary among them a top-heavy bureaucracy, corrupt local administrators, and fragmentation of the country at the hands of numerous warlords. The Ming was caving in on itself; it was only a matter of time before another power would step in. This happened when Manchurian tribes invaded from the north and established the Qing Dynasty in 1644.

The Qing ruled until 1912, at which time they were overthrown under nearly the same chaotic conditions that enabled them to seize control 300 years earlier. Into this vacuum stepped the charismatic Sun Yat-Sen, who established the nation's first republic. But this new order was not to last. Compounding China's age-old problems was a new and darker threat: the specter of foreign imperialism.

You could fill a short volume talking about the injustices and humiliation China has suffered at the hands of foreign powers. It's important for our overall understanding of the PRC chart, so I want to take a moment to look at this chapter in Chinese history. Under the Qing Dynasty in the nineteenth century, foreign countries started moving into mainland China. This initially took place under the rubric of commerce and trade, but the various countries involved ultimately carved out zones of influence. By the late Qing, China had lost control of vital aspects of its commercial, social, and foreign policies.

A pervasive fear began to take hold among many Chinese that their country was being dissolved and its 4,000-year history coming to an end. This feeling intensified during the Opium Wars, at which time British and American traders forced the importation of the drug into the country. The Treaty of Versailles further compounded fears of foreign domination in 1919. Although 100,000 Chinese troops had fought on the side of the Allied Powers in World War I (hoping, in exchange, to reclaim the territory German forces had previously occupied in the country) the treaty stipulated that the territory be turned over to the Japanese. The subsequent atrocities perpetrated by Japan further fueled Chinese rage against foreign powers. Having considered this history, we can now perhaps understand something about those compulsive control needs suggested by the Scorpio Ascendant and the Venus-Mars-Pluto configuration. After more than a century of domination at the hands of foreign powers, anyone would have a compulsive need for control.

Although Sun Yat-Sen had had some success in galvanizing the Chinese against imperialism and unifying the country, the republic started to fall apart when he died in 1925. Into the place of this visionary leader stepped a military man named Chiang Kai-shek. While passionate about uniting the country and fighting imperialism, Chiang lacked the vision and integrity needed for the job. Corruption was rife before long, and the country once again starting falling apart.

However, throughout these turbulent times there was a small band of Communist workers toiling quietly in remote villages throughout the country. When Mao and others started building the Chinese Communist Party in the 1920s, the task looked well nigh hopeless. Here is one account of the dire straits the country was in at that time:

> Vast provinces of the country were caught in a devastating cycle of famine caused by severe droughts, withered crops, and inadequate government relief. In one disaster alone, 500,000 people died, with 19.8 million declared destitute. People were so desperate that houses were stripped of doors and beams so that the wood could be sold or burned for warmth. Refugees crowded roads and railways, with tens of thousands of children sold as servants and prostitutes. Villagers were reduced to eating straw and leaves. Epidemics decimated those too weak to fight back.[1]

While affluent, cosmopolitan Chinese partied in Shanghai and Peking, much of the rest of the country was fighting for its very existence.

How could a small group of insurgent Communists ever hope to overcome problems of such daunting dimensions? Indeed, in 1922 the membership of the Chinese Communist Party numbered only about 200, compared to 85,000 soldiers in Chiang Kai-shek's Guomindang army.

The way they succeeded was through painstaking, backbreaking work. The women and men in the Communist party slaved away for decades in remote backwaters, working with the nation's vast peasant population. "Our China is a rural nation and most of the laboring class is made up of peasants," wrote Li Dazhao, an early Communist organizer, in 1920. "If they are not liberated, then our whole nation will not be liberated; speak out about their sufferings and help them become people who will plan their own lives."

These powerful words led to mass movements in which urban residents—students, well-to-do business people, and others—traveled to the countryside in order to work with the downtrodden peasantry. Through the unswerving dedication of Li, Mao, and others, the nation was unified. When, on the morning of October 1, 1949, Mao mounted the podium in Tiananmen Square and inaugurated the People's Republic, the effect was "electric." The Chinese people, weary from years of war, internal strife, and foreign domination, embraced the triumphant Communist Party with open arms. And who could blame them? For years, the party had selflessly protected and defended the peasantry, and this after centuries of neglect at the hands of the various dynastic orders.

The People's Republic of China: A Crisis of Nurturing

But just what sort of picture of care giving do we see in the PRC chart? In astrology, there are several places that describe the capacity for nurturing. The Moon is the most important. But because the Moon rules Cancer and the Fourth House, both of these areas must be considered as well. In addition, the Moon's Nodes also help describe the manner of care giving.

As already mentioned, the PRC Moon is in Aquarius. Ruled by Uranus, Aquarius is associated with breaking out of old molds and challenging the status quo. Not coincidentally, Uranus was discovered in 1781—fourteen years after the discovery of electricity and five years after the American Revolution. What's also interesting is that Uranus is in Cancer. What we see, then, is a picture of nurturing infused with an erratic, unpredictable energy: not qualities usually associated with the lunar values of nurturing and protection.

Indeed, the Uranus factor in the PRC chart vividly depicts the Communists' particular brand of nurturing. We know that Mao and others dedicated years of their lives to working with the peasantry. But what exactly was happening in those poverty-stricken villages where the seeds of revolution were planted? To gain a glimpse, let's consider Mao's own words: The peasants, he said, ". . .raise their rough, blackened hands and lay them on the heads of the gentry. They alone are the deadliest enemies of the local bullies and evil gentry and attack their strongholds without the slightest hesitation. They alone are able to carry out the work of destruction."

Thus, we see caregiving bound up with destruction and revolution. Indeed, this quote could be seen as a brief explication of the "dictatorship of the proletariat" idea that Marx first proposed 100 years earlier. Li Dazhao, another founding member of the Chinese Communist Party, later wrote of "class struggle" and "race struggle." Another Communist leader, Chen Duxiu (one who'd always been a supporter of the underdog), attacked Confucianism because it "ran counter to the independence of individuals that lay at the center of modern life."

Again and again we see care giving linked with upheaval and revolution. When considered in conjunction with the power needs of the PRC's Scorpio Ascendant, we can understand how this sort of "electrical nurturing" could get out of hand. It evolved, in the early 1950s, into the Party's "struggle sessions"—officially mandated confrontations in which students were pitted against teachers, tenants against landlords, and workers against employers.

By 1952, when the ranks of the party had swelled to 6 million (a far cry from the 200-odd members in the early 1920s), China's business leaders, among others, were forced to undergo group criticism sessions to confess their past economic crimes. "There were parades with drums and banners, door-to-door visits by squads of activists, and use of radio and loudspeakers—all of which put immense psychological pressure on business leaders to "'confess their crimes.'" As one historian noted: "Even those who had never seen a guerrilla unit or experienced life in the countryside now had had at least a taste of revolution." All of this culminated in the horror of the Cultural Revolution: a five-year bloodbath in which over 34,000 were killed and some 730,000 others framed and persecuted.

Acknowledging the emotional need for freedom and upheaval suggested by the Aquarius Moon and Uranus in Cancer is all well and good, but is it enough to understand the darker side of PRC policies? Why would a government—one so invested with taking care of and uniting its people—unleash such a reign of terror? How could this possibly serve the interests and needs of the country? Does the Aquarius and Uranus energy really explain all this?

No, it doesn't. Let's now take a look at the Fourth House, another index of nurturing. In the PRC chart, Pisces is on the Fourth House cusp. Neptune rules Pisces, and Neptune in the PRC chart is conjunct retrograde Mercury, the ruler of the PRC's destiny. Not only that, Neptune is also conjunct the Moon's South Node! Here, then, we begin to see an explanation for the erratic (and deadly) twists in PRC policy: at its core the PRC is confused—not only about its life path (as indicated by the Midheaven/Tenth House) but also about its very heart and soul (the Fourth House).

This is all borne out by some fascinating transits and solar arcs—two techniques for determining current, past, and future astrological influences.

The confusion at the core of the PRC chart can be clearly seen in the transits and solar arcs taking place during the Cultural Revolution. In May of 1966, when the Red Guards were first gearing up and the cycle of destruction just about to commence, transiting Pluto was conjunct the PRC Midheaven. Pluto, as we know, has a reputation for rather violent upheaval, and this was certainly played out in the first pangs of the Cultural Revolution.

A similar dynamic occurred twenty years later on the day of the Tiananmen Square massacre (June 4, 1989) when transiting Uranus was opposing the PRC's natal Uranus. Of this highly significant transit, astrologer Robert Hand says the following: "This is the crisis of middle age when you have to come to terms with a number of realizations that may not all be pleasant. . . . you may become seized with a feeling of urgency that you have only a short time to correct the problem. Consequently, you may begin to act rather disruptively and quickly. Your friends are likely to be rather shocked at the change." On the day of the crackdown, transiting Neptune was also contacting the PRC Neptune/Mercury conjunction, raking up all the regime's anxieties about its goals and objectives, as well as its ideological roots (the Neptune/Fourth House connection.)

Something else was happening as well. A few years earlier, in 1980 and 1981, solar arc Saturn was hitting the PRC's Mercury-Neptune. Again the old fears and anxieties about life path were being raked up, but in a very different way. This is because Saturn, unlike Uranus, Pluto, or Neptune, represents stability and status quo. Saturn is a severe taskmaster, lord of limitation, restriction, and discipline. Suddenly, all the confusion surrounding the nation's life path was being hit by a heavy dose of reality.

Government Enforces One Child Policy

What was happening in China during 1980 and 1981? It was in September of 1980 that the nation's one family/one child policy was implemented, and in 1981 that compulsory sterilizations, abortions, and IUD insertions were enforced. After years of mindless population growth (by some accounts, Mao encouraged rapid population expansion to create a bigger, greater country) the chickens were coming home to roost. The Communist leadership realized the behemoth they'd created, and the impossibility of sustaining the country's population. With nearly 1.3 billion people, China was supporting 22 percent of the Earth's population on about 7 percent of its arable land. At the height of China's population explosion, new babies were being born to over a million families who already had five or more children. For all the criticism that's been leveled at this policy, most experts think that China's policy saved the country 300 million to 800 million people.

There was something else occurring in 1981. In January, the Gang of Four—the people who were responsible for unleashing the terror of the Cultural Revolution—were convicted and sentenced, with two (including Mao's wife) condemned to death. Those responsible for the terror and the insanity of the late 60s and early 70s were finally being made accountable for their actions. China was beginning to take stock of the future and to look realistically at what had to been done.

Conclusion: Challenges for the Twenty-first Century

We've seen the shadow side of some difficult astrological measurements in the chart of the PRC. First, is the compulsive need for power and control (the Scorpio ASC, squaring Mars and Pluto in Leo); and then, the wavering and confusion of the regime's goals and objectives over the past fifty years (seen in retrograde Mercury's rulership of the Midheaven, as well as its conjunction with Neptune.)

However, every difficult aspect or configuration in an astrological chart can be utilized for the good. In fact, it's in the charts of some of the most creative people that one finds the most difficult (i.e., "bad") aspects.

What, then, might be the positive, life-enhancing manifestation of the Mercury–Neptune rulership of the Midheaven? Neptune, when positively expressed, is spirituality and transcendence. What do we see happening in China now? A spiritual group, having expressed no political designs or ambitions whatsoever, being persecuted solely for its practices and beliefs. (And this doesn't mention the PRC's persecution of other sects, Christian churches, for example, or the rampant destruction of the old religious order in Tibet in which 90 percent of the country's 6,000 monasteries were destroyed.) Perhaps part of the challenge of the PRC chart, particularly vis-à-vis the Midheaven, is to embrace the spiritual life of its citizens: to acknowledge people's needs for spiritual as well as material sustenance.

Of course, this would necessitate the leadership letting go of some of its considerable control needs—a big challenge in light of the nation's difficult past at the hands of foreign powers.

However, there are signs—a recent loosening in the PRC's one-family, one-child policy, for example—that the regime might be letting go, just a bit. The government, in fact, now offers a special exemption: if two only children marry, they will be allowed to have a second child. This change echoes the numerous economic liberalization policies initiated under the late Deng Xiaoping. Sadly, there's been no slacking off in the number of political prisoners. Some sources estimate that the human rights situation is getting worse, not better.

Yet another challenge for the PRC in the twenty-first century is the sheer size of the country. "Why are we large and yet weak?" asked scholar and essayist Feng Guifen in the late nineteenth century. In a way, Feng was answering his own question: China is weak because it's large. This idea is directly related to the crisis of nurturing that we've been considering here. A simple example might help make this clear. Imagine a family with, say, twenty-five kids, as opposed to a family with two or three. Which children are going to get more tender loving care and attention? The parents in the two families might equally love their children. But it's going to be a whole lot easier for those in the second to care for their young.

If the government of the People's Republic of China is to survive, it will have to start grappling with these deep-seated problems in a constructive way. If it doesn't, it might be doomed to suffer the fate of Father Sky. According to the

Greek myth, Kronos, one of Sky's children, castrated him with the help of his sister Gaea. From the blood of their father sprang the Furies, the goddesses of revenge, who then unleashed their own brand of terror. Let's hope the Communist leaders in China learn the lessons of the past before things reach that point.

1. *The Search for Modern China* by J. Spense. New York: W. Norton & Company, 1990.

Once in a Blue Moon

By Kathleen Spitzer

I can remember quite vividly the time I asked my mother to go off somewhere by myself, and she replied, "Not once in a Blue Moon!" I was so caught up by the expression, that I totally forgot the question. I did catch on, though, by the tone of her voice that I wasn't going.

The idea that the Moon might be blue was startling to me. In my six years, I had only seen it in analogous shades of cream, yellow, and orange. I watched it carefully for many nights, waiting to catch it wearing its blue hues. I did see it a couple of times in a pale, watery, misty kind of blue, but not the cerulean blue that I imagined or hoped it would be. Eventually, my observations confirmed the tone of my mother's voice. If something was going to happen once in a Blue Moon, it was very rarely.

I did learn that the Moon was blue for about two years after the volcano Krakatoa blew in 1883. Further research showed that the expression was found in print in 1821, even though folk tradition testifies that the expression is older than that. Other things about the Moon began to fascinate me, though, and I left the puzzle of the Blue Moon behind.

Then, in the 1980s, something new about a Blue Moon began to seep into my consciousness, and I realized that a new definition was emerging—

different from the definition my childhood research had produced. By the mid-80s, people were saying that the second Full Moon in a calendar month was called a Blue Moon. It sort of fit with the folklore definition, as it was not very often that two Full Moons appeared in one month, and it also had a very scientific and astronomically authorized feel to it.

The year 1999 had two Blue Moons, one in January and one in March. This new definition for a Blue Moon appeared in newspapers and on radio and television. It seemed to sweep across the country as a folklore truism. Of course, they referred to it as old folklore, when in truth they were helping to make a modern folklore tradition. So where does this modern definition come from? It comes from a series of assumptions, misinterpretations, and miscalculations that can be traced to the 1937 *Maine Farmers' Almanac*.

Almanacs traditionally include astrological data because of an ancient folk tradition still found around the world concerning the relationship of the Sun to the Moon. This relationship has a seasonal effect upon Mother Earth, her inhabitants, and their agricultural lives. In reality, the seasons are not based on the civil calendar, which begins on January 1, but on the tropical year.

The tropical year begins with the Winter Solstice, which is also the first day of winter and Yule. On Winter Solstice, the Sun enters the zodiac sign of Capricorn (Ingress occurs at 0 degree Capricorn.) This is the shortest day of the year and calls for the return of the Sun and lengthening days.

With the returning light, the days get longer until day light equals the dark and we have the ingress of the Sun into the sign of Aries, which is the start of the fertile spring season and of the astrological year. This is the Vernal Equinox (0 degree Aries) or Ostara. Gardens are planted, animals give birth, and people in the Northern Hemisphere rejoice as the earth begins to warm.

Then the lengthening days of sunlight finally reach that northernmost point on the horizon, and the rising Sun appears to stand still for the longest day and shortest night of the year. At Summer Solstice (0 degree of Cancer) or Litha, the Sun moves to the start of the summer season.

However, the Sun's light begins to slacken and lose power, and although the earth is burgeoning with fruits and vegetables, and the waters and woods teem with fish and animals, the hours of day light once again seek to equalize with the dark. The Autumnal Equinox (or Mabon) enters with 0 degree of Libra, and autumn is here. We begin to harvest and store the summer's bounty as the dark hours begin to overtake the day light hours. Each day, as the Sun traverses the sky, it is moving farther south, until it reaches the southernmost point of the horizon. Once again, we experience the shortest day of the year and Winter Solstice.

Because this is the tropical year and not a calendar year, and because the Sun and Moon do not move in perfect mathematical tandem, we have four seasons of three months each, which should mean that we have three Full Moons. But sometimes we have four Full Moons in one season, which equals thirteen Full Moons in a year.

Now, here's the tricky part. The publisher of an almanac uses a civil calendar format of a month per page, but imposes the tropical calendar on it. In order to keep the Full Moons in the proper month, in the year and season where there is an extra Moon; it is called the Blue Moon. This is always the third Full Moon of the four Full Moon seasons, and it can only happen in February, May, August, or November.

Some have suggested that it be called a Blue Moon because the regular Full Moon is indicated on the almanac page in red ink and the extra Moon in the season is printed in blue ink. This is a great explanation, but it isn't true.

The Real Definition of a Blue Moon

Actually, the definition of a Blue Moon as the third Full Moon in a four Moon season has been traced to the *1937 Maine Farmer's Almanac*. And by the way, according to this definition, on August 22, 2002, there will be a Blue Moon. (But, maybe not.)

This, of course, is only half the story. In 1943, a well-meaning columnist wrote in *Sky and Telescope* about the Blue Moon, and listed the *1937 Maine Farmer's Almanac* as his source. In quoting the August page, he failed to mention whether he referred to a calendar year or tropical year. (He also did not read the almanac in careful detail.)

In 1946, this column was used as a source for an article in the same magazine, but by another writer. This writer did his own math and correctly determined that seven times in nineteen calendar years (the Moon's synodic cycle that involves a conjunction of the Sun and Moon, or New Moon), there are thirteen Full Moons. However, he also did not read his source carefully, nor did he go back to the 1937 almanac. He did conclude, however, that during those seven years eleven months would have one

Full Moon and one month would have two Full Moons. This second one would be called a Blue Moon!

By the 1980s, with articles continuing to be published, this definition of a Blue Moon had struck the nation's fancy. It is now commonly understood, according to ancient folklore, that a second Full Moon appearing in a month is called a Blue Moon. Unfortunately, assumptions and miscalculations are the basis for this definition. For those who only understand the civil calendar, or are not exposed to the tropical calendar, this meaning of the Blue Moon has a righteous ring to it that will probably continue until it becomes old folklore! However, by this definition, there are no Blue Moons in 2002.

Blue Moon Salad

1 cantaloupe, halved
Watercress
2 cups low-fat cottage cheese
1 cup blueberries
1 3-ounce package low-fat cream cheese
¼ cup blueberry sauce, jelly, or jam
Low-fat whipped cream
1 teaspoon orange zest

Make melon balls and set aside. Line the empty cantaloupe shells with the watercress. Divide the cottage cheese between the two halves, top with the melon balls and blueberries. Make a dressing with the cream cheese and blueberry sauce and drizzle over the salad. Decorate with a dollop of whipped cream and sprinkle with the orange zest.

Serves 6.

Other Lives and the Moon

By *Leeda Alleyn Pacotti*

Familiarity, a preference for used possessions, that comforting sense of known surroundings—these are all qualities the Moon displays in your horoscope. Ancient interpreters described the Moon as the mother, nurturing, and the home. Modern interpretations not only use these older precepts, but also extrapolate a new meaning to describe the Moon's house, or the Fourth House, as that of foundations.

Seeking to situate twentieth century perspectives into the twelve-house, twelve-sign experience of the individual horoscope, modern astrologers designated the Moon's house as the basis of psychological foundations, drawing on the influences of mother and nurture. As we move into the twenty-first century, the concept of foundations can be expanded to reveal unknown roots for some of our little understood preferences and behaviors.

What are our foundations? Are they strictly those encountered through the direct experiences of nature, nurture, and environment? Have even these been predisposed by yet some other influence?

In astrology relating to health, the Moon rules the cellular development of the organic brain. What the Moon gives, in this circumstance, is the capacity to be receptive. To some extent, this receptivity includes memory of a sort different from what we normally perceive. This memory pertains to predispositions on which the current life is built. Such predispositions have been misnamed as genetic memory or racial memory. In reality, the memories stem from other lives, entwined in our complex of psychological foundations, serving as springboards for encounter and resolution of spiritual dilemmas.

Lives Untold

Most people consider other lives to be past lives only. However, we encounter other lives in a variety of forms. Within our unfolding memories are a bundle of lives: past, future, alternate, and coincident.

Tied to linear time, undoubtedly, past lives are the most acceptable, being the spiritual threshold with which most people are consciously acquainted. The keynote for past lives is a sense of historical confusion. The longer we live and the greater our conscious maturity, we become aware that history is written by the victors, who color historic episodes in flattering terms to heighten their superiority. We also encounter fanciful historic representations in film, made specifically to move a story, which strongly impresses the subconscious mind. The problem of past-life remembrance lies in the conflict between past-life memory from the subconscious and the written word, or introduced picture, from modern fancy. Life, as we know, does not flow in constant high drama. Histories and film cannot relate the intricately woven undercurrents of emotion, deliberation, or unresolved dilemma, which are important perceptions in any life. Further, the nuances of daily living, habits, and lifestyles are lost, when these fail to give any worth to the conqueror's glory or the scriptwriter's sale.

Another memory construct of linear time is the future life. Primarily, we have been conditioned to think we cannot know the future. However, our future selves know us. Most future-life recall is perceived as faded, shimmering memories and is often labeled as fanciful distortions. When the receiver gets even an inkling that these recalls are future memories, he or she tends to dissolve them immediately. Consequently, many important signals, which tell us how well we are dealing with spiritual issues in the present and how these are likely to resolve, are lost. When we can focus on future-life memories, we see whether we are working on resolution, being neglectful of our spiritual development, or creating unnecessary confusions in present reality. The best examples of future-life memories, actively presented, are from fiction writers, especially those writing in the genre of science fiction.

Two other memories arise outside the accepted linear time line. These memories are from alternate lives and coincident lives.

Alternate lives are born from the decisions we make throughout life. Often, after a major choice, we sense the passage of a life-changing episode. The decision can be as obvious as the type of career to pursue or as insignificant, as choosing an apartment with only one bedroom. The choice seems to be made on conditions present in the moment or the immediate past. However, the choice itself is a fixed predeterminant for future choices. Reviewing each choice and its set of consequent choices, we understand why we could not experience certain activities or meet certain people. As humans, we believe we have only one lifetime of living. However, our reality is based in expansiveness. The strength of alternate-life memories rests on a broadly compelling sense of need or accomplishment. We know that we could be a great violinist. We also know that we could be living on the street. The knowledge is so strong we hear the acclaim from the audience or feel the wet, hard pavement against our backs. These memories teach us that the reality of our living self is involved in more than one simultaneous experience. A keynote of alternate life memory is a muffled physical recall of actions and sensations, recognized as unlived in the present life.

The situation of coincident lives also occurs simultaneously with the current life. Unlike alternate lives, a different personality self experiences the coincident life. If alternate lives can be viewed as threads, flowing beside each other in a tapestry, coincident lives are separated planks from a single tree. Each has union with the original tree, but may go to entirely separate places and be used in distinctly different ways. In coincident lives, the soul itself has chosen to live two or more separate existences simultaneously. These do not have similar personality characteristics or awarenesses, except as demanded by the events in surrounding time. These lives are not usually in the same country, do not carry the same sex, or inhabit a similar body build. The overwhelming sense of coincident life memory is an electromagnetic connective to another locality, with extremely vivid memories, as though looking through the eyes of another.

The perception of these various life memories depends on the brain's cellular ability to receive them and the conditioned willingness of the individual to accept the recall. When a memory is consciously accepted and viewed for clues about spiritual problems, certain characteristics provide a telling strength of the memory's truth or significance. Memories, as fleeting mind pictures or conversations, are general indicators of spiritual conditions. When strong smells or tastes accompany them, expect a heightened significance to manifest the spiritual situation in immediate reality. If bodily chills, or a feeling of electrical waves through the nervous system accompanies the memory, the spiritual situation is urgent and capable of instantaneous resolution. A probing self-examination, coupled with a decision to resolve the spiritual issue, propels the individual into a circumstance or series of events, which ingrain the decision to alter the daily perspective permanently.

Other Lives Represented By the Moon

Because the Moon is changeable, no singular type of life will fill every spiritual need. However, an undercurrent spiritual problem is present with each sign where the Moon is placed. The following descriptions tell you about the pressing spiritual dilemma. Examples of possible lives serve as a guideline only. In reviewing them, trust your own memory experiences, which are doorways into understanding your spiritual needs. You may also use these descriptions for the house in which your Moon is placed. These will describe present life activities and help in assessing spiritual needs.

In combining the two, expect to trigger memories similar to those of the sign and house, but uniquely different. The occupations or lifestyles described may be the main part of your memory's reality or a strong peripheral influence. For instance, you may have been in a holy order, or you may have been a Gothic church builder, with your life strongly influenced by those in holy orders.

With the Moon in Aries, or the First House, the primary spiritual problem turned on self-involvement. You were willing to put yourself into any situation, in which you were an active participant, without regard for the needs of others. A prime characteristic was a willingness to go to war. In this life, you are frequently accused of ignoring or minimizing others, or showing a lack of respect. Conversely, you may feel minimized, ignored, or disrespected. Other-life memories include a militarist, a military strategist, a police official, an explorer, a pioneer, a colonist, a soldier, or a mercenary.

From the Moon in Taurus, or the Second House, you have problems with possession and acquisition. Being a form builder, you have gravitated to situations, in which you could mold a social group, or create mental influences through artistic representations. In this life, you may find yourself constantly desiring possession of things or people, or you are overwhelmed with possessions. Other-life memories include an architect, a sculptor, a construction contractor, a money baron, a land baron, or a feudal landowner.

The Moon in Gemini, or the Third House, describes the individual who has refused education. This is the problem of the mental dilettante, who is busy taking in information without learning to evaluate it. Travel has often been used as the excuse to avoid mental discipline. In this life, you are considered too carried away with the moment and lacking depth or the will to see anything through. On the flip side, you may be overwhelmed with meeting educational demands, or torn between responsibilities and a good time. Other-life memories include a correspondent, a cartoonist, a comic, a messenger, a cartographer, a social opportunist, a journalist, or a railway worker.

The Moon in Cancer, or the Fourth House, shows a person who has refused intimacy with others. Although there has been a depth and sensitivity, you have refused to share your feelings with others, or shunned those who touched you with their feelings. Fears of intimacy have forced you into positions in which you could keep others at arms length. In this lifetime, you tend to remain closeted in your own world, letting few in, or you find your emotional world constantly bombarded by others. Other-life memories can include a farmer, an animal tender, a religious celibate, a psychic charlatan, or a sexual Casanova.

With the Moon in Leo, or the Fifth House, problems arose from a refusal to love from the heart. Rather than admit your heart's desire, you pursued activities, persons, or situations, which provided you with some reward. You believed that through these rewards you would either find love, or be more lovable. In this lifetime, you are torn between loving honestly or not at all. You are frequently accused of having a cold heart, no commitment, or being a superior snob. Other-life memories include royalty or nobility, an emperor, an empire builder, a corporate president, a head of state, a slum lord, an actor, a child prodigy, or a prostitution madam or pimp.

Through the Moon in Virgo, or the Sixth House, the spiritual dilemma has been over dedication. You relinquished opportunities to understand yourself and your motives by submerging yourself to a dedicated cause. This led to a misunderstanding that you knew all the rules for living. In this life, you are accused of being too straightlaced or bossy. Without your rules, you feel adrift and unable to fit in with others. Most of the time, you sense there are no rules governing circumstances you encounter, and you often make them up to feel secure. Other-life memories include ritualized behaviors, holy orders, a monk, a nun, a servant, a nurse in catastrophe or war, a medicine woman, a herbalist, and a civil servant.

The Moon in Libra, or the Seventh House, demonstrates the spiritual complements of the passive-aggressive. In relationships, you compromised passively, without question, until you could no longer tolerate the situation. On the flip side, feeling that you had been dominated, you chose domination in other relationships, by using accumulated angers. You learned to misdirect your angers and frustrations. In this life, you are seen as having the will, but no drive. At other times, people find you difficult to work with, sensing anger simmering just below your pleasant surface. Other-life memories include using marriage to rise in society, politics, or career. Relationships involved a diplomat, a politician, an exchange spouse to end war, and a jet setter.

The Moon in Scorpio, or the Eighth House, bears the dilemma of using sex as power. In other lives, sexual prowess, or the promise of it, attained your goals. You lost touch with the pleasure derived from physical union and created the habit of using sexual contact as a reward or punishment. In this life, you are seen as very attractive physically, able to have anyone on whom you set your sights. However, your sexual partners rarely stay around for long and certainly do not consider you a life partner. Other-life memories have included a courtesan, a gigolo, a spy using sexual favors, a power broker in finance, a surgeon, a papal envoy, and a big-game hunter.

The Moon in Sagittarius, or the Ninth House, discloses the spiritual problems of religious extremism and refusal for close or familial relationships. In some ways, these two problems are tied together because dedication to a religious ideal permits or encourages relinquishing personal relationships. You have lost the ability to be close to others, although you consistently attempt to create a sense of familiarity by causing them to laugh or take delight in their circumstances. In this life, you have been called a fool or childish. Because of familial estrangements, others consider you a poor marital and parental risk, and you frequently feel the same way about yourself. Other-life memories include a clown or jester, a vagabond, a prodigal, a lifetime student, a Vatican prelate, an iconoclast, an ecclesiastic, and a roving reporter. In all such lives, there is an element of family

abandonment, whether purposeful or accidental.

The Moon in Capricorn, or the Tenth House, portrays the difficulties of leadership. Similar to the Moon in Aries, you have tended to a self-imposed alienation, however, in this situation, you were aware of others' needs, but chose to ignore them. The dilemma is the requirement to serve others. In meeting this situation, you decided to remove yourself from others, specifically to create a more effective service of broad scope. In some circumstances, you also chose not to accept leadership. In this life, you are considered aloof, uncaring, or insensitive. Actually, you are very sensitive, but you feel that sensitivity overwhelms objectivity, causing you to forsake one person for the group or the group for one person. A continuing sense of weakness, a feeling of distance from others, or a lack of concern are the primary accusations leveled at you. Other-life memories include a judge, a plantation owner, an overseer, a man or woman of God, a business executive, a moneylender, a pawnbroker, a missionary, or a crusader.

From the Moon in Aquarius, or the Eleventh House, the problem of blending with the group conflicts with the need to maintain independence. This conflict exhibits as an overbearing independence in group dynamics or a refusal to participate with a group. The dilemma causes you to focus too strongly on yourself, burdening you with the additional problem of arrogance. A stoic aloofness toward others hides your desire to lend your energies to a common problem. At the worst, you feel you have the answer, but no one wants to listen. In this life, you are often accused of being chilly, cold-hearted, and a smart mouth. Sarcasm abounds when your words are ignored, further alienating others. Other-life memories include a playwright, a screenwriter, an inventor, a magician, a metaphysician, a reformist, and a unionist. In other lives, when you have attempted to blend, but submerged your own needs, memories show a union breaker, a propagandist, and a slave trader.

Through the Moon in Pisces, or the Twelfth House, the primary issue is attaining success. Opportunities for success were abandoned because you believed you would lose your fragile hold on your identity. Consequently, you sought rewards through pitiful means, in which you could be doted on and individually recognized. Because pity creates a vicious cycle, you also turned away from others and entered the only world you trusted—your mind. In this life, you are accused of being out-of-it, in a dream world, or having ideas with no practical basis for implementation. Although your ideas and attitudes are sound, you have skipped lessons in other lifetimes, which would have given you an understanding of how others think. Other-life memories include a recluse, a hermit, a commune dweller, a mystic, an orphan, a widow, or a pauper. Through these memories runs a thread of self-imposed poverty, with consequent shunning and ostracism.

The Real Importance of Other-Life Memories

From a review of the spiritual dilemmas we bring with us into this existence, anyone would question why they should be remembered at all. Simply, no one wants to stay in the rut of a repeated mistake. But how we participate in the repetition is the real key. Other-life memories give us the scenario, which taught us to escape from helpful behaviors into selfish ones.

Using these memories as armor, we have a knowledge that prevents us from inappropriate or delayed action in similar circumstances. Because we tend to enter existence with companion souls, who were involved with our incomplete situations, awareness of carried over psychological and emotional problems lets us pause and allow others to act. Frequently, their unfettered actions assist us in correcting our own behaviors. When we stand back and allow others the freedom to act, we encounter strong inner assurance that correct actions are taking place and an important change is exerting itself on the group dynamic.

A life illustration may help explain what happens. Previously, this writer worked as a department head. Because of her gift for oral presentation, she often preempted coworkers in explaining their position or expressing their feelings. The group dynamic revolved around unconscious recognitions of dependence on strong leadership. During an especially fierce meeting, this writer found herself temporarily blocked from vocalizing an obvious solution to a budget fiasco. Feeling a little dazed, she sat quietly as others looked to her to say something. Suddenly, she experienced a visual overlay from another life in which all present had then been concerned with the need to break from an accepted religious thought. Making the break carried serious consequences of livelihood, because the community would be ostracized by main trade caravans. In that life, this writer outvoiced everyone and bullied them into the religious break. Although their continued survival was quickly secured, individual choices had been pre-empted. In this life, the writer restrained herself, as each person gave ample voice to comments on the budget problem. Surprising solutions were offered, and an innovative budgetary initiative developed. Refusing to act from a second nature habit allowed everyone to develop spiritually from the experience, whether it was speaking up creatively or setting the stage for others to act within their own power.

What If I Don't Want to Remember?

Recalling other lives is not for everyone. These memories, while interesting, can be distracting or confusing. Anything that hampers your ability to act in present time does not have the right to command your consciousness.

Remember an important metaphysical precept: this your life! You and the personality you project live this life, not the personality or recall from any other life. Memories from other lives are shared information, much like that received from your most trusted group of friends. However, when information becomes too overwhelming, you will be distracted from working on the here and now. You also may lose your hold on judgment to decide whether the information is helpful, causing you to mistakenly assess an important situation or action in the present. Sometimes, you just don't want to remember.

In any of these cases, the appropriate inner action is to block the memories, until you want to resume receiving them. The idea of blocking memory is anathema in modern psychological circles. However, other-life memories are shared memories, much like those told to you by your grandparents. They are entrusted to you, but they did not happen to your particular personality, which has responsibility to participate actively in present time.

Three methods, which used individually or as a combined plan, will help you to block out these memories. Using these same methods, with a command to resume memory, will undo the block.

First, give your subconscious a direct command to block the memories. The subconscious is a repository, not a command center. It has no decision over the actions you take; that control is the sole power of the conscious mind.

Your command to the subconscious may be for all other-life memories, several of memories, or one in particular. The command is most effective, when the conscious mind is quiet and focused. A five-minute period of inner silence is adequate. You can also make the command near the end of a meditation or prayer session, during which the conscious mind has been in quiet repose.

In simple terms, give a firm command to your image or sense of your subconscious mind. Be direct and straightforward. Don't bother justifying the command; the subconscious doesn't understand this. But the subconscious does know that it must obey your orders or rules.

Second, some people need extra help in stopping other-life memories. Perhaps the command to the subconscious conflicted with another command or rule, such as a deep-seated desire to remember or a compulsion to avoid missing anything. In this case, when a memory starts to come forward, you will probably notice an emotional signal in advance. That signal may earmark a type of spiritual situation, or it may flag a particular life.

The advance notice warns that a memory is attempting to intrude your consciousness. Immediately refuse the memory, and continue refusing it, until you feel it ebb away. During your next mediation, prayer, or focus session reinforce your original command to the subconscious. Later, examine whether you need to be more specific and directive.

And finally, sometimes the subconscious is heavily conflicted with commands. Because it must obey all commands, the subconscious attempts to fulfill all of them. A direct way of preempting conflicting commands is to utilize deep-refusal writing. Hand write an affirmation seventy times each day, for seven days, giving the exercise your full, uninterrupted attention. The best affirmations are those you design yourself, consisting of ten words or less. If two affirmations are necessary, use the deep-refusal writing method separately for each.

Business &

Legal

Section

How To Choose the Best Dates for Business & Legal Activities

When starting a new business or any type of new venture, check to make sure that the Moon is in the first or second quarter. This will help it get off to a better start. If there is a deadlock, it will often be broken during the Full Moon. You should also check the aspects of the Moon to the planet that rules the type of venture with which you are becoming involved. Look for positive aspects to the planet that rules the activity in the Lunar Aspectarian (pages 34-57), and avoid any dates marked Q or O.

Planetary Business Rulerships

Listed below are the planets and the business activities that they rule. If you follow the guidelines given above and apply them to the occu-pations or activities listed for each planet, you should have excellent results in your new business ventures. Even if it is not a new venture, check the aspects to the ruler of the activity before making moves in your business.

Sun

Advertising, actors and actresses, administrators, executives, finance and financiers, foremen, furriers, gamblers, government and public offices, lawyers, politicians, presidents, prime ministers, princes, racing stable owners, stock brokers, and public relations.

Mercury

Accounting, ad writers, agents, animal trainers, attorneys, auditors, bee keepers, biographers, broad-casting technicians, brokerage, chemists, clerical workers, dieticians, disc jockeys, doctors, editors, employees (in general), inspectors, interpreters, librarians, linguists, mathematicians, medical technicians, opticians, opthamologists, orators, printers, proofreaders, public speakers, pupils, railroads, scholars, scientists, statisticians, tellers, teachers, ticket agents, ventriloquists, writers, publishing, communication, and mass media.

Venus

Amateurs, architects, art curators, artists, associates, bankers, beautician, cabinet makers, candy manufacturers, clothing designers, dancers, duets, fashion, gardeners, hairdressers, hat makers, hotel keepers, juries, limousines, marketing, marriage, motels, negotiators, patrons, music and musicians, poets, restaurants, securities, social functions, and wigmakers.

Mars

Agitators, armies and army officers, athletes, barbers, blacksmiths, bootleggers, butchers, carpenters, charitable institutions, chemists, claims, construction workers, defenders, dentists, embezzlers, fires and firemen, gun makers, locksmiths, lumberjacks, machinists, mechanics, manufacturing, metal workers, profiteers, surgeons, and wrestlers.

Jupiter

Advisors, ambassadors, archers, assessors, attorneys, auditors, brokers, censure, charitable institutions, claims and claimants, corporate law, counselors, doctors, embezzlers, financiers, heirs, horse men and horse trainers, jockeys, juries, judges, legislators, ministers, passports, pharmacists, preachers, professors, psychologists, public analysts, regimes, social clubs, researchers, senate and senators, sheriffs, ships and shipping, storekeepers, and self-improvement.

Saturn

Agriculturists, archeologists, architecture and architects, bailiffs, bankruptcy, buyers, carpenters, carpet layers, cattlemen, cemetery workers, civil engineers, chemists, contractors, debtors, elderly people, farms and farming, felons, funeral directors, gardeners, geologists, hardware manufacturers, historians, mathematicians, miners, misers, mortgages, morticians, organizers, papermaking, plumbers, real estate agents, repairperson, surveyors, tailors, wardens, and watchmakers.

Uranus

Aeronautics, astrologers, agitators, airplane mechanics and pilots, automobile manufactures, aviators, broadcasters, chiropractors, clock makers and repairers, computers, electricians, emancipators, fugitives, gasoline station owners, hydroelectric power, inventing and inventors, lecturing, magicians, photographers, radiology, sudden events, and technical writers.

Neptune

Actors, bartenders, blackmail, bribery, chemical engineers, con men, detectives, divers, druggists, embezzlers, glassware factories, impostors, investigators, magicians, naval men and officers, photographers, oceanographers, resorts, ships and shipping, travel by water, welfare, and wine merchants.

Pluto

Atomic energy, coroners, criminals, demolition, detectives, dictators, disasters, epidemics, gang leaders, global wars, gunmen, magicians, petroleum, racketeering, refuse workers, research, robbery and robbers, therapists, speculators, stockbrokers, and stool pigeons.

Business Activities

Advertising (in Print)

Write ads on a favorable Sun sign day while Mercury or Venus is conjunct, sextile, or trine the Moon. Hard aspects to Mars and Saturn should not occur after the time of your event. Ad campaigns are best when the Moon is well aspected in Gemini (to enhance communication) or Capricorn (to build business).

Advertising (Electronic)

The Moon should be conjunct, sextile, or trine Mercury or Uranus; and in the sign of Gemini, Capricorn, or Aquarius.

Business, Education

When you begin training, see that your lunar cycle is favorable that day and that the planet ruling your occupation is marked C or T.

Business, Opening

The Moon should be in Taurus, Virgo, or Capricorn, and in the first or second quarter. It should also be sextile or trine (X or T) Jupiter or Saturn.

Business, Starting

In starting a business of your own, see that the Moon is free of afflictions and that the planet ruling the business is marked C or T.

Buying

Buy during the third quarter, when the Moon is in Taurus for quality, or in a mutable sign (Gemini, Virgo, Sagittarius, or Pisces) for savings. Good aspects from Venus or the Sun are desirable. If you are buying for yourself, it is good if the day is favorable to your Sun sign.

Buying Clothing

See that the Moon is sextile or trine to the Sun during the first or second quarters. During Moon in Taurus, buying clothes will bring satisfaction. Do not buy clothing or jewelry when the Moon is in Scorpio or Aries. Buying clothes is best on a favorable day for your Sun sign and when Venus or Mercury is well aspected, but avoid aspects to Mars and Saturn.

Buying Furniture

Follow the rules for machinery and appliances but buy when the Moon is in Libra, too. Buy antiques when the Moon is in Cancer, Scorpio, or Capricorn.

Buying Machinery, Appliances, or Tools

Tools, machinery, and other implements should be bought on days when your lunar cycle is favorable and when Mars and Uranus are trine (T), sextile (X), or conjunct (C) the Moon. Any quarter of the Moon is suitable. When buying gas or electrical appliances, the Moon should be in Aquarius.

Buying Stocks

The Moon should be in Taurus or Capricorn, and should be sextile or trine (X or T) Jupiter and Saturn.

Collections

Try to make collections on days when your Sun is well aspected. Avoid days when Mars or Saturn are aspected. If possible, the Moon should be in a cardinal sign: Aries, Cancer, Libra, or Capricorn. It is more difficult to collect when the Moon is in Taurus or Scorpio.

Consultants, Working With

The Moon should be conjunct, sextile, or trine Mercury or Jupiter.

Contracts, Bid on

The Moon should be in the sign of Gemini or Capricorn, and either the Moon or Mercury should be conjunct, sextile, or trine (C, X, or T) Jupiter.

Copyrights/Patents, Apply for

The Moon should be conjunct, trine, or sextile Mercury or Jupiter.

Electronics, Buying

When buying electronics, choose a day when the Moon is in an air sign (Gemini, Libra, or Aquarius) and well aspected by Mercury and/or Uranus.

Electronics, Repair

The Moon should be sextile or trine Mars or Uranus in one of the following signs: Taurus, Leo, Scorpio, or Aquarius.

Legal Matters

A good aspect between the Moon and Jupiter is best for a favorable legal decision. To gain damages in a lawsuit, begin during the increase of the Moon. In seeking to avoid payment, set a court date when the Moon is decreasing. Good aspects between the Sun and Moon strengthens your chance of success. In divorce cases, a favorable Moon-Venus aspect is best. Moon in Cancer or Leo and well aspected by the Sun brings the best results in custody cases.

Loans

Moon in the first and second quarters favors the lender, in the third and fourth favors the borrower. Good aspects of Jupiter and Venus to the Moon are favorable to both, as is the Moon in Leo or Taurus.

Mailing

For best results, send mail on favorable days for your Sun sign. The Moon in Gemini is good, as are Virgo, Sagittarius, and Pisces.

Mining

Saturn rules mining. Begin work when Saturn is marked C, T, or X. Mine for gold when the Sun is marked C, T, or X. Mercury rules quicksilver, Venus rules copper, Jupiter rules tin, Saturn rules lead and coal, Uranus rules radioactive elements, Neptune rules oil, the Moon rules water. Mine for these items when the ruling planet is marked C, T, or X.

New Job, Beginning

Jupiter and Venus should be sextile, trine, or conjunct the Moon.

Photography, Radio, TV, Film, and Video

Neptune, Venus, and Mercury should be well aspected. The act of photographing does not depend on particular Moon phase, but Neptune rules photography, and Venus rules beauty in line, form, and color.

Promotions

Choose a day when your Sun sign is favorable. Mercury should be marked C, T, or X. Avoid days when Mars or Saturn is aspected.

Selling or Canvassing

Begin these activities during a favorable Sun sign day. Otherwise, sell on days when Jupiter, Mercury, or Mars is trine, sextile, or conjunct the Moon. Avoid days when Saturn is square or opposite the Moon.

Signing Papers

Sign contracts or agreements when the Moon is increasing in a fruitful sign, and on a day when Moon-Mercury aspects are operating. Avoid days when Mars, Saturn, or Neptune are square or opposite the Moon.

Staff, Fire

The Moon should be in the third or fourth quarter, but not full. There should be no squares (Q) to the Moon.

Staff, Hire

The Moon should be in the first or second quarter, and preferably in the sign of Gemini or Virgo. The Moon should be conjunct, trine, or sextile (C, T, or X) Mercury or Jupiter.

Travel

See the travel listing in the Leisure & Recreation section.

Writing

Writing for pleasure or publication is best done when the Moon is in Gemini. Mercury should be direct. Favorable aspects to Mercury, Uranus, and Neptune promote ingenuity.

Lunar Effects on Small Businesses

By *Stephanie Clement*

Have you noticed that on some days many of your clients or customers seem to have certain things in common. For example, some days people may only want to window shop, while on other days every customer or client who walks through the doors has a complaint. They are responding to the Moon's energy, which changes approximately every two days.

Being able to assess the customer's needs and desires is key to successful business, and in today's market small businesses need every edge they can find in order to thrive. You may already be aware of the Moon's phases and other attributes, so it will come as no surprise that this heavenly orb also reflects your personal business practices. Knowing and understanding the Moon's day-to-day energy (as determined by zodiac sign) provides a natural rhythm for your life and a significant advantage in business affairs.

The Moon sign in a business' chart indicates how the business is run, in much the same way that the Moon in your personal chart indicates how you tend to approach your day-to-day dealings. If you know the date on which you began your small business, then you can obtain a birth chart for it. If you don't have a specific time, you can use noon of that day for a chart. An almanac for the year you began the business will tell you the Sun and Moon signs on the date you began. Although you will rarely know the Moon sign of your clientele, you can understand people better through the transiting Moon. The Moon on a particular day indicates the people who come to you, and what their emotional, material, mental, and even spiritual needs and desires are.

As you read the rest of this article, you have three things to consider: (1) The sign your Moon is in—this will tell you a lot about how you tend to approach others in your daily work; (2) the Moon's sign in the chart of your business—this reflects the activities involved in your business operations; and (3) the sign the Moon is in today—this will indicate the kind of customers you can expect and what their personal reasons are for coming to you at this particular time.

The Moon in the Signs

When the Moon is in a fire sign—Aries, Leo, or Sagittarius—the modus operandi (how you act when you are not consciously thinking about it) is primarily intuitive. This means that you respond to other people based on what you believe they want or need. Regardless of what service or product you provide, the lasting impact it will have on your customer is a major concern.

When the Moon in an earth sign—Taurus, Virgo, or Capricorn—your approach is primarily that of perceiving through the five senses, and you focus on the practical aspect of your customer interaction. Your concern will be for facilitating the sale, completing the desired service, and managing the day-to-day business to enhance customer interaction.

With the Moon in an air sign—Gemini, Libra, or Aquarius—your approach is primarily intellectual, and working though each customer request logically and rationally will take priority. You'll seek out information that will be helpful to each individual customer, and you'll think through business decisions to their logical conclusion.

When the Moon is in a water sign—Cancer, Scorpio, or Pisces—there is a tendency to approach other people on the feeling level. You judge whether you have the appropriate product or service, not in the basis of a particular customer, but on the business "climate." You sell the customer on the emotional level, appealing to their gut response to your sell, if not to the product or service.

If you and your business have the Moon in the same element—fire, earth, air, or water)—there is a consistency between your own mental process and the way your business can operate effectively. If they are different, however, you can choose between two ways of approaching customers. You can use the personal approach that you are naturally tuned to—an approach that is often successful because people desire the personal touch in their lives and will appreciate that you're offering it. You can also use the approach dictated by the business' own Moon. Thus, if you have the Moon in a water sign and the business has a fire Moon, you can approach customers on the feeling level, while also indicating all the future advantages of the product or service. If you have an air sign Moon and the business' Moon is in an earth sign, you can think through your customer's requests, and then apply all the practical aspects of your business to solving them.

Use the tables in this book, or an astrological calendar, to determine the Moon's sign each day. The Moon Tables (on pages 34–57) will give you the day and time when the Moon changes sign in 2002. Then pay attention to the customers you contact. They will very likely share the characteristics of the Moon's sign. Now, you can blend your own Moon, the Moon of the business, and the daily Moon sign to determine your best approach to doing business!

Moon in Aries

Aries is impulsive, so expect your customers to be more impulsive under an Aries Moon. They may have planned out their shopping needs where large items are concerned, but decide at the last minute on a major upgrade. Aries is associated with the color red and the element of fire. You may find that more products in the warm color range sell with the Moon in Aries. Don't panic and resupply too quickly though—the blue, purples, and greens will sell as the Moon moves through the signs. Oddly enough, the color will matter for products that seemingly have nothing to do with the Moon. You may find that you suddenly have fewer books with red covers, and that all your dictionaries are all blue or brown. Red vegetables may become scarce. You may even sell more marinara dishes and fewer Alfredo dishes.

Keep in mind that you, too, are experiencing the impulsiveness of Aries. This is not the best time to make major inventory decisions that were not planned out in advance. Stick to your dollar limit, even if you see products that call out to you. Remember that if they didn't call out to you yesterday, or the day before, they may not call to your customers tomorrow.

If your business offers a service, expect a few clients who are more than willing to tell you how to run your life, or how to do something better. Listen to them, glean the valuable lesson they offer, but ignore advice that will show its impracticality when the Moon moves into Taurus in a couple of days. Don't redesign the store with the Moon in Aries.

Moon in Taurus

During the earthy Taurus Moon phase of the month, you'll find people want comfort and security. You will want to provide little touches (incense to freshen the air, or comfortable heat or air conditioning) to your business to make your customers relax and spend a few extra minutes shopping. Straightening the shelves and cleaning up around the cash register can also make customers feel that their needs have been addressed. Greet each client or customer warmly, whether in person or over the phone, recall something personal  about people you know and include it in the conversation, or offer a sincere compliment that focuses on their clothing, voice, or appearance.

When helping a customer to select a product, be sure to ask about the intended use. Use key sales points that respond directly to the customer's need or desire, and be sure to incorporate information about the quality of the product or service, its practicality, and durability.

Because you are on a practical roll with the Moon in Taurus, make purchases that you feel will hold up well in your business. Buy shoes that will still feel good when you have been working a long day, and be recalled favorably after they've worn out. Put off shopping for a one-occasion outfit to another day.

Moon in Gemini

When the Moon is in Gemini, you want to be able to change the ambiance to suit each customer. While this may at first sound fickle, it actually means that you are able to respond to individuals, making them feel right at home. Your broad range of interests comes into play as you gather and dispense information to help customers and clientele. While this is not a good day for intense financial planning or for wholesale redesign of your store, it is a good time for creating more temporary displays to showcase new product arrivals, and for making a run to the bank. You may find yourself making long range plans and considering products that will not arrive for several months.

Use this is the time to imagine what products will be hot six months or a year form now, and how you will position them to sell through. Planning for a service business may involve the advertising you plan for an upcoming conference or open house. Product development thrives on the forward thinking of the Gemini Moon. Do some shopping to see what is out there, and even to watch people as they shop.

Moon in Cancer

Regardless of your business or service, you may find that people focus on family matters with the Moon in Cancer. This is a day for nurturing your client, your business, and yourself. Nurturing yourself includes everything from stopping off for a cup of your favorite coffee on your way to work to propping up a good book for a few minutes to working a crossword puzzle. Yes, there is business to attend to, but today will be far more productive if you take breaks and simply enjoy a few minutes to yourself. Nurture your clients by letting them express themselves. You may have the most wonderful new product or service, but it may not be what this person needs, so ask and then listen. When you talk about your product or service, be sure to include information about how practical it is, and also how it will benefit other people besides the person it is intended for.

Nurture your business by taking care of nagging little projects, making sure the paperwork is getting done, or placing the holiday order in time for early shipment. Check your supplies and prepare your reorder, even if the order won't be made until Friday.

Moon in Leo

Everyone wants to be recognized when the Moon is in Leo, and customers will remember that you made them feel special. This is a good time to sell the latest, greatest, new product. "It just came in," or "I've only got a few," or "You can be the first to own one," are all possible approaches. Customers will be pleased to be treated with the respect they so richly deserve.

Treat customers and clients royally by serving samples of food products, including bookmarks in every shopping bag, or offering meaningful discounts on future services or products. Recognize repeat clients or customers in a special way, too. Treat yourself royally and wear clothes that make you feel special, and be sure to include elegant accessories. If you are dress well, clients and customers will believe your did it just for them. In a way you have, but you do this for yourself, too.

Even if your business does not ordinarily focus on humor, Moon in Leo is a good time to incorporate this social element into your business dealings. Humor injects warmth into the most difficult situations. Of course you need to get a reading on your client to be sure that what you feel is funny will appeal to them.

Moon in Virgo

Practical matters and details demand attention when the Moon is in Virgo. This is true for you, your business, and your customer. Perhaps you have noticed that some days all you seem to do is respond to the most detailed, picky questions and complaints. You want to sell an upscale product or making great strides in a client's therapy, and the focus is on the loose thread in your carpet, or a broken fingernail, or an issue from the past that you thought had been laid to rest—the details.

On days like this, a simple approach works best. Get right down to business with each customer, but let him or her tell you what that business is. Expect each customer or client to be somewhat judgmental or critical in their choices. Avoid selling or telling something that only speaks to that moment. Instead, ask how the item fits into the wardrobe, decorating scheme, or personal life of the customer. Oh, and by the way, ask yourself the same questions as you go through the day.

Honesty is always important, and even more so with Moon in Virgo. Without being rude you can let your clients and customers know your true opinion. In this way they will come to trust your judgment and rely on your suggestions. Research new trends in your business while the Moon is in Virgo. Your own skills of discrimination come to the fore, helping you to identify the products or services you can add to your business to attract new customers and keep the old. You may want to think about large purchases, waiting for the Moon to enter Libra before placing the order, however, as this gives you a chance to allow your dreams to speak to you.

Moon in Libra

With the Moon in Libra you may to want to accommodate the customer's every need, which can be either a good or a bad thing. On the one hand, satisfying the customer is what commerce is about. They come to you for some reason, and if you fulfill their need or desire you have transacted profitable business. On the other hand, if you bend over backward too far to satisfy them it'll be difficult for you to maintain a healthy balance in your business or within yourself.

With Libra, the key is finding balance and maintaining it. One sure way to do this is to identify what is truly important to the customer, and keep returning to that point. When the demands tend to side issues, listen, but then reply by moving back to the essentials. Another strategy is to depend on your business partner to help maintain the balance. If, for example, a salesman pressures you to buy a lot more product than you need, your agreement with your partner about large purchases can come into play. Saying, "I have to consult with Mary," postpones the final decision, and gives you time to think over the proposed purchase.

Customers may tend to be self-indulgent with the Moon in Libra, but don't fuel their buying spree; let them do what they want instead. If you encourage them too much, they may feel you took advantage of them later on, and that means they may not be back again.

Moon in Scorpio

The ruthless quality of Moon in Scorpio carries over into the business world, too. Emotional forces that normally don't enter into daily commerce may drive you and your customers. Big sales can make this happen. Everyone wants to take advantage of the sale, and there is a lot of rushing in to grab the merchandise, and not much concern for other people. As the business owner, you occasionally find yourself doing the same thing—for example; buying up all of a product that you believe will be a

big seller. Never mind that this leaves your inventory very one-sided, and that you don't have the resources to balance it out. Never mind that not all of your customers are going to want that one item. You have cornered the market! Later you may wonder why that mattered so much.

Customer relations can also benefit from Scorpio's energy. For example, you can be definite in your opinions without trying to dominate your customer's decisions. You can set competitive prices without reducing your profit margin to zero. You can provide a slightly sexy, emotionally magnetic atmosphere without seeming degenerate. You can focus on the creative and regenerative facets of your business, and even suggest the healing properties of products that are not normally associated with wellness.

Qualities of the Scorpio Moon to de-emphasize include distrust (although you can exercise reasonable care to prevent theft), stubbornness (remember that the customer is always right, even when he or she is wrong), and sarcasm (no matter how much a customer irritates you).

Finally, there is nothing like a Scorpio Moon for pointing out when a relationship with a customer has come to its practical and logical end. You need to know when and how end a relationship with someone. A proven way to do this is to say, "My partner and I have discussed our relationship with you, and we find we are simply unable to achieve an acceptable level of customer satisfaction. We have decided that you will have to take your business to someone who is better equipped to meet your needs." Said without sarcasm, but with meaning, leaving no room for negotiation, you honor the client's needs and your own by taking this action.

Moon in Sagittarius

The tone of the day is inconsistent when the Moon is in Sagittarius. You think you have a plan for what you want to accomplish, but that plan is set aside in favor of something else altogether. You think you have a firm agreement with a customer, a partner, or a supplier, and you find that they (or you) have changed the agreement dramatically. You have ideals popping up to juxtapose themselves with factual realities. A person could become confused!

If you have the Moon in Sagittarius, you are used to this kind of shifting ground. Probably you have learned to depend on other people to point out your inconsistencies. When they suddenly are not playing by those long-established rules, you pessimistically believe that the situation can never work itself out and that all is lost. You probably only feel this way for a few minutes or hours, but the feelings are very strong.

The key focus for Moon is Sagittarius is idealism. You can encourage clients and customers with little bits of wisdom that may have little to do with the chase or service itself, but which nonetheless create a cheerful interchange and set the tone for business. Treat each customer as an individual, because change is the name of the game in every way. Even if three or four people come in asking for the same thing, each has a personal agenda that you can consider. Your customers will come to appreciate the upbeat attitude and look to you to create a bright spot in their day.

Moon in Capricorn

Moon in Capricorn can be a starkly emotionless day or two in your business life. It's not that Capricorn is without emotions—it's more that a sense of duty precludes their expression. This can be a good thing if your are negotiating a deal or tallying receipts. Any activity that demands practical application of your knowledge can be accomplished in such a day. You may lose patience with individuals who want to tell you their sad, happy, or otherwise distracting stories, but your practical business sense suggests to you that listening is often necessary. Use this chance to learn something true about your customer. Your can take in their story without coloring it with your own emotions, and be truly objective while assisting them.

Moon in Capricorn also presents an opportunity to do some basic research in your professional field. Check out the Internet for the latest consumer statistics. See what people are writing about your favorite subjects. People may be feeling reactionary after changeable Sagittarius, but

Capricorn's earthy energy will help people get their feet firmly planted back on the ground. You can look forward to the next Moon sign change, when you and your customers will again shift to a logical, rational mode of communication.

Moon in Aquarius

With the Moon in Aquarius, you are willing to listen to other people's problems. This is a good trait for a shopkeeper, as your approach generally makes people feel better, and this encourages them to return to your shop. Your observation skills allow you to inject something into these conversations that will often help the customer to change in beneficial ways. The ability to listen carries through to sales as well. You let the customer tell you what they want and then you steer them in the right direction. You are also willing to say that you just don't have the product or service they are seeking, and often can recommend someone to them, thereby, providing help indirectly.

Customers with the Moon in Aquarius may feel they need to help you. They will be full of ideas about how to arrange your store, schedule your appointments, and generally, how to run your business. You can listen to what they have to say, however, a planned exit from extended conversations of this type may be needed, as you do have a business to run, after all.

When today's Moon is in Aquarius you will have a mix of ideas that enlivens your day. You have many sales inspirations, perhaps more than you can follow through with, and you also have the sustained mental energy to implement the ones you choose. This is more a mental time than physical, so today is for planning what you will do when the Moon enters Taurus in about five days.

Moon in Pisces

With the Moon in Pisces, you tend to accept ideas from others very readily. You probably recognize the fact that you can be exploited at times, however, you are generally very optimistic. Remember that you can spread that quality to others just as easily as they can influence you. The key is to strike a balance.

If the Moon is in Pisces today, there is a focus on your emotional nature. You may wish to be alone in the back room sorting through catalogs, entering product into inventory, or fantasizing about your next major project. To the extent that this is possible, do it. Naturally, not all the staff in your business can be in the back room if the front door is open, but you can take the feeling into the shop and even impart the peaceful calm that you wish to engender in yourself. You can rearrange shelves, restock product, and generally use your imaginative touch to refine the look of your establishment.

Customers with the Moon in Pisces may be wishing for this calm and order when they come to your business. They too are subject to exploitation, to some extent, and you want to be respectful of their emotional tenderness. If you are showing them particular products, you will want to reshelf the items, letting them go back to pick things out for themselves. This is not a time to hover too close either. The Moon in Pisces customer wants to ramble around. By letting them do this, you may find that you make a larger sale.

Summary

Competition in sales and service businesses is aggressive. Any tools you can find that give you an edge will reap big benefits. Understanding the nature of the Moon for you, your business, and your customer can provide just such an advantage. Your own Moon sign provides information about how you tend to engage the world on a less conscious level (the Sun reflects your conscious approach). The Moon sign for the chart of your business tunes you into the way you engage the customer or client, regardless of the product or service involved. While you will generally not know your customer's Moon sign, you can often detect the unconscious urge that brought them to you, and then try to meet that need. Finally, this book provides the information you need to keep track of the sign the Moon is in each day. Try planning a month or two around the Moon's sign, and observe the difference it makes to the flow of your business.

Closing on a personal note, as you become familiar with your own lunar cycle, you may identify certain signs that are better for one kind of activity than another. To the extent that you can accommodate your personal lunar cycle, give yourself a break on days when you expect to be more sensitive. Push yourself on the days when you think can accomplish more. You don't have to be consistent (unless your Taurus Moon demands it). By respecting your own cycles, you will be far more successful in the long run, and you may feel a lot better in the short run.

I wish you great success!

Love in the Work Place

By Alice DeVille

Work place dynamics highlight your astrology chart's Sixth House of employment, a key area of interest in this article. Other houses (departments of your life) related to work are the Second House, which indicates how you earn and spend your income; and the Tenth House of career, ambition, and authority figures—such as bosses.

Your chart also holds major clues about your dating style and love life. If you are involved in the dating game, you'll want to consult it for information about your prospects and the way your social life plays out. You've probably given consideration to the best places to meet dates. What appeals to you? Where do you go? Can you honestly say that you meet potential partners at these places? Where did you meet the last person you dated? Was it a champagne experience? Or was it a bust?

Once you have assessed your preferences, you're apt to fuel your expectations by seeking out enjoyable companions and favorite haunts. You need, assuming you want to get in the game, a social life. How is yours?

Both relationship astrologers and dating experts say that over 25 percent of their clients blame job or career pressure for their inability to pursue or sustain a romance. If they have to choose how they spend their time after work, it often means that they sacrifice their social life. Why? Many say they are just too tired to think about dating and end up on the couch eating ice cream and chips. What is your experience? Are you too busy to date because of a daunting workload? Well, bag that alibi. You're about to learn a few new dating secrets.

You could find the relationship of your dreams right under your nose. Did you ever think of the work place as a primary source of dating opportunities? If you are thinking: *not me; no way!*, well, stop and reconsider. Coworkers may be the very people who fill the most cherished places in your life.

Dating Do's and Don'ts

Much has been said about not dating coworkers, and there are good reasons to follow that advice. However, you're options are seriously limited if you eliminate the place you spend most of your time from your scope. There are, however, special considerations to take into account.

First, the work place is not the environment to try out the spiciest dating trends. The suggestions I will offer for meeting partners relate mostly to extracurricular activities and not to the arena where you do your work. Then, once the two of you become an item, new rules kick in. If you use discretion you will never give a boss or a coworker an uncomfortable moment. I do recommend that you let others know you are dating. That way, if they see you on the street they won't be shocked since they normally see you interacting in a professional capacity.

Second, although your jobs may require that you collaborate in your work, be sure neither of you lingers too long at the other's workstation. Keep the doors open. Don't get lost at lunch either, or come back with lipstick on your cheek or shirt collar. Coworkers have radar. When they know you are dating, you can be sure they will look for telltale signs. So will your boss.

That brings me to rule number three, please don't date the boss—unless the two of you keep it strictly out of the work place. If you become serious about each other, make quiet plans to relocate one of you to another position. Once the word gets out subordinates may be looking for signs of favoritism and the dynamics get messy.

Fourth, talk yourself out of dating a married coworker—no matter how magnetic the attraction! People pick up vibes on affairs. Your visible dating space has limits and you could do something foolish, like baring your passions on the boss' desk. (I'm not kidding.) An example of this scenario involved an air Moon secretary and a fire Moon telephone repairman (both married) who carried on a hot romance for years. When she knew her boss would be stepping out for a few hours, the air sign would summon the fire sign to fix the ailing phones. Yep, those wires went on the fritz several times a week. Within moments of the boss' departure, the faithful fire responded to her urgent call. The real fire was in the boss' darkened conference room where the lovebirds would retreat for their afternoon delight. Everyone in the office knew about it except the boss until the fateful day that he returned unexpectedly. Can you imagine his shock when he flung open the door of his conference room to retrieve a presentation portfolio and got an X-rated view of his secretary and her lover in the throes of passion?

And finally, while not everyone in love takes the bare approach in the actual work setting, other indiscretions do occur. Avoid sending love letters via e-mail, or chain mail, or any form of communication that others may see. It doesn't matter whether your loved one is a client or an off-site contact. You'll stimulate the office grapevine because your unprofessional behavior wastes company time and money. Ditto for you frequent flyers. When traveling together for legitimate work commitments, don't book connecting rooms in your hotel. Who are you kidding? If you meet while on a trip, remember that long-distance romances are among the most difficult to sustain.

So, as I said, you can find the relationship of your dreams right under your nose, so lets proceed and check it out.

Houses of Intimacy

Your astrology chart has twelve major segments called houses. Planets that reside in these houses, or rule the cusps (doors) of the houses, describe the nature of your life's activities. Houses Five through Eight explore some of the relationships you are likely to encounter in this lifetime. We call this grouping the Zone of Intimacy or the Zone of Relationships. When the Moon resides in this sector, you experience firsthand how others affect your emotions. The Moon monitors and helps you balance your emotions.

These houses and the planets that fall in them describe the people you meet and the nature and type of activity that occurs. Knowing the birth dates of potential partners helps you discover whether their intimate planets fall (are placed in the same sign or degree) as some of your own planets in these key houses—information that reveals the nature of the relationship and the level of compatibility you'll share.

Briefly, the Fifth House describes your social life, how you recreate, where you vacation, whom you date, your lovers, and your affairs. Think of this house as an attraction-generating zone that lets you assess potential of partners. The Sixth House—the focus of this article—describes the general nature of the employment scene, which includes your colleagues, coworkers, clients, contacts, and service personnel. We'll look at a wide range of settings that explore relationships that evolve through work connections. Partnerships of all types fall in the Seventh House—marriage or business partners, roommates, significant others, advisors, consultants, and the public. The Seventh House actually describes qualities you desire in a partner. For a view of sex and intimacy, look at the Eighth House for planets that describe your receptivity and compatibility to romantic and sensual relationships. As the relationship evolves, you'll see the big picture and know whether you and your partner have magnetic chemistry, or are destined for a brother-sister relationship.

Individuals with planets in these houses usually have a high degree of interaction with other people. When three or more planets fall in the Sixth House, the work setting often becomes the focal point of considerable social activity related to the job scene. You easily find best friends among coworkers, bosses, or contacts. Be on the lookout for workaholics as well and avoid becoming one yourself. Placement of a combination of the personal planets—Sun, Moon, Mercury, Venus, Mars, and sometimes Jupiter—in this house heighten the opportunity for work place romance. If the thrill of love in the work place appeals to you, be sure you understand the rules of engagement before you take the plunge.

The Work Scene

This dating arena, also known as your work environment, varies in tone given the diversity of professions. Work place politics influence the climate.

Liken the possible scenarios to the many colors in the spectrum. Opportunity is either enhanced by an open, people-friendly setting, or diminished by a business-only outlook. Understanding the underlying philosophy will give you a clue about how intracompany dating might be viewed. Be sure you understand existing policies. Many companies discourage employee fraternization. What's it like where you work? If you are clueless, check out the organizational directory for evidence of employed couples and the grapevine for an informal read.

Larger organizations seem more open to employing bonded couples if there are no conflicts of interest along supervisory lines. Some companies are okay with hiring married couples, but discourage pursuit of a hot romance on company time. Officials would rather see Mars and Venus do their thing on neutral turf, and embarrassing moments disrupt productivity. Employee discomfort mushrooms when they see coworkers sneaking a smooch in the hallway or necking in the parking lot after lunch. Not all work settings involve large numbers of other employees observing the love bug in action. Sometimes your future partner comes to you in response to your need for help. A variety of circumstances may create the Sixth House romance setup. Employees in service industries report meeting future partners while responding to a call to duty. Think of repair specialists who visit your home when the air conditioning, plumbing, or electricity is on the fritz. The cop on the beat can have fluttery heartstrings while gathering information from an attractive victim of an office mugging. She may even call back to make sure the victim is healing and check out the left hand for signs of a wedding band.

Consider the opportunities of personal care providers such as hair stylists, fitness trainers, and estheticians who meet a variety of people on a daily basis. Individuals who seek their services come to them and talk about their lives. The client's love life is often the chief topic of discussion. Before long a level of trust develops and you are trading notes. (They already have your telephone number!) True to the nature of the

Sixth House, the service provider is not only a good listener but knows the state of your emotions by touching your hair, feeling your tense muscles, or observing your skin's reaction when you are under stress. When you are happy, they can see your glow. Best of all, they know whether you are available or between relationships. According to my case files, many a friendship or a romantic union forms under these circumstances.

A vivacious client of mine met her future mate on the job. She is a mover-shaker real estate professional who sold a widower's home for him. When he settled on his dream home several months later he had a new companion—my client. Yes, she had me compare their charts for compatibility. The match was a winner. His Sun and Venus fell (were conjunct in the same signs and approximate degrees) on her Moon, Mercury, and Mars in the Sixth House of work.

If you are self-employed you might have reservations about dating your clients. Maybe you even have a policy, but if you don't have one, prepare for the day when a client puts you on the spot and asks for a date. Business owners often cite their experiences of clients making a move even though the owners thought of the relationships as purely professional. Of course, that can change if you are available and responsive. But if you are not, the moment becomes embarrassing for both of you.

Think about the advantage an astrologer has over other professions—he or she already knows your sign and whether the sparks between you have the potential to develop. I'm often asked if people are afraid to date astrologers since we know so much about a prospective partner's astrology chart. Believe me, it doesn't stop a flirt from using creative pick-up lines.

Elements and Signs

To understand more about the nature of your Sixth House of work, look at the sign and element on the cusp of the house, as well as planets that fall there. The more planets that reside within, the greater the importance of the house in terms of relationships and involvement in your work. The twelve astrological signs are divided by element (property or quality) into four groups: fire, earth, air, and water. Are you curious about compatibility with your coworkers or important work contacts? The sign on the cusp or the planets within have been known to describe dominant characteristics of colleagues, if not their actual Moon (and often Sun) signs. Compatibility simply means that your astrology sign seems to work well with those of your coworkers. Signs in the fire element (Aries, Leo, and Sagittarius) and air element (Gemini, Libra, and Aquarius) relate favorably to one another. Likewise, the earth signs (Taurus, Virgo, and Capricorn) get along with signs in the water element (Cancer, Scorpio, and Pisces).

So where does love come in? Just think about the amount of time spent interacting with others in the work place. You meet people who share common interests, educational experiences, philosophies, and maybe similar goals. Individuals with Moons in harmonious astrological elements seem to get along better in relationships. Communication flows from the boardroom to the lunchroom and beyond.

Although an understanding of Moon sign compatibility gives you insight into the possible dynamics, it is seldom enough proof that a relationship is solid. Your astrology chart reflects your blueprint for this lifetime, and presents a total picture of your emotional needs and passions through the expression of your personal natal planets: Sun, Moon, Mercury, Venus, Mars, and Jupiter. If you have these planets in the Sixth House, you automatically increase your chances for meeting someone through your work that becomes a dating partner. The odds go up tremendously when a prospective partner has planets in favorable aspect to your Sixth House placements. If the natal planets make contact with transiting planets (current movement of the planets), the relationship develops. That means your adrenaline starts pumping every time this wonderful person comes near you. You may not remember anything you say because the transiting planets are generating activity. Just shake up Venus and Mars and you have a little heart action.

Style and Substance

If you are wondering how the elements express their love in the work place, this overview may give you the information. Fire Moons (Aries, Leo, and Sagittarius) demonstrate their passion and responsiveness. This element has a deep awareness of their magnetism and falls in love easily. Once attracted, fire signs put considerable energy into getting to know you. Regardless of gender, they facilitate private encounters to find out what makes you tick. They want to eliminate competition, so before long you'll be sharing lunch, discussing your favorite recreation spots, and exploring weekend plans. Leave it to fire signs to find a way to get you to say "yes" to that first date. These high-energy types will include you in work-related projects or social events and off-site get-togethers with their friends. Do these qualities appeal to you? Know that with fire ruling your Sixth

House of work, you could attract this type of partner. If you are not interested, it won't take a fire sign long to catch on and quickly back away. Pride is a big thing with them, and they won't want colleagues to catch them in the throes of rejection.

Members with earth Moons (Taurus, Virgo, or Capricorn) develop a work place relationship much more slowly than their fire peers. If you are particularly grounded and committed to your career, you'll probably catch the eye of an earth sign when this element influences your Sixth House of work. They'll probably start out by looking at your place in the organization and evaluating your contributions. For earth signs, passion often begins after they've observed outstanding performance in the work place. Earth looks for a strong work ethic, ambition, and financial security in prospective partners. When an earth sign discovers your charms, you may find yourself under quiet surveillance. This more reserved type makes it a point to engage you in conversations or pick your brain at meetings and conferences. Since they enjoy self-development, don't be surprised if a smitten earth supervisor or colleague shows up in the same training session as you more than once—it is no coincidence. Earth may also show an interest in your travel schedule and look for opportunities to link up in distant places. Rather than meet you for lunch in the company cafeteria, a normally discreet earth may feel more comfortable dining with you while you are both in travel status. If you don't mind talking shop in the early stages of the relationship, rapport with an earth type could take you out of the dating loop and into a secure partnership.

With the air element (Gemini, Libra, and Aquarius) affecting your Sixth House, the world of communication influences dating opportunities. For one thing, air Moons are generally talkative and prefer intellectual rapport with partners. Their interests are very diverse. They quickly assimilate workplace dynamics, first out of curiosity and then to impress colleagues with their smarts. Air signs wrote the book on networking and unless they are writers, they'll rarely spend a workday in seclusion. If they are interested in you, you will feel like air types are popping up everywhere you go. And in between those physical meetings, members of this element find every imaginable way to connect with love interests—the Internet, e-mail, telephone, pager, snail mail, interoffice memo, or a witty verbal exchange over an office partition. Make eye contact with them across a crowded room and expect a wink. Yes, they are flirts, and you may have competition because others are attracted to their easygoing mannerisms. You can count on air sign's sense of humor and calm facade to reduce tension when the work place has one of those Murphy's Law days. Air signs hope you value their intelligence and problem-solving skills. Dating a member of the air element assures you of an active social life and a variety of mind-expanding experiences.

When the water element (Cancer, Scorpio, and Pisces) influences your work house, you need emotional commitment and support from others. This requirement often emerges in the form of a mentor who notices your potential and coaches your professional development. Initially, they may show a strong protective attitude toward you and be unaware of their growing personal interest. Water signs, with their developed sixth sense, have the inside track on your moods and feelings. They have excellent people skills and feel flattered when you seek their counsel and guidance. One or more water sign coworkers, clients, or contacts may develop a crush on you and find reason to visit your work place frequently. Members of this element usually sense your receptivity. They will almost surely treat you to an impressive meal, or offer to cook one for you, when the relationship progresses. Don't be surprised if they invite you to family gatherings early in the game. Once love blossoms, the water Moon may pursue you relentlessly and smother you with attention. With the Sixth House water emphasis, you're going to draw partners who show compassion and a desire to cherish their beloved. Since you need depth and intensity in your relationships, you'll soon have evidence of a lasting commitment. Just make sure you save the bear hugs for after hours.

Formula for Work Place Dating

Do you want to know where to find single men and women? I hope you can keep a secret so there won't be a stampede. The fire, earth, air, and water Moons are right under your nose at the work place. All you have to do is get going, and not necessarily out of your way.

Take an inventory of your typical workday. Where do social opportunities occur? The best time to meet a working person is early in the morning, at lunchtime, or after work. As you get to know more about a work colleague, the optimal meeting time will extend to weekend activities.

First, how do you get to work? If you travel alone, consider answering an ad to join a carpool. There may not be a single in the group, but the camaraderie that develops usually leads to social invitations and access to members' friends who are single. Join members for lunch occasionally. They may introduce you to unattached colleagues who have interests you share.

If you ride public transportation, chances are you see the same people at the same bus or subway stop. Have you ever initiated a conversation with another rider? Travel-related exchanges, especially weather conditions, are an easy entry. Ever notice how a snowstorm or sudden downpour serves as an icebreaker for usually stoic passengers? Other starters cover destination, jobs, and companies. Remember that you aren't the only single who is riding. Once you make the right connection, you may be saving a permanent seat for your favorite commuter. I know two couples who met this way.

Don't forget to check a potential date's reading material. You may be able to spot a prospect with a compatible Moon sign. Fire signs read sports, politics, and entertainment materials; earth signs look at the stock market, read historical novels and how-to-get-rich guides; air signs go through at least two magazines per trip and carry the current bestseller; and water signs like the biographies and self-help manuals. "Are you enjoying that book?" is a comment that is sure to get a response when you ask your seatmate for a reading recommendation.

What do you do when you get to work? Do you make a quick stop at the coffee shop before you head to your cubicle? Ever notice that employees from other divisions besides your own stop there also? Some workers are eating breakfast, not just running in for a cup of coffee. Many of them are single. You could leave home a little earlier once or twice a week and have breakfast, too. You could be looking at the sunny

side of a relationship in no time. And if your organization has a coffee break ritual, make it a point to set your work aside and join colleagues. This way you'll pick up information on social gatherings and learn all about company-sponsored events.

Remember your opening lines when you spot an interesting single reading in the work place lunchroom or cafeteria. "Mind if I sit here?" seldom gets a turndown, especially if you show an interest in the person's reading material. If bowling, tennis, or softball interest you, find out who is on the team and join it. Does your company have a fitness center? That's where you'll find those fire and earth Moons working out, often over lunch. I'm not saying the airs and waters are not fit, but they will probably use the facilities after hours, so go there to meet new singles.

The best way to meet singles at your work place is to make yourself visible. Volunteer to chair the charity campaign, the holiday dance, the company picnic, or the blood drive. You'll be able to keep your thumb on the pulse beat when it comes to spotting other singles. Do attend conventions, conferences, and off-site meetings. Each event has built-in social opportunities like mixers, awards banquets, and tours that offer a chance to bond. If you have a flair for entertainment or a gift of gab, offer to emcee or present a skit. Each of the elements has a bit of ham in them, especially the fires and airs. Don't pass up training when it is offered either. Your water Moon classmate may be the object of your earth sign desire.

Love in Bloom

If you have personal planets in the Sixth House you are bound to form close ties with work contacts at sometime during your trek through the wonderful world of work. Be open to the possibilities. Potential dates are those very individuals who influence a part of your workday. Some common denominator binds you together whether you share adjoining space or provide a needed service for a client. Savor your good fortune when romance blossoms through your career connections. Your biggest bonus is yet to come. Just make sure you check with me to select the ideal wedding date. See you at the altar.

Work in Sync with Eight Lunar Phases

By Maria Kay Simms

Notches of the lunar cycle carved on bones by cave people offer evidence that since the most ancient of times, humans have looked to the Moon for timing the events in their lives, and in hopes of predicting what may lie ahead. It is obvious why this has been so—the Moon is by far the fastest changing and easiest to observe of all lights in the sky. Even skeptics of astrology have acknowledged observable influences of the Moon on the Earth and on human life. From her pull on the ocean tides to the increased intensity of stress most often associated with her full and new phases, her influence can be felt.

Each lunar month (about twenty-nine days) we can see the Moon go through the same predictable phases, from waxing crescent to full and then gradually diminishing until she vanishes from the night sky. About three nights later, she'll reemerge as a thin crescent once again. She passes through the entire zodiac during each monthly cycle.

But, sadly, we look at the sky much less than our ancestors did. Instead, we rely on calendars, ephemerides, computers, or the TV news to tell us what is happening in the sky. Even with an ephemeris (book of tables denoting the planets' positions) or a computer program to provide us with astrological data, much useful and valuable information about the Moon that would be very obvious if you look at the sky, goes undetected. One thing that you'd notice is that the Moon has more than four phases!

Eight Moon Phases

Most basic astrological guides show only the New Moon, first quarter, Full Moon, and fourth quarter Moon. Actually, there are eight clearly observable phases. These eight phases were first articulated by the great astrological philosopher, Dane Rudhyar, in his book *The Lunar Phases*.

I have found these eight phases illuminate the following three things: (1) they are a primary indicator of eight basic personality types, (2) they coincide with the life phases in a twenty-nine year cycle of personal experience, and (3) they indicate the most obvious times for choosing to do various activities. Living and working in sync with the Moon's changing phases can move you toward success by providing you with that edge that comes from choosing the best time to undertake important activities.

You can find current transiting lunar phases in your ephemeris or computer programs, if you know where and how to look—or you can go outside at night and see them! But, since most resources will not have an eight-phase calendar readily available to you, let's look at the sky!

Bear with me for a month and use the guidelines that follow to observe the changing faces of the Moon. It will be healthy for your soul as you work to be more in sync with her cycles. If you do, you'll never be satisfied to look only at a computer screen, a book, or a table of numbers again as your sole sources for astrological information. If you stick with it for a month, you'll gain a useful tool for the timing of your life, and you'll feel more in harmony with the universe's natural cycles.

New Moon Means No Visible Moon

For about three nights each month the sky is dark, with no Moon visible. That because the Moon is conjunct (in the same or very near the same degree) as the Sun. During this time, the Moon rises with the Sun, but we can't see her because the Sun's light is too strong. We'd have to look directly at the Sun, which can't be done without hurting our eyes. Since the Moon at conjunction also sets with Sun, the night sky is left completely dark except for the stars. At the clock time given on your calendar as New Moon, the night sky is dark. I emphasize this point because most people think of New Moon when they see the Moon's second phase, or crescent Moon, appear. The crescent is a distinct phase with a different meaning for your life, which we will consider after we deal with how to observe the distinct phases.

Crescent Phase Observed

After the night sky has been void of the Moon for three nights, begin looking to the western sky shortly after the Sun sets, and you'll soon spot the slender crescent Moon, with her curve on your right, and her tips pointing toward the left.

First Quarter Phase Observed

Three or four days after the crescent appears, the waxing (gradually increasing) Moon can be seen as a half-circle. The right side will be light and the left side dark. During the waxing phases, the Moon appears a bit further east each night, and she is visible for longer periods.

Gibbous Moon Observed

When, three or four nights after first quarter (or half Moon), we see an orb that is almost, but not quite, a full circle, we are at the gibbous phase. The Moon is now round on the right and a bit flat on the left. She will be clearly visible as the Sun sets, remaining up most of the night.

Full Moon Observed

At about two weeks past New Moon phase, the Moon has traveled 180 degrees (or opposition aspect) away from the Sun. She shines as a full, bright orb, illuminating the sky for at least three nights as she approaches, opposes, and begins to move away from the opposition degree to the Sun. The Full Moon can be observed rising in the east just as the Sun is setting in the west, and she shines all night long. For the following two weeks, until the Moon and Sun are conjunct once again, her cycle will be waning (gradually decreasing) in light and shape.

Disseminating Moon Observed

When the Moon begins to appear flattened on the right, she has entered her disseminating phase, and she will rise later after sunset each night.

Last Quarter Phase Observed

When the Moon can be seen as a half-circle of light again, but now the left side is light and the right side dark, she is at last quarter phase. Now it will be several hours after sunset before she appears. Still, be aware that she is not following Sun. Ever since she separated from the conjunction, she has been racing around the entire zodiac to catch up with Sun again.

Balsamic Phase Observed

Stay up very late, or rise in the wee hours of the morning, to see the lovely balsamic Moon (commonly referred to as the waning crescent or crone Moon). This time she curves toward the left with her tips pointing toward the right. Normally, she'll be observable for only a brief time because the rising Sun's light is so strong that the Moon disappears from our view. (Sometimes the balsamic Moon can be seen in daylight, but this is much more likely to happen at the full or near-full phases.)

Within just three or four days after the balsamic phase, the fast-moving Moon will conjunct the Sun once again, having completed an entire 360-degree circle of the zodiac, while the Sun has plodded along through only one degree. (It takes the Sun one year to travel through all 360 zodiac degrees.)

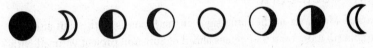

Eight Moon Phases

Understanding Yourself Through the Moon's Phases

Now, with awareness of all eight phases of the Moon and how to observe when they are occurring, let's consider what that means in terms of every cycle of experience. This knowledge is useful in understanding yourself, for the phase of the Moon at the time of your birth is a factor in your basic personality. It is also useful in understanding the changing phases of your life, for the 29-year-cycle of the progressed Moon is one of the most useful interpretive tools in astrology for understanding the larger patterns in the ebb and flow of your life. Last, but certainly not least, the transiting phases of the Moon that occur every month of every year, as Moon orbits Earth, give valuable keys to making good choices in timing.

Let's begin with interpretations of the birth phases, and then the progressed phases. Understanding the themes of these first can increase your ability to understand yourself, as well as to effectively use the shorter-term transiting phases. Suggestions for timing the most appropriate activities for the transiting phases will conclude this article. In your birth chart, your lunar phase is determined by the positions of your Sun and Moon in relation to each other.

The easiest, and by far the least expensive, resource for determining the current monthly transiting phase is to go out and look at the sky. Each phase lasts for about three-and-one-half days, and the changes will be visible unless your sky is very cloudy for days at a stretch. It is important to know the exact time of the New Moon. Many calendars, including Llewellyn's *Astrological Calendar*, will list the clock time of the New Moon. The reason you should check this is because the difference is quite dramatic between what activities are appropriate for New Moon and what would be best done during the preceding balsamic Moon. The other phases indicate an evolving process for which the exact times of change in phase are far less critical.

New Moon Born

Sun and Moon are in the same sign, or the Moon is in the sign after the Sun, but no more than 44 degrees ahead of Sun. You project yourself with a creative sense of new beginnings, and often feel urged to move forward just to get things moving. You may not have the process well thought through. When challenged, you operate best on instinct.

Crescent Moon Born

The Moon is 45 to 89 degrees ahead of the Sun. Your impulse is to take action that will improve your status in life, but you frequently find yourself involved in intense challenges, in which breaking from the past may be a factor.

First Quarter Moon Born

The Moon is 90 to 134 degrees ahead of the Sun. You are attracted to action, noise, movement, and excitement; and feel a constant urge to progress, even if the end goal is a bit hazy. You are strong willed and likely to develop managerial skills.

Gibbous Moon Born

The Moon is 135 to 179 degrees ahead of the Sun. You are very involved in self-discovery, constantly asking: "Why?" or "Where am I going?" or "How am I growing?" It is important for you to discover better ways of doing things, and you may get caught up in advocating a cause.

Full Moon Born

The Moon is 180 to 224 degrees ahead of the Sun. More than other phase type, it is through relationships that you gain clarity and objectivity about your own purpose. Considerable crisis in relationships is likely until you discover that true completion is within yourself. Fulfillment is not enough—you must find illumination, a worthwhile reason for your life.

Disseminating Moon Born

The Moon is 225 to 269 degrees ahead of the Sun. You are a natural communicator capable of disseminating ideas that are important to you. You may be a born teacher, and you could be an effective crusader if a particular cause becomes important. Your purpose to share your wisdom, your beliefs, your interests.

Last Quarter Moon Born

The Moon is 270 to 314 degrees ahead of the Sun. You feel that you don't quite fit in to the accepted mold, but you try. You are likely to seem different to others than you really feel inside, and you could even seem inflexible, for on the surface you stick to structures because you are not yet ready to "come out" with what you are really thinking. One day, you might surprise others and let them know the thinking that was going on inside you.

Balsamic Moon Born

The Moon is 315 to 359 degrees ahead of the Sun. You are likely to be openly out-of-sync (or outright eccentric) with the mainstream; one who hears a different drummer. Sure that you have a destiny, you are ready to flow with life, even if you're not too clear on just what it is or where you are going. There may be a sense of the prophet about you.

Progressed Lunar Phases

Each progressed phase, in succession, represents about a three-and-a-half-year period of your life in which the things you are working through are similar in theme to the birth phases just given. The total cycle begins with your birth phase and lasts about twenty-nine years. Then, the wheel turns again. A full life span could encompass three full cycles, and more. For your progressed lunar phase, you need your calculated position of progressed Sun and progressed Moon. Consider the exact conjunction as zero, and then find your progressed phase by how many degrees your progressed Moon is ahead of your progressed Sun according to the same formula as is given above. A number of astrological computer programs will do the calculations for you. Or, you can get your birth phase plus dates of all the progressed phases for your lifetime in an inexpensive one-page report, *Lifetime Lunar Phases*, from Astro Communications Services in San Diego, by calling 1-800-888-9983.

Progressed New Moon

It's a time of some significant new beginning, but because you are likely to begin on instinct, you may not even be fully aware of the nature of its importance until you look back on it later. It may come more as a gradual awakening of new goals.

Progressed Crescent

What began at New Moon begins to take form. You want to move forward, but sometimes it may seem as though you are taking two steps forward and one step back. You may have to break away from something in the past, or resist the naysayers around you.

Progressed First Quarter

It's a crisis of action in the new direction you are establishing. This is the time to make it happen. Be aggressive in pursuing your goals. If there are obstacles from the past holding you back, this is the time to clear them away decisively.

Progressed Gibbous

This is a skill-building period. You can clearly visualize the fulfillment of your goal, but you need to perfect the techniques and strategies that will get you there. Analyze, evaluate, reorganize, improve, and develop.

Progressed Full Moon

This can be a time of climax or fulfillment of the new direction that began at New Moon. It's likely to be a high-impact period where what you've been building works, but it is also likely to be a time when balance and integration are required. If some issues in your life are out of balance, you'll probably know it. A challenge is to find illumination, a meaningful purpose for what you have built. If you don't, enthusiasm may wane. If illumination is found, you have much to give back to the world in the coming phase.

Progressed Disseminating

During this period you build on the successes of your Full Moon period, and demonstrate what you have learned. To disseminate is to spread. Share the fruits of your achievements and the wisdom of your illumination with your world. Teach what you have learned.

Progressed Last Quarter

This period has been called the "crisis of consciousness." At first, you continue to do well what you've done in the past, but you may be asking yourself, "Is this all there is for my life?" Inside, you are likely to be finishing up parts of your life because what you are doing lacks the zing it once had. You're looking for something new, but may not show it.

Progressed Balsamic

This is a period of experimentation in which you may try several new starts. Some may fall by the wayside, but some, or one, may later prove to be the seed of a whole significant new cycle. Do not mourn for what is past. Let it go—try out the new! Have faith that every ending is the seed of some new beginning.

Using the Lunar Phases In the Current Month

For any use of astrological timing, it is important to know yourself, and how you are likely to act or respond in any given situation. Your birth lunar phase is part of the general personality profile that is indicated by your birth chart.

By now, from reading the birth and progressed phases, you should be aware of the general theme of each phase. Using them in current transits is similar, although three-and-one-half days does go by quite fast. A complete cycle of experience, or one work project, may well take longer than one Moon cycle of twenty-nine days. Even so, awareness of the phase you are in may help you in making significant steps in a long-term project, as well as to successfully time short-term activities.

From New Moon until first quarter is the best time to start something new. At New Moon instinctive ideas emerge; hunches can be especially valuable. As you move toward first quarter, plans take shape; projects get off the drawing board and begin to manifest. Be aware of when New Moon actually occurs before starting a new project or initiating an activity. If you have no calendar to tell you the time, it would be better to wait until you see the first slender crescent Moon appear.

Don't get discouraged if something begun at New Moon encounters some resistance at the crescent phase. If its important to you, your challenge is to get past your own self-doubts, or feelings of lethargy. Keep the naysayers in perspective, and keep nudging things forward.

At first quarter, it's decision time. Get that project off the ground and running! Confront obstacles and clear them away. Organize. Be assertive in going after what you need to move forward.

From first quarter to Full Moon is the time to take decisive action and move forward. During the gibbous phase, revise and develop your strategies and techniques, evaluate what has happened so far and learn from it. Keep focused on your goal.

At Full Moon, results should be evident. If ideas that emerged at New Moon look to be winners, go for it. Even if you're not yet completely sure, don't give up. Keep working. This is a high time for accomplishment. Illumination may come regarding a nuance of what you're doing that is beyond what you thought before. That could spur you on with additional energy, or it could possibly provoke reevaluation.

Full Moon to last quarter is a time when you can effectively consolidate your gains on that "winner." If more development time seems to be needed, you'll wind down a bit, reevaluate, and tie up loose ends. (Hey, this is only a one-month cycle.) This project may just take more time and thought. During the disseminating period, you'll likely be more involved with communicating what you are doing with others on your team, sharing your ideas, enlisting support.

Last quarter to New Moon is a good time for reflection and revise. At last quarter, a short-term project may have come to fruition, and now that it is successfully handled, you're beginning to wonder what's next. This may be the time when you are thinking about delegating the project to others so you can move on to something else. If something hasn't worked out as you once hoped, you could be coming to terms with that, and thinking about where to go from here. The project that had potential may yet be reincarnated with some introspection and revised plans.

During the balsamic period, you are at the most favorable time for bringing things to closure, for eliminating that which is not working, for clearing out the clutter, for letting go. It is a good time to dream about new ideas, or perhaps for noncritical experimentation, or for routine continuation of long-term projects, but wait until after New Moon occurs before initiating a new activity.

To be aware of and in sync with the phases of the Moon is to live in harmony with the ebb and flow of nature. The Sun is the center of our solar system, the vitality of our lives, but the full and constant brilliance of that light is blinding, just as being up and running all the time can cause burnout. Our Moon reflects the Sun's bright light in measured phases that shine on the Earth with a message that life is an endless cycle. There is a time to plant seeds of activity, to nurture them, to watch them bloom, to reap the harvest, and then to let what has been created wane and die in the appropriate time, so that new seeds can germinate and we can begin again. Look to the sky and at the phases of the Moon to learn her cycles. In so doing, you'll be nurtured in spirit.

Economic Forecasts
for the Year 2002

By Kaye Shinker

Since ancient times astrologers have looked at a select number of charts set for the capital of their country to determine the future economic picture. Today, financial astrologers look at the same charts to study the position of the Sun, Jupiter, Saturn, and now Uranus. First, they look at the these planets in the equinox charts. (Equinox charts are representative of the time when the Sun reaches 0 degree of the cardinal signs Capricorn, Aries, Cancer, and Libra.) Next, they look at these planets in solar eclipse charts. There will be two solar eclipses in 2002.

My descriptions of the transiting planets through the signs are meant to give you an overview of economic trends for the year, and I will give you ideas as to where to invest your time and money. I am using the term North Americans this year because Jupiter will transit through Cancer and Leo, and both Canada and the USA have Sun sign Cancer. (Yes, I know Mexico is in North America, and they will benefit from the prosperity later in the year.)

The Market's Schedule

The markets (that means all of them) will dip about 1 percent around January 18, but by February 8 they will begin to recover. March 1, the Bull will be uncaged and this trend will continue adding as much as 20 percent, on average, to all markets until May 15, 2002. A 2 percent breather down will then go into effect until June 10, when the other shoe falls and 5 percent more gets knocked off of the indexes. From July until September, the markets inch back up, and then they take a time out September 15. By October 11, they are through climbing and once again do their October thing of running right back down 15 percent. Around November 3 the tech stocks will finally start to trend up. However, there will not be a Christmas bounce in December. Save your money and expect an up trend in March 2003.

A tax surplus and assorted insurance plans will be the business topic of the year. Everyone has something to say about these issues and tells their congressman. Throughout the year various tax laws will be enacted and inefficient collection techniques will be scrapped. The marriage penalty and a lower tax rate will be the first new bills to make their impact on the paycheck. Capital gains tax cuts and withdrawal of the inheritance tax will also put extra money into the economy. Of course, these changes will not make paying taxes less difficult. The tax laws will remain complicated.

Insurance companies are creating new products for their customers. They are making changes on their own to avoid problems with public relations. Quite a few of the large companies have merged. Old customers are cashing out of unnecessary policies. Their source for new customers is a much smaller population group, and they are searching for ways to entice their older customers to buy new products.

Pensions and Social Security are also important topics throughout the year. The baby boomers are ready to retire, and they will not be told what they ought to do. People have their own agenda and are setting goals and achieving them. Municipalities and high-tax states will find their older population moving. Baby boomers put their houses on wheels and leave. This new group of retired folks will not wait for changes in laws they consider being an unfair burden.

The price of fuel is holding steady since there has been a systematic decrease in consumption. People are using their communications equipment to conserve fuel and save time. Wage inflation is the cause of higher interest rates and higher prices for consumer goods.

The housing stock will be plentiful throughout the year. Office building managers will be challenged to keep their spaces rented. Problems continue with city infrastructures. Impatient CEOs suggest that moving is a fine solution, however, hospitals, museums, government offices, and universities do not move easily. Therefore, they will dominate the downtown scene. Folks have moved their traffic to the countryside.

Jupiter and the Economy

The sign Jupiter transits indicates the areas of the economy where there will be abundance. Jupiter has been in Cancer since July 13, 2001, and will remain in Cancer until August 2, 2002. Jupiter will begin its transit of Leo on August 2, 2002, and remains in Leo through August 27, 2003.

Jupiter in Cancer

Look for post-baby boomers to show an increased interest in genealogy. They'll do their research on the Internet and accomplish much through e-mail to all the relatives. In abundant supply are things associated with water sign Cancer—water, bath houses and bathing places, bathrooms, environmental issues, gardens and gardening equipment, taverns and restaurants, sheep, food, houses, shops and shopkeepers, home-based businesses, silver, plumbers, social workers, flowers, and milk. In short supply are things associated with the earth sign Capricorn—masons and masonry, minerals that are black in color, salt, civil servants, coffins, animals with cloven feet and horns, fine furniture, watch repairers, and leather goods.

Jupiter in Leo

People benefit from the urge to play more, and from an abundance of entertainment. You can expect to see this trend building throughout the summer as Jupiter makes it's way through Cancer and into then enters Leo. In abundant supply are things associated with fire sign Leo—hot and humid air, heat exhaustion, almonds, ballrooms, children in general (but especially, first children), circuses, government officials and activities, gold, golf, casinos, entertainment (including showboats), stadiums, picnics, romance, royalty, solariums, the colors orange and gold, stocks and stock brokers, stoves, and sunflowers. In short supply are things associated with Aquarius—cooperative effort, counselors, automobiles, batteries, free thinkers, humanitarianism, airplane pilots, telephone wires, radio receivers and wide-band radio frequencies, photographic supplies, and researchers.

Live entertainment is inexpensive and there is plenty available. Copyrights from the 1920s are expiring and these old songs and plays furnish new material for aspiring actors and musicians. You realize that live entertainment is more fun, and when possible, you'll find time to enjoy the theater or a concert. "Play ball" is the expression, and opportunities abound for trying new games. Participation in a sport is "in," serious competition is "out." Beautiful bodies are in, and so are spas and health clubs. The spark is within folks to experience an adventure, take a chance, risk an encounter—or all of the above. People are hiking, gambling, and finding romance.

Saturn in Gemini

Saturn began its transit of Gemini April 20, 2001, and remains in the sign until June 4, 2003. The organization, efficiency, cost, and utility of elementary education, transportation, highway systems, and neighborhoods are under scrutiny. Parents and teachers are serious and determined that reading, writing, and arithmetic will be the first priority of their children. Hiring teachers is expensive. Outdated retirement plans, low salaries, and challenging students have left many communities with a very real shortage of elementary teachers. Neither public nor private schools can budget enough money to encourage recent college graduates to seek employment, and finding teachers for the extremely bright and mentally challenged students is difficult. Taxpayers will feel the pressure to vote to increase their real estate assessments.

States want to raise gasoline taxes. Highway maintenance is a huge problem for local and state governments. Too much traffic, expensive public transportation, potholes, and bridge repairs are the issues. The freeways are jammed twenty-four hours a day. Some folks are moving away from it, others are arranging flex hours or computer commuting. Truckers and delivery people just have to deal with the problem.

The problem of tire treads separating made headlines when Saturn made its first appearance in Gemini in August 2000. North

Americans' demands for safe products have slipped through the cracks, causing major public relations difficulties. This is especially true of vehicles and various communication devises. Litigation seems to be fashionable. The Internet has made researching liability law a new game for the ordinary citizen.

As the transit of Saturn through Gemini ends, expect announcements of mergers between powerful companies in the telecommunications, media, automobile, and trucking industries. They will site the economy of scale. Qualified commercial drivers are scarce. Vehicle repair folks have their appointment books filled.

Uranus in Aquarius

Uranus entered Aquarius January 13, 1996, and will depart December 3, 2003. Aquarius (the sign of invention and electronics) is ruled by Uranus. Computers were born under the air sign Aquarius, as was the NASDAQ stock exchange.

Personal cell phones, book bags on wheels, and laptop computers are required at private schools, therefore these things will soon be on the lists of public school students.

Energy costs will continue to encourage retailers to find new ways to keep prices down and margins up, and windmill and solar panel farms find a good market for their electricity. North Americans will demand megawatts. Grocers will continue to install self-check-out equipment. Other retail businesses solve the problem by finding more ways for you to do-it-your-self. The desk on wheels looks like carry on luggage until it unfolds to reveal an array of tools. The ability of the cell phone to operate worldwide allows employees and technicians to roam the countryside. Many will have their computer attached to the cell phone. Work time is when you do it.

The sign for Aquarius is two parallel zigzag lines. The NASDAQ likes its week-to-week result to imitate the glyph for the sign. Zigzag lines will describe the results of the market with a bias for going up. The NASDAQ's average at year's end ought to be 8,000. Various sectors will lead the market throughout the year, but biotech trends down losing favor as the year progresses. Always friendly to new ideas, the NASDAQ will continue to find new companies ready to sell shares in their business every week.

Neptune in Aquarius

Every new gadget is touted as an energy-saving device, but there's a catch. Each one requires a four-hour videotape to teach you how to operate it. An incredible number of inventions have appeared since November 28, 1998, when Neptune entered Aquarius, and new applications will appear throughout the Aquarius transit that ends February 4, 2012.

People are buying glossy, sleek, one-of-a-kind items to decorate their homes. They're expensive, but beautiful. Fashion, drama, music, painting, and literature have made a quantum leap. If it is outrageous it will sell. Three-dimensional art is favored, especially if light and shadow change the painting. There will be many new ways to sell and distribute the arts. All of these innovations in the arts will require expensive risk taking by the artists. Artists in every medium will go public to get them through the lean times. No longer is there a need to find a wealthy patron or corporate sponsor; it's less of a hassle just to go public. In drama, expect characters with a definitive philosophy expressed in the story line.

Pluto in Sagittarius

Pluto has been in Sagittarius since November 11, 1995, and will leave the sign on Thanksgiving 2008. In the middle degrees of Sagittarius, the tough problems come from Russia and the Middle East. Russia with her vast natural resources continues to rewrite her economy. North Americans have grown impatient with the off-and-on oil crisis, and they're telling the Near East, "We'll invent ourselves out of this one."

We are a people who love travel and consider it fun. Trains, planes, and automobiles are about to find new sources of fuel and all of this will cause an enormous reinvention of the world and economy.

Pluto represents scandals, and in the case of the wireless Internet, there will be plenty of e-mail on the subject. When something is new and free, all sorts of shady characters infiltrate. Software to prevent theft will become very sophisticated, with volume of sales making it cheap. Still the opportunities for the entrepreneurs are limitless.

The old rules simply do not work, and new rules must be devised to maintain order in international communications. Worldwide conferences of all varieties are being called by organization with interests in higher education, religion, law, and travel.

The computer industry has been using its opportunities to form businesses without the benefit of all the forms and licenses of government. This trend will continue. The various governments around the world are trying to think of ways to regulate and tax this enterprise. But the trouble is that techies who could possibly think of a way to collect a tax are employed by the computer companies and not by the government. That is the real reason that the Internet is escaping the tax man.

The first week in November finds a shift in attitude among the users of technology. No longer amused by the antics of hackers, they are insisting on regulations. Software developers have determined that ethics education is their priority. They also insist that international legal systems provide new methods of copyright enforcement.

Eclipse in Sagittarius

The December 14, 2001, eclipse at 23 degrees Sagittarius forced a lot of old-line industries to retool, therefore plants have given their employees an extra Christmas break. With bonuses to spend, extremely cheerful moods started us into the holiday season with high spirits.

Capricorn Ingress

The Capricorn ingress December 21, 2001, saw businesses begin the celebration with bonuses to their employees. Taxes, insurance, health and safety awards, and incentive bonuses that had accumulated throughout the year needed to be paid. Better than expected earnings meant larger dividends were due to the shareholders.

With plenty of cash for investments, the stock and bond markets will be good investments. Most investors will wait for their tax forms and then begin to set investment objectives. January will be dominated by creative investment suggestions. February and March will find people making decisions by adding to their portfolios. The Dow and other averages will climb throughout the spring and summer with only a few dips greater than 2 percent. However, September and October always put the market in a bearish mood. December holidays will witness a major tax sell-off. Investment opportunities abound if you are clever and choose wisely.

Aries Ingress

The Aries Ingress is March 20, 2002, and it foretells conditions concerning agriculture. There is more than enough rainfall, and some farmers give up trying to plant their crops. Last year's volcanic activity is the cause. Backyard gardeners are having the same problem with seeds washing away and the root systems of perennials rotting.

Food will cost more. Weather is the biggest concern, but wage inflation is the other problem for agriculture. Not only do farmers have to pay their temporary workers more, but they also have to pay higher interest on farm loans. Their crops command higher prices, but they have to grow first. Agriculture exports are in demand, but the exchange rate for currency is difficult to calculate and constantly fluctuating. Fortunately, farmers who have spent the winter studying wireless communications will be able to hedge the crops they can plant.

All of the market indexes are going up. The earnings reports in both the new and old economy are good. Most companies have enjoyed increased sales and profits. Investors are optimistic and anxious to buy. This type of run up in the markets also brings dishonest charlatans. Although these speculators are always present, this time they are forcing the rules to be rewritten. Too many people have horror stories of money lost to the unscrupulous scoundrels or due to plain stupidity. Thinking for yourself is required in this environment. Dreams and schemes are abundant. Make you own decisions about investments and don't quit your day job. There is plenty of advice available on line.

Manufactures of aerospace and military equipment are working hard to fill their orders. Engineers will need to redesign the systems that produce the energy that make the machines work. The domestic fleet requires new airplanes, and the congress and administration request military preparedness. North American peacekeeping units need armaments that discourage riots without injuring the rebels. Finally, there are enough incentives and young people to fill the ranks of the military.

The next few months will find various religious groups concerned about their aging leaders. Many will retire from public life and new leaders will be selected. Conventions will be convened specifically for that purpose. Pope John Paul II is among the group. It would be precedent setting if he retired. If he chooses to retire it will be during this, or the previous, Easter celebration.

Gemini Eclipse

The eclipse occurs on June 10, 2002, at 19 degrees Gemini (almost conjunct Saturn) and will be visible along the western coast of North America. The best view will be in Hawaii. Visible over the Pacific suggests weather problems, cyclones, volcanic eruptions, and earthquakes around the Ring of Fire.

Everyone is complaining that they are tired. They are tired of paperwork, housework, and especially tired of their boss. Family reunions, weddings, and graduations are exhausting. Folks want to escape. Vacation requests are the first order of business this week.

Folks are tired of commercial broadcasting. Equities in media corporations are suffering, advertising revenues are down, and the evening weather report is about the only reason people turn on the TV. Newspapers are available on the Internet, but radio stations are being turned on, instead, because they report on traffic conditions.

The market indexes usually go down right after an eclipse. This time it will last for about two weeks, and on then June 14 they will begin to inch up. The indexes are not tired, they are slowly setting new highs and adding new industries to their listings. The media describes these as "old techs" and "new techs," "old biotechs" and "new biotechs," etc.

The landscape of the brokerage industry has changed dramatically. Offices are used for teaching and seminars. Most trading is done on the Internet. Only a few elderly folks are trading stocks and bonds with a live broker.

This means the providers of electric power are required to maintain a steady supply.

North Americans are increasing their percentage of the world's wealth at a phenomenal rate. The actual currency is fluctuating with world news, but the real currency is market equities. They are stronger than ever. Revenues from taxes are at an all-time high in spite of cuts made during the past eighteen months. The various government agencies have no idea what to do with the money.

Cancer Ingress

The Sun's ingress into Cancer is June 21, 2002, and suddenly, the pressure is off. Stressful situations are resolving themselves. People refuse to listen to any more bickering or stupid arguments. Flowers proliferate across the landscape. Folks are involved in lots of activities with their friends. Entertainment events at outdoor theaters, concerts, fairs, and amusement parks are attracting large crowds. Everyone is excited to visit with their friends and neighbors, and their relatives.

Automobile and truck dealers are caught with an oversupply. The new and old models are very similar in design. People have shortened their road trips and simply do not need to replace their current vehicles. Also, the advice of friends is to keep the old one. Gadgets designed to make them safer, or more fuel-efficient, do not work as well as they should. Most folks do not have time to hassle with the service departments. Instead, they take their neighbor's advice and keep their old vehicles.

Imported technical labor is going home. The tech revolution has given these folks lots of entrepreneurial skills. They will seize new opportunities in their native lands, now that they have learned physical location is irrelevant. Technology specialists are changing the role of international partnerships. They have learned how to circumvent old business practices with technical skills.

Day traders and other gamblers are taking a time-out. There is not much action. All of the markets are fluctuating at less than 1 percent a week. Therefore it is boring. Even the casinos and racetracks are caught in a period of oversupply. High-rolling gamblers will not play when the pay-offs are too numerous and too small.

Decisions concerning Social Security have congressional lawmakers locked in serious debates. A healthy population that works smarter is pushing up the retirement age. New types of tax-deferred retirement

schemes are being introduced. The average investor is concerned about what are his or her real goals. Discussions center on the topic of funds allocation, as well as returns on investments. Advice is plentiful and people are thinking seriously about what they ought to do.

Libra Ingress

The Libra Ingress is September 23, 2002, and it describes our relationship with the rest of the world.

Behind the scenes the boardrooms of huge corporations are changing. More women are in positions of power. They are able to command higher salaries, stock options, and more perks. No longer in the shadow of a male mentors, these women have stepped out and taken command. But don't expect to see them in designer clothes pacing in front of a flow chart. Many haven't seen the boardroom since they were given a sightseeing tour of famous buildings twenty-five years ago. These women are last year's hands-on managers.

Another group of CEOs started the company on their own and it just kept growing. Their stories start at the kitchen table. They know how to inspire creative thinking, and they have invented their own rules. They understand their customers, and they know how to keep their employees on task. They have also taken the time to learn another language.

October is approaching and the stock market indexes are not going down. Volume, however, is low. The second week of October makes the bargain hunters happy, when share prices finally move down. Tax incentives, earnings reports, and international currency have all been favorable to the market. Sales of consumer goods and new machinery are strong but working with very thin profit margins. Spending on new equipment by government agencies is at the approval stage. Therefore companies are optimistic and anticipate future earnings will be great. But for now they aren't so good. Still, it isn't time to go bargain shopping for equities.

The dollar has finally forced other currencies to behave. Exports are up because business has found markets for used equipment. The trade deficit is low and more employers find employees through immigration to replace retiring skilled personnel.

Those who are successful and wealthy set the trends in what we wear. They will choose attire plain, loose attire made from natural fibers for the workplace. Clothing with designer signatures is definitely out of style. Shoes are custom-made in light colors and without heels. Eveningwear consists of flashy sleep shirts.

Sagittarius Eclipse

The total solar eclipse occurs at 11 degrees Sagittarius on December 4, 2002, and is not visible in North America. Southeast Africa and western Australia will have the best view from land. The effect of Indian Ocean winter storms will be a problem for both areas.

Romance is the theme for the next six months. Gold jewelry is a wonderful holiday gift and there will be a wide selection at bargain prices. Tickets to various musical and sporting events are plentiful and easy to obtain.

International markets are upset. Their averages appear to have dropped double-digit percentage points. This, of course, upsets American markets and they drop an equal number of percentage points. Every corporate officer assures the public that there is nothing to worry about. The accounting departments are fine and everything is under control. (It is a weird week.) Communications blunders seem to be everywhere, and sorting through misinformation is a challenge.

The old industries and the new industries have decided to get along together. They are working out their differences and designing new and better toys for all of us. New companies have taught the old ones how to save money and work efficiently. Old companies have taught the new ones how to sell their ideas to the public.

Retail is divesting itself of inventories. Evaluate your needs and start bargain shopping. Holiday merchandise will be marked down, as will all kinds of electronic devices. Mall owners finally realize they need to be creative with their real estate. The world of dot.coms can make them obsolete. Regional malls will find the need to specialize. Some will sell only furniture; others will offer apparel and shoes. Some will find ways to convert their space to offer convention space; venues for live entertainment, special events, or product demonstrations similar to those at a state fair.

Competition and new inventions have made a lot of things obsolete. Desktop computers are at the top of the list. Cell phones have been practically reinvented. Computer chips with all sorts of gimmicks embedded in them will be designed into every home appliance. They are tiny and cheap. Electronics and vehicles will be extremely different in 2004. If you anticipate the need for a new appliances or vehicles, start saving for them now.

Capricorn Ingress

The Capricorn Ingress is December 21, 2002. This ingress foretells the activities of business during the year ahead.

Anticipate a wet winter with snow shovels and rain gear in short supply. Check the house for cracks and leaks even if it is new. This will be a good year for visiting with the world via the Internet. (Cover the woodpile, though, just in case the electricity fails and you are reduced to using battery power.)

Equities have a difficult year ahead. Investors have turned conservative. Year-end bonuses will be earmarked for home improvements. Companies are spending their extra cash on research and industrial design. Marketing and advertising strategies will be changed throughout the year. Shareholders can expect their dividend checks will be much smaller.

Itty-bitty chips have changed industry, and it is time to retool. Therefore most manufacturing companies will spend their profits on designing new products. The new industries to watch are new energy sources, food service, accounting and consulting businesses. Financial institutions, banks, and brokerage houses are also growing. These very old companies have spent the last two years divesting themselves of obsolete

products and personnel. Many have merged with other financial groups to bring in new efficiencies and skilled employees.

Health care will move back home. Hospitals have determined that they are either trauma centers or diagnostic centers. With the help of tiny computer chips doctors will be able to monitor their patients from the golf course or the ski slopes.

Children are the focus of business throughout the year ahead. Their education is the major issue. Conventional wisdom holds that education through entertainment works. However, skilled labor is in very short supply, which requires workers with self-discipline. Business is demanding that the philosophy of educators change to allow skilled labor to share their knowledge. Cash rewards from business will be the incentive.

Editor's note: While there are others goods, services, and items that are ruled by the signs mentioned in this article, the lists are far too extensive to include here. If you are interested in knowing more about a specific sign or planet, Rex E. Bills *The Rulership Book* (American Federation of Astrologers, 1971) is an excellent resource.

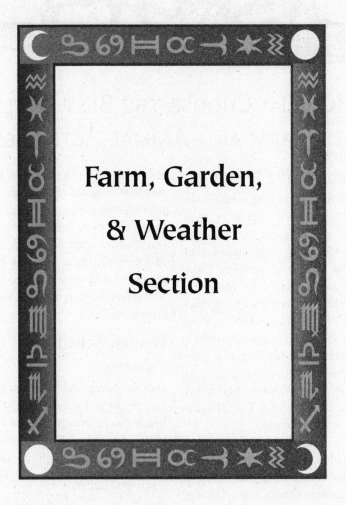

Farm, Garden,

& Weather

Section

How To Choose the Best Dates for Farm and Animal Activities

Animals and Breeding

Animals are easiest to handle when the Moon is in Taurus, Cancer, Libra, or Pisces, but try to void the Full Moon. Buy large animals when the Moon is in Sagittarius or Pisces, and making favorable aspects to Jupiter and Mercury. Buy animals smaller than sheep when the Moon is in Virgo with favorable aspects to Mercury or Venus. Neuter or spay animals in Sagittarius, Capricorn, or Pisces. Slaughter for food in the first three days after the Full Moon in any sign except Leo.

To encourage healthy births, eggs should be set and animals mated so births occur when the Moon is increasing in Taurus, Cancer, Pisces, or Libra. Those born during a semi-fruitful sign (Taurus and Capricorn) will produce leaner meat. Libra yields beautiful animals for showing and racing. To determine the best date to mate animals or set eggs, subtract the number of days given for incubation or gestation from the fruitful dates given in the following tables. For example, cats and dogs are mated sixty-three days previous to the desired birth date. See tables on pages 314.

Garden Activities

Cultivating

Cultivate when the Moon is in a barren sign and waning, ideally the fourth quarter in Aries, Gemini, Leo, Virgo, or Aquarius. Third quarter in the sign of Sagittarius will also work.

Cutting Timber

Cut timber during the third or fourth quarter in Taurus, Gemini, Virgo, or Capricorn—especially during the month of August. Look for favorable aspects to Mars.

Fertilize and Composting

Fertilize when the Moon is in a fruitful sign (Cancer, Scorpio, Pisces). Organic fertilizers are best when the Moon is waning, chemical fertilizers when the Moon is waxing. Start compost when the Moon is in the fourth quarter in a water sign.

Grafting

Graft during the first or second quarter Capricorn, Cancer, or Scorpio.

Harvesting Crops

Harvest root crops when the Moon is in a dry sign (Aries, Leo, Sagittarius, Gemini, or Aquarius) and waning. Harvest grain for storage just after Full Moon, avoiding water signs (Cancer, Scorpio, Pisces). Harvest in the third and fourth quarters in dry signs. Dry in the third quarter in fire signs.

Irrigation

Irrigate when the Moon is in Cancer, Scorpio, or Pisces.

Lawn Mowing

Mow in the first and second quarters (waxing phase) to increase growth and lushness, and in the third and fourth quarters (waning phase) to decrease growth.

Picking Mushrooms

Gather mushrooms at the Full Moon.

Planting

For complete instructions on planting by the Moon, see Gardening by the Moon on page 292, A Guide to Planting on page 299, Gardening Dates on page 304, and the Companion Planting Guide on page 316.

Pruning

Prune during the waning phase (third and fourth quarters) in Scorpio to retard growth and to promote better fruit, and in Capricorn to promote better healing.

Spraying and Weeding

Destroy pests and weeds during the fourth quarter when the Moon is in Leo or Aquarius, and making favorable aspects to Pluto. Weed during a waning Moon in a barren sign. For the best days to kill weeds and pests, see pages 310–311.

Weather

For complete weather forecasts for your zone for this year, see page 317.

GARDENING BY THE MOON

Today, people often reject the notion of Moon gardening. The usual nonbeliever is not a scientist, but the city dweller who has never had any real contact with nature and no experience of natural rhythms.

Camille Flammarian, the French astronomer, testifies to Moon planting: "Cucumbers increase at Full Moon, as well as radishes, turnips, leeks, lilies, horseradish, and saffron; onions, on the contrary, are much larger and better nourished during the decline and old age of the Moon than at its increase, during its youth and fullness, which is the reason the Egyptians abstained from onions, on account of their antipathy to the Moon. Herbs gathered while the Moon increases are of great efficiency. If the vines are trimmed at night when the Moon is in the sign of the Lion, Sagittarius, the Scorpion, or the Bull, it will save them from field rats, moles, snails, flies, and other animals."

Dr. Clark Timmins is one of the few modern scientists to have conducted tests in Moon planting. Following is a summary of his experiments:

Beets: When sown with the Moon in Scorpio, the germination rate was 71 percent; when sown in Sagittarius, the germination rate was 58 percent.

Scotch marigold: When sown with the Moon in Cancer, the germination rate was 90 percent; when sown in Leo, the rate was 32 percent.

Carrots: When sown with the Moon in Scorpio, the germination rate was 64 percent; when sown in Sagittarius, the germination rate was 47 percent.

Tomatoes: When sown with the Moon in Cancer, the germination rate was 90 percent; but when sown with the Moon in Leo, the germination rate was 58 percent.

Two things should be emphasized. First, remember that this is only a summary of the results of the experiments; the experiments themselves were conducted in a scientific manner to eliminate any variation in soil, temperature, moisture, and so on, so that only the Moon sign is varied. Second, note that these astonishing results were obtained without regard to the phase of the Moon—the other factor we use in Moon planting, and which presumably would have increased the differential in germination rates.

Further experiments by Dr. Timmins involved transplanting Cancer and Leo-planted tomato seedlings while the Moon was increasing and in Cancer. The result was 100 percent survival. When transplanting was done with the Moon decreasing and in Sagittarius, there was 0 percent survival. The results of Dr. Timmins' tests show that the Cancer-planted tomatoes had blossoms twelve days earlier than those planted under Leo; the Cancer-planted tomatoes had an average height of twenty inches at that time compare to fifteen inches for the Leo-planted; the first ripe

tomatoes were gathered from the Cancer plantings eleven days ahead of the Leo plantings; and a count of the hanging fruit and its size and weight shows an advantage to the Cancer plants over the Leo plants of 45 percent.

Dr. Timmins also observed that there have been similar tests that did not indicate results favorable to the Moon planting theory. As a scientist, he asked why one set of experiments indicated a positive verification of Moon planting, and others did not. He checked these other tests and found that the experimenters had not followed the geocentric system for determining the Moon sign positions, but the heliocentric. When the times used in these other tests were converted to the geocentric system, the dates chosen often were found to be in barren, rather than fertile, signs. Without going into a technical explanation, it is sufficient to point out that geocentric and heliocentric positions often vary by as much as four days. This is a large enough differential to place the Moon in Cancer, for example, in the heliocentric system, and at the same time in Leo by the geocentric system.

Most almanacs and calendars show the Moon's signs heliocentrically—and thus incorrectly for Moon planting—while the *Moon*

Sign Book is calculated correctly for planting purposes, using the geocentric system. Some readers are confused because the *Moon Sign Book* talks about first, second, third, and fourth quarters, while some almanacs refer to these same divisions as New Moon, first quarter, Full Moon, and fourth quarter. Thus the almanacs say first quarter when the *Moon Sign Book* says second quarter.

There is nothing complicated about using astrology in agriculture and horticulture in order to increase both pleasure and profit, but there is one very important rule that is often neglected—use common sense! Of course this is one rule that should be remembered in every activity we undertake, but in the case of gardening and farming by the Moon it is not possible to use the best dates for planting or harvesting, and we must select the next best and just try to do the best we can.

This brings up the matter of the other factors to consider in your gardening work. The dates we give as best for a certain activity apply to the entire country (with slight time correction), but in your section of the country you may be buried under three feet of snow on a date we say is good to plant your flowers. So we have factors of weather, season, temperature and moisture variations, soil conditions, your own available time and opportunity, and so forth. Some astrologers like to think it is all a matter of science, but gardening is also an art. In art, you develop an instinctive identification with your work and influence it with your feelings and wishes.

The *Moon Sign Book* gives you the place of the Moon for every day of the year so that you can select the best times once you have become familiar with the rules and practices of lunar agriculture. We give you specific, easy-to-follow directions so that you can get right down to work.

We give you the best dates for planting, and also for various related activities, including cultivation, fertilizing, harvesting, irrigation, and getting rid of weeds and pests. But we cannot tell you exactly when it's good to plant. Many of these rules were learned by observation and experience; as the body of experience grew we could see various patterns emerging that allowed us to make judgments about new things. That's what you should do, too. After you have worked with lunar agriculture for a while and have gained a working knowledge, you will probably begin to try new things—and we hope you will share your experiments and findings with us. That's how the science grows.

Here's an example of what we mean. Years ago, Llewellyn George suggested that we try to combine our bits of knowledge about what to expect in planting under each of the Moon signs in order to gain benefit from several lunar factors in one plant. From this came our rule for developing "thoroughbred seed." To develop thoroughbred seed, save the seed for three successive years from plants grown by the correct Moon sign and phase. You can plant in the first quarter phase and in the sign of Cancer for fruitfulness; the second year, plant seeds from the first year plants in Libra for beauty; and in the third year, plant the seeds from the second year plants in Taurus to produce hardiness. In a similar manner you can combine the fruitfulness of Cancer, the good root growth of Pisces, and the sturdiness and good vine growth of Scorpio. And don't forget the characteristics of Capricorn: hardy like Taurus, but

drier and perhaps more resistant to drought and disease.

Unlike common almanacs, we consider both the Moon's phase and the Moon's sign in making our calculations for the proper timing of our work. It is perhaps a little easier to understand this if we remind you that we are all living in the center of a vast electromagnetic field that is the Earth and its environment in space. Everything that occurs within this electromagnetic field has an effect on everything else within the field. The Moon and the Sun are the most important of the factors affecting the life of the Earth, and it is their relative positions to the Earth that we project for each day of the year.

Many people claim that not only do they achieve larger crops gardening by the Moon, but that their fruits and vegetables are much tastier. A number of organic gardeners have also become lunar gardeners using the natural rhythm of life forces that we experience through the relative movements of the Sun and Moon. We provide a few basic rules and then give you day-by-day guidance for your gardening work. You will be able to choose the best dates to meet your own needs and opportunities.

Planting by the Moon's Phases

During the increasing or waxing light—from New Moon to Full Moon—plant annuals that produce their yield above the ground. An annual is a plant that completes its entire life cycle within one growing season and has to be seeded each year. During the decreasing or waning light—from Full Moon to New Moon—plant biennials, perennials, and bulb and root plants. Biennials include crops that are planted one season to winter over and produce crops the next, such as winter wheat. Perennials and bulb and root plants include all plants that grow from the same root each year.

A simpler, less accurate rule is to plant crops that produce above the ground during the waxing Moon, and to plant crops that produce below the ground during the waning Moon. Thus the old adage, "Plant potatoes during the dark of the Moon." Llewellyn George's system divided the lunar month into quarters. The first two from New Moon to Full Moon are the first and second quarters, and the last two from Full Moon to New Moon the third and fourth quarters. Using these divisions, we can increase our accuracy in timing our efforts to coincide with natural forces.

First Quarter

Plant annuals producing their yield above the ground, which are generally of the leafy kind that produce their seed outside the fruit. Some examples are asparagus, broccoli, Brussels sprouts, cabbage, cauliflower, celery, cress, endive, kohlrabi, lettuce, parsley, and spinach. Cucumbers are an exception, as they do best in the first quarter rather than the second, even though the seeds are inside the fruit. Also plant cereals and grains.

Second Quarter

Plant annuals producing their yield above the ground, which are generally of the viney kind that produce their seed inside the fruit.

Examples include beans, eggplant, melons, peas, peppers, pumpkins, squash, tomatoes, etc. These are not hard- and-fast divisions. If you can't plant during the first quarter, plant during the second, and vice versa. There are many plants that seem to do equally well planted in either quarter, such as watermelon, hay, and cereals and grains.

Third Quarter

Plant biennials, perennials, and bulb and root plants. Also plant trees, shrubs, berries, beets, carrots, onions, parsnips, peanuts, potatoes, radishes, rhubarb, rutabagas, strawberries, turnips, winter wheat, grapes, etc.

Fourth Quarter

This is the best time to cultivate, turn sod, pull weeds, and destroy pests of all kinds, especially when the Moon is in the barren signs of Aries, Leo, Virgo, Gemini, Aquarius, and Sagittarius.

Moon in Aries

Barren, dry, fiery, and masculine sign used for destroying noxious weeds.

Moon in Taurus

Productive, moist, earthy, and feminine sign used for planting many crops when hardiness is important, particularly root crops. Also used

for lettuce, cabbage, and similar leafy vegetables.

Moon in Gemini

Barren and dry, airy and masculine sign used for destroying noxious growths, weeds, and pests, and for cultivation.

Moon in Cancer

Fruitful, moist, feminine sign is used extensively for planting and irrigation.

Moon in Leo

Barren, dry, fiery, masculine sign used only for killing weeds or for cultivation.

Moon in Virgo

Barren, moist, earthy, and feminine sign used for cultivation and destroying weeds and pests.

Moon in Libra

Semi-fruitful, moist, and airy, this sign is used for planting many crops, and producing good pulp growth and roots. A very good sign for flowers and vines. Also used for seeding hay, corn fodder, and the like.

Moon in Scorpio

Very fruitful and moist, watery and feminine. Nearly as productive as

Cancer; used for the same purposes. Especially good for vine growth and sturdiness.

Moon in Sagittarius

Barren and dry, fiery and masculine. Used for planting onions, seeding hay, and for cultivation.

Moon in Capricorn

Productive and dry, earthy and feminine. Used for planting potatoes and other tubers.

Moon in Aquarius

Barren, dry, airy, and masculine sign used for cultivation and destroying noxious growths and pests.

Moon in Pisces

Very fruitful, moist, watery, and feminine sign especially good for root growth.

A Guide to Planting

Using Phase & Sign Rulerships

Plant	Phase/Quarter	Sign
Annuals	1st or 2nd	
Apple trees	2nd or 3rd	Cancer, Pisces, Taurus, Virgo
Artichokes	1st	Cancer, Pisces
Asparagus	1st	Cancer, Scorpio, Pisces
Asters	1st or 2nd	Virgo, Libra
Barley	1st or 2nd	Cancer, Pisces, Libra, Capricorn, Virgo
Beans (bush & pole)	2nd	Cancer, Taurus, Pisces, Libra
Beans (kidney, white, & navy)	1st or 2nd	Cancer, Pisces
Beech Trees	2nd or 3rd	Virgo, Taurus
Beets	3rd	Cancer, Capricorn, Pisces, Libra
Biennials	3rd or 4th	
Broccoli	1st	Cancer, Pisces, Libra, Scorpio
Brussels Sprouts	1st	Cancer, Scorpio, Pisces, Libra
Buckwheat	1st or 2nd	Capricorn
Bulbs	3rd	Cancer, Scorpio, Pisces
Bulbs for Seed	2nd or 3rd	
Cabbage	1st	Cancer, Scorpio, Pisces, Libra, Taurus

Plant	Phase/Quarter	Sign
Cactus		Taurus, Capricorn
Canes (raspberries, blackberries, and gooseberries)	2nd	Cancer, Scorpio, Pisces
Cantaloupes	1st or 2nd	Cancer, Scorpio, Pisces, Libra, Taurus
Carrots	3rd	Taurus, Cancer, Scorpio, Pisces, Libra
Cauliflower	1st	Cancer, Scorpio, Pisces, Libra
Celeriac	3rd	Cancer, Scorpio, Pisces
Celery	1st	Cancer, Scorpio, Pisces
Cereals	1st or 2nd	Cancer, Scorpio, Pisces, Libra
Chard	1st or 2nd	Cancer, Scorpio, Pisces
Chicory	2nd, 3rd	Cancer, Scorpio, Pisces
Chrysanthemums	1st or 2nd	Virgo
Clover	1st or 2nd	Cancer, Scorpio, Pisces
Corn	1st	Cancer, Scorpio, Pisces
Corn for Fodder	1st or 2nd	Libra
Coryopsis	2nd or 3rd	Libra
Cosmos	2nd or 3rd	Libra
Cress	1st	Cancer, Scorpio, Pisces
Crocus	1st or 2nd	Virgo
Cucumbers	1st	Cancer, Scorpio, Pisces

Plant	Phase/Quarter	Sign
Daffodils	1st or 2nd	Libra, Virgo
Dahlias	1st or 2nd	Libra, Virgo
Deciduous Trees	2nd or 3rd	Cancer, Scorpio, Pisces, Virgo, Taurus
Eggplant	2nd	Cancer, Scorpio, Pisces, Libra
Endive	1st	Cancer, Scorpio, Pisces, Libra
Flowers	1st	Libra, Cancer, Pisces, Virgo, Scorpio, Taurus
Garlic	3rd	Libra, Taurus, Pisces
Gladiola	1st or 2nd	Libra, Virgo
Gourds	1st or 2nd	Cancer, Scorpio, Pisces, Libra
Grapes	2nd or 3rd	Cancer, Scorpio, Pisces, Virgo
Hay	1st or 2nd	Cancer, Scorpio, Pisces, Libra, Taurus
Herbs	1st or 2nd	Cancer, Scorpio, Pisces
Honeysuckle	1st or 2nd	Scorpio, Virgo
Hops	1st or 2nd	Scorpio, Libra
Horseradish	1st or 2nd	Cancer, Scorpio, Pisces
House Plants	1st	Libra, Cancer, Scorpio, Pisces
Hyacinths	3rd	Cancer, Scorpio, Pisces
Iris	1st or 2nd	Cancer, Virgo
Kohlrabi	1st or 2nd	Cancer, Scorpio, Pisces, Libra

Plant	Phase/Quarter	Sign
Peonies	1st or 2nd	Virgo
Peppers	2nd	Cancer, Pisces, Scorpio
Perennials	3rd	
Petunias	1st or 2nd	Libra, Virgo
Plum Trees	2nd or 3rd	Taurus, Virgo, Cancer, Pisces
Poppies	1st or 2nd	Virgo
Portulaca	1st or 2nd	Virgo
Potatoes	3rd	Cancer, Scorpio, Taurus, Libra, Capricorn
Privet	1st or 2nd	Taurus, Libra
Pumpkins	2nd	Cancer, Scorpio, Pisces, Libra
Quinces	1st or 2nd	Capricorn
Radishes	3rd	Cancer, Libra, Taurus, Pisces, Capricorn
Rhubarb	3rd	Cancer, Pisces
Rice	1st or 2nd	Scorpio
Roses	1st or 2nd	Cancer, Virgo
Rutabagas	3rd	Cancer, Scorpio, Pisces, Taurus
Saffron	1st or 2nd	Cancer, Scorpio, Pisces
Sage	3rd	Cancer, Scorpio, Pisces
Salsify	1st or 2nd	Cancer, Scorpio, Pisces

Plant	Phase/Quarter	Sign
Shallots	2nd	Scorpio
Spinach	1st	Cancer, Scorpio, Pisces
Squash	2nd	Cancer, Scorpio, Pisces, Libra
Strawberries	3rd	Cancer, Scorpio, Pisces
String Beans	1st or 2nd	Taurus
Sunflowers	1st or 2nd	Libra, Cancer
Sweet Peas	1st or 2nd	Cancer, Scorpio, Pisces
Tomatoes	2nd	Cancer, Scorpio, Pisces, Capricorn
Shade Trees	3rd	Taurus, Capricorn
Ornamental Trees	2nd	Libra, Taurus
Trumpet Vines	1st or 2nd	Cancer, Scorpio, Pisces
Tubers for Seed	3rd	Cancer, Scorpio, Pisces, Libra
Tulips	1st or 2nd	Libra, Virgo
Turnips	3rd	Cancer, Scorpio, Pisces, Taurus, Capricorn, Libra
Valerian	1st or 2nd	Virgo, Gemini
Watermelons	1st or 2nd	Cancer, Scorpio, Pisces, Libra
Wheat	1st or 2nd	Cancer, Scorpio, Pisces, Libra

2002 Gardening Dates

Dates	Qtr	Sign	Activity
Jan. 2, 6:34 pm– Jan. 4, 8:23 pm	3rd	Virgo	Cultivate, especially medicinal plants. Destroy weeds and pests. Trim to retard growth.
Jan. 6, 11:41 pm– Jan. 9, 4:57 am	4th	Scorpio	Plant biennials, perennials, bulbs and roots. Prune. Irrigate. Fertilize (organic).
Jan. 9, 4:57 am– Jan. 11, 12:18 pm	4th	Sagittarius	Cultivate. Destroy weeds and pests. Harvest fruits and root crops for food. Trim to retard growth.
Jan. 11, 12:18 pm– Jan. 13, 8:29 am	4th	Capricorn	Plant potatoes and tubers. Trim to retard growth.
Jan. 13, 8:29 am– Jan. 13, 9:41 pm	1st	Capricorn	Graft or bud plants. Trim to increase growth.
Jan. 16, 9:00 am– Jan. 18, 9:35 pm	1st	Pisces	Plant grains, leafy annuals. Fertilize (chemical). Graft or bud plants. Irrigate. Trim to increase growth.
Jan. 21, 9:47 am– Jan. 21, 12:47 pm	1st	Taurus	Plant annuals for hardiness. Trim to increase growth.
Jan. 21, 12:47 pm– Jan. 23, 7:28 pm	2nd	Taurus	Plant annuals for hardiness. Trim to increase growth.
Jan. 26, 1:17 am– Jan. 28, 3:31 am	2nd	Cancer	Plant grains, leafy annuals. Fertilize (chemical). Graft or bud plants. Irrigate. Trim to increase growth.
Jan. 28, 5:50 pm– Jan. 30, 3:40 am	3rd	Leo	Cultivate. Destroy weeds and pests. Harvest fruits and root crops for food. Trim to retard growth.
Jan. 30, 3:40 am– Feb. 1, 3:44 am	3rd	Virgo	Cultivate, especially medicinal plants. Destroy weeds and pests. Trim to retard growth.
Feb. 3, 5:35 am– Feb. 4, 8:33 am	3rd	Scorpio	Plant biennials, perennials, bulbs and roots. Prune. Irrigate. Fertilize (organic).
Feb. 4, 8:33 am– Feb. 5, 10:21 am	4th	Scorpio	Plant biennials, perennials, bulbs and roots. Prune. Irrigate. Fertilize (organic).
Feb. 5, 10:21 am– Feb. 7, 6:08 pm	4th	Sagittarius	Cultivate. Destroy weeds and pests. Harvest fruits and root crops for food. Trim to retard growth.
Feb. 7, 6:08 pm– Feb. 10, 4:15 am	4th	Capricorn	Plant potatoes and tubers. Trim to retard growth.
Feb. 10, 4:15 am– Feb. 12, 2:41 am	4th	Aquarius	Cultivate. Destroy weeds and pests. Harvest fruits and root crops for food. Trim to retard growth.
Feb. 12, 3:53 pm– Feb. 15, 4:26 am	1st	Pisces	Plant grains, leafy annuals. Fertilize (chemical). Graft or bud plants. Irrigate. Trim to increase growth.
Feb. 17, 4:58 pm– Feb. 20, 3:50 am	1st	Taurus	Plant annuals for hardiness. Trim to increase growth.
Feb. 22, 11:16 am– Feb. 24, 2:36 pm	2nd	Cancer	Plant grains, leafy annuals. Fertilize (chemical). Graft or bud plants. Irrigate. Trim to increase growth.

Dates	Qtr	Sign	Activity
Feb. 27, 4:17 am– Feb. 28, 1:47 pm	3rd	Virgo	Cultivate, especially medicinal plants. Destroy weeds and pests. Trim to retard growth.
Mar. 2, 1:51 pm– Mar. 4, 4:55 pm	3rd	Scorpio	Plant biennials, perennials, bulbs and roots. Prune. Irrigate. Fertilize (organic).
Mar. 4, 4:55 pm– Mar. 5, 8:25 pm	3rd	Sagittarius	Cultivate. Destroy weeds and pests. Harvest fruits and root crops for food. Trim to retard growth.
Mar. 5, 8:25 pm– Mar. 6, 11:48 pm	4th	Sagittarius	Cultivate. Destroy weeds and pests. Harvest fruits and root crops for food. Trim to retard growth.
Mar. 6, 11:48 pm– Mar. 9, 9:56 am	4th	Capricorn	Plant potatoes and tubers. Trim to retard growth.
Mar. 9, 9:56 am– Mar. 11, 9:56 pm	4th	Aquarius	Cultivate. Destroy weeds and pests. Harvest fruits and root crops for food. Trim to retard growth.
Mar. 11, 9:56 pm– Mar. 13, 9:03 pm	4th	Pisces	Plant biennials, perennials, bulbs and roots. Prune. Irrigate. Fertilize (organic).
Mar. 13, 9:03 pm– Mar. 14, 10:34 am	1st	Pisces	Plant grains, leafy annuals. Fertilize (chemical). Graft or bud plants. Irrigate. Trim to increase growth.
Mar. 16, 11:01 pm– Mar. 19, 10:20 am	1st	Taurus	Plant annuals for hardiness. Trim to increase growth.
Mar. 21, 7:06 pm– Mar. 21, 9:28 pm	1st	Cancer	Plant grains, leafy annuals. Fertilize (chemical). Graft or bud plants. Irrigate. Trim to increase growth.
Mar. 21, 9:28 pm– Mar. 24, 12:12 am	2nd	Cancer	Plant grains, leafy annuals. Fertilize (chemical). Graft or bud plants. Irrigate. Trim to increase growth.
Mar. 28, 1:04 am– Mar. 28, 1:25 pm	2nd	Libra	Plant annuals for fragrance and beauty. Trim to increase growth.
Mar. 30, 12:21 am– Apr. 1, 1:48 am	3rd	Scorpio	Plant biennials, perennials, bulbs and roots. Prune. Irrigate. Fertilize (organic).
Apr. 1, 1:48 am– Apr. 3, 6:58 am	3rd	Sagittarius	Cultivate. Destroy weeds and pests. Harvest fruits and root crops for food. Trim to retard growth.
Apr. 3, 6:58 am– Apr. 4, 10:29 am	3rd	Capricorn	Plant potatoes and tubers. Trim to retard growth.
Apr. 4, 10:29 am– Apr. 5, 4:07 pm	4th	Capricorn	Plant potatoes and tubers. Trim to retard growth.
Apr. 5, 4:07 pm– Apr. 8, 3:57 am	4th	Aquarius	Cultivate. Destroy weeds and pests. Harvest fruits and root crops for food. Trim to retard growth.
Apr. 8, 3:57 am– Apr. 10, 4:40 pm	4th	Pisces	Plant biennials, perennials, bulbs and roots. Prune. Irrigate. Fertilize (organic).
Apr. 10, 4:40 pm– Apr. 12, 2:21 pm	4th	Aries	Cultivate. Destroy weeds and pests. Harvest fruits and root crops for food. Trim to retard growth.

Dates	Qtr	Sign	Activity
Apr. 13, 4:55 am- Apr. 15, 3:56 pm	1st	Taurus	Plant annuals for hardiness. Trim to increase growth.
Apr. 18, 1:01 am- Apr. 20, 7:20 am	1st	Cancer	Plant grains, leafy annuals. Fertilize (chemical). Graft or bud plants. Irrigate. Trim to increase growth.
Apr. 24, 11:22 am- Apr. 26, 11:15 am	2nd	Libra	Plant annuals for fragrance and beauty. Trim to increase growth.
Apr. 26, 11:15 am- Apr. 26, 10:00 pm	2nd	Scorpio	Plant grains, leafy annuals. Fertilize (chemical). Graft or bud plants. Irrigate. Trim to increase growth.
Apr. 26, 10:00 pm- Apr. 28, 12:13 pm	3rd	Scorpio	Plant biennials, perennials, bulbs and roots. Prune. Irrigate. Fertilize (organic).
Apr. 28, 12:13 pm- Apr. 30, 4:03 pm	3rd	Sagittarius	Cultivate. Destroy weeds and pests. Harvest fruits and root crops for food. Trim to retard growth.
Apr. 30, 4:03 pm- May 2, 11:43 pm	3rd	Capricorn	Plant potatoes and tubers. Trim to retard growth.
May 2, 11:43 pm- May 4, 2:16 am	3rd	Aquarius	Cultivate. Destroy weeds and pests. Harvest fruits and root crops for food. Trim to retard growth.
May 4, 2:16 am- May 5, 10:46 am	4th	Aquarius	Cultivate. Destroy weeds and pests. Harvest fruits and root crops for food. Trim to retard growth.
May 5, 10:46 am- May 7, 11:22 pm	4th	Pisces	Plant biennials, perennials, bulbs and roots. Prune. Irrigate. Fertilize (organic).
May 7, 11:22 pm- May 10, 11:32 am	4th	Aries	Cultivate. Destroy weeds and pests. Harvest fruits and root crops for food. Trim to retard growth.
May 10, 11:32 am- May 12, 5:45 am	4th	Taurus	Plant potatoes and tubers. Trim to retard growth.
May 12, 5:45 am- May 12, 10:04 pm	1st	Taurus	Plant annuals for hardiness. Trim to increase growth.
May 15, 6:33 am- May 17, 12:52 pm	1st	Cancer	Plant grains, leafy annuals. Fertilize (chemical). Graft or bud plants. Irrigate. Trim to increase growth.
May 21, 7:19 pm- May 23, 8:38 pm	2nd	Libra	Plant annuals for fragrance and beauty. Trim to increase growth.
May 23, 8:38 pm- May 25, 10:20 pm	2nd	Scorpio	Plant grains, leafy annuals. Fertilize (chemical). Graft or bud plants. Irrigate. Trim to increase growth.
May 26, 6:51 am- May 28, 1:54 am	3rd	Sagittarius	Cultivate. Destroy weeds and pests. Harvest fruits and root crops for food. Trim to retard growth.
May 28, 1:54 am- May 30, 8:35 am	3rd	Capricorn	Plant potatoes and tubers. Trim to retard growth.
May 30, 8:35 am- Jun. 1, 6:37 pm	3rd	Aquarius	Cultivate. Destroy weeds and pests. Harvest fruits and root crops for food. Trim to retard growth.

Dates	Qtr	Sign	Activity
Jun. 1, 6:37 pm- Jun. 2, 7:05 pm	3rd	Pisces	Plant biennials, perennials, bulbs and roots. Prune. Irrigate. Fertilize (organic).
Jun. 2, 7:05 pm- Jun. 4, 6:51 am	4th	Pisces	Plant biennials, perennials, bulbs and roots. Prune. Irrigate. Fertilize (organic).
Jun. 4, 6:51 am- Jun. 6, 7:07 pm	4th	Aries	Cultivate. Destroy weeds and pests. Harvest fruits and root crops for food. Trim to retard growth.
Jun. 6, 7:07 pm- Jun. 9, 5:29 am	4th	Taurus	Plant potatoes and tubers. Trim to retard growth.
Jun. 9, 5:29 am- Jun. 10, 6:46 pm	4th	Gemini	Cultivate. Destroy weeds and pests. Harvest fruits and root crops for food. Trim to retard growth.
Jun. 11, 1:15 pm- Jun. 13, 6:39 pm	1st	Cancer	Plant grains, leafy annuals. Fertilize (chemical). Graft or bud plants. Irrigate. Trim to increase growth.
Jun. 18, 1:11 am- Jun. 20, 3:42 am	2nd	Libra	Plant annuals for fragrance and beauty. Trim to increase growth.
Jun. 20, 3:42 am- Jun. 22, 6:42 am	2nd	Scorpio	Plant grains, leafy annuals. Fertilize (chemical). Graft or bud plants. Irrigate. Trim to increase growth.
Jun. 24, 11:01 am- Jun. 24, 4:42 pm	2nd	Capricorn	Graft or bud plants. Trim to increase growth.
Jun. 24, 4:42 pm- Jun. 26, 5:36 pm	3rd	Capricorn	Plant potatoes and tubers. Trim to retard growth.
Jun. 26, 5:36 pm- Jun. 29, 3:00 am	3rd	Aquarius	Cultivate. Destroy weeds and pests. Harvest fruits and root crops for food. Trim to retard growth.
Jun. 29, 3:00 am- Jul. 1, 2:49 pm	3rd	Pisces	Plant biennials, perennials, bulbs and roots. Prune. Irrigate. Fertilize (organic).
Jul. 1, 2:49 pm- Jul. 2, 12:19 pm	3rd	Aries	Cultivate. Destroy weeds and pests. Harvest fruits and root crops for food. Trim to retard growth.
Jul. 2, 12:19 pm- Jul. 4, 3:16 am	4th	Aries	Cultivate. Destroy weeds and pests. Harvest fruits and root crops for food. Trim to retard growth.
Jul. 4, 3:16 am- Jul. 6, 2:01 pm	4th	Taurus	Plant potatoes and tubers. Trim to retard growth.
Jul. 6, 2:01 pm- Jul. 8, 9:36 pm	4th	Gemini	Cultivate. Destroy weeds and pests. Harvest fruits and root crops for food. Trim to retard growth.
Jul. 8, 9:36 pm- Jul. 10, 5:26 am	4th	Cancer	Plant biennials, perennials, bulbs and roots. Prune. Irrigate. Fertilize (organic).
Jul. 10, 5:26 am- Jul. 11, 2:08 am	1st	Cancer	Plant grains, leafy annuals. Fertilize (chemical). Graft or bud plants. Irrigate. Trim to increase growth.
Jul. 15, 6:39 am- Jul. 16, 11:47 pm	1st	Libra	Plant annuals for fragrance and beauty. Trim to increase growth.

Dates	Qtr	Sign	Activity
Jul. 16, 11:47 pm– Jul. 17, 9:13 am	2nd	Libra	Plant annuals for fragrance and beauty. Trim to increase growth.
Jul. 17, 9:13 am– Jul. 19, 1:02 pm	2nd	Scorpio	Plant grains, leafy annuals. Fertilize (chemical). Graft or bud plants. Irrigate. Trim to increase growth.
Jul. 21, 6:26 pm– Jul. 24, 1:40 am	2nd	Capricorn	Graft or bud plants. Trim to increase growth.
Jul. 24, 4:07 am– Jul. 26, 11:04 am	3rd	Aquarius	Cultivate. Destroy weeds and pests. Harvest fruits and root crops for food. Trim to retard growth.
Jul. 26, 11:04 am– Jul. 28, 10:39 pm	3rd	Pisces	Plant biennials, perennials, bulbs and roots. Prune. Irrigate. Fertilize (organic).
Jul. 28, 10:39 pm– Jul. 31, 11:17 am	3rd	Aries	Cultivate. Destroy weeds and pests. Harvest fruits and root crops for food. Trim to retard growth.
Jul. 31, 11:17 am– Aug. 1, 5:22 am	3rd	Taurus	Plant potatoes and tubers. Trim to retard growth.
Aug. 1, 5:22 am– Aug. 2, 10:46 pm	4th	Taurus	Plant potatoes and tubers. Trim to retard growth.
Aug. 2, 10:46 pm– Aug. 5, 7:02 am	4th	Gemini	Cultivate. Destroy weeds and pests. Harvest fruits and root crops for food. Trim to retard growth.
Aug. 5, 7:02 am– Aug. 7, 11:27 am	4th	Cancer	Plant biennials, perennials, bulbs and roots. Prune. Irrigate. Fertilize (organic).
Aug. 7, 11:27 am– Aug. 8, 2:15 pm	4th	Leo	Cultivate. Destroy weeds and pests. Harvest fruits and root crops for food. Trim to retard growth.
Aug. 11, 1:38 pm– Aug. 13, 3:01 pm	1st	Libra	Plant annuals for fragrance and beauty. Trim to increase growth.
Aug. 13, 3:01 pm– Aug. 15, 5:12 am	1st	Scorpio	Plant grains, leafy annuals. Fertilize (chemical). Graft or bud plants. Irrigate. Trim to increase growth.
Aug. 15, 5:12 am– Aug. 15, 6:25 pm	2nd	Scorpio	Plant grains, leafy annuals. Fertilize (chemical). Graft or bud plants. Irrigate. Trim to increase growth.
Aug. 18, 12:15 am– Aug. 20, 8:16 am	2nd	Capricorn	Graft or bud plants. Trim to increase growth.
Aug. 22, 5:29 pm– Aug. 22, 6:11 pm	3rd	Aquarius	Cultivate. Destroy weeds and pests. Harvest fruits and root crops for food. Trim to retard growth.
Aug. 22, 6:11 pm– Aug. 25, 5:48 am	3rd	Pisces	Plant biennials, perennials, bulbs and roots. Prune. Irrigate. Fertilize (organic).
Aug. 25, 5:48 am– Aug. 27, 6:32 pm	3rd	Aries	Cultivate. Destroy weeds and pests. Harvest fruits and root crops for food. Trim to retard growth.
Aug. 27, 6:32 pm– Aug. 30, 6:45 am	3rd	Taurus	Plant potatoes and tubers. Trim to retard growth.

Dates	Qtr	Sign	Activity
Aug. 30, 6:45 am– Aug. 30, 9:31 pm	3rd	Gemini	Cultivate. Destroy weeds and pests. Harvest fruits and root crops for food. Trim to retard growth.
Aug. 30, 9:31 pm– Sep. 1, 4:14 pm	4th	Gemini	Cultivate. Destroy weeds and pests. Harvest fruits and root crops for food. Trim to retard growth.
Sep. 1, 4:14 pm– Sep. 3, 9:36 pm	4th	Cancer	Plant biennials, perennials, bulbs and roots. Prune. Irrigate. Fertilize (organic).
Sep. 3, 9:36 pm– Sep. 5, 11:16 pm	4th	Leo	Cultivate. Destroy weeds and pests. Harvest fruits and root crops for food. Trim to retard growth.
Sep. 5, 11:16 pm– Sep. 6, 10:10 pm	4th	Virgo	Cultivate, especially medicinal plants. Destroy weeds and pests. Trim to retard growth.
Sep. 7, 10:57 pm– Sep. 9, 10:48 pm	1st	Libra	Plant annuals for fragrance and beauty. Trim to increase growth.
Sep. 9, 10:48 pm– Sep. 12, 12:44 am	1st	Scorpio	Plant grains, leafy annuals. Fertilize (chemical). Graft or bud plants. Irrigate. Trim to increase growth.
Sep. 14, 5:47 am– Sep. 16, 1:54 pm	2nd	Capricorn	Graft or bud plants. Trim to increase growth.
Sep. 19, 12:18 am– Sep. 21, 8:59 am	2nd	Pisces	Plant grains, leafy annuals. Fertilize (chemical). Graft or bud plants. Irrigate. Trim to increase growth.
Sep. 21, 8:59 am– Sep. 21, 12:11 pm	3rd	Pisces	Plant biennials, perennials, bulbs and roots. Prune. Irrigate. Fertilize (organic).
Sep. 21, 12:11 pm– Sep. 24, 12:55 am	3rd	Aries	Cultivate. Destroy weeds and pests. Harvest fruits and root crops for food. Trim to retard growth.
Sep. 24, 12:55 am– Sep. 26, 1:26 pm	3rd	Taurus	Plant potatoes and tubers. Trim to retard growth.
Sep. 26, 1:26 pm– Sep. 29, 12:01 am	3rd	Gemini	Cultivate. Destroy weeds and pests. Harvest fruits and root crops for food. Trim to retard growth.
Sep. 29, 12:01 am– Sep. 29, 12:03 pm	3rd	Cancer	Plant biennials, perennials, bulbs and roots. Prune. Irrigate. Fertilize (organic).
Sep. 29, 12:03 pm– Oct. 1, 6:58 am	4th	Cancer	Plant biennials, perennials, bulbs and roots. Prune. Irrigate. Fertilize (organic).
Oct. 1, 6:58 am– Oct. 3, 9:52 pm	4th	Leo	Cultivate. Destroy weeds and pests. Harvest fruits and root crops for food. Trim to retard growth.
Oct. 3, 9:52 pm– Oct. 5, 9:51 pm	4th	Virgo	Cultivate, especially medicinal plants. Destroy weeds and pests. Trim to retard growth.
Oct. 6, 6:18 am– Oct. 7, 8:57 am	1st	Libra	Plant annuals for fragrance and beauty. Trim to increase growth.
Oct. 7, 8:57 am– Oct. 9, 9:21 am	1st	Scorpio	Plant grains, leafy annuals. Fertilize (chemical). Graft or bud plants. Irrigate. Trim to increase growth.

Dates	Qtr	Sign	Activity
Oct. 11, 12:45 pm– Oct. 13, 12:33 am	1st	Capricorn	Graft or bud plants. Trim to increase growth.
Oct. 13, 12:33 am– Oct. 13, 7:51 pm	2nd	Capricorn	Graft or bud plants. Trim to increase growth.
Oct. 16, 6:07 am– Oct. 18, 6:13 pm	2nd	Pisces	Plant grains, leafy annuals. Fertilize (chemical). Graft or bud plants. Irrigate. Trim to increase growth.
Oct. 21, 2:20 am– Oct. 21, 6:57 am	3rd	Aries	Cultivate. Destroy weeds and pests. Harvest fruits and root crops for food. Trim to retard growth.
Oct. 21, 6:57 am– Oct. 23, 7:17 pm	3rd	Taurus	Plant potatoes and tubers. Trim to retard growth.
Oct. 23, 7:17 pm– Oct. 26, 6:10 am	3rd	Gemini	Cultivate. Destroy weeds and pests. Harvest fruits and root crops for food. Trim to retard growth.
Oct. 26, 6:10 am– Oct. 28, 2:20 pm	3rd	Cancer	Plant biennials, perennials, bulbs and roots. Prune. Irrigate. Fertilize (organic).
Oct. 28, 2:20 pm– Oct. 29, 12:28 am	3rd	Leo	Cultivate. Destroy weeds and pests. Harvest fruits and root crops for food. Trim to retard growth.
Oct. 29, 12:28 am– Oct. 30, 6:59 pm	4th	Leo	Cultivate. Destroy weeds and pests. Harvest fruits and root crops for food. Trim to retard growth.
Oct. 30, 6:59 pm– Nov. 1, 8:28 pm	4th	Virgo	Cultivate, especially medicinal plants. Destroy weeds and pests. Trim to retard growth.
Nov. 3, 8:10 pm– Nov. 4, 3:34 pm	4th	Scorpio	Plant biennials, perennials, bulbs and roots. Prune. Irrigate. Fertilize (organic).
Nov. 4, 3:34 pm– Nov. 5, 8:01 pm	1st	Scorpio	Plant grains, leafy annuals. Fertilize (chemical). Graft or bud plants. Irrigate. Trim to increase growth.
Nov. 7, 9:59 pm– Nov. 10, 3:27 am	1st	Capricorn	Graft or bud plants. Trim to increase growth.
Nov. 12, 12:42 pm– Nov. 15, 12:38 am	2nd	Pisces	Plant grains, leafy annuals. Fertilize (chemical). Graft or bud plants. Irrigate. Trim to increase growth.
Nov. 17, 1:23 pm– Nov. 19, 8:34 pm	2nd	Taurus	Plant annuals for hardiness. Trim to increase growth.
Nov. 19, 8:34 pm– Nov. 20, 1:25 am	3rd	Taurus	Plant potatoes and tubers. Trim to retard growth.
Nov. 20, 1:25 am– Nov. 22, 11:48 am	3rd	Gemini	Cultivate. Destroy weeds and pests. Harvest fruits and root crops for food. Trim to retard growth.
Nov. 22, 11:48 am– Nov. 24, 8:00 pm	3rd	Cancer	Plant biennials, perennials, bulbs and roots. Prune. Irrigate. Fertilize (organic).
Nov. 24, 8:00 pm– Nov. 27, 1:42 am	3rd	Leo	Cultivate. Destroy weeds and pests. Harvest fruits and root crops for food. Trim to retard growth.

Dates	Qtr	Sign	Activity
Nov. 27, 1:42 am– Nov. 27, 10:46 am	3rd	Virgo	Cultivate, especially medicinal plants. Destroy weeds and pests. Trim to retard growth.
Nov. 27, 10:46 am– Nov. 29, 4:54 am	4th	Virgo	Cultivate, especially medicinal plants. Destroy weeds and pests. Trim to retard growth.
Dec. 1, 6:15 am– Dec. 3, 6:58 am	4th	Scorpio	Plant biennials, perennials, bulbs and roots. Prune. Irrigate. Fertilize (organic).
Dec. 3, 6:58 am– Dec. 4, 2:34 am	4th	Sagittarius	Cultivate. Destroy weeds and pests. Harvest fruits and root crops for food. Trim to retard growth.
Dec. 5, 8:39 am– Dec. 7, 12:54 pm	1st	Capricorn	Graft or bud plants. Trim to increase growth.
Dec. 9, 8:46 pm– Dec. 11, 10:49 am	1st	Pisces	Plant grains, leafy annuals. Fertilize (chemical). Graft or bud plants. Irrigate. Trim to increase growth.
Dec. 11, 10:49 am– Dec. 12, 7:58 am	2nd	Pisces	Plant grains, leafy annuals. Fertilize (chemical). Graft or bud plants. Irrigate. Trim to increase growth.
Dec. 14, 8:43 pm– Dec. 17, 8:43 am	2nd	Taurus	Plant annuals for hardiness. Trim to increase growth.
Dec. 19, 2:10 pm– Dec. 19, 6:30 pm	3rd	Gemini	Cultivate. Destroy weeds and pests. Harvest fruits and root crops for food. Trim to retard growth.
Dec. 19, 6:30 pm– Dec. 22, 1:48 am	3rd	Cancer	Plant biennials, perennials, bulbs and roots. Prune. Irrigate. Fertilize (organic).
Dec. 22, 1:48 am– Dec. 24, 7:05 am	3rd	Leo	Cultivate. Destroy weeds and pests. Harvest fruits and root crops for food. Trim to retard growth.
Dec. 24, 7:05 am– Dec. 26, 10:53 am	3rd	Virgo	Cultivate, especially medicinal plants. Destroy weeds and pests. Trim to retard growth.
Dec. 28, 1:41 pm– Dec. 30, 4:01 pm	4th	Scorpio	Plant biennials, perennials, bulbs and roots. Prune. Irrigate. Fertilize (organic).

2002 Dates to Destroy Weeds & Pests

Jan. 2	6:34 pm	Jan. 4	8:23 pm	Virgo	3rd
Jan. 9	4:57 am	Jan. 11	12:18 pm	Sagittarius	4th
Jan. 28	5:50 pm	Jan. 30	3:40 am	Leo	3rd
Jan. 30	3:40 am	Feb. 1	3:44 am	Virgo	3rd
Feb. 5	10:21 am	Feb. 7	6:08 pm	Sagittarius	4th
Feb. 10	4:15 am	Feb. 12	2:41 am	Aquarius	4th
Feb. 27	4:17 am	Feb. 28	1:47 pm	Virgo	3rd
Mar. 4	4:55 pm	Mar. 5	8:25 pm	Sagittarius	3rd
Mar. 5	8:25 pm	Mar. 6	11:48 pm	Sagittarius	4th
Mar. 9	9:56 am	Mar. 11	9:56 pm	Aquarius	4th
Apr. 1	1:48 am	Apr. 3	6:58 am	Sagittarius	3rd
Apr. 5	4:07 pm	Apr. 8	3:57 am	Aquarius	4th
Apr. 10	4:40 pm	Apr. 12	2:21 pm	Aries	4th
Apr. 28	12:13 pm	Apr. 30	4:03 pm	Sagittarius	3rd
May 2	11:43 pm	May 4	2:16 am	Aquarius	3rd
May 4	2:16 am	May 5	10:46 am	Aquarius	4th
May 7	11:22 pm	May 10	11:32 am	Aries	4th
May 26	6:51 am	May 28	1:54 am	Sagittarius	3rd
May 30	8:35 am	Jun. 1	6:37 pm	Aquarius	3rd
Jun. 4	6:51 am	Jun. 6	7:07 pm	Aries	4th
Jun. 9	5:29 am	Jun. 10	6:46 pm	Gemini	4th
Jun. 26	5:36 pm	Jun. 29	3:00 am	Aquarius	3rd
Jul. 1	2:49 pm	Jul. 2	12:19 pm	Aries	3rd
Jul. 2	12:19 pm	Jul. 4	3:16 am	Aries	4th
Jul. 6	2:01 pm	Jul. 8	9:36 pm	Gemini	4th
Jul. 24	4:07 am	Jul. 26	11:04 am	Aquarius	3rd
Jul. 28	10:39 pm	Jul. 31	11:17 am	Aries	3rd
Aug. 2	10:46 pm	Aug. 5	7:02 am	Gemini	4th

Dates to Destroy Weeds & Pests

Aug. 7	11:27 am	Aug 8	2:15 pm	Leo	4th
Aug. 22	5:29 pm	Aug 22	6:11 pm	Aquarius	3rd
Aug. 25	5:48 am	Aug 27	6:32 pm	Aries	3rd
Aug. 30	6:45 am	Aug 30	9:31 pm	Gemini	3rd
Aug. 30	9:31 pm	Sep 1	4:14 pm	Gemini	4th
Sep. 3	9:36 pm	Sep 5	11:16 pm	Leo	4th
Sep 5	11:16 pm	Sep 6	10:10 pm	Virgo	4th
Sep. 21	12:11 pm	Sep 24	12:55 am	Aries	3rd
Sep. 26	1:26 pm	Sep 29	12:01 am	Gemini	3rd
Oct. 1	6:58 am	Oct 3	9:52 am	Leo	4th
Oct. 3	9:52 am	Oct 5	9:51 am	Virgo	4th
Oct. 21	2:20 am	Oct 21	6:57 am	Aries	3rd
Oct. 23	7:17 pm	Oct 26	6:10 am	Gemini	3rd
Oct. 28	2:20 pm	Oct 29	12:28 am	Leo	3rd
Oct. 29	12:28 am	Oct 30	6:59 pm	Leo	4th
Oct. 30	6:59 pm	Nov 1	8:28 pm	Virgo	4th
Nov. 20	1:25 am	Nov 22	11:48 am	Gemini	3rd
Nov. 24	8:00 pm	Nov 27	1:42 am	Leo	3rd
Nov. 27	1:42 am	Nov 27	10:46 am	Virgo	3rd
Nov. 27	10:46 am	Nov 29	4:54 am	Virgo	4th
Dec. 3	6:58 am	Dec 4	2:34 am	Sagittarius	4th
Dec. 19	2:10 pm	Dec 19	6:30 pm	Gemini	3rd
Dec. 22	1:48 am	Dec 24	7:05 am	Leo	3rd
Dec. 24	7:05 am	Dec 26	10:53 am	Virgo	3rd

Gestation & Incubation

Animal	Young/Eggs	Gestation/Incubation
Horse	1	346 days
Cow	1	283 days
Monkey	1	164 days
Goat	1–2	151 days
Sheep	1–2	150 days
Pig	10	112 days
Chinchilla	2	110 days
Fox	5–8	63 days
Dog	6–8	63 days
Cat	4–6	63 days
Guinea Pig	2–6	62 days
Ferret	6–9	40 days
Rabbit	4–8	30 days
Rat	10	22 days
Mouse	10	22 days
Turkey	1–15	26-30 days
Guinea Hen	15–18	25-26 days
Pea Hen	10	28-30 days
Duck	9–12	25-32 days
Goose	15–18	27-33 days
Hen	12–15	19-24 days
Pigeon	2	16-20 days
Canary	3–4	13-14 days

2002 Egg Setting Dates

Jan. 16 9:00 am-Jan. 18 9:35 pm	Pisces	1st	Dec. 26
Jan. 21 9:47 am-Jan. 21 12:47 pm	Taurus	1st	Dec. 31
Jan. 26 1:17 am-Jan. 28 3:31 am	Cancer	2nd	Jan. 5
Feb. 12 3:53 pm-Feb. 15 4:26 am	Pisces	1st	Jan. 22
Feb. 17 4:58 pm-Feb. 20 3:50 am	Taurus	1st	Jan. 27
Feb. 22 11:16 am-Feb. 24 2:36 pm	Cancer	2nd	Feb. 1
Mar. 13 9:03 pm-Mar. 14 10:34 am	Pisces	1st	Feb. 20
Mar. 16 11:01 pm-Mar. 19 10:20 am	Taurus	1st	Feb. 23
Mar. 21 7:06 pm-Mar. 21 9:28 pm	Cancer	1st	Feb. 28
Mar. 28 1:04 am-Mar. 28 1:25 pm	Libra	2nd	Mar. 7
Apr. 13 4:55 am-Apr. 15 3:56 pm	Taurus	1st	Mar. 23
Apr. 18 1:01 am-Apr. 20 7:20 am	Cancer	1st	Mar. 28
Apr. 24 11:22 am-Apr. 26 11:15 am	Libra	2nd	Apr. 3
May 12 5:45 am-May 12 10:04 pm	Taurus	1st	Apr. 22
May 15 6:33 am-May 17 12:52 pm	Cancer	1st	Apr. 24
May 21 7:19 pm-May 23 8:38 pm	Libra	2nd	Apr. 30
Jun. 11 1:15 pm-Jun. 13 6:39 pm	Cancer	1st	May 21
Jun. 18 1:11 am-Jun. 20 3:42 am	Libra	2nd	May 28
Jul. 10 5:26 am-Jul. 11 2:08 am	Cancer	1st	Jun. 19
Jul. 15 6:39 am-Jul. 16 11:47 pm	Libra	1st	Jun. 24
Aug. 11 1:38 pm-Aug. 13 3:01 pm	Libra	1st	Jul. 21
Sep. 7 10:57 pm-Sep. 9 10:48 pm	Libra	1st	Aug. 17
Sep. 19 12:18 am-Sep. 21 8:59 am	Pisces	2nd	Aug. 29
Oct. 6 6:18 am-Oct. 7 8:57 am	Libra	1st	Sep. 15
Oct. 16 6:07 am-Oct. 18 6:13 pm	Pisces	2nd	Sep. 25
Nov. 12 12:42 pm-Nov. 15 12:38 am	Pisces	2nd	Oct. 22
Nov. 17 1:23 pm-Nov. 19 8:34 pm	Taurus	2nd	Oct. 27
Dec. 9 8:46 pm-Dec. 11 10:49 am	Pisces	1st	Nov. 18
Dec. 14 8:43 pm-Dec. 17 8:43 am	Taurus	2nd	Nov. 23

Companion Planting Guide
Plant Helpers and Hinderers

Plant	Helped By	Hindered By
Asparagus	Tomatoes, Parsley, Basil	
Beans	Carrots, Cucumbers, Cabbage, Beets, Corn	Onions, Gladiola
Bush Beans	Cucumbers, Cabbage, Strawberries	Fennel, Onions
Beets	Onions, Cabbage, Lettuce	Pale Beans
Cabbage	Beets, Potatoes, Onions, Celery	Strawberries, Tomatoes
Carrots	Peas, Lettuce, Chives, Radishes, Leeks, Onions	Dill
Celery	Leeks, Bush Beans	
Chives	Beans	
Corn	Potatoes, Beans, Peas, Melons, Squash, Pumpkins, Cucumbers	
Cucumbers	Beans, Cabbage, Radishes, Sunflowers, Lettuce	Potatoes, Aromatic Herbs
Eggplant	Beans	
Lettuce	Strawberries, Carrots	
Melons	Morning Glories	
Onions, Leeks	Beets, Chamomile, Carrots, Lettuce	Peas, Beans
Garlic	Summer Savory	
Peas	Radishes, Carrots, Corn, Cucumbers, Beans, Turnips	Onions
Potatoes	Beans, Corn, Peas, Cabbage, Hemp, Cucumbers	Sunflowers

Plant	Helped By	Hindered By
Radishes	Peas, Lettuce, Nasturtium, Cucumbers	Hyssop
Spinach	Strawberries	
Squash, Pumpkins	Nasturtium, Corn	Potatoes
Tomatoes	Asparagus, Parsley, Chives, Onions, Carrots, Marigold, Nasturtium	Dill, Cabbage, Fennel
Turnips	Peas, Beans	

Plant Companions and Uses

Plant	Companions and Uses
Anise	Coriander
Basil	Tomatoes; dislikes rue; repels flies and mosquitos
Borage	Tomatoes and squash
Buttercup	Clover; hinders delphiniums, peonies, monkshood, columbines
Chamomile	Helps peppermint, wheat, onions, and cabbage; large amounts destructive
Catnip	Repels flea beetles
Chervil	Radishes
Chives	Carrots; prone to apple scab and powdery mildew
Coriander	Hinders seed formation in fennel
Cosmos	Repels corn earworms
Dill	Cabbage; hinders carrots and tomatoes
Fennel	Disliked by all garden plants
Garlic	Aids vetch and roses; hinders peas and beans
Hemp	Beneficial as a neighbor to most plants
Horseradish	Repels potato bugs

Plant	Companions and Uses
Horsetail	Makes fungicide spray
Hyssop	Attracts cabbage fly away from cabbages; harmful to radishes
Lovage	Improves hardiness and flavor of neighbor plants
Marigold	Pest repellent; use against Mexican bean beetles and nematodes
Mint	Repels ants, flea beetles and cabbage worm butterflies
Morning Glory	Corn; helps melon germination
Nasturtium	Cabbage, cucumbers; deters aphids, squash bugs, and pumpkin beetles
Nettles	Increase oil content in neighbors
Parsley	Tomatoes, asparagus
Purslane	Good ground cover
Rosemary	Repels cabbage moths, bean beetles, and carrot flies
Sage	Repels cabbage moths and carrot flies
Savory	Deters bean beetles
Sunflower	Hinders potatoes; improves soil
Tansy	Deters Japanese beetles, striped cucumber beetles, and squash bugs
Thyme	Repels cabbage worms
Yarrow	Increases essential oils of neighbors

2002 Weather Forecast

By Kris Brandt Riske

Astrometeorology—weather forecasting through astrology—is one of the oldest branches of the science. For thousands of years, before the invention of radar, satellites, and other modern technology, astrologers used the positions of the planets to forecast weather.

Based on the cardinal ingresses (Summer and Winter Solstices, and Spring and Fall Equinoxes) and the four monthly quarterly lunar phases in combination with the transiting planets, astrometeorology reveals seasonal and weekly weather trends.

The outer planets and the signs they're transiting set major, long-term trends, such as hot or mild summers, cold or temperate winters, droughts or excessive precipitation. This year, a Jupiter-Pluto combination will contribute to extremes of heat and cold, as well as precipitation. Saturn trine Uranus will bring cold and cloudy conditions to some regions, and Saturn trine Neptune adds excess precipitation. Where these weather phenomena manifest depends on the longitude and latitude affected by the transiting planets.

Another factor that contributes to weather trends is eclipses. Planets situated along a certain meridian (longitude) at the time of an eclipse tend to activate that area according to the planetary significance, creating "hot spots" of extreme weather potential. Although the effect of an eclipse lasts from six to twelve months, it will only be activated if transiting planets strongly connect with the point. Eclipses affecting 2002 weather are:

December 30, 2001

Mars—heat and stormy conditions from Wisconsin to New Orleans

Uranus—high pressure systems and storms from Montana to Arizona; cooler east, warmer west

May 26, 2002

Neptune—excessive precipitation, above normal temperatures, humidity from Montana to Arizona

Uranus—high pressure systems and storms from Minnesota to Houston; cooler east, warmer west

June 10, 2002

Neptune—excessive precipitation from Seattle to San Francisco

Uranus—high pressure systems and storms from the Montana-Wyoming border through eastern New Mexico; cooler east, warmer west

June 24, 2002

Jupiter—pleasant and fair to above normal temperatures from Seattle to San Francisco

Venus—cloudy and warm, with precipitation from the mid-Dakotas to San Antonio

Uranus—high pressure systems and storms (hurricanes) from Ohio south to Florida; cooler east, warmer west

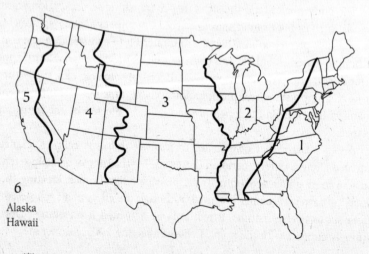

6
Alaska
Hawaii

Winter 2002

Zone 1: precipitation above normal, especially Northeast to mid-Atlantic states; temperatures below normal in Florida

Zone 2: temperatures slightly below normal; cooler and stormy in eastern areas; heavier precipitation northern two-thirds of zone

Zone 3: temperatures normal to above, but major storms with heavy precipitation and cold temperatures; windy, stormy, and cooler to the west

Zone 4: above normal precipitation north and in mountainous areas; warm south with normal precipitation

Zone 5: normal to above normal temperatures, precipitation above normal with cold

Zone 6: cold with normal to above normal precipitation in Alaska; seasonal to cooler temperatures and normal to above normal precipitation in Hawaii

January 2002

Zone 1

January 1–5: cold and wet northeast and mid-Atlantic region; drier south

January 6–12: windy northeast with possible precipitation; locally heavy precipitation in Florida

January 13–20: overcast, windy, cool; colder northeast; heavy precipitation

January 21–27: very windy, cloudy, stormy, heavy precipitation with blizzard potential north, cold

January 28–31: heavy precipitation with flooding potential; cold and thunderstorms south

Zone 2

January 1–5: cold with precipitation east

January 6–12: cold and windy; precipitation heavier east

January 13–20: temperatures seasonal to above west; cold with precipitation east

January 21–27: stormy east with blizzard potential; cloudy and cool with precipitation in Gulf states

January 28–31: partly cloudy to overcast, seasonal to cold, blustery with precipitation in Ohio

Zone 3

January 1–5: cold in the Plains, Montana, Wyoming; storms north; warmer south

January 6–12: blustery, cold, overcast, some heavy precipitation

January 13–20: windy, especially east; heavy precipitation and cold in Plains states

January 21–27: seasonally cool, fair, cooler; chance of precipitation northwest

January 28–31: overcast, stormy, cold in the Rockies through Plains; precipitation heavier in the north

Zone 4

January 1–5: cold northwest and in mountains; storms north; cool south with precipitation

January 6–12: very cold west and in mountains; windy, cold south with precipitation

January 13–20: cool to cold, cloudy, precipitation

January 21–27: fair; above normal temperatures north; cooler south

January 28–31: windy and chance of precipitation north; warmer south, with chance of precipitation in the mountains

Zone 5

January 1–5: overcast with locally heavy precipitation, stormy north, warmer south

January 6–12: cool, precipitation

January 13–20: cool and windy; precipitation north

January 21–27: cool, fair north; warmer, windy south with precipitation

January 28–31: stormy south; cool and windy all areas

Zone 6

January 1–5: seasonal to above normal temperatures with precipitation in Alaska; warm with precipitation in Hawaii

January 6–12: overcast, precipitation in Alaska; cloudy, precipitation Hawaii

January 13–20: cold, overcast, heavy precipitation in Alaska; cool, cloudy, precipitation in Hawaii

January 21–27: cold, chance of precipitation in Alaska; cool, windy, precipitation in Hawaii

January 28–31: heavy precipitation and cold in Alaska; major storm and cold in Hawaii

February 2002
Zone 1

February 1–3: cold, precipitation, very windy south

February 4–11: seasonal temperatures, precipitation in coastal areas
February 12–19: clear, cold, and windy; chance of precipitation south
February 20–28: significant precipitation Gulf and Southeast with flooding potential; colder south

Zone 2

February 1–3: seasonal to cool, wind; very windy east with precipitation
February 4–11: overcast and cold, heavier precipitation north
February 12–19: windy and cold west; cloudy and warmer south and east
February 20–28: windy, cloudy, stormy with heavy precipitation in Great Lakes and areas south; cold with flooding potential south

Zone 3

February 1–3: cooler west; warmer central Plains with some thawing; precipitation east
February 4–11: major storm with blizzard potential across the Plains; cold, freezing rain, sleet south
February 12–19: cold and overcast; heavy precipitation western and central Plains
February 20–28: precipitation and wind; cold east and north

Zone 4

February 1–3: temperatures seasonal to above; windy and warmer south with precipitation
February 4–11: cold and windy south with significant precipitation; major winter storm with blizzard potential in the Rockies
February 12–19: cold east with precipitation; warmer west
February 20–28: cold and cloudy; significant precipitation north and in mountains

Zone 5

February 1–3: windy; chance of precipitation inland; windy cool and south
February 4–11: precipitation heavier in north; fog and cooler in northern California; overcast south
February 12–19: significant precipitation and overcast northern coastal areas; cold inland; precipitation south
February 20–28: cool, breezy, and precipitation north; windy and precipitation south

Zone 6

February 1–3: cold, precipitation in Alaska; seasonal to cool, precipitation east in Hawaii

February 4–11: cold in Alaska, precipitation west; cool with precipitation in Hawaii

February 12–19: cold and precipitation in Alaska; Hawaii, coo and clear

February 20–28: cold, windy in Alaska, precipitation west; cool and precipitation west in Hawaii, seasonal east

March 2002

Zone 1

March 1–5: windy, heavy precipitation southeast with flooding potential; seasonal temperatures

March 6–13: cool and cloudy northeast; warmer south; thunderstorms southeast and Florida

March 14–20: significant precipitation and fog northeast; windy, warm, and humid to the south

March 21–27: cold northeast; warmer, windy, and humid south with a chance of showers

March 28–31: fair northeast; humid and thunderstorms—some strong—in the mid-Atlantic states and areas south

Zone 2

March 1–5: cool west; warmer south and east; precipitation in the Ohio Valley and areas east and south; very windy east

March 6–13: fair west with scattered storms; stormy Ohio Valley and areas south with tornado potential; cooler east with storms

March 14–20: windy; fair to partly cloudy, cool; precipitation in western two-thirds of zone; cloudy Ohio Valley and areas south

March 21–27: windy, fair, warm west; warm, humid with precipitation east

March 28–31: cloudy west with a chance of precipitation; fair southeast; precipitation in Ohio and Pennsylvania

Zone 3

March 1–5: partly cloudy to cloudy with temperatures seasonal to above, a chance precipitation

March 6–13: cool and fair northwest; windy with thunderstorms and tornado potential in the Plains

March 14–20: fair and breezy northwest; cool with precipitation, some locally heavy rain with flooding potential in the Plains

March 21–27: precipitation northwest and west; seasonal temperatures, windy, partly cloudy in the Plains, with a chance of showers south

March 28–31: warm and very windy west; warmer and a chance of precipitation east; humid south

Zone 4

March 1–5: windy north; cloudy with precipitation south; temperatures normal to above

March 6–13: overcast, cool, and precipitation west; warmer, fair and partly cloudy to cloudy east and south

March 14–20: windy, cool; chance precipitation north and in the mountains; warm desert Southwest

March 21–27: seasonal temperatures and a chance of precipitation north; warmer and precipitation south

March 28–31: warm, fair, cooler; precipitation in mountains; windy north

Zone 5

March 1–5: clear to partly cloudy and cool north; colder and overcast in California; precipitation and windy south

March 6–13: overcast, cool, damp; precipitation heavy to the south,

March 14–20: cool, fair to windy with precipitation south

March 21–27: fair, warm, windy north; partly cloudy south with a chance of precipitation

March 28–31: fair and pleasant north; chance of precipitation south; overcast south and inland

Zone 6

March 1–5: seasonal west, cold with precipitation in eastern Alaska; precipitation, windy, cool in Hawaii

March 6–13: cold, windy, stormy in eastern Alaska; locally heavy precipitation and windy in eastern Hawaii

March 14–20: overcast, precipitation, cool in Alaska; seasonal temperatures, partly cloudy to cloudy with precipitation in Hawaii

March 21–27: overcast, precipitation, cool in Alaska; precipitation, mostly fair to partly cloudy in Hawaii

March 28–31: mostly fair and seasonal, precipitation in eastern Alaska; fair, seasonal, chance of precipitation in Hawaii

Spring 2002

Zone 1: more precipitation northeast; fair and drier south, warm, breezy, and humid

Zone 2: seasonal temperatures and precipitation normal to above to the west; cool east with seasonal conditions and thunderstorms

Zone 3: seasonal in the northwest; fluctuating temperatures and normal precipitation west and east, but drier in the central Plains; prevalent cloudiness, but fairer north

Zone 4: temperatures above normal, especially in the desert Southwest; normal precipitation and seasonal conditions

Zone 5: windy, cloudy, cooler with precipitation north; fair south with average precipitation

Zone 6: cloudy, above normal temperatures and precipitation in Alaska; stormy, seasonal to above normal temperatures and precipitation with flooding potential in Hawaii

April 2002

Zone 1

April 1–3: precipitation in southeast and Florida; humid and overcast in northeast

April 4–11: fair north; cloudy south with thunderstorms

April 12–19: windy with precipitation south; dry north; cool in coastal regions; warm inland

April 20–26: stormy from northeast to mid-Atlantic states with heaviest precipitation northeast; windy southeast

April 27–30: fair south; cool, windy, and precipitation northeast

Zone 2

April 1–3: fair, warm, and windy

April 4–11: cloudy and chance of precipitation west; overcast and thunderstorms with tornado warnings Ohio Valley and south

April 12–19: precipitation and thunderstorms west to Ohio Valley

April 20–26: above normal precipitation with flooding potential south; windy east and partly cloudy

April 27–30: seasonal; chance of precipitation west; warm south; windy east

Zone 3

April 1–3: warm and windy with a chance of precipitation

April 4–11: heavy precipitation and stormy northwest and west; severe thunderstorms with tornado warnings in the Plains

April 12–19: windy, partly cloudy with a chance of precipitation north and northwest; Plains mostly fair; above normal precipitation with flooding potential east

April 20–26: windy and cloudy west; scattered thunderstorms central and eastern Plains

April 27–30: cool, stormy, very windy north; precipitation west; severe thunderstorms with tornado potential in the Plains

Zone 4

April 1–3: warm, fair, windy, with chance of precipitation in the mountains

April 4–11: stormy with heavy precipitation in the mountains and throughout the zone's central area

April 12–19: fair with a chance of precipitation; windy, especially in mountains; partly cloudy south

April 20–26: breezy north with a chance of precipitation; warm south and partly cloudy

April 27–30: fair and warm north; cooler and windy east with precipitation

Zone 5

April 1–3: precipitation north; fair and windy south

April 4–11: cloudy with precipitation north; partly cloudy and warm south with coastal precipitation

April 12–19: fair to partly cloudy north

April 20–26: fair to partly cloudy; chance of precipitation

April 27–30: precipitation north in coastal areas; foggy and warm; fair south

Zone 6

April 1–3: cloudy with precipitation in Alaska; windy, seasonal conditions in Hawaii, with precipitation

April 4–11: fair to partly cloudy in Alaska—cool east, warmer west; fair with precipitation in eastern Hawaii

April 12–19: very windy, cloudy, cool in Alaska; windy, fair to partly cloudy in Hawaii,

April 20–26: windy, fair to partly cloudy in Alaska; seasonal, fair to partly cloudy in Hawaii

April 27–30: windy, cool, with precipitation in Alaska; precipitation east, fair west in Hawaii

May 2002

Zone 1

May 1–3: thunderstorms, seasonal conditions

May 4–11: fair to partly cloudy and cool northeast; severe thunderstorms with high winds and tornado warnings in the mid-Atlantic states and southeast

May 12–18: temperatures above normal northeast with scattered thunderstorms; very humid south; cloudy and cooler mid-Atlantic states; temperatures above normal and scattered thunderstorms south

May 19–25: sultry, afternoon thunderstorms; heavy precipitation in Florida

May 26–31: seasonal and fair northeast; overcast with showers mid-Atlantic states; hot and humid in Florida

Zone 2

May 1–3: windy west; humid east; thunderstorms in the Ohio Valley

May 4–11: windy, cool, and cloudy; severe storms with high winds tornado warnings in the Ohio Valley and south

May 12–18: partly cloudy west; temperatures above normal; humid and scattered thunderstorms south and east

May 19–25: hot and humid; afternoon thunderstorms with high winds east

May 26–31: hot and fair west; cooler, cloudy, precipitation east

Zone 3

May 1–3: windy and cool west; cool east; severe thunderstorms and tornado warnings in the Plains

May 4–11: humidity with temperatures above normal, thunderstorms and tornado warnings

May 12–18: temperatures above normal, especially northwest and west with chance of precipitation; slightly cooler, partly cloudy and humid in the Plains; windy south with scattered thunderstorms

May 19–25: windy, partly cloudy, humid west; overcast and hot in Plains with scattered strong thunderstorms, high winds, and tornado warnings

May 26–31: windy and a chance of showers west; above normal temperatures, humid, and partly cloudy north with high winds

Zone 4

May 1–3: windy and cool east; warm throughout most of the zone; chance of precipitation south

May 4–11: fair, warm, precipitation west; hot, humid, partly cloudy to cloudy south with a chance of precipitation

May 12–18: fair and windy, turning hot and humid south

May 19–25: windy with thunderstorms west; windy, partly cloudy, dry, and hot south

May 26–31: showers, partly cloudy, above normal temperatures; humid south; windy north

Zone 5

May 1–3: windy, cloudy, heavy precipitation north; warm and seasonal in the south

May 4–11: overcast, cool, precipitation north; breezy, fair, and cool south

May 12–18: cool with precipitation north; fair south

May 19–25: warm and fair with a chance of showers; cloudy and cooler in the south

May 26–31: windy, partly cloudy with a chance of showers north; cloudy and showers south

Zone 6

May 1–3: seasonal conditions with precipitation in Alaska; precipitation and cooler in Hawaii,

May 4–11: precipitation and cool in Alaska; seasonal, breezy, a chance of precipitation in Hawaii

May 12–18: fair and cold in Alaska; cool, windy, overcast, precipitation in Hawaii

May 19–25: overcast and cool in Alaska; fair to partly cloudy and seasonal in Hawaii

May 26–31: cloudy and cool, becoming fair and warmer in Alaska; showers, cooler and cloudy eastern Hawaii

June 2002

Zone 1

June 1–9: warm and breezy northeast; humid with precipitation to the south

June 10–16: warm and breezy; chance of precipitation north; humid south with showers likely

June 17–23: cool and windy mid-Atlantic states; thunderstorms, some severe with tornado warnings in the south

June 24–30: cloudy, cool, thunderstorms northeast; windy mid-Atlantic states and warmer in coastal areas; cooler with thunderstorms south

Zone 2

June 1–9: humid and overcast; strong thunderstorms with tornado warnings; locally heavy precipitation

June 10–16: cloudy and cooler with a chance of strong thunderstorms and high winds

June 17–23: humid, scattered thunderstorms, stronger north; thunderstorms, locally heavy precipitation and tornado warnings Ohio Valley and south

June 24–30: hot and dry west; cooler and scattered thunderstorms east

Zone 3

June 1–9: hot and dry west; slightly cooler, windy, and severe thunderstorms with tornado warnings in the Plains

June 10–16: unseasonably warm west; windy, humid, fair and slightly cooler central and eastern Plains

June 17–23: temperatures seasonal to below; cloudy with precipitation west; thunderstorms central Plains

June 24–30: hot with precipitation west; hot and humid in the Plains with scattered thunderstorms

Zone 4

June 1–9: hot, partly cloudy; chance of precipitation north

June 10–16: unseasonably warm and cloudy north; hot desert Southwest

June 17–23: very windy, fair, chance of precipitation west; seasonal temperatures, but hot and humid south

June 24–30: fair with temperatures seasonal to above; partly cloudy and precipitation north; hot, humid, and a chance of showers south

Zone 5

June 1–9: breezy and partly cloudy; warm with some precipitation south

June 10–16: precipitation and fog north; warm and breezy south

June 17–23: temperatures above normal north; windy and cooler south and inland with a chance of showers

June 24–30: stormy, cloudy, cool north; fair, breezy, cool south

Zone 6

June 1–9: precipitation, windy, warm in Alaska; temperatures above normal, fair with seasonal showers in Hawaii,

June 10–16: windy with precipitation in Alaska; warm, windy, humid, with showers in Hawaii

June 17–23: partly cloudy with precipitation in eastern Alaska, and fair and warm west; seasonal temperatures and showers in Hawaii

June 24–30: cloudy, precipitation, cool in Alaska; windy, humid, with precipitation in Hawaii

Summer 2002

Zone 1: temperatures seasonal; humid, more precipitation south; precipitation heavier in coastal areas with potential flooding

Zone 2: temperatures normal to above, but cooler with more precipitation east; windy west; more cloudiness north

Zone 3: warm and dry northwest; normal precipitation and seasonal temperatures in the mountains; hot, humid and precipitation normal to below Plains; more cloudiness south

Zone 4: precipitation and seasonal temperatures north; temperatures normal to above south; hot and dry desert Southwest

Zone 5: above normal temperatures north; cooler and cloudy south with normal precipitation coastal areas; fair and warmer inland

Zone 6: cooler east, above normal precipitation and warmer west, strong storms eastern Alaska; warm with normal to above precipitation in Hawaii

July 2002

Zone 1

July 1–9: hot and thunderstorms northeast; hot, humid, scattered thunderstorms south

July 10–16: humid and windy south; chance of precipitation throughout the zone, especially the mid-Atlantic states

July 17–23: warm with thunderstorms; partly cloudy and humid south

July 24–31: warm with precipitation north; hot and fair south

Zone 2

July 1–9: fair and dry west; hot with scattered thunderstorms—some strong—in the east

July 10–16: cloudy with scattered thunderstorms west; more precipitation north; windy south; hot, dry, windy east

July 17–23: warm, humid, chance of precipitation west, especially the Gulf states; partly cloudy and scattered thunderstorms east

July 24–31: thunderstorms, some severe, throughout the zone except for the northeast

Zone 3

July 1–9: warm north; cooler, overcast, and wind, with scattered thunderstorms west; hot and humid with scattered thunderstorms in the Plains

July 10–16: precipitation north; fair and windy west; temperatures seasonal to above, humid, with scattered thunderstorms in the Plains

July 17–23: hot northwest; cloudy and cooler west with a chance of showers; hot and humid central Plains; cooler east

July 24–31: hot and dry west; cooler and fair east; humid and scattered thunderstorms in the Plains

Zone 4

July 1–9: thunderstorms and warm north; hot, windy, humid, a chance of precipitation south

July 10–16: temperatures above normal west; cooler east; cloudy with precipitation in mountains and south

July 17–23: hot, fair, windy north; precipitation mountains; partly cloudy, hot and a chance of showers south

July 24–31: hot and dry, turning partly cloudy

Zone 5

July 1–9: cool with precipitation north; seasonal conditions south

July 10–16: windy, partly cloudy south; temperatures above normal

July 17–23: warm with a chance of precipitation north; hot, partly cloudy and precipitation south

July 24–31: cloudy with precipitation, some heavy, to the north; fair and warm south

Zone 6

July 1–9: fair, pleasant, windy, with precipitation in Alaska; precipitation, cooler east, warmer western Hawaii

July 10–16: precipitation and cloudy in Alaska; warm, cloudy, with heavy precipitation in Hawaii

July 17–23: stormy, heavy precipitation, and cool in Alaska; windy and warm in Hawaii, with showers

July 24–31: seasonal conditions with precipitation in Alaska; fair, and a chance of showers in Hawaii

August 2002

Zone 1

August 1–7: heavy precipitation from mid-Atlantic states north, hurricane potential; cloudy and precipitation south

August 8–14: cloudy and chance of precipitation northeast; hot, humid, windy south

August 15–21: humid; scattered thunderstorms, some strong, south

August 22–31: stormy; hurricane potential mid-Atlantic states and New England

Zone 2

August 1–7: dry and fair west; cloudy, precipitation east

August 8–14: windy west; fair and humid east

August 15–21: windy with scattered thunderstorms; tornado warnings in the Ohio Valley; fair in the east

August 22–31: cloudy, precipitation—some heavy—west; fair and breezy in the east

Zone 3

August 1–7: stormy northwest; hot, fair, and dry in the Plains

August 8–14: hot, dry, and partly cloudy north

August 15–21: precipitation west; other areas hot, dry, turning humid

August 22–31: scattered thunderstorms; hot west; fair in the Plains

Zone 4

August 1–7: breezy north with chance of precipitation; overcast and thunderstorms with flash flooding south

August 8–14: warm with precipitation, some heavy, north; hot and humid south

August 15–21: hot and stormy south with flash flood potential

August 22–31: thunderstorms north followed by windy, cooler conditions; mostly fair south with scattered thunderstorms

Zone 5

August 1–7: fog and showers north; warm and fair south

August 8–14: fair to partly cloudy north; warm with a chance of showers south

August 15–21: fair, warm, and breezy, with a chance of precipitation; turning cloudy and cooler south and inland

August 22–31: fair and warm; hot south with chance of precipitation

Zone 6

August 1–7: stormy, heavy precipitation with potential flooding in Alaska; significant precipitation, high winds with hurricane potential in Hawaii

August 8–14: stormy, heavy precipitation in Alaska; overcast and cool in Hawaii, with heavy precipitation

August 15–21: warm east, cool west with precipitation in Alaska; temperatures above normal, some thunderstorms in Hawaii,

August 22–31: cool east, warmer and precipitation west in Alaska; precipitation, thunderstorms, typhoon potential in Hawaii

September 2002

Zone 1

September 1–6: breezy and fair north; cloudy to the south with chance of precipitation

September 7–12: fair north; cloudy and breezy south with scattered thunderstorms

September 13–20: windy, fair, and warmer south

September 21–28: seasonal north; stormy with heavy precipitation southeast and moving north; hurricane potential

September 29–31: partly cloudy, chance of precipitation north; warm and windy south with precipitation

Zone 2

September 1–6: cloudy and cool west; precipitation east

September 7–12: cool with precipitation west; chilly north; cloudy and windy south; warmer east

September 13–20: fair and breezy west; cold and overcast Ohio Valley and areas south

September 21–28: cool, overcast, stormy, heavy precipitation and high winds east; hurricane effects

September 29–31: warm and windy west; precipitation in the Ohio Valley; seasonal temperatures

Zone 3

September 1–6: cloudy, cool, precipitation northwest; above normal temperatures west; dry and windy in the Plains states

September 7–12: windy and cool northwest; fair to partly cloudy west with showers; fair to partly cloudy in Plains states

September 13–20: scattered thunderstorms; breezy and mild in the Plains

September 21–28: windy, cool, stormy mountains; clear to partly cloudy in the Plains; windy north

September 29–31: windy and cloudy northwest; precipitation in the Plains; windy south

Zone 4

September 1–6: fair north with a chance of precipitation; overcast, cool, and precipitation south

September 7–12: windy, fair to cool and partly cloudy south

September 13–20: breezy, partly cloudy, cool north; seasonal south

September 21–28: windy west; precipitation east and south; cool and stormy mountains

September 29–31: cloudy, cool, precipitation north; windy, cloudy south

Zone 5

September 1–6: partly cloudy and cooler north; fair south

September 7–12: overcast, cool, precipitation in the north; fair and warm in the south
September 13–20: mild to partly cloudy; cooler inland
September 21–28: overcast, heavy precipitation, and cool; hurricane effects
September 29–31: windy and partly cloudy north; precipitation south; seasonal temperatures

Zone 6
September 1–6: overcast with precipitation in Alaska; cloudy and cool in Hawaii
September 7–12: cloudy with precipitation in Alaska; cool and partly cloudy with showers in Hawaii
September 13–20: seasonal temperatures, partly cloudy in Alaska; fair and pleasant in Hawaii
September 21–28: cold, cloudy, and windy in Alaska; partly cloudy, warm west, cool and windy in eastern Hawaii,
September 29–31: cloudy and warm in Alaska; partly cloudy with seasonal temperatures in Hawaii

Autumn 2002

Zone 1: windy, precipitation northeast; cloudy in the mid-Atlantic states and areas south with storms and heavy precipitation
Zone 2: stormy with high winds west; cool, fair, and more precipitation south; cold, overcast, heavy precipitation east
Zone 3: cool, windy, cloudy west; warmer in the Plains with average precipitation, some major storms and partly cloudy to cloudy; storms more prevalent in the central Plains
Zone 4: temperatures normal to above normal; windy, cooler, and cloudy east
Zone 5: cloudy and wet, with the heaviest precipitation in the south
Zone 6: very windy, stormy, with temperate to cool in Alaska; windy, normal to above normal precipitation, seasonal temperatures, and storms in Hawaii

October 2002
Zone 1
October 1–5: warm south; precipitation and windy north
October 6–12: fair and cool north; precipitation heavy south and mid-Atlantic states

October 13–20: precipitation north; cloudy and cool south

October 21–27: stormy northeast; windy and partly cloudy south

October 28–31: cool, precipitation, cloudy; abundant precipitation southeast

Zone 2

October 1–5: warm west; very windy and overcast with precipitation and cooler in the east

October 6–12: stormy; precipitation heaviest to the east

October 13–20: fair and chance of precipitation west; cooler and cloudy east

October 21–27: cold and windy in the east

October 28–31: cloudy, precipitation, some heavy with potential flooding in the south, Gulf states, Kentucky, and Tennessee

Zone 3

October 1–5: precipitation northwest; warmer east; precipitation in Plains; windy and cooler north

October 6–12: major storm, abundant precipitation in the Rockies, moving into the Plains where there will be blizzard potential; high winds; cold

October 13–20: stormy in mountains and western Plains; seasonal in the Plains; precipitation south

October 21–27: cloudy with precipitation; heavy precipitation in the Plains; heaviest south; cold north

October 28–31: precipitation northwest; fair west; windy, cool, and partly cloudy in the Plains

Zone 4

October 1–5: cloudy and cool with precipitation in the mountains; windy north; cloudy south

October 6–12: chance of precipitation; partly cloudy and cooler in the mountains; warmer south

October 13–20: precipitation, high winds east; seasonal to cooler temperatures west

October 21–27: cloudy and cool with precipitation; warmer south

October 28–31: precipitation mountains; windy north; partly cloudy to cloudy and breezy south; temperatures declining

Zone 5

October 1–5: precipitation north; windy south; seasonal temperatures

October 6–12: windy and partly cloudy; cooler and precipitation northern coast; seasonal south

October 13–20: partly cloudy north; precipitation and windy south

October 21–27: windy and cool with precipitation north; fair and windy south

October 28–31: precipitation north; cloudy south; chance of precipitation

Zone 6

October 1–5: cooler with precipitation in Alaska; cloudy with precipitation in Hawaii

October 6–12: cloudy and breezy in Alaska; partly cloudy to cloudy, and cool in Hawaii

October 13–20: precipitation, fog, temperatures normal to above in Alaska; seasonal and balmy in Hawaii

October 21–27: cloudy with seasonal temperatures in Alaska; precipitation, windy, overcast, and cool in Hawaii

October 28–31: cold, precipitation, and windy in Alaska; temperatures seasonal to below, windy in Hawaii

November 2002

Zone 1

November 1–3: cool, cloudy, precipitation southeast—some heavy

November 4–10: fair, turning cloudy and cooler north; windy, precipitation south

November 11–18: windy north with seasonal temperatures; precipitation mid-Atlantic states; cooler south

November 19–26: cool and windy, partly cloudy to cloudy; warmer south; chance of precipitation northeast

November 27–30: partly cloudy and cold north; warmer and cloudy south; precipitation mid-Atlantic states

Zone 2

November 1–3: overcast and windy; precipitation—some heavy—in Gulf states, Tennessee, and Kentucky

November 4–10: cool and overcast; precipitation, some locally heavy

November 11–18: windy and cool west with precipitation; fair to partly cloudy east

November 19–26: fair to partly cloudy; cool and windy east

November 27–30: cool, cloudy, and windy east with precipitation, some heavy

Zone 3

November 1–3: fair west; precipitation and cloudy in the Plains

November 4–10: partly cloudy west with temperatures normal to above;

cooler and windy east with chance of precipitation

November 11–18: fair with a chance of precipitation west; cold and overcast in the Plains; precipitation east

November 19–26: cool; partly cloudy to cloudy; precipitation Plains

November 27–30: windy and cool northwest with precipitation; cold Plains; very cold north

Zone 4

November 1–3: partly cloudy to cloudy and seasonal to the south; precipitation east

November 4–10: cloudy and precipitation in the mountains; fair and temperatures normal to above south and east

November 11–18: fair, temperatures normal to above, partly cloudy west; cooler east with precipitation

November 19–26: cool, partly cloudy to cloudy and windy; chance of precipitation east

November 27–30: seasonal, windy, cloudy south

Zone 5

November 1–3: precipitation north; overcast and cool, precipitation south

November 4–10: partly cloudy and chance of precipitation north; cooler, cloudy, with precipitation south

November 11–18: breezy and partly cloudy; temperatures normal to above; mostly fair

November 19–26: cloudy and cool north; warmer south and inland

November 27–30: cold and overcast north with precipitation; windy and fair south

Zone 6

November 1–3: cold and partly cloudy in Alaska; temperatures seasonal to below, warmer and breezy in western Hawaii

November 4–10: seasonal, windy, with precipitation in eastern Alaska; fair and becoming warmer in Hawaii

November 11–18: precipitation, overcast and cold in Alaska; cloudy, heavy precipitation east, fair in western Hawaii

November 19–26: cloudy, windy, with seasonal temperatures in Alaska; breezy, fair to partly cloudy in Hawaii

November 27–30: seasonal west, cold and cloudy with precipitation east in Alaska; seasonal conditions, temperatures seasonal to below in Hawaii

December 2002

Zone 1

December 1–3: partly cloudy and cold; cloudy and warmer south; precipitation southeast

December 3–10: cloudy north; fair to partly cloudy south; seasonal temperatures

December 11–18: partly cloudy, with precipitation north and south; cool southeast

December 19–27: cold northeast; cloudy, cool, precipitation south

December 28–31: fair to partly cloudy and seasonal; cloudy, cool, windy south

Zone 2

December 1–3: cool, windy, and cloudy

December 3–10: cloudy with precipitation; cooler and partly cloudy east

December 11–18: windy and fair west; precipitation south; cold and partly cloudy east

December 19–27: windy, cold, cloudy; precipitation moving west to east, heavy in the Ohio Valley

December 28–31: seasonal west; windy north; cooler and cloudy south and Ohio Valley; fair east

Zone 3

December 1–3: cool to cold, with storms in Plains states; heavy precipitation east

December 3–10: very windy and overcast; cold with precipitation

December 11–18: stormy with heavy precipitation mountains and into central Plains; overcast

December 19–27: overcast and cold northwest; precipitation west and moving across Plains; windy and cool in Plains states

December 28–31: overcast and windy west; precipitation throughout the zone; warmer in the Plains

Zone 4

December 1–3: seasonal to cool; windy and cloudy

December 3–10: windy with temperatures above normal; cloudy and precipitation east

December 11–18: cold and cloudy west; partly cloudy and cool east; chance of precipitation

December 19–27: cold east and south with precipitation; overcast and warmer west

December 28–31: cloudy with temperatures seasonal or above; cooler east

Zone 5

December 1–3: cold and overcast north, with some precipitation; fair south

December 3–10: temperatures above normal; mostly fair; partly cloudy south

December 11–18: cool north; warmer, partly cloudy south

December 19–27: fog and partly cloudy; warmer and fair south

December 28–31: windy, seasonal temperatures, a chance of precipitation

Zone 6

December 1–3: cold and windy in Alaska; overcast and cool in Hawaii

December 3–10: cold and cloudy in Alaska; precipitation—some locally heavy east—and cloudy in Hawaii

December 11–18: precipitation, seasonal temperatures, windy in Alaska; abundant precipitation, overcast, and cool in Hawaii

December 19–27: heavy precipitation, seasonal temperatures, overcast in Alaska; cloudy, cool, precipitation in Hawaii

December 28–31: precipitation, overcast and fog in Alaska; seasonal and windy with precipitation in eastern Hawaii

Permaculture: A Permanent Agriculture

By Penny Kelly

Imagine stepping out your back door and picking a bunch of juicy grapes hanging from the trellis overhead, plucking a few kiwi from their vines, and cutting a delicious cucumber or melon away from the trellis. Along the walkway, tomatoes in their cages form a hedge and backdrop against a profusion of flowers, carrots, pole bean tents, cauliflower and broccoli bushes, green and red peppers. See yourself gathering a handful of edible flowers to toss in the salad greens that are growing underneath the pole bean tents. Herbs are interspersed with onions, garlic, beets, and berries. Melons and squash grow profusely from one or two of last years compost pits, while dwarf fruit trees and numerous bulb flowers create additional microclimates with moving shady spots or weed suppression.

This is the vision of what is called "the kitchen garden," and in it, everything is well mulched, leaving a minimum of weeding. Paths and access to all plants have been carefully designed and laid out for easy care and easy harvesting. You see the garden in considerable detail every day because you have to walk through it to get in or out of the house. It is beautiful to look at and a joy to be in, as well as a means of sustenance for the family.

Many people do not realize that the food-getting practices of a culture go hand-in-hand with the outlines and schedules of daily living. Two thousand years ago you could not just drive over to the local grocery store to pick up milk, beer, a bag of chips, and a few fruits or vegetables. Two thousand years ago people grew their own fruits and vegetables, raised animals for meat and milk, wove much of their own cloth, and made most of what they needed by hand. Their lifestyles were the result of an interlocking set of pieces that all fit together sensibly.

Today, our lifestyles are also the result of interlocking pieces that fit together. The grocery stores, financial systems, manufacturing plants, containers, cars, trucks, and highways all exist in tandem with our lifestyle choices. Regardless of which system we live in—working for ourselves or working for someone else—in order to survive we need a permanent and reliable source of food.

To be considered permanent, a food supply must be stable, plentiful, and sustainable. *Stability* avoids the chaos caused by alternating feasts and famines. *Plenty* means having enough food to satisfy your belly and provides enough of the essential amino acids, vitamins, and minerals to keep a population healthy, peaceful, and able to reproduce successfully. *Sustainability* ensures that the methods of obtaining food can be continued again and again without endangering or exhausting either the population gathering it, or the source from which the food comes.

One method of creating a stable food supply is to incorporate the practice of permaculture into you life. Permaculture is the study, design, and implementation of enduring, functional, sustainable, and integrated systems that support us and our environment. Permaculture designs integrate energy-efficient houses with permanent, sustainable food gardens, and the animals necessary to do this. It is a commonsense approach to using technology and energy that saves labor.

In essence, it is a system of permanent agriculture that builds an entirely new set of interlocking pieces for daily living that promotes healthy, peaceable people who work from home in a culture based on wise ethics, self-sufficiency, extensive access to complete information, and creative trade. On a national and world level, it is an approach that revamps our cumbersome, ineffective systems of government, finance, education, and agriculture by bringing together landscapes and peoples in harmonious villages that make a future possible.

Where Did Permaculture Begin?

Bill Mollison developed the concept of permaculture in the 1960s and 70s as the result of his extensive study of Earth care, first as a scientist, naturalist, and university professor, then as a vigorous political activist against environmental and social exploitation. The science of permaculture was a proactive means to restore nature's balance. Mollison was twenty-eight when he began to realize that the self-sufficient ways of his youth were disappearing along with fish, birds, water, animals, and the ability of the land to snap back into productivity after being disturbed by man. He had learned much from sophisticated Aboriginal belief systems. When he compared Aboriginal belief systems, ethics, and lifestyles, to the lifestyles dictated by corporate cultures, the ways of modern man appeared crude, shallow, and selfish. In contrast, all indigenous cultures that had demonstrated an ability to survive over time held to a set of ethics that were used to guide choices and decision-making. He realized that any kind of sensible agriculture would have to be founded on a set of ethics that would guide human effort and form a system of priorities.

He also began to compare the dramatic differences between how nature and man arranged things. This led him to a deepening grasp of the basic elements of wind, water, trees, soil, plants, animals, man, and the individual patterns of each of these, along with the necessary interactions among all of them. These interactions were the basis of man's safety and security in nature, as well as our source for a permanent supply of food.

As modern corporate lifestyles continued to carry each generation into greater dependency on the state, Mollison began teaching people how to return to a much more dependable way of life within nature. In his words, "The only ethical decision is to take responsibility for our own existence and that of our children." Experience and observation had taught him that the most important ethic we could hold and honor was caring for the Earth. From this came a second ethic: that of caring for people. And holding to the first two ethics produced a third: the necessity of setting limits to population and consumption. Gradually, with these ethics as his foundation, he developed a set of practices and teachings that came to be called permaculture.

In permaculture, the goals are to work with nature rather than against it, and to make the least number of changes for the greatest possible effect. The basic strategy is to design a home and garden that integrates people, animals, and food, that eliminates the *make-work* (extra work) that fills our needs, while creating a surplus of yield for trade. Permaculture defines a yield is that which is produced over and above the needs of the gardener. All yields must be sustainable—without damage to Earth or people—and can only be counted after upstream costs such as energy, and downstream costs such as health have been taken into consideration. Any yield that costs more time, energy, and money to produce than the yield is worth, or that causes health problems later on, is not a yield at all, it is the symptom of poor design in a system that will soon become unworkable, causing many people pain or grief.

Designing for Cooperation and Connections

To anchor the design process in reality and create a truly workable system, permaculture starts with a complete analysis of your entire site. This includes its elevations, types of soil, amount of slope, water supply, sun and shade, position of existing homes or other buildings, and kinds of plants and trees already present. Once the analysis is completed, a total design is created that maximizes or even reworks the entire site and perhaps its structures. The new design integrates appropriate structures, materials, techniques, and technologies (both old and new) for your particular climate. It puts heavy emphasis on water collection for irrigation, temperature modulation, fire protection, support for animals and aquaculture, and for plain old pleasure such as swimming. On every site there is the sensible generation and use of energy from as many natural sources as possible. All designs incorporate a series of gardens that produce foods natural to the bioregion, and on each site there is an attempt to nurture as much interaction as possible between overlapping biological systems such as forest and open field, or open field and marshy areas. What emerges is a way of life, complete with food and energy systems that is nothing less than revolutionary.

Once the site has been analyzed, permaculture uses a series of concentric circles as *zones of activity* and places your home in Zone 1 as the center of human activity. This is where the kitchen garden, herbs, annual vegetables, and dwarf fruit trees will be placed. Zone 2 contains small domestic stock, the greenhouse, barns, poultry shed, along with larger orchard and nut trees. Zone 3 is for a main crop (e.g., potatoes, corn, wheat); some forage for rabbits, goats, chickens, or even cows; water storage for fire control; and perhaps one or more field shelters for animals. Zone 4 is for forests that supply wood for fuel and furniture, for gathering herbs or wild plants in forests and fields, for some pasture, some forage, and perhaps a barn for storing hay. And Zone 5 is strictly for wildlife.

The rule is that every system, plant, animal, or structure must be placed so that it serves at least two or more functions, and is served in at least two or more ways. This rule is based on the understanding that there are many

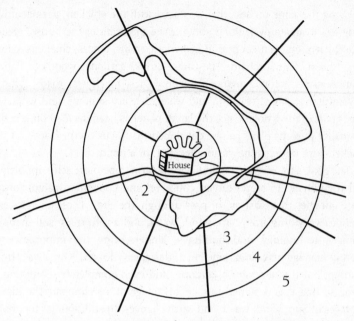

Permaculture Zone Map

necessary connections between the components of living, biological systems, and as in nature, the goal is to honor these connections and set up life in order to survive. Mollison uses the example of a chicken to demonstrate this.

A chicken has needs and behaviors, and it provides products. It needs water, shelter, grit, dust, air, food, a healthy life of moderate stress, and other chickens. It produces eggs, meat, feathers, more chickens, manure, methane, and carbon dioxide. Its behaviors include scratching, foraging, flying, fighting, dusting itself, and mating. Since extra work is caused when any need is not filled automatically by another component of the system, and *pollution* is created when any product is not used productively by any other component of the system. A good design will arrange to make the needed connections between the chicken, its needs, and its products. By asking where a component, in this case the chicken, best fits in the overall design, you end up with a plan of relative placement. Things are placed in relationship to each other so that we can relax and let this part of the system self-regulate. Mollison calls this the principle of self-regulation that works best in a system of open exchange.

Using the same process that was used with the chicken, permaculture designers evaluate everything about a site or location: the house, greenhouse, barn, chicken coop, ponds, hedges, trellis, fences, chickens, cows, pigs, sheep, fish, orchards, pastures, crops, gardens, woodlots, labor, finance, skills, people, markets, technologies, machines, roads, accessways, water storage, irrigation and water delivery systems, and whatever else is part of the whole. Once the larger plan has been decided on, a series of smaller nucleus plans can be developed that focus on the house, or the chicken-run, perhaps the pasture fencing, or a pond.

The goal is to recreate the home or the farm to be more self-supporting, and the aim is "to store, direct, conserve, and convert to useful forms, those energies that exist on, or pass through, the site." These energies can include everything from Sun, wind, water, and air, to trees, soil, people, animals, technology, and buildings. Underscoring the importance of energy management and efficiency, designers do not shy away from pointing out the necessity of altering, and even completely rebuilding, a home so that it is designed to take advantage of, or eliminate the disadvantages of Sun, wind, water, and earth changes. In addition, far too many homes are built without a single thought as to whether or not the home's design would support a family who wanted to live, educate, work, and feed itself from home. Since all cultures and civilizations change constantly, this kind of flexibility only makes sense and serves to provide a stable framework for those who practice permanent agriculture.

Even when rebuilding of a home is not required, the addition of a greenhouse—either to the house proper, or as an add-on to the chicken coop—is advocated. Methane from decomposing chicken manure can be used to help heat the greenhouse, and if the greenhouse is attached to the house itself, this will help heat the house in winter.

Several design features often encouraged in permaculture include super insulation, the installation of heated floors in cold climates, and the necessity of setting up extensive trellising around the house. The insulation and heated floors are so energy efficient and comfortable anything else is considered wasteful. As for the trellises, not only do they provide support for a much wider selection of foods close to the house, the trellis reduces the wearing effects of full Sun on many kinds of paint and wood, and helps save on the energy needed for air conditioning. Trellising also helps create many small microclimates for successfully growing a variety of foods with a wide range of environmental needs.

Once you have a design for the entire site, you can begin to lay out the kitchen gardens that surround the house. Mollison's advice is to start with a small, manageable chunk at the back door of your home. He uses the humorous, yet accurate, example of a woman who grows a large garden that is a hundred or more feet from the house, out behind the garage, or across the yard in an old field to teach the importance of putting the garden immediately outside the back door. This woman is having company and is making something for lunch or perhaps dinner. She needs a pepper or tomato from the garden but it's raining, she's not dressed yet, and is wearing a pair of big, pink, fuzzy slippers while she cooks. There is no way she is going to run across all that wet grass and into a muddy garden to get what she needs. If the garden were right outside the back door, designed and mulched according to permaculture principles, she would be able to step out, fuzzy pink slippers and all, and quickly pick that tomato or pepper.

This highlights some serious problems with modern garden design and placement. Out of sight is often out of mind. If the garden is in a nice-but-out-of-the-way place, it is frequently too far off the daily track to be easy and convenient to go and visit. We tell ourselves we'll get out there, but we don't. Weeds get a head start and we become reluctant to go out to a patch of weeds that remind us of our neglect. Then fruits and vegetables ripen and we're too busy to notice. For a huge number of people, far too much garden produce is never harvested at all. Putting the garden right outside the back door proves to be an effective strategy for reminding us to notice. Seeing the ripening food as we come and go over the day also sparks ideas about how to use what is ripe, and running out to the garden can replace running to the store for something you forgot to pick up.

When it comes to garden design, one of the principles that permaculture goes to great effort to teach is the difference between order and chaos. "Order is found in things working beneficially together," says Mollison. It is not the forced condition of neatness, tidiness, and straightness, all of which are, in design or energy terms, disordered. True order may lie in apparent confusion if it produces energy to or beyond consumption, it is ordered—natural. It follows then that you can reduce disorder, or eliminate much of the waste that results from poor garden placement and design, by changing your perception of what is order and what is chaos. This may take a bit of effort but it can be done. I know because I have managed to change my own ideas about how things should be.

We live in southwest Michigan, in an area called the Fruitbelt, where there are hundreds of orchards, vineyards, and fields of small fruits. I remember a time not so long ago when I would drive by these vineyards or fields and admire the nice straight rows, neatly tilled soil, and complete absence of weeds. If I happened to pass by a field where there were *weeds* among the plants, I would think to myself, "That looks awful! Why don't they get out there and take care of that mess?" We have two vineyards ourselves, and when we decided to practice organic *viticulture* (grape growing) and let the soil restore itself, we stopped spraying herbicides and tilling the soil to keep the weeds down. At first, I thought it looked messy and uncared for. But after a few years I got used to it. I knew that I had changed my perception when one day I was driving past one of those perfectly sprayed, tilled, and manicured vineyards and my first, gut-level thought was, "Look at that poor vineyard, it's got no life in it!"

Creating replicas of the nice straight rows that appear in garden magazines is forcing disorder upon a system. This is not the way things grow in nature, and anyone who has tried to maintain nice, straight, clean rows knows that they simply cannot be maintained without extraordinary amounts of time, human energy, and perhaps the mechanical energy of a rototiller complete with fuels. If you get busy and the weeds get bad enough, even the rototiller is no match. When gardens are surrounded by neatly edged grass and lawn, we are reluctant to build a messy-looking compost pile next to it. So either we don't have a compost pile at all, or we put it somewhere out of sight, which becomes make-work when we have to haul the compost to the garden in the spring, or whenever we want to do some top-dressing. Other piles, such as mulch, paramagnetic rock, and bags of lime or bone meal are just as unwelcome, and if left sitting on the lawn for a few days or a week, they leave nice areas of dead grass where they sat.

Lest you think that permaculture results in a sloppy, trashy looking yard, rest assured that quite the reverse is true. Due to the intense planning and design work that is carried out beforehand, the use of zones, and the careful set-up of systems and access-ways to allow both self-regulation and evolution, the only things that are lost in a permaculture system are the uselessness of today's suburban yards, and the artificial look that plagues many of them. Indeed, with an emphasis on balance and greatly expanded diversity, sometimes as many as 4,000 trees and plants per acre are carefully selected and added to a single site in order to restore the natural order and beauty.

Dense Plantings

By Harry MacCormack

For more than five thousand years of annually tilled and planted food and fiber crops, arguments over plant spacing have abounded. Variant planting patterns have evolved as a result. Some appear to reflect cultural bias, even cosmological viewpoints. But in all cases yield seems to be a factor in choice. After all, our primal desire is to produce food easily in enough quantity to perpetuate our species. Other animals have to hunt or forage. We can use our minds to plan and execute. So one of the primary questions for any grower of food is, "How can we get the most with the least amount of effort?"

Multistoried diversity abounds in nature. Where desertification hasn't denuded the ancient greening of our planet, it is common to see many species growing together. Symbiosis (two organisms living together in close proximity) has been established. Visually, what is always apparent, is that there exists a kind of harmony between various trees, shrubs, flowers, grasses, insects, birds, animals, and yes, invisible microbes. One way or another the brown of earth is covered. Commercial growing fields exhibit just the opposite tendencies. For much of the year they are intentionally left without crop. Often, whatever would or could grow gets coated with herbicides. Many home gardens suffer from similar practices. Anything growing without our permission is determined to be a pest, and is killed, if not with chemicals, then with black plastic or continual tillage. Integrated natural growing systems are destroyed through human manipulation. We tend to elevate this destruction by using the term "management."

In the 1970s, during the back-to-the-land movement in the U.S., many of us were reacting to degradation that resulted from intensive monoculture management schemes. Most of us began growing gardens with a lot of intelligence and very little know-how or money. Through observing plant organization patterns in forests, meadows, areas of natural prairie, we saw not only diversity, we saw density. It was obvious that plants liked growing in very close proximity to other plants. There seemed a natural vigor—a perennial health in those nonhuman schemes. Many of us read of cultures whose ancient gardens mimicked such dense plantings. Chinese gardens are legend. I knew of such gardens in South America, and I had observed tightly managed gardens grown in old monasteries in Europe. Based on that knowledge and a will to experiment, the bio-intensive gardening techniques developed by horticulturist Alan Chadwick appeared in the now classic book *How to Grow More Vegetables Than You Ever Thought Possible on Less Land Than You Can Imagine: A Primer on the Life-Giving Dynamic of Biodynamic/French Intensive* by John Jeavons (now in its fifth revised edition, but out of print). On our Sunbow Farm market gardening operation we have used variants of intensive, dense planting management schemes.

For this *2002 Moon Sign Book* we revisited the theory and practice of organically based dense planting. We've always done tight plantings in our hoophouses where early and late season's crops are grown. To varying extents we've carried some of that methodology into fields where we work with green-manure crops, machinery, and much larger beds. So we have years of observations to draw from. This season we decided to take a more careful look at what we're doing and why we're doing it, and report our findings on these pages.

Light, Fertility, and Moisture

The mantra for growers of plants is "Light, fertility, moisture." Over and over we deal with these illusive plant requirements. In previous editions of this annual I've discussed a fourth, and perhaps primary requirement— subtle wave energies. All of this requisite plant culture affects and is effected by plant spacing.

So let's look at one example and extrapolate from it. It is midwinter. I've got a tray of baby lettuces and I'm going to set these lettuces into a hoophouse bed. The bed is raised, three-feet wide and twelve-feet long. In many conventional gardens you would see two rows of lettuce on such a bed, maybe twenty-four heads. It might be considered radical to move these lettuce plants toward the edge of the bed and plant a third row. That would give thirty-six heads. But using John Jeavons' charts we cover the entire bed with baby lettuces on eight-inch centers. We cram sixty-four lettuces on this bed. At something over $1.50 per head midwinter this small bed should yield about $100.00 worth of product. Can I get away with this?

Light

Light in winter is low on the horizon. By the time these lettuces are mature it will be much higher, providing minimally, light for ten hours a day. Because of the effect of plastic over this area of beds light-heat hours will translate into solar gain in the soil, warming the roots of these plants considerably, especially when compared with soil outside the hoophouse. Light intensity will not be a problem. There may be too much heat for a crop that prefers cool. Light seems not to be a problem in this dense planting until plants are near maturity. Then we've observed a reaching, particularly in this hoophouse-plastic cover condition, but also outside. That stretching causes a reshaping of the plant. There seems to be a speeding-up of growth. We can loose saleable production, as the plant seems stimulated to produce seed. Does light/heat act the same way when plants are spaced further apart? We've experimented with this premise. Plants on twelve-inch, rather than eight-inch, settings grow more broadly. They tend to "lay-open." What seems a constant is that various kinds of lettuce require space suitable to their type. A French Butter lettuce requires much less space than a Red Sails Looseleaf. Light and heat seem to be a determining factor in that observation.

Fertility

We turn to the question of fertility. How potent is potent? When dealing with very dense plantings do we need to add proportionately more fertilizer?

Fertilization may be a bad concept in our fast paced world. We tend to think it in terms of replacement, cookbook chemistry. Most of us tend to forget that we are not feeding foods directly to plants. Instead, we are feeding a microherd, billions of organisms in a handful of rich garden soil. These organisms are interactive (they live together in symbiosis). They eat each other and any amendments we add, making available residues of their interactiveness as foods for plants. The previous discussion of light/heat is relevant here because crucial bacteria operate in very narrow temperature ranges. Most true bacteria require temperatures in at least the fifty-degree Fahrenheit range to be active in soils. Some combination bacteria/fungi critters can be active in lower soil temperatures. But fertility is less in cooler soils; or in soils that are too hot—above ninety degrees Fahrenheit.

So, how do we know if we've got enough fertility to sustain a dense planting? This one question is probably what drives the art of agriculture. There is no scientific formula for fertility. What we add as amendments to one soil in one season may differ widely from what gets added another season. There now exist through Soil Food Web1 living soil tests telling us microbial counts in various soils. These tests allow us to guess more clearly what a soil needs to support a crop. But fertility is still a creative process based on alertness of the practitioner. Care of the soil, like care of the soul, is mysterious. It differentiates one garden and gardener from others.

From experience we know that composted organic materials, alive with microorganisms and their residues, always enhance soil life. How much compost is needed on a bed? It depends. I know of situations where too much compost over the years has resulted in a lack of fertility. So, along with compost should be a program of additions of a good nitrogen compound. (We tend to use fish-based compounds.) Also, minerals broken-down by microbes and utilized by plants need to be replaced. Depending on previous cropping, we might use on our lettuce planting a sprinkling of rock phosphate, rock dust, a source of calcium like oyster shell powder, or a sprinkling of lime.

Fertility observations will tell you very rapidly if you have too little of a nutrient balance to sustain a tight planting of a crop. If the crop looks weak, use liquid teas: compost tea, liquid fish/kelp. Spray or sprinkle these teas over the crop. You should see an almost immediate improvement in growth and overall healthy look of plant life. In nature, you might observe such a change following a rain after a dry period. Rain carries nutrients in solution—a power drink for the microherd. And actually, plants can uptake liquid nutrition directly through the stoma, or breathing pores, in the epidermis of plants.

Moisture

Moisture is very critical in dense plantings. With a crop like lettuce it is very easy to start fungal diseases, rot, if there is too much water. Too little moisture and you get stunting and wilt. How do you maintain proper levels? I suggest a water meter. Test several places in a bed. If at all possible in a dense planting use drip irrigation. Drip lines keep the water in the soil, off the plant, which can help with fungal problems.

Outside a covered hoophouse situation, in the field, later in the season, tight plantings of lettuce are handled similarly. Less compost is required because green manure is plowed into the soils. Light is usually only a problem when a tender leafy crop needs to set roots while it is too hot. We often use floating row covers to help temporarily modulate light/heat/moisture.

The critical disease factor in tight plantings of most crops, as related to moisture, is air circulation. What we've observed is that when dense plantings of tender leafy crops—lettuce, basil, spinach, etc.—mature to a stage where they touch plant to plant, and air either doesn't clear them of moisture or is not circulating much at all, fungal rot sets in. This condition can be alleviated somewhat by selling smaller plants, or thinning. Sometimes, if markets are jammed and we wish to save bigger plants for later markets we are forced to thin, eat a lot ourselves, or toss plants on the compost heap. Thinning opens up the stand.

Now, for my favorite mystery—plant harmonics. I have been interested for a long time in plant communication. Plants utilize wave energies. I've written about these subtle energy relationships in previous *Moon Sign Books*. Questions relevant to this article are: do plants (say lettuces) communicate differently when planted in a monocropped bed as distinct from a mixed bed where they have companions? Observation says, "yes." We get much more even, much more lettucey lettuce on a bed that is all lettuce than we do when lettuce is intercropped with say carrots, marigolds, spinach, or kale. Some of the plant harmonics probably reflects root exudates (to be discharged or discharge slowly) and their interactions with soil microlife. We know little of how various root exudates might clash. And we know almost nothing about how these root exudates interact with microlife either singly or in combination. What seems obvious from my knowledge of subtle energies is that each plant is an individual. Individuals have field-energy requirements. We can't see the field energies around a plant, usually, but we sense them in terms of a requirement for space. Imagine yourself in a densely human situation and how you feel crammed. How is that different from being where you are in relationship, but with an openness—a space—around you so that your energy field can be completed, outward thrust, openly transmittive?

Our observations suggest that having crops in adjacent beds is usually preferable to interplanting in terms of yield. One effect of tight planting of dissimilar crops seems to be elongation. Again, lettuce: elongation is fine if you're growing a Romaine variety. It is a disaster if you're marketing large, leafy, more rounded forms. The lettuce may taste fine, but it just doesn't look as people expect the form to look. This season we did further experiments with dense plants of various root crops: beets, onions, carrots, and potatoes, with some interesting results.

Onions were planted on four and six inch centers in rows with a foot of opening between them. The rows had to be weeded four times. Hand weeding right around the plants was necessary because mechanical tools cannot get that close without plant damage. The tighter plantings also had to be hand weeded. But per square foot we were dealing with much less weed pressure. Usually, one weeding was all that was needed.

Although onions on the dense plantings were never as large as onions from the rows, overall yield in terms of poundage per square foot of ground was much greater. Even if tonnage is the same, we utilized much less soil to get it, less water, less fertilizer, less time. In the marketplace, our smaller onions went for a higher price than other's larger onions. Another interesting factor is that the onions in the dense planting seemed to mature faster. This allowed us to clear the bed sooner and put in another crop. (Double and triple cropping is often a result of dense planting schemes.)

We had similar experiences with beets and carrots. Dense plantings of each of these crops yielded well. Beets in particular were very easy to keep clear of weeds. Their larger leaves formed a tight canopy shading out smaller seedlings. After one weeding, carrots did likewise. We've always planted potatoes on two-foot centers, allowing us a double zigzag row system down our beds. In other words, we're doubling our production per square foot when compared with more accepted row-planting schemes. We grow only gourmet or specialty varieties, which are usually mature in sixty days. Tight plantings and fast growth usually allow us to get by with one light hoeing and hilling just before blossom time. We are able to harvest the potato beds mechanically.

So, do dense plantings of larger plants such as broccoli, kohlrabi, or cabbage fare? Jeavons recommends eighteen-inch centers. We follow a diamond pattern when setting out these plants. Or if direct seeded, we thin to that pattern. We know that eighteen inches leaves a lot of room for early weed growth. But, a hoe can work those areas fairly rapidly. This season we tried broccoli on one-foot centers. We got beautiful heads, the leaves touching closed the canopy, so weed pressure was a lot less. However, we used compost tea weekly on these plants. They are all heavy feeders. The secret to pulling off dense plantings is often faster than normal growth, especially in early stages after transplant. Kohlrabi seemed much better on smaller centers. Cabbage, on the other hand, may need two feet. Small heads were the result of even eighteen-inch plantings.

We also tried broccoli, cabbage, and kohlrabi, scattered in diverse plantings of mizuna, parsley, lettuce, and carrots. The larger brassicus (tall, branched herbs of the mustard family) plants overpowered the smaller lettuce and carrot family. Some carrots were entirely wiped out by cabbage leaf sprawl. So much for companion planting on the same bed. From a vibrational/wave-energy standpoint, adjacent plantings on diverse beds did well. Insect pressure seems disrupted as thoroughly as it does when everything is mixed together.

Tomatoes

We are major tomato growers. We are always looking to get more production from our three-foot wide interior beds and our four-foot wide outside beds. Usually, we've found we can use a zigzag transplant pattern on approximately eighteen-inch centers and do one weeding with good production. However, if plants are trellised (indeterminate varieties that climb), we've gotten by with one-foot centers. Make certain that fertility is high. And use drip irrigation.

This season we experimented out of necessity, because of wet weather at transplanting time and too many plants, with a three-row zigzag pattern on a four-foot bed. The variety was Early Girl. We knew these plants wouldn't grow really tall, but they would need some kind of trellis to get full production. It was not fun, but after the floating row covers came off, when the weather had warmed, we did manage to weave a makeshift trellis among plants that were literally pushing up against each other. Surprise to us, production was good. Picking was kind of a pit. But the tomatoes were good sized, and there were no weeds.

Strawberries

Another place we've tried dense plantings is on Everbearing strawberries. We set them out on eight-inch centers, theorizing that when mature a strawberry plant is about the size of a lettuce. We put drip irrigation lines between plants to lower the possibility of fungal rot from overhead irrigation, particularly early in the season. The plants have done quite well. (Production is good for everbearing plants.)

In our climate, in the hot summer, drip lines do not provide enough water for such a dense planting. So overhead sprinklers are used. One of the secrets to providing a steady flow of strawberries is to keep them wet enough. Picking is done easily from two sides of a bed. Runners are pruned for new plantings. Weeds will eventually become a problem and hand weeding is a difficult job. But at $2.50 a pint basket, it is worth it.

Fruit Trees

Some of our friends have experimented with tight plantings of fruit trees. From what I've seen, dwarf and semidwarf trees can attain full size in these systems. But they require extensive pruning and usually some kind of irrigation. Also trees in a dense system seem to require more fertilizer inputs, and seem to be more susceptible to both insect damage and disease. Getting beneath trees that are planted very densely, to pick, mow, and cultivate can be tricky. To a certain extent the canopy does provide enough shade to keep competitive weeds down. But in our orchard I've stopped thinking about grasses, etc., as competition. In fact, there may be herbs and other cash crops, which would grow just fine as an understory in these orchards providing not only ground cover and a secondary income, but an insectary where beneficial balancing of insect populations is enhanced.

The whole concept of multistory plantings takes us back to where this essay began, namely the naturally occurring interactive forests, trees, and complex systems of smaller plants. Gardens should reflect this layering. However, the more interwoven species you've got jammed together, the more tiptoeing you do when working in the garden. Maybe that's a good thing, a practice for walking lightly on this Earth.

Given adequate light, fertility, and moisture, you need only be concerned about proper spacing to allow for total energy flow needs of all plants. Imagine yourself as any one plant. Imagine what it would feel like to not be able to spread fully. Give everyone enough room. You'll see happy plants supporting each other. Orchards or permaculture crops are not the only multistoried designs we've tried. One classic is the corn/bean/squash combo. The beans do grow up the corn. To a certain extent so do the squashes. Everyone is having fun. It's simply an awful place for a human to harvest. Especially if beans come on ahead of corn ahead of squashes.

Wave Energies

Our universe, and therefore our gardens, manifest through interactive subtle wave energies. Oscillations influencing plant growth, or coming from plant growth, have been measured. In general, we are the outcome of cosmic wave energies merging with bioactive wave energies. According to Dr. O. Ed Wagner, cosmic wave constants (always in motion) such as gravity or background W-waves, which are everywhere in our universe, may be changed by plants. Plants may even affect the proposed curvature of space. If we understand plants and ourselves as resonators, how then do plant spacings enhance or thwart that resonance?

In a forest or open meadow we might expect to respond to plant resonances differently than from a garden. Gardens are, after all, human designs. The difference between a forest and a garden is that the garden represents human intention. If that intention includes tight plantings, then how might human organizational patterning affect plant growth? And how might that plant matrix influence even gravity?

These questions relate to a sacred geometry. Dan Winter is among those working in this field. He notes that the principle structural ratio of DNA, the Golden Mean Ratio, permits waves to add and multiply implosively. Human structural design intention is wave interference in DNA. In other words, designing a garden with dense plantings rather than open rows affects biological ordering. Intention is a thrust into rather steady state wave realities, cosmic and biological, creating an amperage shift we experience as future. He uses the term *dilation* to describe this process.

That we humans can steer wave energies through our choices has vast implications for all of creation. Just in the realms of garden plantings, what is the difference between a monocropped bed of lettuce, vibrationally speaking, and a bed the same size planted with say five randomly spaced crops? Each crop is emitting a different kind of resonance. Does a mix of resonances send a different message back into the universe about the state of our intelligence, different from a more intensely formed resonance from one sort of plant? And let's expand this to look at dense plantings such as those seen in commercial agriculture from Indiana all the way to Colorado, monocropped corn and soybeans, thousands of miles of one, or sometimes two, vibratory resonances. How does that human intervention with earth differ from natural prairie grasses and trees? What might diversity have to do with overall health? If we should, as a species, decide to regreen our Earth—move toward a perennial agriculture, stop desertification—would our future look brighter? Hertz readings from monocrops are quite different from those in mixed natural plantings. Is one more in unity with universal energy than another?

When I go into the garden for noneconomic reasons, I sense that our beds are happier when all kinds of plants are stimulated there. I watch layers: herbs growing in partial shade from beans, carrots popping through a squash. The whole concept of dense planting changes when variety is introduced. On the other hand, the most boring agriculture ever introduced graces much of our country with very dense plantings of corn and soybeans. Although lush and green at late summer, there's a vibrational flatness that probably didn't exist when the buffalo roamed. We can, with machinery, plant a single crop every foot year after year. Does that mean we should?

The politics of dense planting is most often that of commodity marketing. It could just as easily be that of the much smaller, more diverse market garden. Or humans could do dense planting design to preserve the natural diversity of our planet with no eye to production and marketing? These are choices we must make, soon. How we choose to clothe our soils determines what kind of future our species will or won't have.

How High Is the Moon?

By *Valerie Vaughan*

The complex motions of the Moon form an intricate pattern of cycles—a celestial dance that has fascinated skywatchers for millennia. Perhaps the most obvious cycle is the repeating phases of New and Full Moons, but there are other noticeable differences in the Moon's behavior that repeat on a regular basis. One of these changes, which the ancients observed (and you may have noticed as well), is the height of the Moon. It is not always the same.

If you pay attention to the Moon's movement, you will see that its path across the sky (as the Earth rotates) looks like an arc that stretches from the eastern to the western horizon. At one time during each month, this arc seems to be lower in the sky. The height of this arc changes gradually, until about two weeks later, the Moon is moving in a relatively higher arc across the sky. And if you consult the calendar in the *Old Farmer's Almanac*, you will see that these monthly extremes are indicated as days when "the Moon rides low" or "the Moon rides high." Astrologers and astronomers refer to this change in height as the declination, which is measured in degrees north or south of the Earth's equator and is listed in any good ephemeris.

Even beyond these regular monthly extremes, there are certain years when the lunar path is especially low or high. (Most people become aware of these special extremes when the Moon starts shining through certain windows where it had not previously appeared.) If you observed the Moon continuously, as the ancients did, you would eventually discover that the full cycle of these extreme declinations is 18.61 years. This number may sound familiar because it's the cycle of the Moon's nodes.

The 18.6–Year Lunar Nodal Cycle

A little astronomy can explain this cycle. The Moon orbits the Earth in a slightly different path than the ecliptic (where the Sun appears to move). The paths of the Sun and Moon cross each other at two points called the North and South Nodes. Because of a wobble in the lunar orbit, there is a gradual drift in the position of the nodes, and they appear to move backwards through the zodiac. The North Node returns (in retrograde motion) to the 0 degree of Aries once every 18.61 years.

Every time the North Node passes through 0 degree Aries, the Moon's orbit is more tilted with respect to the Earth's equator, so the greatest declination occurs (28 degrees north or south), and that's when the Moon moves in its most extreme high and low arcs across the sky. The last time this occurred was in late 1987, and the next time will be in 2006. In the middle of this cycle, when the North Node is at 0 degree Libra, the Moon reaches its least declination (18 degrees north or south), and the twice-monthly difference in height is not so noticeable. This last occurred in early 1997.

The Long History of Natural Astrology

The lunar node cycle was one of the earliest discoveries of ancient sky-watchers. In fact, the very oldest part of Stonehenge was built to measure this pattern of 18.61 years. Why were the ancients so concerned with tracking this cycle? Most archeo-astronomers believe the reason was to predict eclipses, because the nodes determine when the paths of the Sun and Moon are aligned. But that answer simply begs the question of why someone would want to predict eclipses in the first place. Many archeo-astronomers believe that the ancient skywatchers did this in order to appear knowledgeable of magic and thus maintain control over the masses of supposedly fearful people. This interpretation is unfortunately based on a negative view that modern science has of astrology, and it assumes that the ancients were either power-hungry astrologers, or completely stupid, gullible people.

If we take a different approach to history and give the ancients the credit they deserve for being intelligent observers, we soon realize there was a very practical reason for tracking the lunar node cycle. The ancients recognized that this cycle correlated with patterns of change in natural phenomena, such as weather and the behavior of animals. They sought to understand this cycle because their very livelihood depended on knowing when the fish were biting, or when to protect crops from frost or flood. They also noticed that human behavior changed according to this cycle because people reacted differently when their bellies were full or there was a good wine harvest. It is only a modern (and very mistaken) notion to think that humans can exist independently from their environment.

One of the most amazing things about the lunar nodal cycle is that there is so much scientific proof of its presence as a cyclical influence in nature. Numerous studies have shown that the 18.61-year cycle correlates with patterns of drought, flooding, tree growth, fish population, earth-quakes, and many other phenomena. But scientific researchers who perform these studies are careful to avoid mentioning the "A" word. Scientists who study cycles would be appalled if they knew they were actually practicing the oldest form of astrology. Medieval and Renaissance astrologers called it natural astrology, and it encompassed the astrological study of all sorts of natural phenomena—weather, meteors, ocean tides, and the behavior of plants and animals.

The Proof That Astrology Works

Once we acknowledge that lunar cycles correlate with natural phenomena, it is easy to see how this could influence human behavior. To demonstrate this, let's suppose that you're a farmer in Iowa in the 1950s. You have learned from your grandfather (who was also a farmer) that severe droughts tend to occur in the Great Plains every nineteen years or so, as they did in the 1890s, 1910s, and 1930s. You know that the area is currently due for another drought, but you plant anyway. The drought occurs right on schedule with the nodal cycle, and your crop fails (as does your neighbor's). Since much of the world's entire grain crop is grown in the

Great Plains, there are widespread consequences for the world's economy. Grain prices soar.

Essentially, the drought has started a domino effect. First, it affects you personally, because the crop failure spells financial doom for your farm. You try to borrow money or sell part of your land, but most of the other farmers are doing the same, which drives interest rates up and land prices down. Cheap land attracts developers, and suddenly there's a new highway being built that alters the countryside, along with your personal driving habits. Some of the farmers organize to demand government subsidy. Overwhelmed by the changes, people become more conservative, less likely to take a risk. You, like everyone else, start behaving differently. All because of a crop failure caused by a drought, which was brought on by changes in the atmosphere, which was altered by certain alignments of the Sun, Moon, and Earth. As a farmer, you've lost a lot, but you also understand now why astrology works.

Long-Term Effects of the Nodal Cycle

The ups and downs of rainfall are not the only natural phenomena that follow the nodal cycle. Major climate events such as El Niño and severe winters seem to follow this cycle. The reason is that long-term trends in temperature and air pressure are affected by what scientists call the "tidal forcing positions" of the Sun, Moon and earth. Just as the Moon exerts an effect on the ocean tides, there is a similar astronomical tidal pull on the Earth's ocean of air, causing mass interactions in the atmosphere that result in stormy weather, lightning, and changes in ozone.

In the final analysis, everything on our planet is affected by the weather. A cycle that brings damp, cool summers, or harsh, snowless winters has a large effect on the reproduction and growth of plants and animals. Research has revealed a regular nodal cycle pattern (or half-cycle of nine years) in the growth of plants and the population of salmon, lynx, tent caterpillars, and many other fauna.

Humans must rely on these weather-affected plants and animals for survival, so ultimately, all human activity is dependent on the weather. This is why researchers have found rhythms of nine and eighteen years in business, such as wholesale prices, stock prices, industrial activity, and building construction. Even marriage rates have been shown to follow the ups and downs of the eighteen-plus year cycle. The nodal cycle of weather changes can also be correlated with alterations in human emotion, disease, and death (more people die during lousy weather). A review of history will show that the increase in technological progress can be linked to cyclical weather patterns. In the final analysis, civilization itself is stimulated or repressed by conditions of climate. Is it any wonder that early civilizations built sacred monuments to measure and worship the cycles of the Moon?

In and Out of Fashion

Apparently the Moon's nodes reflect the public mood and the changing focus of public interest. We can observe this in the periodic changes that occur in popular fads and fashions. As styles go in and out of fashion, they seem to follow a pattern of the nodes moving retrograde through the signs of the zodiac. The sign that the node is in seems to represent the quality

of what's currently popular. For instance, when the North Node was in Sagittarius in the mid-1970s, a new activity called skateboarding swept across America. This is an active sport that involves thigh muscles (ruled by Sagittarius) and represents a Sagittarian mixture of fun and mobility.

One nodal cycle earlier, when the North Node was in Sagittarius in the mid-1950s, it was a fad for college students to see how many could stuff themselves into an automobile (another Sagittarian example of combining fun with transportation). Also at this time, the popularity of TV's *Davy Crockett* led to millions of children wearing coonskin caps, a symbol of the Sagittarian interest in hunting and the wild frontier. The most popular hairstyle for America's young girls in the mid-50s was the ponytail, showing the horsey influence of the node in the sign of the Sagittarian Centaur. The latest fashion in clothing at the time was Bermuda shorts, which of course revealed the thighs. When the node was again in Sagittarius eighteen years later, a popular clothing fad was the string bikini, which revealed even more of the thigh and buttocks (both ruled by Sagittarius).

When the North Node is in Leo, fashion trends focus on individuality and a showiness that seems to shout, "I'm special!" In 1980, when the node was in Leo, a popular item of clothing was designer jeans, which were conspicuously labeled by top fashion houses. One nodal cycle earlier, in 1961, women's clothing trends were set by that regal Leo-Sun herself, First Lady Jackie Kennedy.

Scorpio is a dark, powerful sign. In 1957, with the North Node in Scorpio, teenage boys departed from usual fashion customs by wearing black leather jackets. Bouffant (puffed-up) hairdos became popular as women sought to create a more powerful appearance. Also during this Scorpio nodal passage, a New York businessman discovered a warehouse full of British bobby (policeman) capes, which led to a brief but profitable clothing craze. Scorpio rules profitable schemes, hidden storehouses, and the police.

The youthful look of Gemini became fashionable during the mid-1960s when the North Node transited Gemini. The boyish look of the Beatles became popular, as did the flower-child image and the little-girl style of miniskirts. Gemini is an air sign that rules the intellect. It was during this period that teenagers began cutting holes in their sneakers, seeking an air-conditioned effect, and it was also a fad to acquire an intellectual look by wearing open-air glasses (frames without lenses).

When the node is in unique Aquarius, styles tend to become weird, nerdy, or controversial. When this occurred in 1952, over thirty million American children could be seen wearing propeller-topped beanies. When the North Node returned to Aquarius in 1970, hot pants were a popular but highly controversial clothing item, and men began wearing flamboyant bow ties. In the mid-1980s, the node was in Taurus, the powerful sign of the Bull, which rules thick necks and wide shoulders. This is precisely the period when women began dressing up in power suits that were beefed up with thick, wide shoulder pads.

Fun and Games

What people do for fun and games can also go through phases of popularity, again corresponding to the change in nodal sign. In 1902, the first teddy bear was sold, a warm-fuzzy toy that offered pleasant company for little children. At this time, the North Node was in Libra, the sign of pleasant companionship. In 1909, jigsaw puzzles became enormously popular, a game with numerous and scattered individual parts (just like

Gemini, the sign the node was in). In 1919, with the North Node in secretive and occult-oriented Scorpio, the first Ouija boards went on sale.

In 1924, with the node in logical Virgo, the first crossword puzzle book was published. At the time, this new interest in crossword puzzles was blamed for the downfall of the previous game fad, Mah-jong. This Chinese game had been introduced in 1922, when the node was in relationship-oriented Libra. Getting together to play Mah-jong was an important social event for many women. Later, in the mid-1920s, the node moved through Leo, and various attention-getting marathons became all the rage, such as individuals sitting on top of a flagpole for hours.

Signs of War

Because the nodes move backward through the zodiac, they enter the back door of a sign through its last degree. In October 2001, for example, the North Node finished up nineteen months of being in Cancer as it passed through the 0 degree of Cancer, and then entered the last degree of Gemini. The ingress of the node into a new sign is usually highlighted by important events.

If we track the sign ingresses of the node through the history of war, we find that an important battle, or the start of a war, is often concurrent with a nodal sign change. The first battle of the American Revolution, a war fought for independence and individual identity, took place in April, 1775, within a few weeks of the node changing to Leo. When Hitler invaded Poland and started World War II in September 1939, the node was at 0 degree Scorpio. The massive Normandy invasion of June 6, 1944, took place within days of the node reaching 0 degree Leo. In July, 1950, the U.S. entered the Korean War, within a few weeks of the node at 0 degree Aries.

The United States began its involvement in the Vietnam War by sending in the first 20,000 troops in 1961, within days of the node being at exactly 0 degree Leo. In August 1964, within days of the node reaching

0 degree Cancer, the Gulf of Tonkin Incident occurred, which President Johnson later used as the basis for his buildup of troops in Vietnam. When the node was at 0 degree Aries in April 1969, the number of U.S. troops in Vietnam had reached the highest of the entire war, over half a million. Then, as the node moved through Pisces, the sign of withdrawal, more and more troops began to be withdrawn. President Nixon announced his intention to withdraw 150,000 troops by the end of 1970, precisely when the node reached 0 degree Pisces.

Public Mood and Politics

The quality of nodal sign can be observed in recent American presidential elections. In 1980, with the node in Leo, we elected a former movie star, and then in 1984, with the node in consistent, never-changing Taurus, we opted for four more years of the same thing. In 1988, the node was in Pisces, a relatively conservative sign, and Republican George Bush was elected. In 1992 and 1996, the nodes were in the social, liberal signs of Sagittarius and Libra, and we elected a sociable, Democratic president, Bill Clinton.

The nodal hits on the cardinal direction points (zero degree of Aries, Cancer, Libra, and Capricorn) tend to mark especially important watersheds. As the node passes through one of these points, major events that represent a distinct directional shift in public attitudes are likely to occur. A quick look at the last two nodal cycles will make this clear. In 1964, when the node passed through 0 degree Cancer, Congress passed the Civil Rights Act. The entire country became more concerned with the protection (Cancer rules protection) of equal rights. As the node passed to the next cardinal sign, warlike Aries, the Vietnam War had replaced civil rights as the central national issue. By the time the node passed through zero Aries in 1969, the country was clearly divided between the hawks and doves (symbolized by the North Node in aggressive Aries opposed the South Node in peace-loving Libra). In 1973, as the node passed through Capricorn—the sign of administration, but also loss—the U.S. stopped fighting (and lost) the Vietnam War, and the Watergate scandal was in full form as numerous members of the Nixon administration resigned.

As the node entered Cancer in 1981, the public became aware of a new, incurable disease called AIDS, which initiated a Cancerian mood of vulnerability and caution. Also at this time, the national budget deficit had reached a high mark of one trillion dollars, and people became concerned about the Cancerian need to reduce government spending. Within days of the nodal passage through zero degree Cancer, Reagan announced his "solution" for protecting the U.S.—the Star Wars defense plan. Just as the node entered explosive Aries in 1986, the Soviets announced that a nuclear accident had occurred at Chernobyl. As the node moved through Aries, the public was made aware of the Iran-contra affair, in which the Reagan administration had been secretly selling arms to Iran and diverting sales money to rebels in Nicaragua. In 1987, as the node closed in on zero degree Aries, Reagan signed a treaty providing for the dismantling of all United States and Soviet intermediate-range nuclear weapons.

Financial Cycles

Economic crises such as financial panics and market crashes tend to center around the passage of the nodes through the cardinal signs. This nodal pattern (and its multiple, 54–56 years) has long been recognized by economists who study cycles. Many important financial events in history have coincided with the beginning or end of wars, because both were riding on the same lunar cycle.

The great financial crisis of 1763 occurred as the node passed through Aries, just at the end of the Seven Years War in Europe. The French economy went into severe decline in 1787 just prior to the French Revolution, with the node in Capricorn. A major financial crash occurred in 1797, precisely when the node crossed 0 degree Cancer, and another in 1811, exactly when the node crossed 0 degree Libra. The crisis of 1815, related to the end of the Napoleonic Wars, occurred with the node in Cancer. In the twentieth century—right at the end of the Vietnam War, and within days of the nodal passage through 0 degree Capricorn (late 1973)—the Arab oil embargo began, setting off an oil crisis and economic decline. A few weeks before the node reached 0 degree Aries in 1987, the stock market plunged in the largest drop in history.

Of the twenty-eight major economic crises that occurred between 1763 and 1987, four happened with the node in Cancer (1797, 1815, 1907, 1981–82), six happened with the node in Libra (1773, 1810, 1828, 1847-48, 1866, 1920–21), and seven with the node in Aries (1763, 1819, 1837–38, 1857, 1893, 1930–31, 1987).

Economists who study cycles have noticed another important eighteen-plus year pattern, one that exists in real estate activity. From 1783 through 1987, there were eleven nodal cycles. In a remarkable display of coincidence, there was a peak in real estate activity and new building construction once in every nodal cycle—whenever the North Node was in Cancer, the sign of home and property ownership.

The Cycle–Behavior Link

Most activities and natural phenomena are not static; they follow an up-and-down pattern of development, and many of these wave patterns appear to correlate with the 18.61-year nodal cycle. The following example will demonstrate how one such pattern can translate into human behavior.

Between 1838 and 1931, there were six periods of nodal cycle. Each time the North Node passed through Pisces and then Aquarius, the signs associated with spiritual, religious, and group affiliation, church membership increased and reached the highest peak for each 18.61-year period. This pattern of behavior can be understood by recalling the retrograde motion of the nodes. Because the nodes move backward, the development of a pattern follows the reverse order of the zodiac. The node enters Pisces right after it has been in Aries. As we have seen from the examination of wars, droughts, and economic crises, the nodal passage through Aries tends to be a disruptive time. It makes perfect sense that, following such a challenging period, more people would be drawn to seek peace through spiritual attunement as the node passed through Pisces, and then harmony through group bonding as the node entered Aquarius.

The North Node in Gemini

This year, 2002, the node will move backward from 27 degrees Gemini (in January) to 8 degrees of Gemini (in December). We can expect to see some developments in 2002 that will match what happened during previous years with the node in Gemini. Earlier passages occurred in the years of 1983–84, 1964–65, 1946–47, and 1927–28. With the node in the information-oriented, communicative sign of Gemini, these were all-important years for the development of computers and telecommunications.

In 1927, the first public demonstration of television took place the same week that the node entered Gemini. In 1928, color television was demonstrated for the first time. Two nodal cycles later, in 1964, color television sets became popular and soon replaced black-and-white sets.

In 1946, the first all-purpose electronic computer (ENIAC) came on line. In 1947 came the invention of the transistor, one of the most important developments for computers. This was also the year of the first nationwide telephone strike. In 1964–65, the first commercial telephone communications satellite was launched, and the public saw the first demonstration of television via satellite. This was also the year that picture-phone appeared, combining television with telephone. Gemini rules language, and in 1965, IBM-BASIC appeared, the first all-purpose computer programming language. Also this year, astronauts were orbiting the Earth in Gemini capsules. In 1983, the computer mouse was introduced, a device for the hand (ruled by Gemini). In 1984, the first CD laser disks appeared, providing the ability to deal with ever-growing amounts of information.

If the nodal cycle runs true, events in 2002 are likely to match these previous years. Progress, as well as problems, will likely center around information technology such as telephones, computers, television, and communication satellites. There may be important developments in information transfer, and television over the Internet will probably be popularized. Information overload may drive the public mood to distraction, reaching a peak of Gemini data frenzy. The pace won't settle down until the node enters stabilizing Taurus in 2003. The Moon's nodal cycle will continue moving, and we humans will keep on dancing to its rhythm.

Trees: Living Energy Beings

By Penny Kelly

I live in an old hayloft. A couple of giant linden trees, a silver maple, two red maples, and a Chinese elm extend their lacy boughs onto the third-floor deck that surrounds my loft. Just out of reach are a few river birch, several spruce, cedars, and pines, a magnolia, and a mountain ash. At times it seems I am living in the trees, so close are these leafy neighbors. Living up here has opened a small window into their community, introducing me more personally to the domestic habits of birds, squirrels, butterflies, beetles, cicadas, moths, and several families of tiny organisms that create a variety of bumple-sized dwellings on the undersides of leaves.

By May, you can easily see a dozen nests among the branches, even though the deciduous trees are partly dressed in their summer greens. The birds that go south for the winter and return in the spring squabble over choice locations and begin building immediately. It is clear, however, that the evergreen trees—the spruce, cedars, and pines—are prime real estate as far as birds are concerned. Their large, secluded branches offer year-round comfort in the form of protection from blustery winds, driving rain, and hot sun while Mama Bird sits on her nest. In addition, they maintain high levels of privacy from the eyes of predators, nest-thieves, and those neighbors who don't mind renting the nest for an hour to lay an egg among the eggs already there, then vacate, leaving the hatching and raising of the step-chick to the original inhabitants.

Over the past ten years I have become more and more interested in my tree neighbors and their daily life. Trees are master alchemists, translating the energy gifts of Sun, wind, and water into wood. Wood is a marvelous substance! We use it as fuel to keep us warm; for building boats, homes, garages, picnic tables, telephone poles, and everything else from rake handles to hairbrushes.

Too often we think of trees only as useful after they have been cut down. There are many useful gifts from living trees that we just take for granted, and so many things that trees do that we don't even know about. They are not just major producers of oxygen for our planet, they are the producers, and I wonder who will supply us with oxygen when the trees are all gone? I hope we won't be foolish enough to think that the government will take care of it, or that we can turn it into a business and let some commercial producer supply us with oxygen that we have to earn dollars to buy. It seems a bit silly to dig ourselves deeper into the financial hole by having to pay for something that Mother Nature offers for free. We've already made that mistake with water and land.

Oxygen is one of the most powerful antibiotics in the entire world, and already the amount of available oxygen in our world has dropped by 50 percent compared to what it was one hundred years ago. This has led to a steep increase in breathing difficulties, infections, and cancers, many of which miraculously heal when exposed to higher levels of oxygen!

Walter Schauberger, a brilliant scientist who spent his life studying trees and water, and the motion of the living energies in them, once calculated that by the time a tree is 100 years old, it:

a. Has processed the carbon dioxide in 18 million cubic meters of air and fixed it as 2,500 kg of pure carbon.

b. Has photochemically converted 9,100 kg of carbon dioxide and 3,700 liters of water.

c. Has made 6,600 kg of molecular oxygen available for humans and animals.

d. Has drawn 2,500 tons of water from the roots up through the crown, working against the forces of gravity, and evaporated it into the atmosphere.

e. Has supplied one member of society with enough oxygen for 20 years.

Besides oxygen, trees have been building layer upon layer of topsoil for thousands of years. During the growing season they send roots deep into the subsoil, some even into the deep rock layer. A good gauge of how deep the roots go is to look at how high the tree grows. Although some trees do not go very deep and prefer to spread their roots out laterally, there is often as much or more mass below ground as there is above ground. The roots that do tunnel their way through the subsoil and rock layer create a small mineral mining operation in which they release mild acids through their root hairs. These acids dissolve tiny amounts of a variety of minerals from the rock, and these minerals are then transported up the trunk to the leaves where they are used to build the trunk, the branches, and thousands of thick, sturdy, glossy leaves. When autumn arrives and the trees shed their leaves, they fall to the ground, leaving a fresh deposit of organic minerals on the surface, which are then processed by insects.

The new leaf layer offers fresh roofing material for worms and ground-dwelling insects that make their homes under sticks, stones, leaves, tufts of thick grass, and anything else that provides a sense of shelter. Yet in a quirk of nature, the insects end up eating their house! Worms consider leaves to be an extraordinary delicacy and will make their way through a leafpile with great relish, digesting the carbon-based green matter, and leaving mineral-rich worm-castings behind. Other insects live and die among the fallen leaves, creating a tremendous amount of waste material, all of which helps to further decompose the leaves.

Each year a new layer of growth decays into dark, moist, composted soil, now becoming home to millions of micro-organisms, bacteria, fungi, and other mycorrhiza that survive best on heavily decayed material. When these microorganisms have done their share of work on the leaf pile, it becomes a rich humus, building up slowly over time to create thick, organic topsoil that provides the perfect nutrient bed for other plants, be they flowers, fruits, grains, or vegetables.

Topsoil used to be measured in yards. Now it is measured in inches. The ability of this luxurious topsoil to produce was recorded in *The Farmer's Every-Day Book* by the Reverend John Blake in 1851. Corn yields in 1822 were 172 bushels per acre, the next year they were 170 bushels per acre. Yearly corn yields from 1822 to 1850 ranged from 118 bushels per acre at the low end to 174 bushels at the high end. In the same period, farmers harvested 800 bushels of potatoes per acre. All of this—without chemical fertilizers to push it, special genetics to modify it, or other agents, such as pesticides or herbicides, to protect the weak crop until it gets to the barn or the granary. All of this in Mother Nature's brand of soil—a rich, friable humus—that was made slowly, renewed yearly, and given freely.

This same layer of loosely stacked humus also works as a layer of insulation over the surface of the earth, keeping the roots of trees cool and moist. When the surface of the earth is kept cool and porous, rainwater will easily penetrate and begin to sink into the soil. There are 43,560 square feet of topsoil in an acre (208 feet x 208 feet = 43,560 sq. ft.). If the top six inches of topsoil is a biologically active, carbon-based material—the kind created by trees year after year—this six inches of soil will hold up to four times its own weight in water. There are two million pounds of topsoil in the top six inches of an acre of land. This means that only one acre of good topsoil will hold eight million pounds of water before it starts to run off. Twelve inches of topsoil would hold up to sixteen million pounds of water. That's 8,000 tons of water in the space of about four city lots measuring roughly 75 feet x 150 feet. Quite a reservoir, not to mention protection from floods! Seems to me that we ought to be planting a strip of trees at least a couple acres wide along each side of our rivers—not houses, levees, roads, and high-rise buildings.

When my husband and I were first married we had a beautiful chalet in the forests of northern Michigan. Even when the wind blew with quite a bit of force, you could hear it, and you could see the tallest treetops moving, but on the ground the air was quiet, and still. When it rained, it had to rain long enough and hard enough to get to the "through-fall" stage where it actually hit the ground because so much was collected by the trees first. Mud puddles were rare because the soil was so absorbent. I thought it was my imagination that things rarely got dusty, but later, when I began to study trees, I discovered that 3,000 feet inside the edge of a forest, the trees have cleaned and sifted the air to a sparkling, dust-free state. This, combined with the cool, moist, oxygenated air made it easier to breathe. My husband's asthma eased greatly. Fatigue disappeared and we were left feeling energized.

If you look back just a bit you will see that for thousands of years our leafy allies stood quietly on mountainsides, holding onto the soil, keeping it from sliding away in the rain and piling itself onto villages below. Trees that didn't mind wet feet stood at the edges of the sea to catch the waves that came with great storms and kept the land from being washed away. Great swamps formed at land's end, and whole trees went down in them becoming huge masses of carbon to hold water, creating unique neighborhoods for a whole new assortment of flying, crawling, swimming creatures, and an even more varied collection of water-loving plants, flowers, vines, and bushes.

Today, mud slides and floods are a yearly problem. We spend billions of dollars to build dams and dikes, and tell ourselves we have "created jobs," when a more accurate perception is that we have "made more work for ourselves." We spend millions of dollars on artificial fertilizers to douse our fields, and we tell ourselves we have more food, when the truth is that food grown in today's agricultural system is seriously short of the minerals that build good teeth and bones and then maintain them. The three inches of good topsoil left in most parts of the world makes it almost impossible to grow food with a high levels of vitamins and amino acids, so we are forced to spend millions of dollars on artificial supplements to shore up our ailing bodies. When it comes right down to it, we could not find enough men and money to do the work that trees used to do, and if we could, the quality of their work would not come close to the expertise and quality of the work done by trees.

A full-size tree has been estimated to have as many as 100,000 growing tips on it, and research now suggests that each tip is a unique genetic individual. Cutting a branch off a deciduous tree in order to graft it or reroot it elsewhere has occasionally resulted in the unexpected growth of an evergreen tree! When a mammal produces seed, all the seeds come from within that one body. But when a tree produces seed, each seed comes from a different flower, which may have picked up genes from something in the air or the water; or maybe the seed is responding to a unique set of microclimate conditions on one side of the tree. It is possible that a tree is "a collection of compatible genetic individuals, each with a set of persistent characteristics which may differ from place to place on the tree, and each of which may respond differently to energy and other stimuli."[2] If this is so, then cutting trees down wholesale is the same thing as destroying 100,000 possibilities for genetic adaptation with every tree that is lost to the saw.

If you drive along a certain street just outside our community, there are huge lots with big, beautiful, expensive houses on them. There may be $10,000 worth of landscaping around the foundation and deck of each of these houses, with two, maybe five, or even a dozen young trees planted in the yard – some leafy deciduous, and some evergreen. If you drive by on a hot summer day, the sprinkler system may be on watering the trees, flowers, and bushes; the air conditioning may be running full tilt, and there isn't a human in sight. The place may be lovely overall, but it is clear that we no longer know much about trees.

The evergreen trees, which collect and then radiate heat, are clustered around the air conditioning unit because the wide branches at the base of the tree hide the unit from the neighbors or the street. It would make more sense to shade the compressor unit with a tree that offers a bit of shade, but too often we do things for looks only.

Trees are extremely sensitive to light and heat. In the forest, young trees grow to maturity under the shady protection of the mother trees. In a cool atmosphere rich with carbon dioxide, they are protected from strong wind and rain. They are healthiest, strongest, and produce the best wood when grown slowly in diffuse light. Their annual tree rings are small and close together. Their trunks are wide at the bottom and taper nicely to the top. Those with smooth bark prefer dim light and will often be found in the center of the forest. Those with rough or shaggy bark will be okay in the Sun at the edge of the tree line.

When shade-loving trees are grown in full Sun, their temperature rises and this is equivalent to being in a "fevered" state. Their internal metabolism is disrupted, and they may be unable to fight invasion by parasites, fungi, or bacteria. We experience the same thing when we get a fever! When trees sitting in full Sun are watered freely with dead or immature water, they grow too quickly and their annual rings become widely spaced and corky, and results in a weak tree that is not only susceptible to disease. Or the tree may suffer violent damage or the loss of limbs during periods of high wind or ice storms. When grown in the Sun, trunks tend to be straight and cylindrical all the way up rather than tapering, and this tapering shape is the key form by which a tree maintains the high-energy metabolism it needs to continue developing and stay healthy throughout its life.

Industry prefers the quick growing, straight trunks of modern tree farms, but much of the wood is weak, twists out of shape when dried in the kiln, and rots too quickly at the lumberyard. It is ironic that a tree that has stood outside through winter snows, summer rains, spring winds, and numerous temperature changes must now be sheltered from all these once it gets to the lumberyard lest it rot before it is incorporated into a house and sheltered by aluminum siding. My mother worked in a lumberyard when I was a girl and I remember running and climbing among the piles of pine and oak that sat outside. Nowadays if you leave piles of wood outside for any length of time they curl up enough to be suitable only for the bottoms of rocking chairs.

Besides its preference for light and shade, each tree has a personality expressed in its patterns of shape, color, the texture of its bark, and personal rhythms for leafing out, flowering, or closing down for winter. The trees outside my loft also have a language of sounds by which they send messages to those who are listening. There is the soft hissing sound that can be heard at the start of a light summer shower when you can't yet see or feel the first drops of rain. There is the soft soughing sound the pines begin to make when the winds of spring arrive and there will be no more severe winter storms. Once in a while they have great, roaring conversations with a gale wind that comes by to prune dead or weakened limbs. I also overhear shimmery, rustling conversations among them. I sometimes strain to hear their whispers. Other times, am in awe of their towering silence. How can anything be so huge and so quiet?

Once I had a conversation with a tree. I asked if it had anything to add to what I was writing about it. "Yes," it replied, "the very page from which your words rise is a transformed tree, sacrificed to make paper. Why don't you people learn to communicate and leave us alone?" Needless to say my shock was complete. After that, I was aware that every piece of paper expressed the silent voice of a tree. The tree's thoughts and words were woven among the words we placed upon that paper. How many trees had given their life that we might send letters, invoices, newspapers, and advertisements back and forth, and then into the wastebasket?

When I go into the city I am appalled at the thin, sickly looking trees cemented in place along the edges of sidewalks, or marooned in an ocean of asphalt laid down to make a parking lot.

"Look at those poor trees," I said to a friend one time. "Why did they even bother to plant them in this kind of environment?"

"People like trees," she said, "they like a little greenery."

"But what about the trees?" I asked.

"What about them?" she replied with a small shrug. It was an eloquent testament to the divorce that took place between humans and nature long before I was born.

Sometimes I look out across the field and see the ghosts of lost trees, thousands of them. I look around my loft and see that the place I live has a framework of tall, strong tree trunks. The bark is still on them. I wonder if the family who built this barn gave any thought to replacing the fifteen trees they cut from the woods and planted in cement to stand for at least a hundred years holding up the small forest of rafters, roof boards, and siding that make this a barn.

Whether they did or not, it is time for us to be thinking about such things . . . umbrellas in a light rain . . . specialists in chemical manufacture . . . modifiers of the wind . . . end posts to a hammock . . . monkey bars to a five-year-old . . . landlord to ten thousand Others. The tree is a world in itself, a living being that makes it possible for us to share this time and place with it.

1. *Living Energies* by Callum Coats, published in 1996 by Gateway Books, Bath, UK.

2. *Permaculture: A Designer's Manual* by Bill Mollison, published in 1996 by Tagari Publications, New South Wales, Australia.

Parting the Seasons

By Lynne Sturtevant

The Japanese have a long tradition of cherishing nature and its creations. All aspects of the landscape are honored, but over the centuries, certain plants and natural phenomena have gained special symbolic significance. Moments that seem to capture the transition from one season to another, such as spring snow falling on plum blossoms, are especially revered. These transitional moments, called "partings of the seasons," continue to inspire artists, poets, factory workers, and students to pause and reflect on nature's eternal rhythms.

The tradition of observing the changing pattern of the year is deeply rooted in Japanese culture. Like other Asian peoples, the ancient Japanese used the lunar calendar, which is based on the phases of the Moon. However, the lunar calendar does not account for all of the days in a solar year and it cannot predict the dates of solstices and equinoxes. The lunar calendar's shortcomings caused serious difficulties for the Japanese. They were farmers, and forecasting the annual cycles of rain, drought, heat, and cold were critical to their survival. Astronomers solved the problem by dividing the year into twenty-eight Moon stations or *sei shuku,* which signaled subtle changes in the seasonal cycle, star positions, wind, or weather.

The lunar calendar and Moon stations were officially abandoned in the nineteenth century, but the habit of carefully monitoring natural changes survived. Even though the Japanese people live in the most technologically advanced nation on Earth, they maintain their connection with the land, sky, and agricultural traditions of their ancestors by honoring the unique beauty of each of the four seasons.

Spring

The highlight of spring is the opening of the *sakura* (cherry blossoms). The appearance of the blossoms is so important that TV stations chart the progress of the "Sakura Line" from the moment the first tree opens in southern Japan until the last petals fall in the northernmost islands. People travel great distances to participate in *hanami* (flower viewing), and to picnic under the trees. Cherry blossom season is a time to celebrate the arrival of spring and to compose short poems known as haiku. But because the delicate blossoms' flowering cycle is so short, it is also a time to contemplate life's impermanence.

After the cherry trees finish blooming, the *shobu* (irises) open. The iris is an ancient symbol of male virtue and perfection. The long, pointed leaves resemble samurai swords and the flowers' full ranges of hues, from white to purple, are considered masculine colors. Although not as important as cherry blossom viewing, many people visit parks and public gardens in late spring to admire iris displays.

Summer

Summer is the season to celebrate bamboo and rice, the most revered and respected plants in Japan. *Take* or bamboo symbolizes strength through flexibility. It is honored for its versatility and many practical uses. The tender young sprouts are delicious and the mature wood is used in projects ranging from light construction to the manufacture of chopsticks, umbrellas, and birdcages. The powerful and complex symbolism associated with rice or *ine* includes nationalistic elements. Rice represents Japan's ability to feed its population, resist foreign influence, and maintain its independence.

August is *tsukimi* time (Moon viewing). In medieval Japan, poets toasted the August Full Moon with rice wine or sake and allowed its "pure brilliance" to shine on their faces. Even in today's crowded, light-polluted cities, people gather at dusk to relax on mats and spend the evening watching the August Moon float through the clear night sky.

The *kiku* (chrysanthemum) is the symbol of the Imperial family and the most beloved flower of autumn. In Japan, chrysanthemums are not considered outdoor garden plants. They are grown exclusively in pots. Hundreds of exotic varieties have been developed and chrysanthemum shows are popular fall events. People appreciate the hybrid forms for the obvious patience that goes into their cultivation.

Autumn

Autumn is also *mojimi* (tinted leaf) viewing season. Families and groups of students and workers travel to the mountains in September and October for mojimi hunting excursions, to gather mushrooms known as "the children of the forest," and to listen to the humming cicadas or "voices of autumn."

Winter

Winter is the time to walk through the countryside and admire the quiet beauty snow gives to rocks, frozen streams, and bare trees. In the bitterly cold northern islands, huge bonfires are built from pine branches. The pine tree or *matsu* symbolizes long life and burning its branches helps to chase away the cold and encourage an early spring.

When it seems winter will never end, the *ume* (apricot blossoms) open. Another parting of the seasons occurs and the cycle continues. Soon the insects will awaken, the tiny buds on the cherry trees will begin to swell and the icy Moon will be softened by the warm mists of spring.

Living Water

By Penny Kelly

If you could float above the Earth high enough to get a bird's eye view of the landscape, and if there were a natural river flowing across the land, you would see that the river twists and turns like a snake making its way through that landscape. You would also see that the banks of the river were lined with trees and bushes. If the water in that river was healthy, living water you would be able to see the stones and the sand in the riverbed clearly—even if the water was several yards deep.

Now imagine that you are a molecule of water in that river. You are part of only one specific stream of colder water spiraling forward at a given rate within the river, and moving beside you are one or two other "streams within the river stream," each of a slightly different temperature and rate of spiraling flow. The two or three different streams are winding around one another like long, thin DNA strands laid out horizontally above the shady riverbed. This spiraling motion allows you to continuously dig out your own river course, throwing sand, gravel, and other matter outward toward the riverbank, which helps to build good banks naturally, and keep you contained and on course. It also keeps your main flow clean and clear.

Now, you move through a stretch where there are no trees, the heat of the Sun warms you. You become tired and lethargic. The spiraling motion slows considerably and you feel lazy. Without the spiral motion throwing particulate matter off toward the riverbank the water becomes thick and cloudy. You can't see where you're going and your depth becomes shallow, so the Sun warms you even more. You feel sick. Many of your companion molecules are giving up and evaporating into the great blue above.

Suddenly you move into the shade again, ever grateful for the trees that line the riverbanks. Your temperature begins to drop and you have hope that you can begin to be yourself again. You have your greatest strength and activity when your temperature is at 4° C (about 39° F). Above this temperature your internal metabolism begins to disintegrate. As your temperature drops, you regain strength and vigor. Your spiraling motion takes on new energy. You throw larger particulate matter off toward the riverbanks, and head clearly downstream once more.

This little river journey gives but a small view of the life of water in a living river system. Interest in water is skyrocketing today, partly because there are such serious shortages of it, and partly because the work of Viktor Schauberger is finally having an impact. Schauberger, who was born in 1885 and spent much of his life in the wilderness areas of Austria studying trees, water, and subtle energies in nature, came to the conclusion that water was born, developed to maturity, and sought to change itself into higher forms of energy.

After watching the poor effect of watering crops, with what he termed "immature" or "devitalized" water, Schauberger spent years trying to teach people that water matures when it is allowed to move through its full cycle from the earth to the atmosphere and back again. Trees are a major player in this cycle, which begins when the water "dies" by evaporating into the atmosphere. Once aloft, it is carried by wind until enough of it accumulates for a good cool breeze to cause the condensation we call rain. The rain falls to the earth among the trees and sinks into the surface soil, which is kept cool and porous by the trees. The water continues to sink downward through the cool root zone, losing temperature rapidly as it passes through the roots. Continuing to descend, the water reaches a level where its pressure deep in the soil is equal to the weight of the water pressure in the atmosphere. At this level, the heat from deep in the Earth begins to heat and pressurize the water and some of it becomes steam. The steam now binds with carbon and a chemical reaction takes place: carbon + water, changes to carbon dioxide + hydrogen gas ($C + H_2O = CO_2 + H_2$). As a hot gas, the hydrogen now seeks to rise upward. As it pushes its way up through the soil, it dissolves some of the surrounding mineral salts into itself, carrying these toward the surface. When the rising gas reaches the cool root zone of the trees, near the surface once again, some of the mineral salts precipitate out and are deposited in the root regions to become nutrients for vegetation. In this way, trees and plants are fed in a slow-growth system that results in good health for the trees, and superior quality wood for building projects.

As the cooling hydrogen gas moves through the crust of the earth, its internal motion is centripetal, also known as "magnetic" energy. The cooling hydrogen magnetically bonds oxygen to itself to form new molecules of water. Because the magnetized hydrogen was carrying some dissolved mineral salts from its sojourn through the deepest regions of Earth, the resulting water carries a good supply of minerals in it. As the water reaches the surface and enters streams, rivers, artesian springs, or other natural sources, it is considered mature, ready to be used for drinking and irrigation.

Schauberger deplored the pumping of "immature" water from deep in the earth and insisted that it was ready to drink only when it came to the surface on its own. His research showed that the carbon matter in gaseous form carried by the water molecule amounted to traces of all the elements known to man, including minerals, metals, and even a number of compounds, and that when the water was healthy, these minerals were in a form that could be absorbed by the human body.

He also discovered that the internal motion of the hydrogen atom at the time of its bonding with oxygen was critical in the quality of water. Centripetal motion is an inward drawing force, and in a body of any kind it is centripetal motion that helps maintain shape, form, strength, and vitality. Centrifugal motion is an outwardly exploding force, and in a body of any kind it is this force that helps to speed disintegration and dissolution. As it turns out, there are two ways to make water, and the two different results can have subtle but powerful long-term effects on health depending on the motion of the hydrogen.

Cooling hydrogen that has been through the full water cycle will be carrying dissolved mineral salts and carbonic gasses. It will have a centripetal motion when it goes after inactive oxygen to form a water molecule. This water will have the effect of helping the body stay in good shape, remaining healthy and strong. When hydrogen warms up, its motion changes from centripetal to centrifugal, and it tends to throw off its precious load of minerals and trace elements. It becomes slow, relatively inactive, and does not seek much bonding with oxygen.

When oxygen warms up, its motion also becomes centrifugal, but rather than becoming sluggish, oxygen becomes highly active the warmer it gets. The highly active oxygen now seeks out the slow-moving hydrogen and bonds with it, but the result is a subtle change in the effect of the water. The internal centrifugal motion of the water molecule and tends to have a dissipative, degenerative effect on the body. When coupled with the other degenerative pressures of our culture, the effect is to reduce our life span to a mere seventy years, when it is fairly well-known that the human lifespan would normally be somewhere between 120 years and 160 years.

Living water turns out to be water that has matured by passing through the full atmosphere-to-earth-to-atmosphere cycle. Photographs of the inside of a drop of living water reveal extraordinary structure, in what appear to be the currents and waterfalls and oceans of motion by which the water maintains itself and carries the gift of nutrients to the plants and animals and people that drink it!

Dead water, on the other hand, has not passed through the full atmosphere-to-earth-to-atmosphere cycle. Its inner motion is sluggish, explosively centrifugal, or nonexistent. It carries no gift of nutrients to other living beings, and sometimes carries the dissolved salts of numerous pesticides, fertilizers, and fungicides. Since many of these chemicals have an estrogen-like effect in the body, we grow too quickly, are weak and sickly, and leave too soon.

To many of us alive today, water is water. Our education has left us woefully unschooled in nature's classroom. Said Schauberger, "Water in its natural state shows us how it wishes to flow, so we should follow its wishes." Those twisting, turning, snakelike bends that we see in every natural river are the water's way of constructing its own path to maintain its high energy and keep itself "in bounds." When we straighten out a river, we ruin the water's spiraling motion. When we cut the trees along the banks the water warms up and becomes lazy. When we cut too many trees from the land, the surface soil swells then collapses and falling rain cannot sink in deeply, it just runs off, carrying the topsoil with it. Most of that topsoil ends up in the river, choking the waterways and filling in the channel the river creates for itself. The result is that the water does not pass through the entire water cycle and we end up drinking dead water with no nutrients. We water the plants in our garden with dead water and wonder why we're fighting fungus and mildew all season long. The missing minerals leave us with plants that are structurally weak. In the same way that we use calcium, magnesium, iron, and other minerals to build good bones, plants use the same minerals to build good structure. Without it they are highly susceptible to molds, mildews, and rots.

In the same way we were once ignorant of the fact that the soil was alive, we didn't know that water was alive. We didn't know that when we captured water out of the rivers and underground reservoirs, forcing it into pipes, tanks, and drainage ditches that we were interfering with the internal motion it used to sustain itself. We didn't know about water's maturity and its living qualities. Schauberger tried to get authorities to use pipes that were not perfectly round but were ovoid instead, and to teach the concept that water should be kept circulating in contact with metals—especially silver and gold—in an attempt to preserve its motion and some of its healing effects on the body and the mind. He predicted the day when a barrel of water would sell for more than a barrel of oil, and he was right. These days a 55-gallon barrel of oil runs between $29.00 and $39.00. We pay $.89 for a quart of good mineral water at the store. That puts the cost of the water at about $195.80 per barrel. Perhaps Schauberger's favorite saying points the path for all of us, "Study Nature and then copy Her."

Gloria Star's
Personal
Lunar Forecasts
for 2002

Understanding Your Personal Moon Sign

By Gloria Star

She's there, a constant companion to Earth, a part of our skyscape. The Moon sends forth light against the night sky, showing an ever-changing reflection of the Sun's fiery radiance. Not only can we see the Moon, we feel her power. Physically, her cycles control the continual ebb and flow of Earth's tides. Yet, there is something more that has lead to our unique and eternal fascination with the Moon. Since the time of the Sumerians, written records have linked the Moon's cycles with alterations in nature and changes in behavior. Recorded musings about the Moon and her influences are scattered over time and throughout the art and literature of human history. But do you realize that you have your very own personal Moon? It is one of the many features of your astrological chart, and it is a significant indicator of your emotional nature and the way you express your needs.

Your horoscope is the picture of your personal astrological chart based upon precise calculations. An astrologer charts the positions of the Moon,

Sun, and planets based upon the exact date, time, and place of your birth. This detailed picture of your natal horoscope symbolizes the complex levels of energy that are part of your whole being. You probably know about your Sun sign, which describes the ways you express your ego and your drive to be recognized—something easy to see and even easier to show to others. Your Moon tells an intimate story; it describes your sub-conscious nature. You feel your Moon.

The exact position of your personal Moon sign is indicated in your astrological char. Since the Moon enters a new sign every couple of days, you can understand why an accurate calculation is necessary. To obtain your chart, you can visit a competent astrologer, or order your chart directly from Llewellyn Chart Services. (Ordering information is at the end of this article.) You may also use the handy tables and simple calculation method described on page 66 of this book. These guidelines provide a close approximation of your Moon's sign, but to determine the precise placement of your Moon, you'll need a copy of your astrological chart.

You are intimately acquainted with the energy of your Moon, even if you are not familiar with astrological vocabulary. Whenever you tune into your basic feelings about anything, you're connecting through the energy of your Moon. Imagine that your Moon is a finely tuned recording device that is constantly collecting, storing, and assimilating everything you experience and feel. These messages replay themselves in the form of your habits and attitudes. You can add more information at any time, and you can make alterations. However, since you hold these impressions at a very deep level it's not always easy to change or erase an old internal message, even when you want to. Your habits are part of this same message system, stored through the experience of your lunar energy.

What can you learn from your Moon sign? When you explore your Moon, you gain insights into your inner strengths. The Moon shows where you feel most vulnerable; it also stimulates your underlying emotional nature. The characteristics of your Moon sign symbolize the filter through which you absorb your impressions about your life experiences. Your Moon Sign describes the nature of your emotional filter, depending on the qualities of her astrological sign in your natal chart.

Through your Moon you also create what gives you that special feeling of "home." As you learn more about yourself and your needs through experiencing life, you gain an understanding of what you need to feel comfortable and secure. You can explore the meaning of your

Moon sign to help you tap into the best ways to assure that you create a personal environment that provides for your unique needs. Once you're in the flow of the energy of your Moon, you carry your sense of home into every life situation.

You're using your lunar energy whenever you reach out to nurture and support anyone or anything, and your Moon's sign shows how you express these sentiments toward others and yourself. Whether you're male or female, your Moon indicates the way you mother others. Psychologically, your Moon portrays your archetypal feminine and represents your relationship with mother, with women, and with the feminine part of your own psyche. Your Sun, on the other hand, represents the archetypal male quality and illustrates your connection to men, father, and the masculine elements of your inner self.

When you probe more deeply into the mystery of your Moon you uncover the cradle of your soul. At this level, your Moon contains all that you have been, and therefore influences all that you can become. Shining forth from deep within your eyes, the light of your Moon reflects the inner, soulful, aspects of yourself—your most dominate emotional tendencies and needs. It is the part of you that has flown to the pinnacle of ecstasy, but remembers the true emptiness of despair. Your capacity for contentment increases when you strive to fulfill the needs defined by your Moon's sign. Essentially, you will feel most satisfied when you embrace your Moon!

This part of the *Moon Sign Book* is designed to help you understand the basic planetary cycles throughout the year 2002 that will influence you at an emotional level. The planetary transits to your Moon stimulate change, and you may discover that some of the cycles help you reshape your life, while others stimulate a desire to delve into the mystery of yourself. Astrology can show you the cycles, but you are the one who determines the outcome through your responses. By opening to your own needs and responding to the planetary energies in a way which allows you to fulfill these needs, you can experience a renewed sense of self confirmation and a deepened feeling of personal security.

ARIES MOON

Full steam ahead! You're ready to take the initiative, and you have a prolific and creative essence. Your Aries Moon fuels the spirit of a warrior, and when you really want something, there's little that can stop you from going after it. Eager to experience the thrill of meeting your challenges head-on, you have the ability to forge ahead while others are paralyzed or uncertain. Yet, it is your need to feel truly free to pursue your dreams and desires that keeps you moving further into the creation of a life that is uniquely your own.

A spirit of adventure shines in your eyes. Whether you're in pursuit of career aims or a personal relationship, it's necessary to feel that your passion is fully engaged in whatever you do. Once your mission is underway, you can lose your enthusiasm unless there are a few unpredictable or challenging circumstances. People who are willing to sit back while life stirs around them may be completely uninteresting to you, although you do need a few willing followers so you can be the one in the lead.

In a crisis, you're the one whose action can solve the problems at hand. The game of life keeps you on your toes, and your ever-youthful vivacity can be a powerful magnet in your personal and professional relationships. You enjoy challenge, and might relish competitive situations like sports, the military, crisis counseling, or emergency rescue. If there's not a crisis, you might create one just to keep boredom at bay. (Remember that when things get quiet in your close relationship.) After all, your flirtation with disaster can be fun for you, but others can feel insecure if you seem to be interested only when there's a risk involved. Some things simply take time, and while your childlike impatience was understandable during your youth, as an adult, however, it can be downright frustrating (for you and for others). At home is where you laugh, love, and create—with gusto, of course!

Famous Individuals with Aries Moon
Antonio Banderas, Peggy Fleming, Lily Tomlin

The Year at a Glance for Aries Moon

Your enthusiasm is on the rise during 2002, and it strengthens your sense of security. While you may be tempted to promise more than you can deliver, for the most part you're able to evaluate situations and make determinations that keep you on an even keel. Your ideals and hopes light your way, and cooperative ventures work to your advantage. However, your independent drive is also very powerful, and you're not likely to become involved in situations where your individuality is undermined or compromised.

Saturn's stabilizing influence helps you establish a clear direction, but it is the flash of inspiration from Uranus' cycle that opens the way to make your dreams come true. You're waking up to different drives and needs, and less inclined to do things that will stand in the way of your need to express yourself. Jupiter's cycle brings temptation your way from January through July. This seduction can be in the form of overindulgence, especially on a dietary level. Give yourself a little room to partake without going overboard, since absolute restraint can be too frustrating. Starting in August, you're more inclined to indulge in pleasures that stem from directing your creativity and artistry. Jupiter's cycle in Leo adds a rich level of self-confidence, and your ability to express and fulfill your deepest needs is strengthened under this influence.

You can feel impelled to explore the deeper question of your life or soul purpose this year if your Moon is from 0–9 degrees of Aries. It's time to listen to the voice of your inner healer, since Chiron's cycle encourages you to strip away the habits that stand in the way of your ability to fulfill your needs. In addition, Neptune's cycle brings vision to your dreams this year, too. The spiritual impulse from Neptune can prompt you to become more involved in charitable outreach, but you might also be more inclined to bring your spirituality into your daily life.

If your Moon is 10–20 degrees Aries, then you're experiencing the influence of Pluto in a supportive trine aspect to your Moon. This cycle stimulates your need to establish a home space, which you can grow and prosper from. Changes in your family can be especially significant now. During the first six months of 2002, you are also experiencing the valuable support from Saturn transiting in sextile to your Moon, bringing a period of emotional maturity.

You're ready for change if your Moon is 21–29 degrees Aries. You may decide to move or renovate while Uranus invites your Moon to dance with joy this year. The stimulus to try something completely different can be pure delight. Fortunately, you're also feeling some stability from Saturn's cycle starting in July, and that means you're likely to make changes that have some permanence to them.

All Aries Moon individuals can make tremendous headway in family relationships this year. Your ability to communicate your needs and feelings is strengthened as you find ways to become more responsible. That doesn't mean you have to take on heavy burdens, but that you're ready to embrace your needs and to take actions that assure you are fulfilling them.

Affirmation for the Year

My life is filled with wonder, love, and pure joy!

January

Staying in touch with the present moment is your challenge this month. Your dreams and hopes take center stage, but outside requests from others can complicate matters until your priorities become clear during the New Moon on the 13th. Still, knowing where to draw the line can be difficult, since you're eager to get things moving and hesitation from others can be a bother. Once Mars enters Aries on the 19th your patience grows short for a few weeks, and you'll be much more content if you see signs of progress. Start a project around the house, or take the lead in family matters. An escape from the ordinary beckons during the Full Moon on the 28th, when festivities bring special joy and an escape with your sweetie ignites the pleasures of love.

February

Fasten your seatbelt! Your emotions are in high gear, and there's little to stop you from accomplishing your aims. However, you can go overboard and intimidate others with your assertiveness, so watch for reactions from others to avoid alienating those you're trying to win over. It's all about Mars, and this contact to your Moon literally lights up your needs and feelings. Exciting changes arrive with the New Moon on the 12th, when a surprise can lead to options you had not even considered. Your magnetism intensifies, and you can be quite persuasive. Of course, it helps if you know precisely what you want, since focused action brings more satisfying results. A situation from your past can slow your momentum from the 17th to 22nd, especially if you have unfinished business. Tie up those loose ends before the Full Moon on the 27th.

March

Now that you've cleared the way, it's time to let your creativity shine. Your fresh way of doing things lifts a tired situation out of the doldrums, and you can also revitalize a love relationship that's grown stale. There's no rush. A more leisurely approach to love gives you a chance to enjoy sharing what's in your heart. Lucky you: Venus enters Aries on the 7th, and it's easier to attract the things (and people) you desire for the following few weeks. But you can also be too self-indulgent around the time of the New Moon on the 14th, so be careful not to get in your own way. It's a test of knowing the difference between what you want and what you need. Drat! There's good news for relationships during the Full Moon on the 28th—if you know what you need, that is.

April

It's time to talk about your feelings and needs. Mercury's impulse prompts you to confess what's on your mind and in your heart from the 1st to 13th. Changes at home work quite nicely, too—whether you're decorating, renovating, or moving. You're ready to clear out to make room for your personal projects or special needs. Are you thinking of self-improvement? If so, the Aries New Moon on the 12th marks a great time to toss bad habits in favor of a more nourishing daily routine. A change of focus leads you to see yourself and your life from a different viewpoint, and you're ready for a few innovations where they will make the greatest impact. It's one time when "me first" can serve you well. This is your time to renew yourself at a soulful level.

May

On the move and ready for a change of scenery, you'll appreciate a chance to make new friends and explore new paths. An open-minded attitude leads to discovery of ideas, or sparks a series of changes that can help you reshape your life. This is definitely a time to get out into the world and enjoy the adventure. Once Mercury turns retrograde on the 14th you might feel more inclined to get back in touch with friends and family, especially if you have important news to exchange. This is an excellent time to mend fences in those relationships that have suffered from misunderstandings. Reach out during the lunar eclipse on the 26th. It's the perfect time to show how much you do care.

June

Friction arises close to home, but may simply be the result of increased interaction with one another. Do you feel a need to head off on your own? Clarify your intentions if you want to avoid the hassle of hurt feelings, since impulsive actions on your part can wound someone close to you. You can also be extrasensitive, particularly if your expectations are met with disappointment. There's a kind of emotional clumsiness prompted by the collision to your Moon from boisterous Mars connecting with bombastic Jupiter during the last half of the month—when impulsive actions lead to one problem after another. However, a more careful approach can help you uncover the mystery of a close relationship during the Moon's eclipse on the 24th.

July

Before you take someone up on that challenge early this month, think twice. Is it really worthwhile? You can get in over your head, and might end up damaging something precious. However, measured risk could be worth the effort. Your heart's on the line, and that ache you feel can be just what you need to uncover the truth of a relationship. If your impulse is to run away, ask yourself why before you surge away from the starting block. The fun starts after the 12th, when your playfulness works to your advantage. Then, during the Full Moon on the 24th, your desire to bring someone closer can add a spark to your flirtatious charm. Laughter definitely has its appeal.

August

Despite the impulse to throw caution to the winds, you'll do yourself a favor if you make a careful evaluation of the situation before you take action. There's plenty of room to make headway, and even more opportunity to let your courage rise to the forefront. However, too much bravado can leave you looking like a blowhard while someone else gets all the credit! Fortunately, your self-confidence gets a boost from Jupiter's change of attitude. Fresh faces and different options appear on the scene during the New Moon on the 8th, and pure fun is featured for the Full Moon on the 22nd. Leave room in your schedule for spontaneity, since the keynote for this cycle is serendipity.

September

Double-check your itinerary and keep a close watch on your schedule, since it appears that other people have plans for you. Cooperative ventures can be especially satisfying, but only if you know what's expected. Watch out for those carrying a checklist, since you could be on it. It's time to see how others handle their power and to avoid stepping into a battle zone that has nothing to do with you. Awkward situations can emerge near the time of the Full Moon on the 21st, when you may feel like the uninvited guest at the party. Your intuition tells you if you should step in the door and check your coat, or if you should turn around and find something better to do.

October

Creative directions for your passionate drive lifts your spirits, even if you're stuck doing a few things you'd rather not write about in your diary. The New Moon on the 6th sparks a period of excitement in your relationship, but it can also lead to an exploration of the things you do not like about one another. Sometimes, it's good to accept the things you cannot control. Circumstances that can benefit from your action. Venus retrogrades, and that means you need to be clear about your true feelings. Confrontation may not be the answer, but honest communication can definitely improve the situation. Listen to your heart, and make time for the good stuff during the Aries Full Moon on the 21st.

November

That itch to get moving comes from Mars acting like a thorn against your Moon, but any discontent you feel can arise from the blocks that keep you from getting started in the first place. Team efforts provide a great opportunity to use your initiative, especially if you feel that you're not ready to put all your effort behind a personal project. Despite your usual independent streak, you'll enjoy the experience of others helping to share the burden of responsibility. After the lunar eclipse on the 20th you may feel that most of your obligations are out of the way so you can have more freedom to start something that allows you to shine on your own.

December

Sometimes, solar eclipse cycles bring more intensity into a situation you've needed to change. Turn your attention to your inner, spiritual needs during the Sun's eclipse on the 4th. This can be an excellent time to fine-tune your life and incorporate spirituality into your daily routine. A more mindful focus makes all the difference, when you'll feel that you have a stronger grasp on your ability to direct your life on your terms. Your connections with others take on a different meaning, and you may want strengthen the commitments that have real importance. Pure fun is on the agenda around the time of the Full Moon on the 19th, when special moments add to your scrapbook of memories.

TAURUS MOON

Endurance is one of your outstanding qualities—and it comes from your Taurus Moon. You have the ability to create a stable, consistent, and solid footing that gives you a great foundation from which you can build your dreams. You view life through a soulful yearning for love and beauty, and as a result, may spend much of your time growing one thing or another. There's an earthiness about your needs, and you'll feel a surge of happiness when you're standing on solid ground enjoying the sweet fruits of life.

You can be conservative, since the idea of wasting anything simply does not make sense to you. That same focus adds an element of patience to your personality, since you understand that some things (and people) are definitely worth the wait. Love brings life into full bloom for you, but that does not mean you're likely to rush toward commitment. You know that once you promise yourself to an idea, situation, or a person that you're likely to remain committed. So, taking time to determine whether it's real and can withstand life's trials is a key factor in any situation requiring you to make a pledge. For you, a solid footing means a lot, and long-term growth reassures your faith in yourself. Change is never easy—especially if it's not your idea. Anything that shakes your foundations triggers an uneasy anxiety, and that can quickly undermine your confidence. Sometimes "no" is simply your first response because your stubborn resistance requires it. But others will accuse you of simply being ornery. Are they right?

You can see the beauty in the simplest things and appreciate lasting values. It is an embrace of the quintessential beauty of life that inspires you to build a beautiful home, to nourish those you deeply love, and to develop your artistic sensibilities. The music of life is simply part of you, and your close relationships inspire your greatest accomplishments. Letting go of anyone or anything can hurt, because you feel that you are losing part of yourself. Those who have your love understand your motivation to hold on, but will appreciate it when you give them room to follow their own paths and make their own choices. Fortunately, your heart reminds you that evolutionary change requires certain ingredients: trust, time, and, most of all, love.

Famous Individuals with Taurus Moon

Jesse Helms, Jr.; Elton John, Meryl Streep

The Year at a Glance for Taurus Moon

You may feel that life is spinning out of control if there are too many things changing around you. Fortunately, you can create a strong footing that allows you to bend like a tree in the wind. Your ability to reach into a deeper quality of understanding adds flexibility. It's called self-confidence. In many ways, this is a year that involves reshaping your foundations, and enhancing your life experience. To empower yourself, remember that even when situations change beyond your control—your have a choice in the way you respond.

Careful steps and practical planning help you make the best use of your time and resources this year. Saturn's influence provides a series of stepping stones that allow you to nurture growth where it counts most. Small maneuvers give you more breathing room. Think of this cycle as clearing your garden for the new growth of springtime.

Jupiter's cycles stimulate recognizable progress, and from January through the end of July you'll feel your timing is most reliable. Improvements at home can make a huge difference in your sense of security, and changes within your family may be most welcome. When Jupiter moves into Leo in August, you may feel an uncomfortable level of expansion, since some things can get too large, too fast. Measuring your limits becomes more difficult, since your list of wants can get long—quickly. For that reason, you'll operate more effectively if you try to follow a plan of action whenever possible.

The confusion created by Neptune's cycle is most notable if your Moon is from 0–9 degrees of Taurus. You can feel emotionally scattered, or like you've lost your center, when what's happening is a change in your priorities. It's time to let go of the things that keep you weighted down and that prevent you from connecting with your spirituality. However, you do need to take special care with practical matters, since your desire to escape is pretty strong, too.

If your Moon is 10–19 degrees of Taurus, you're making a series of adjustments while Pluto transits in an irritating connection to your Moon. This cycle prompts you to look at the areas of your life where you're feeling a bit of a pinch. Is there a relationship that's more work than joy? How can you change your attitudes toward it? Most important, this cycle helps you explore your habits and your daily routine. It's time to get rid of destructive habits and focus on healing.

If your Moon is 20–29 degrees of Taurus, then you're on an emotional roller coaster this year. Uranus' cycle conflicts with your Moon, bringing an unsettled and highly changeable period. Other people can change, leave, or play a different role in your life, leaving you to fill the void some way. Or, you might decide that you've reached your limit in a situation and that it's time to seek out different options. This is even stronger after June, when Saturn's influence helps you trim away what you no longer need.

For all Taurus Moon individuals there's a heightened creative sensibility under the year's planetary cycles. Fresh ideas stem from changing your focus and opening to a different way of doing things. You may also have a chance to polish your talents or dust off your special skills.

Affirmation for the Year

In all things, I listen to the song of my heart!

January

Start the year off with a focus on beautifying your personal surroundings, and incorporate the things you love most as enhancements. If you enjoy travel or cultural exchange, explore options that stimulate your appreciation for the artistic. An interesting connection can develop as a result of your exploration or creative self-expression. The New Moon cycle on the 13th opens the way for improvement in a love relationship, but your connections at work can also be enhanced. After Mercury turns retrograde on the 18th you may feel uneasy, especially about unfinished business. Some of your anxiety may be justified, since hidden elements or a deceptive attitude from others can undermine your plans during the Full Moon on the 28th.

February

A difference of opinion or values can throw you off balance emotionally early in the month, especially if you're at odds with someone you love. Take a second look from the 4th to 11th, when your common ground is easier to identify. Even if your viewpoints are not the same, there's room for diversity. Your opportunity to make lemonade from those lemons arises after the 18th, when just the right amount of sweetness makes all the difference in the way others respond to you and your ideas. By the time the Full Moon arrives on the 27th, you may see your way clear to reach a reasonable settlement, especially if you're getting something you want in the process.

March

If you're wondering what's triggering hidden hostility, it's the cycle of Mars trudging through Taurus. All those things you thought were buried or tucked away in a safe zone seem to poke their heads out—and at the most inconvenient time, too! This can be particularly troubling midmonth, when the illusions are blown away and you have to deal with things at their most basic level. You're more vulnerable then, too—if you've been denying the reality of a situation in favor of what you want to see. The good news is that this is a great month to take the initiative when it matters most. Expressing what's on your mind is easiest from the 12th to 28th, when you'll also have better luck making contact.

April

Pesky Mars remains in Taurus through the 13th, although you can't blame Mars alone. It's the friction from unpredictable Uranus that rocks your boat. Your efforts to keep everything under control may not work the way you intend, although you're likely to weather the storm just fine. Lovely Venus travels in Taurus, too, and brings a calm quality to your emotions despite all the craziness happening around you. Common sense comes to the rescue just after the New Moon on the 12th. Your ability to hold things together in a crisis works to your advantage. But it's the passion stirring near and during the Full Moon on the 27th that you'll remember most. The ecstasy may be fleeting, but the effect is definitely long term.

May

Your resilience (or lack of it) is tested in situations when others seem to be distracted from what's most important. The underlying problem is that you don't want to be saddled with responsibilities that belong to someone else. So, if you find yourself asking whether you should step in and put your finger in the dike, think again—especially if your obligations are already taxing. Your practical resourcefulness comes to the rescue during the Taurus New Moon on the 12th. It's a good time to let someone in on the secrets of your needs, too, since you're more in touch with the essence yourself. Changes beyond your control can upset the apple cart near the time of the lunar eclipse on the 26th, when old reliable elements are showing some wear and tear.

June

Your self-confidence surges forth and works like a magnet to draw the kind of support you were wishing for last month. Better late than never, although in the cosmos, things are usually right on time. Love blossoms from the 1st to 14th, when reaching out to others warms your own heart, and momentum in a passionate relationship grows more intense. While the solar eclipse on the 10th stimulates your need to strengthen your resources, you're more focused on building a commitment that fits into your long-range plans. You can be distracted by something (or someone) that looks more appealing on the surface, but has little substance. It's the open exchange of ideas and common spiritual ties that you uncover during the lunar eclipse on the 24th which serve to deepen your affections where it counts most.

July

Diversity adds intrigue and interest, but you can feel like a fish out of water if the contrast is too sharp. Clarify your common threads during the New Moon on the 10th, but make room to weave your differences into the tapestry of your relationship, too. Connections with those whose ideals and interests support your own can be especially significant from the 7th to 21st, when you're more inclined to be more open about your feelings. Watch your personal boundaries, though, since it's easy to go too far, or to try to take up slack for someone else. By the time the Full Moon occurs on the 24th you can feel emotionally exhausted if you've pushed beyond your emotional limits. Give yourself a break and indulge in a bit of healthy pampering for a soulful recharge.

August

Jupiter enters Leo, and the temptation to bury yourself under too much indulgence can slow your momentum. This can be particularly notable in matters of diet and daily routine, since the temptation is to go overboard. If you're making improvements at home, or considering a move you can also bite off more than you can chew. Family gatherings can be great fun this month, but the politics can get out of hand near the Full Moon on the 22nd, when the more disruptive members of your clan can be a bother. Or you may decide that you don't fit into the same old picture any longer, and you'd like to do things your way for a change. Either way, rebellion is in the air.

September

For the remainder of the year, everything is about striking a balance between your wants and needs and those of others. This month, your productivity shines, although your focus is more on expressing the depth of your feelings through a creative avenue. Working cooperatively with others can be a challenge if you feel that your needs are being overlooked, and the only way to change things is to speak up about it. To avoid creating an unnecessary stir, you might be tempted to swallow your feelings, but that could lead to feelings of resentment. Talk to a friend if you need to vent, since unspoken hurt can pollute the purity of your heart. And allow plenty of time for romance to work its magic during the Full Moon on the 21st.

October

The universe gives you a second chance. Hurt feelings resulting from those power struggles back in August may need resolution. From the 2nd to 10th there's an opening in the scheme of things that allows an opportunity to reach an understanding and put old hurts behind you. You may simply need to acknowledge the individual responsibilities involved, but it's time to move on. If you're wondering about the effect of Venus retrograde from October 10 until November 11, it definitely has an influence in your life.

This is the time to search your own heart for your true feelings about yourself and about others. The questions that arise over your relationship may be whether or not your current needs are being met, or if you're stuck in the past. It's a new century, and you have different needs. Make room for them.

November

Gentle persuasion is the name of the game, and you're usually a master at it. Venus moves in opposition to your Moon sign, and you can see more clearly how your relationships reflect your values and needs. Encourage others to do their part. Fortunately, the balance of power in your relationships may be more to your liking, although you may wonder if you're getting the whole story. Explore your concerns after the New Moon on the 4th, but expect to get your information in bits and pieces. It's like working an emotional puzzle, and things may not fall into place until just before the Taurus lunar eclipse on the 20th. This Full Moon (the eclipse) can mark a turning point in a relationship, but even more important, it's a time when you can let go of the past and move on.

December

Sumptuous delights await your magic touch. Your ability to pour yourself into whatever you're doing is enhanced by the dance of Venus and Mars in opposition to your Moon. Mixed signals can confuse the issue from the 1st to 14th, particularly if your aims contrast with somebody else's. However, if your desire is to create beauty and harmony, then you can bring things back into balance. It's easy to go overboard, or to feel that someone is pressing issues long after they've been decided, so before the Full Moon comes around on the 19th, let others know your plans and your limitations. After the 23rd, you're ready to sit back and enjoy the quiet moments of the season. This time invites you to turn inside and reflect on your hopes for the future.

GEMINI MOON

The world holds tremendous fascination for you, since your Gemini Moon is nurtured when you exercise your endless curiosity. Your appetite for information helps you stay young, and whether you're exploring ideas, talking with ordinary people, reading a book or attending a stimulating class—you yearn to learn. Your independent streak is a reflection of Gemini Moon, too. Changeable situations are most interesting to you, and relationships that give you plenty of room for personal development have the best chance of succeeding.

Your need to experience new places, careers, or people helps keep you going, although you can distract yourself and may have trouble finishing things when you lose your focus. Before you know it, you can be up to your ears with so many things to do that you have difficulty keeping up with yourself. That burning desire to know somehow gets lost in the shuffle, and then you can feel frustrated because you're not getting anywhere. Despite all the fast-paced changes, you can keep your wits about you, especially in the midst of a crisis. It's then that your objectivity and logic can come to the rescue.

Highly emotional situations can be uncomfortable for you, particularly when things don't make sense. Unfortunately, life is often illogical when it concerns matters of the heart. However, your feeling of connection to people and places can be quite powerful, especially if you can strengthen your interests and ideologies through your association. Your life journey can lead you through all sorts of fascinating possibilities. For you, home can be almost anywhere, since your adaptability and objectivity allow you to make the most of your circumstances. However, real security happens when you are unified with the essence of personal freedom that stems from an outpouring of the unfettered expressions of your mind as it links harmoniously to higher truth.

Famous Individuals with Gemini Moon

Fred Astaire, George Carlin, Barbara Walters

The Year at a Glance for Gemini Moon

Your sense of emotional stability continues to grow during 2002, although you may alter your priorities more than once. The cosmic climate produces the right atmosphere for you to breathe life into your creativity, strengthen your relationships, and lay a strong platform for long-term growth. You're taking a serious look at your needs, and may break away from situations and change attitudes that stand in the way of your personal fulfillment. However, circumstances that support your growth will become reinforced.

Saturn continues its transit in Gemini (a cycle which began in mid-2000), stimulating your need to be clear about your feelings. You're testing yourself and the people around you, and may feel more in touch with the passage of time. The pressing need to establish a firm foundation can lead you to purchase a home, strengthen your family ties, or put down roots—one way or another. Whether you realize it or not, the commitments you make now are likely to last.

If your Moon is 0–7 degrees Gemini, you may feel that you're finally stepping into the sunlight after a trying period of swollen responsibility. The heavy-duty cycles of Saturn and Pluto are over, and it's time to build on the foundations you created last year. However, if your Moon is from 7–12 degrees Gemini, you're experiencing a sense of expanded consciousness while Neptune makes a harmonious connection to your Moon. Your impressions and intuitive sensibilities can be enhanced, and since you have the benefit of Saturn helping to ground you, it's likely that you'll make choices that can take you somewhere. Be particularly aware of your feelings during the Sun's eclipse on December 4th, since this cycle marks a time of completion and new beginnings.

If your Moon is 13–20 degrees of Gemini, then you're dealing with the unsettling energy of Pluto in a confrontational opposition to your Moon this year. You may feel that you're being uprooted, and that some of these changes are happening without your permission. However, if you bring your focus onto your priorities, you may realize that you're only losing what you no longer need. Still, your vulnerability is exposed, and you may need time to retreat and reflect. The Gemini solar eclipse on June 10th has special impact in your life, and indicates the possibility that this year will be one of critical change. A move or shift in family structure can dramatically alter your life.

If your Moon is 21–29 degrees Gemini, you're experiencing a period of awakening and a drive to commit to a life path that fulfills your highest needs. Saturn is exactly conjunct, or joined with, your Moon during the last half of 2002, and brings stability and focus your way. However, it's the lightning flash from Uranus that serves to awaken your feelings. You may be more creatively inspired, or have opportunities than were previously unavailable to you. Either way, it's time for a change. Fortunately for you, you can make these alterations without undermining your security. (That's the support from Saturn working to your advantage.)

For all Gemini Moon individuals, this is a year to be more in touch with your underlying feelings and motivations. You cannot escape yourself, and will not want to run away, either. The insight and clarity you can gain may serve you well into the future.

Affirmation for the Year

I am always honest with myself and with others.

January

Hostility is a feature of the first half of the month, when power issues come to the surface whether you want them to or not. You can be especially frustrated if someone seems to say one thing, and then do another. You're looking for focus and clarity, and you're also eager to keep progress rolling along. Choosing your battles makes all the difference, since there may be trouble whirring around you. (You may not have to fix it.) A positive mental focus works wonders, although you may not see evidence of this until after the 18th. Relationship issues smooth over, and becoming closer to the one you love is easier after the 20th. The soulful connection you share is even more intensified during the Full Moon on the 28th.

February

It's time to get in touch with an old friend or close relative to share stories and renew your connection. Staying active feels great. Perhaps you and your buddy can stir up interest in something you've longed to accomplish? Fresh ideas inspire your creative drive, too. So whether you direct this toward making improvements at home or bettering communication at work, you're likely to add spark and spice to whatever you do. The New Moon on the 12th is a highly productive stimulus, and you may discover that you've accomplished quite a lot during this short month's duration. Watch for potential disagreements over matters of taste and priority after the 17th. These can show up around the dinner table during the Full Moon on the 27th.

March

Ideas are coming along at faster than you can turn them into something, but at least you can talk about your inspirations. Writing and communication fare quite nicely, and innovative changes occupy your time from the 1st to 13th. Unrealistic expectations from others can temporarily thwart your progress near the New Moon on the 14th, when you may have to take extra time to explain yourself. Everyone may not grasp things as quickly as you do, so a bit of patience on your part can go a long way toward improving your ability to work cooperatively. From the 21st through the Full Moon on the 28th there's a lot going on at home. Entertaining friends can be fun, but you might also feel like putting extra energy into redecorating or rearranging your personal space.

April

An open-minded exchange of ideas builds a bridge of understanding. However, outlining expectations takes extra patience from the 1st to 10th, since everyone seems to be jumping to conclusions. The time you spend working with others can be quite gratifying, despite the fact that you're moving at a different pace. You can be more easily agitated after the 13th, when Mars enters Gemini and stirs up your emotions for the following six weeks. You're experiencing a strong desire to express what's on your mind; it's time to be aware of the way you handle anger. Venus calms the winds of discontent on the 25th, and others may warm to you more easily. Until then, it's up to you to keep a level head whenever you can.

May

You'll wonder why every month can't be like this one. Mercury, Venus, Mars, and Saturn all team up in Gemini, adding a great combination of ingredients to your life experience. It's easier to talk about your feelings. Others seem more receptive. Your common sense is working nicely with your intuition. And, to top it off, progress is made in the areas that mean the most to you. But there's a trickster waiting in the wings. You have to know when you've reached your limit. If not, someone or something will set it for you—and that's never much fun. Power plays can arise, just to test your popularity and influence. Do you handle these with grace and even hand, or do you lower yourself to their level? The answer sounds easy, but accomplishing the task can be quite a feat. The truth arrives with the lunar eclipse on the 26th, and it's staring at you in the mirror. Smile!

June

The Gemini solar eclipse on the 10th brings critical situations to a peak, and from there you're ready to start over. Oh, you don't exactly get a clean slate, but you are facing a different horizon. The links you forge with others now can be quite inspiring as a meeting of the minds can get your creative juices flowing. However, there are earmarks that indicate some things are ended, once and for all, and despite the new freedom you feel as a result, you can be a bit grief-stricken. Maybe you're just abandoning a bad habit. Still, you'll grieve. And with every tear, your heart opens more fully until you can see yourself and your new path with greater clarity. Celebrate the endings and the new beginnings, since acknowledging change increases your inner strength.

July

The nagging feeling that you're nearing the limits of your emotional capacity can be the result of Jupiter's cycle. It's not just you. The emotional climate surrounding you is on the brink of change, and since you're moving into different directions, you can feel more uncertain of yourself. The impulse to push onward with caution works to your advantage from the 1st to 7th, as long as you're attentive to the storm clouds nearby. A break in the action gives you a chance to cool your jets from the 1st to 20th, and then you're off into yet another exploration. This time, your ideas and insights garner the attention of others in need of inspiration, and that keeps you going, too. But do watch for another power issue to emerge during the Full Moon on the 24th.

August

An even pace and confident attitude work to your advantage as Jupiter changes signs and moves into Leo. It adds special zip to your step and a sparkle to your smile. The sudden changes from the 1st to 5th open the way for you to step in and work your own magic, although you'll have to pay homage to the more conservative factions if you want to get anywhere. A difference of opinion gets you going from the 6th to 26th, but you may find that the debate itself inspires a fresh direction for your ever-fertile mind. It's easy to fly off into several directions at once during the Full Moon on the 22nd, when you'll do yourself a favor if you keep a close watch on your priorities. You still have to stay on track with what's really important.

September

It's a good thing you like variety, since there are several things happening at once for you this month. Mentally and creatively, you're in a great space, with ample support from Mercury to help you get your point across. However, Mercury does turn retrograde on the 14th, and so you may feel that you're repeating yourself more often than you like. Think of it as education. The tricky elements come from Mars and his stranglehold with Pluto. The pressure can explode right on your front door, with argumentative power struggles happening just when you thought you had better things to do. The test is about whether or not you'll be drawn into a situation that has nothing to do with you. Clarity emerges, but not until after the Full Moon on the 21st.

October

It's a good thing your self-confidence is strengthened, since the less tolerant types may be pointing their fingers in your direction. This is when your wit can work to your advantage. Your task is to know when to take the critics seriously, and when to ignore them. Expectations run high since Venus and Jupiter are bumping heads, and tried and true rules seem to be bending in odd places while Mars and Saturn square off.

Watch for an opening during the New Moon on the 6th, when a healthy alliance gives you a chance to make headway. Then, after the 12th, communication improves and your team starts to take shape. Family matters improve dramatically by the Full Moon on the 21st, when you're also more optimistic about a situation that you've been fretting over. Take things one day at a time.

November

With Mars traveling under the guise of Libra's charm, hostilities can take place while the combatants remain courteous to one another. The trouble comes from those who seem to have a hidden agenda, and if you look closely, you'll be able to identify them before you fall under their spell. Keep a low profile until the 22nd if you want to stay out of the line of fire. Otherwise, just wear your bulletproof vest when you're out for your morning walk. Seriously. You can be caught in the crossfire of unruly battles from others, and that proves very little in the long run except that you were in the wrong place at the wrong time. Those with emotionally charged ideals can be the most difficult right now. Even your exceptional logic may not get through.

December

Your "heads up" for the solar eclipse on the 4th is in the area of relationships, although you may not see the final results until the Gemini Full Moon on the 19th. Those who've been unwilling to listen may be more open to your ideas from the 1st to 8th, although they could just be waving you off to get you out of their way. Focus instead on your friends and others who share your ideals. Make room to enjoy the pleasures of family and children, and when you have the time, give your own inner child a chance to play, too. Which dreams are still alive for you? What are you doing about making them a larger part of your reality? This insight is the basis for something more than a resolution for the year ahead. It's your ticket to getting what you need from life.

CANCER MOON

Your Cancer Moon helps you stay in touch with the cyclical nature of life itself. There's no doubt that you can tune in to the tides of human emotion, and you can also be deeply intuitive. The more you trust and open to the natural rhythms of life, the more connected you are to your own heart. It's more like you to become intimately involved in whatever you're doing, and you need to take an active part to assure that those you love are protected and nurtured. You simply do not like the feeling you get when you have to stand on the sidelines.

Comfort and support are easy outpourings of your soul, and you have a knack for making others feel better. Is it any wonder that they come to you for support? That same energy extends into your personal space, since feathering your nest is one of your favorite focal points. You are definitely into comfort zone amenities. However, the haven you create is more than a place: it's the essence of your being. Your insightful, protective guidance and care shine through whether you're raising kids, encouraging students, or directing a company. You may be a fabulous cook, and even if you are not, you know the significance of gathering around the table with those you adore. You understand the value of the things that tie people together, and may have a passion for history, genealogy, antiques, or collecting. The pain in your life comes when you have to let go, particularly when it's time for your innocents to face the world. Yet, the connection you've created will always remain, if you have faith in the purity of love. Sometimes, changes that require you to step into the unknown can leave you feeling vulnerable and uncertain, and letting go of the past can have the same effect.

Through celebrating the progressive stages of life, you can always move back into the beautiful, natural rhythms that calm your soul. As you merge with this flow, your eyes glow with contentment that comes from the peace arising from your awareness of the timeless truth of life. From that space, you are whole.

Famous Individuals with Cancer Moon

Claude Debussy, Harrison Ford, Nancy Reagan

The Year at a Glance for Cancer Moon

The jubilation and confidence you feel this year can carry you through the ups and downs, and may even attract exceptional opportunities. Most of the trouble spots show up when you have to deal with changes beyond your control, and steering your ship through uncertain waters can be frustrating. Love itself grows and prospers, and it's by listening to the song of your heart that you rise above the inevitable upsets.

The year 2002 begins with Jupiter continuing its cycle in Cancer. Through the end of July this cycle opens the way for you to establish a positive connection with yourself. This is your time to explore the deeper and higher purpose of your soul. Your reach into a more profound understanding of yourself and your needs can instill a kind of strength that creates an unshakable foundation based on higher Truth. However, there can be a down side to the time Jupiter transits through your Moon's sign. It's easy to overindulge, to overspend, or to push beyond your limits. The effects might not be immediate, but you'll certainly notice them once Jupiter moves on into its next cycle starting in August. As Jupiter moves into Leo, you'll start to see the costs of any overextending you've done during the previous twelve months. To avoid having to pay more than necessary, try to keep your limitations in mind during the first seven months of this year.

If your Moon is 0–7 degrees Cancer, you're experiencing a year of insightful understanding of your drives and needs while Chiron travels in opposition to your Moon. This cycle helps you unlock many of your underlying motivations, almost like giving you a glimpse of your soul's most intense yearning. You can also see ways you hurt yourself, and may find that it's time to deal with destructive habits once and for all. However, if your Moon is from 7–13 degrees Cancer, you may feel that it's finally time to forgive some situations from your past. You're feeling the influence of Neptune's transit in a ticklish quincunx aspect to your Moon as this cycle stirs some uncomfortable old memories and repressed emotions. As you release these things, you can feel a strange emptiness, but will eventually find that there is an openness that allows you to become more fulfilled on a spiritual and emotional level. You're also bidding goodbye to an old way of life while Saturn completes its cycle in semisextile to your Moon during the first four months of 2002.

If your Moon is from 14–21 degrees Cancer, you can feel fairly uneasy. You can reel from the shock waves of Pluto transiting in quincunx aspect to your Moon, since some of your deepest attachments may be exposed. Think of this as a time of emotional renovation, when you're tearing down old defenses in order to create a more hospitable emotional environment for yourself. From February through June, Saturn adds an extra punch in a semisextile transit to your Moon, and your support system can be more unreliable than you like. However, it's most likely that you are losing what (and whom) you no longer need. If your Moon is 22–29 degrees of Cancer, you're experiencing the restless vibrations of Uranus transiting in quincunx to your Moon. This cycle is like dealing with a lot of thunderstorms, except they occur on an emotional level.

For all Cancer Moons, there's hope through these stormy times. It comes from your ability to keep track of your most important priorities, and the need to set aside the things that are not as significant as you may have thought.

Affirmation for the Year

I am open to new possibilities, and welcome change!

January

You're motivated to demonstrate how you feel, and can certainly get your point across, even if indirectly. Relationships improve as you open to the needs of the other person, although you'll be happier if there's balance in the process. In other words: your needs count, too! It's easy to feel overwhelmed by outside demands during the New Moon on the 13th, when you may have to put your personal plans on hold in favor of something more pressing. Try to squeeze in a little time for romance, or just take a break from the action to keep things in their proper perspective. Friction with others escalates after the 18th, although the biggest problem during the Full Moon on the 28th is likely to stem from unfulfilled expectations.

That crestfallen experience can be minimized when you stay in the moment, instead of pining over what could have been.

February

Misunderstandings are part of the Mercury retrograde cycle, but they can lead to hurt feelings—especially if you feel left out. Unfamiliar situations, or a new relationship, can be difficult to figure out, and you can over-compensate by becoming too protective too quickly. After the 12th, Venus comes to the rescue and you may find that you're on familiar turf once again. Generosity from others soothes you and it's easier to confirm who appreciates you. This little confidence booster allows you to let your guard down just a bit. Time spent sharing your favorite pleasures can strengthen a close relationship, and snuggling together under the covers on cold winter nights can be simply divine. Leave room for romance during the Full Moon influence from the 26–27th, when a fabulous dinner can be the key to opening your heart.

March

The cosmic melodies play a tune that prompts you to sing along. Tap into your creativity, and let your heart show you the way to happiness. Romance sparkles from the 1st to 8th, although you may feel more com-fortable if your keep your desires away from public scrutiny. Since your tastes and priorities might not mesh with others after the 9th, you may wonder if you've made the right choices on the home front. It's not the best time to redecorate, although playing with plans and shopping for options can be interesting. Mixed signals can create a problem from the New Moon on the 14th until the 17th, when you may feel that you're on a different wavelength from the rest of the world. Take comfort in the things and people you know, and if you're traveling, bring something along that reminds you of home.

April

Fasten your seat belt, since the ride gets bumpy from the 1st to 13th! The problem is that your friends or loved ones may arrive on your doorstep with unexpected news. It can be fun, but disruptive, and unless you have an open mind you may feel that you're left out. Before you jump to con-clusions, look around. It could be that the backdrop is changing now. Selfish attitudes from others will not be welcome, and can be a signal that you need to pull away and give them space to make their own mistakes. After the 14th, calm descends under the heavenly influences. Your designs or plans for improvements at home will definitely make a positive impact. Romance is best from the 14th–26th. Do something fabulous the night before the Full Moon on the 27th.

May

That pesky distraction you feel comes from all the mutable energy stirring up change around you. You can be out of sorts when others rely too much on logic and scrap their intuitive sensibilities—or worse, demean the value of yours. It's a test of your ability to allow the intellectual element to flourish, but not at the expense of a more soulful quality. Fortunately, you are protected when it counts. Besides that, once Mercury turns retrograde on the 15th all those purely logical arguments may be in trouble. Venus saunters into Cancer on the 20th, opening the way for tender moments. Then, on the 28th, Mars moves into Cancer, too. The home front is definitely activated, and those you love most may even show up at the dinner table in time to talk about the lunar eclipse happening on the 26th.

June

With plenty of news to share, your connection to those around you can be supercharged. You're busy at home with improvements, moving, or increased family activity throughout the month. Loving moments fill your days and nights while Venus activates your Moon through the 14th. It's also an excellent time to beautify your home in some way. The solar eclipse on the 10th may mark the beginning of uncovering a few secrets from the past, but it's the lunar eclipse on the 24th that's most significant to your life. If you're thinking of making a move, or doing repairs, you may get more help from other people after the 23rd. You can be extra sensitive emotionally, though, and may feel unusually frustrated if others fail to live up to your expectations.

July

The surge of energy from Mars coupled with Jupiter in Cancer can feel like a tidal wave of emotion early in the month, and while you may feel that you're riding high, it can be an exhausting ride. Still, you're likely to dive right in, since it's not every day that circumstances fall into place that allow you to bring your dreams to life in such a magnificent way. A blend of practical solutions and soulful communication goes a long way toward mending old problems in your personal life after the 7th. Consider the Cancer New Moon on the 10th to be a time of emotional rebirth, when you can leave behind your old attachments and focus your energy on nurturing your personal growth. First, you have to decide what you need. After the 21st, your focus is on building your dreams.

August

It's time to take everything down a couple of notches while you concentrate on establishing a new set of priorities. With the groundwork accomplished, you can feel a bit off balance, and may need additional time to regain your focus. Consider this an excellent period to evaluate your physical needs, and to make alterations in your diet and daily routine that will bring more stability and consistency. The Venusian sparks of temptation to indulge in too many sweets, or to spend too frivolously, can be the result of your need for a little extra pampering. There are healthy ways to reward yourself, but they may require extra effort. Just for kicks, try something completely different during the Full Moon on the 22nd. Maybe those tofu burgers are better than you think.

September

Have you ever wished that you could just transmit what you need without having to talk about it? That desire can be especially powerful, since words can actually get in the way of what you really want to express, or it can seem that way. The marvelous thing is that your heart is open, and the love you feel can actually radiate into everything you do—particularly when you're reaching out to others. The New Moon on the 7th marks a time to refocus, although you may also be dealing with endings. Are there habits you want to change? This is the time to determine a fresh pathway. Anticipation gets your pulse racing from the 13th to 22nd, and romantic action during the Full Moon on the 21st can be divine. Take your cue from the music of your heart.

October

It's one of those months when it may not be easy to understand what you feel. The contrast between need and want can be rather powerful, and if you're overdoing it in the want category, some of your real needs can be pushed aside. You can also run into the problem of trying too hard to make sure that everybody else gets what they want, but at a dear cost to yourself. The question rests in whether or not you love yourself enough to put your needs somewhere near the top of your priority list. Part of the experience of Venus retrograde from 10/10 to 11/21 is the process of uncovering the essence of love in your life. The irritation you experience in a relationship after the 15th only amplifies the need to determine how you really feel about your situation. Take your time. The process is like peeling an onion—there are plenty of layers.

November

To absorb the healing qualities of the planetary cycles, give your inner child some room to dance. Whether you spend more time with children, or exercise your creativity more fully, your need to express feelings that stem from the depths of your soul can thrust you into a transformation. The New Moon on the 4th marks a time to open your heart and allow the love you feel to pour into everything you say and do. Some confusion can result if you try to make sense out of it all. From there, changes begin to take shape; then, little by little, you can crack the code that helps you expose what's on the next horizon. Old anger can surface, too—just in time to break away from a situation you no longer need in your life. Tune in to what stirs your soul during the lunar eclipse on the 19th–20th.

December

Ride the wave of bliss generated while Venus and Mars dance together. Bring together the people you love. Take pictures. Enjoy the bounty of your lives. Make memories. The changes happening in the world around you during the Solar eclipse on the 4th can seem like stories on the news, even if they're happening at your back door. What matters most now is that you make the connections that give you a chance to deepens your commitment. Watch a tendency to push beyond your limits during and after the Full Moon on the 19th, since you could end up paying a price that you'd rather not endure. It's like saying "no" at the buffet table. Except this time, your plate can be filled with responsibilities that are not yours to carry.

LEO MOON

The fire in your soul conveys a warmth and adds drama to your personality. Your heart of gold shines forth from your Leo Moon, and—whether you want to be or not—you are often the center of attention. When your passions are aroused, you simply don't do anything halfway. Your creativity is food for your soul, and when there's a lot at stake, you perform at your very best. After all, the thought of letting down those who count on you is totally unacceptable. Your love for life drives you onward, and can inspire those who need encouragement through their personal journey.

For you, there's nothing like the feeling that you've brought pride through your actions to the hearts of those you admire and love. Their appreciation can keep you going when you're down, just as your support, generosity, and loyalty provide tremendous support for them. You have a lot invested in promises. Expect the same from those who have made commitments to you. Anyone who violates a promise or shows disloyalty can wound you deeply, and you may find it difficult to forgive such actions. It's when you feel most insecure that your selfish resistance takes over. Then you're likely to alienate those you want most to impress. You can even fall into a rut of stubborn willfulness, that can continue a vicious cycle of hurt. As you uncover broader options for exercising your creativity and imagination, you'll be better able to reach beyond yourself and move forward through life's inevitable ups and downs.

Once you feel in control of your life, your flair for the fabulous emerges. Your house can be a showplace, and even if your surroundings are simple, a quiet elegance helps you feel at home. You need plenty of opportunities to express the love in your heart. Your artistry may be the best way to give love to the world, and developing your talents helps to assure that your bond with a higher power is intact. After all, you are the ultimate performer in the drama of life—never far from the hearts of those who adore you, even when you cannot hear the applause.

Famous Individuals with Leo Moon

Tom Cruise, Queen Elizabeth II, Mohandas Ghandi

The Year at a Glance for Leo Moon

With all the challenges and changes you've experienced during the past few years, you're ready for some good news. Thank your lucky stars because this year, Jupiter's benevolence shines on your Moon! More than that, solid support from Saturn's time-tested discipline aids your ability to make choices that lead to a true feeling of personal security. There are still likely to be a few surprises, but consider them to be a little extra spice in the recipe.

From January through July, Jupiter transits in Cancer. During these months, you may feel an enhanced sense of vision, and your dreams can reveal future possibilities. However, your dreams also provides clues to the things you need to release so that you can open up to fresh possibilities. You'll feel a joyful anticipation. Then, starting in August, Jupiter will spend the next twelve months in Leo, bringing an expanded sense of optimism and good fortune your way. The year Jupiter transits in conjunction to your Moon can be a remarkable time, especially if you have some clarity about what you truly need. This energy aids your ability to fulfill those needs. The only downfall is that you can be shortsighted, and may be too self-indulgent.

If your Moon is from 0–6 degrees Leo, you're experiencing a mixture of testing and opportunity. From March through October, Saturn transits in a frustrating connection (a semisquare) to your Moon. You have to determine your real priorities during this time, since the manner in which you handle your personal responsibilities will determine whether or not you can take advantage of the opportunities that come your way. That period of enhanced good fortune occurs during August and September. However, if your Moon is from 7–12 degrees Leo, you're ready to let go and explore your inner self more fully. Neptune opposes your Moon, opening your consciousness to a deeper understanding. The difficult part of this cycle is determining healthy escapes, since addictive and self-abusive possibilities are enhanced under this influence.

If your Moon is from 13–20 degrees Leo, this is your year to experience healing from the inside, out. With Pluto's cycle in supportive trine to your Moon, it's easier to release the things you no longer need—ranging from bad habits to outworn relationships. A move may also be in order!

If your Moon is from 21–29 degrees Leo, you're ready to try something completely different while Uranus travels in opposition to your Moon. Fortunately for you, Saturn's practicality helps you keep one toe on the ground until you're really ready for launch. The first half of the year may be the most unsettling, since Saturn's influence is stronger after June. For that reason, if you're changing residence early in the year, remember that this is a transitional phase, and you may yet make another change before the year is over.

All Leo Moon individuals experience support from Saturn's cycle this year. The things you've learned about yourself can be quite valuable, as long as you use what you know. The commitments you make this year are also likely to last.

Affirmation for the Year

I value the insights arising from my intuition.

January

There are plenty of disruptions popping up, making it tough to get into your groove. Consider this a test of your flexibility (or lack of it), since your attempts at keeping things under control will definitely be met with resistance. You're likely to run into a different style of doing things—either at work or at home—and while you might not agree, you'll at least have a chance to see diversity in action. After the 18th a few things start to fall into place, and your emotional energy seems more focused. However, vague circumstances in a close relationship can create confusion during the Leo Full Moon on the 28th. Just remember that although you prefer to know where you stand, some people operate in a state of flux! It's all a matter of knowing when to paddle and when it's safe to sit back and see where the tide takes you.

February

With a few disputes circling about, you can feel unsettled—especially if you jump in unnecessarily. You have your own priorities, and stepping into a battle zone that has little to do with you can result in a costly setback. Inventive changes, renovation, or repair can certainly simplify your life during the New Moon on the 12th, even if it does take you a while to figure out how to work everything. Some of the problems or issues bandied about last month resurface after the 14th. If you've been wondering what someone really meant by what they said, this is the time to clarify. After the 23rd, you may have to deal with others whose values or tastes clash with your own. A gracious and accepting attitude on your part can keep the peace—for the time being, at least.

March

Mars travels in bullheaded Taurus, challenging you to deal with a bit of stubborn resistance from others. It's time to concentrate on practical matters, even if you don't want to. The problems arise when you start organizing things and realize that the support you expected may not be there. After the 7th, your talented team starts to fall into place under your leadership, although you can still feel vulnerable if someone is continually challenging your authority. Before you vote them off the island, consider whether or not they're bringing anything valuable into your life. While you cannot tolerate deceit, you can understand if the situation warrants your support. Family gatherings provide plenty of entertainment after the 20th, but romance may be on your mind during the Full Moon on the 28th.

April

Tension in the form of arguments, disrupted schedules, and angry outbursts spring up from the 1st to 10th, and you can be on the receiving end of somebody's frustration. Fortunately, open communication helps diffuse the friction, although establishing trust can be a chore. Patience works to your advantage, and even if you've been hurt by unfounded accusations you're at least learning about triggers in your relationships. At home, you may feel unappreciated despite your best efforts to get a smile from the folks who share your personal space. No need to despair, since a playful exchange opens the way for acceptance and understanding during and after the New Moon on the 12th. A break from daily hassles works wonders, and may be an absolute requirement if you want to feel more centered during the Full Moon on the 27th.

May

Now that the storm clouds are clearing away, you may feel like celebrating! It's the perfect time to bring friends together and catch up on all the news. At home, you're ready to open up more space and feel the air moving around you. That makes this a great time to clear away clutter, make repairs, and bring more light into your personal environment. If your plans call for a move or remodel, you'll have an easier time of it from the 1st to 14th. Others may come to you for comfort or advice if they're dealing with an emotional crisis. Although you're not required to fix anything, your warmth may be just what they need to get back on track. The lunar eclipse on the 26th emphasizes a need to find common threads amidst the diversity. This means that if someone's viewpoints are different from your own, you can each make space for the others' voice.

June

Observation serves you well, and experimentation works to your advantage while Mercury completes its retrograde through the 8th. By maintaining a lower profile early in the month you can be in a better position to launch your ideas or plans after the solar eclipse on the 10th. If you're still uncertain, evaluate your designs and desires after Venus moves into Leo on the 14th. You may discover that you need something different, and that what once seemed like a pressing need doesn't matter anymore. Your flair for the dramatic can be even more effective during the Moon's eclipse on the 24th. Your heart beats to pure love, and expressing the depth of your feelings can bring you closer to the fulfillment of your deepest yearnings.

July

A change of heart leads to a more profound connection in a relationship, although you may have to be willing to risk giving up control for a while. Why not? Perhaps it will feel good to surrender the driver's seat and enjoy the beauty surrounding you. Some elements of control are only an illusion anyway, and as the cycles move along through the month, keeping this in mind can give you reasons to smile. Projects around the house may keep you busy after the 11th, although a restless energy can stimulate your desire to be on the go once Mars enters Leo on the 13th.

Watch your tendency to get a bit pushy (especially if you've grown impatient), since others might make themselves scarce if you go too far. Reflect on what you feel and need because next month you have a chance to revitalize your needs.

August

This is your time to renew your commitments to the things that fill your heart with joy. Open your mind to unusual options, or ideas, that challenge your old perceptions from the 1st to 6th. Then, initiate changes in your daily routine during the Leo New Moon on the 8th. Seek out opportunities to enhance your energy. Bring more play into your life. Dietary changes that add vitality can make a huge difference, and increased physical activity can also have an amazing effect from the 8th to 27th. Unique situations give you every reason to marvel at life, so be on the lookout for a chance to try something completely different during the Full Moon on the 22nd. Taking an emotional risk can lead to ecstasy, but only if you're comfortable with the situation.

September

It's a mixed bag. The cosmic forces bring experimental and delightful changes your way from the 1st to 9th, but you may have to make room for some situations (or people) that are uncomfortable in the beginning. There can be turmoil around you that distracts from the things you want most to do, but that could just be a test of your priorities. Watch for situations to trigger your tolerance during the New Moon on the 7th. Then, after the 14th, be attentive to the problems that can result from holding unrealistic expectations. You could be the one on the receiving end of trouble if you fail to deliver what someone else anticipates—so be sure to clarify what's expected before you promise to show up for dinner. Circumstances improve after the 24th, but not before you have a chance to witness an abuse of power. The question is whether or not you're supposed to do anything about it.

October

Your list of wants is probably larger than your checkbook will allow. The same can apply to your personal life. You may really want somebody you cannot have, or may desire something from someone that they cannot give. On the home front, you may feel that you need more space, or something grand, in the way of your personal surroundings. Before you curl up in despair because things are not as you want them to be, reflect on your intrinsic values. What's driving your desires? Venus turns retrograde on the 10th, prompting you to question love and all its trappings. Talk about your concerns with your best friend, and then take small steps after the 16th to trim down that very long list of yours. By the time the Full Moon rolls around on the 21st you should have a good idea about what's really important—to you.

November

Contrast can be a good thing when it broadens your perspective on life. But it can hurt, too. The hurtful elements of contrast can occur this month if you feel that you simply cannot give someone what they need or want from you. Call it a growth cycle. It's time to address the difference between the situations you can control, and those you can only watch and wonder over. You're also grappling with a pressing need to make changes that give you more room to express yourself and to grow emotionally without leaving behind someone you hold dear to your heart. To reach an understanding, you may have to step aside and listen for a while. Reflect on your underlying drives during the lunar eclipse on the 20th, and seek out creative ways to express them in the days that follow. Laughter softens the tension after the 21st.

December

Fortunately for you, assuring that you please everyone all the time may not be a big drive. However, that's not going to stop more than a few people from asking—especially right now. It's more than the holidays. It seems your attention is required, even needed, by more people than you realized. Sort through your priorities during the solar eclipse on the 4th. Offer up apologies where necessary, since evading issues only leads to trouble. Leaving others to draw their own conclusions can put you in more hot water than you ever imagined. By the time the Full Moon occurs on the 19th, you're ready for a chance of scenery. Look for something cool, calm, and away from the beaten path.

VIRGO MOON

Details, details. Your Virgo Moon thrives on details, and your keen observational abilities and sense of discrimination are a testimony to that fact. It's those fine points that titillate your interest in anyone or anything and add to your desire to experience perfection. Since you tend to take a practical approach to life, you can seem emotionally conservative—something that often belies your exceptional sensitivity.

At the end of a productive day, you feel great. In fact, it's doing nothing that can be troublesome because you prefer to stay busy. Your analytical mind is frequently occupied figuring out how to improve something (or someone). Most content when things fit into sensible categories, you can feel uncomfortable in the midst of emotional turmoil. Natural surroundings or a pristine and serene environment help counterbalance the scattered emotions you experience when there's too much tension in your life. Patience is hard to come by when others fail to understand that your ideas about how to do things are correct, or when you see someone repeating mistakes without learning from them. That's one of the things that create worry, and that can result in your tendency to fret too much over the inconsequential or the things you cannot control.

It is the process of personal development that will ultimately allow you to accept yourself and your individual power and worth. Helping others is part of that. Improving the quality of life around, or teaching what you've learned can be an easy outreach for this driving need. In relationship, a partner appreciates your perceptive ability and understands that you can be grumpy when things don't work out according to your careful plans.

While you might find that you believe in someone else and their abilities, self-confidence is not easy for you. It's through your exploration of the transcendent qualities of love and compassion that you can reach peace and self-acceptance. Even though you may think you need perfection, you may mostly desire unqualified acceptance. It begins when you look in the mirror and see the light from your soul reflecting through your eyes.

Famous Individuals with Virgo Moon

Deepak Chopra, Jodie Foster, Robert Redford

The Year at a Glance for Virgo Moon

This is a year to slow your pace and concentrate on your most significant needs. Since you're naturally driven toward the process of self-improvement, incorporating innovative and alternative methods into your health regimen and daily routine can give you a new lease on life. Consider this the year to eliminate habits and attitudes that block your ability to feel whole.

The positive benefits that arise from Jupiter's cycle in connection to your Moon can be seen when you open to a more optimistic attitude. From January through the end of July, Jupiter's contact stimulates your ability to take better care of yourself and those you love. Your hope can inspire others, but—even more importantly—it keeps you going. Then, from August through December, you can expand your outreach and may want to be more involved in charitable efforts. However, it is a spiritual yearning that calls to your soul, and the remainder of the year involves an ability to delve more deeply into your inner self.

If your Moon is from 0–7 degrees Virgo, you're experiencing a time of fruitful self-discovery under the influence of Chiron's supportive contact to your Moon. The emotional tension and testing you experienced last year may have left you feeling exhausted, and this cycle can bring healing into your life. It's time to rejuvenate.

If your Moon is from 7–12 degrees Virgo, you're feeling stimulated to follow the whispers of your intuitive voice while Neptune transits in quincunx aspect to your Moon. This is not an easy cycle, since the temptation to escape at almost any cost can lead you to make choices that undermine your real needs. The more time you spend grounding your energy, the better your choices and more extensive your options will be.

If your Moon is from 13–19 degrees Virgo, you're undergoing huge changes while Pluto travels in a tense square connection. This is your breakaway year, when it's time to leave behind habits and circumstances that are simply not good for you. During the first six months of the year, Saturn adds tension and testing, and it can be difficult to break free. Persistence, patience, and determination will work to your benefit.

If your Moon is from 20–29 degrees Virgo, you can feel unsettled and tested at the same time. Uranus' disruptive energy brings friction to your Moon, and you can feel unsettled by changes which result from the actions and attitudes of others. After June, Saturn moves into an edgy square to your Moon for the remainder of the year. You can feel that your needs are being blocked. It's up to you to determine where those blocks originate, and to take greater responsibility for yourself and your feelings.

All individuals with Virgo Moon are challenged to uncover real feelings and motivations, since this is a year to find and focus on your priorities. Even if you're unhappy, it will do you little good to point out blame. Concentrate instead on using your practicality to create solutions. From there, you can accomplish a sense of fulfillment.

Affirmation for the Year

I appreciate myself and show gratitude for the abundance in my life.

January

After a bumpy start, your productivity gets into gear and continues strong through most of the month. Friction with others can be problematic unless you establish reliable guidelines, since power struggles seem to be lurking around every corner. You can be pulled into conflicts even if you do not have a vested interest, so be alert to the possibility of falling victim when you're trying to help. Concentrate on the completion of an old project, or deal with continuing family business, until the New Moon on the 13th. Then, turn your attention to a different set of priorities. Despite Mercury's retrograde that starts on the 18th, you're likely to trudge onward, shouldering your responsibility. Use your discrimination to determine the limitations of what you can safely carry.

February

Your fix-it ability comes to the rescue, although you may celebrate a quiet victory. Those who are part of your inner circle are likely to offer greater support and understanding, which helps you deal with some of the frustrations you face on a daily basis. Have your first-aid kit handy, during the New Moon on the 12th, or you may stand by watching while somebody else jumps hastily into a situation unprepared. Your careful ministrations do not go unnoticed, although you may not be comfortable if others make too much of your help. Consider it a learning experience, since accepting praise has probably never been very easy for you. Despite differences in taste or values at work, closer to home you have a lot to enjoy during the Virgo Full Moon on the 27th.

March

The strength you feel comes through on every level, but starts with a surge of assertiveness about meeting your needs. Mars lends support to your Moon, which means it's easier to get things done. On top of that, other factors indicate that if you ask for help, you might get it. (When the job is done, remember to offer up praise, even if others are not quite up to your exacting standards.) In your relationship, look for new ways to communicate your feelings and needs. Start with small steps during the New Moon on the 14th. Listen to your partner, too, since you may discover that you're actually on the same wavelength. Unfulfilled expectations can come crashing down around you during the Full Moon on the 28th. Before you start picking up the pieces, think about it. You might do better to walk away.

April

Everything's coming together, but not without a few surprises. Unanticipated actions from others can interrupt progress, although the end result could be to your benefit. If anybody can make lemonade out of those lemons, it's you. Your down-to-earth attitude helps maintain calm while others feel uncertain or insecure. Besides that, you're seeing results for the effort you've been putting out there, adding confidence and clear-mindedness to your increasing attributes. This is the time to put your talents to work, and to invite those you respect to join your team. Close relationships improve while you work side-by-side to bring your dreams to life. Make room to enjoy the fruits of your labors during the Full Moon on the 27th. And this time, those fruits are not of the sour variety.

May

Maintaining your concentration can require extra effort, since distractions are everywhere. Part of the problem involves the endless list of requests from other people. To stop the never-ending flow you may have to resort to using that voice mail system after all. Certainly, there's a level of excitement in all this, and you may even have reasons to celebrate. Remember that there is value in delegating tasks, since your expertise may be needed in a particular area. Set your priorities during the New Moon on the 12th, when a project at home may have to be pushed aside in favor of work. The lunar eclipse on the 26th is a time of reorganization, when old power struggles push to the surface and upset the status quo. However, with your priorities in order, you can determine how you fit into the picture, and continue to offer your services where they're most needed.

June

The fallout from a change of the guard can be a good thing, since your confidence in your abilities may be strong. While the solar eclipse on the 10th draws your attention to recently exposed information, you can quickly evaluate and determine where to go next. It's time to make the most of your circumstances. Involve your friends and their talents when it's appropriate. Your enthusiasm can be contagious, and others are likely to enlist your support. Love and passion fill your days and nights, and you may have much to be grateful for. If there's a cause that's close to your heart, put your energy into it and watch the progress! Let others know your feelings, since the lunar eclipse on the 24th stimulates your desire to allow love to lead the way.

July

Yes, this can be a time when you feel frazzled, but with potentially good results. The anticipation and excitement builds as you work toward a meaningful goal or the climax of a creative endeavor. Take steps to assure the success of your efforts during the New Moon on the 10th, when your vision merges with your capacity to get the job done. Despite a few disruptions, your self-confidence grows. Expressing how you feel is easier after the 7th, and an old emotional wound may be ready for healing. Then, on the 10th, Venus moves into Virgo, bringing a quality of tenderness and grace into your life. At home, it's a fabulous time to redecorate, design, or improve your landscape. But in your heart, this is your time to let the good things in life flow to you, and to test your ability to accept the gifts of love.

August

The voice of your soul may be singing so quietly that you have to withdraw from the noises of daily life to hear it. You're ready to listen, and pulling away from the intense activity that kept you so busy for the last couple of months may be necessary to return a balance to your life. You'll feel more in the mood to share your perceptions and feelings while Mercury travels in Virgo from the 6th to 26th, but not just anybody will do. Tender expressions are meant for a quieter space, where every nuance can be better appreciated. Consider taking a vacation, or break up your routine, so you have time to bring your emotional priorities back into focus. It's time to sort through what you need for yourself versus what others demand from you. The Full Moon on the 22nd beckons you to open to your visionary sensibilities. What do your dreams tell you?

September

All the inner work you've done lately has helped to create a space for self-renewal. It's the Virgo New Moon on the 7th that marks a time of fresh direction. Let go of attitudes that block your ability to fulfill your needs, and while you're at it, clear out a few closets, too. A health assessment could help bring you on track physically, and you might also feel ready to delve into your feelings more carefully through counseling or other self-discovery processes. With Mars traveling in Virgo until 10/15, you're experiencing an urge to assert your needs more fully, but you also feel the urge to get the things done that have fallen by the wayside. This can be a productive month on every level. Watch for a challenge during the Full Moon on the 21st, especially if your cleanup efforts have stepped on somebody's sensitive toes.

October

With a second chance to explain how you feel, or talk about what's really on your mind, you may be able to push beyond an impasse in a relationship. Mercury's cycle works to your benefit, since this expressive energy slips back into Virgo from the 2nd to 10th, giving you an opportunity to reconsider something you may have blocked or overlooked back in August. The big story involves the feeling that your needs are squeezed by pressures from the push-pull battle between Saturn and Mars from the 1st to 17th. It's a test of how well you handle your obligations, and how clear you are about your personal needs. Plus, unresolved anger works against you. For that reason, a bit of soul-searching can reveal the real source of any discontent. Start by giving yourself permission to feel what you feel, not what you think you should be feeling.

November

The depth of emotions you experience can feed your creativity, but will also enrich every part of your life. Despite the questions you have about the experience and expression of love while Venus retrogrades until the 21st, the planetary picture suggests that you are ready to address your resistance against creating true personal fulfillment. Reflect on your dreams and desires during the New Moon on the 4th, when you can see positive ways to strengthen your self-worth while helping to lift others, too. Then, by the time the lunar eclipse occurs on the 20th, you can open more fully to embrace the essence of your soul. Focus on your personal environment, too, since this can be an excellent time to fine-tune your home space so that you feel truly serene, secure, and comfy.

December

Even with the clattering voices giving you a long list of wants, your perspective on your real priorities can remain intact. The greatest distractions can come during the solar eclipse on the 4th, when family or career demands can lead you away from the things you needed to do for yourself. Consider it a momentary test, and then move on. Practical matters and activities around the house give you plenty of ways to use your artistic talents, and your motto, "The simpler, the better," works quite nicely amidst the fluster of holiday events. Still, the temptation to overdo it can take its toll after the 21st. No matter how many carrot sticks are on that buffet table, you're likely to be drawn to the scrumptious goodies that scream "cholesterol!" If you're a real health nut, you could even indulge in too many tofu treats.

LIBRA MOON

Your dreams of paradise feature a world where peace and harmony reign supreme, where you live together with the perfect partner by your side. Through your Libra Moon, you seek symmetry and beauty, and you prefer to present yourself in the most gracious manner possible. As a result, you possess a distinctive style. You may also be called on to exercise your exceptional diplomacy at home, at work, and in your community.

Your need for fairness is likely to be evident in everything you do. Most of all, though, you need acceptance, since your sense of perfection can cause you to doubt yourself from time to time. In relationships, you may need time to explore your search for a soul mate, since finding the right ingredients for a healthy relationship can be one of your primary life lessons. One thing you may discover early on is that the fairy tales promising "happily ever after" forgot to mention that human imperfections (including your own) would have to be addressed somewhere along the way. As you experience life, the wisdom you gain helps you make space for the ever-changing balance of needs that help you create an ideal relationship. It is that same desire for balance that can frustrate your decision-making ability. Others may have to learn that you need space and time to carefully weigh your options.

At home, your environment reflects your expression of beauty, and you may have an elegant sense of taste. Artistry inspires you, and surrounding yourself with lovely things and beautiful people seems only natural. Your quiet charm can fool people, though. A passionate heart beats beneath your calm exterior. When confronted by hostility, your vulnerability can send you running for cover. However, when it's important, you can definitely take a stand, and may win the day through your logical argument. To stabilize your emotions, you may need a regular time in your schedule to connect with your inner self. It is the bond you create with your inner partner that will allow you to mirror the self-assurance you need which will ultimately attract all that you need from life—including your partner.

Famous Individuals with Libra Moon

Elizabeth Barrett Browning, Julia Child, Leonardo DiCaprio

The Year at a Glance for Libra Moon

The skyscape shows a positive outlook for your emotional needs during 2002. Even if other factors in your life are undergoing change or challenge, your ability to handle those situations is strongly supported. Responsible choices bring your priorities into focus, and stability shows up on the home front. All in all, there's reason to make significant commitments that will help you fulfill your real needs.

Jupiter's cycles challenge you to identify your limitations, since your confidence is growing stronger—but will you be able to tell when you've reached your capacity? From January through the end of July, Jupiter's expansive energy tempts you to promise more than you can deliver. That can be especially true if you have to choose between two excellent options. A part of you will think, "Why not do both?" Fortunately, Saturn's clarity and focus helps you see the better alternative. The test is whether or not you'll do it anyway! By August, Jupiter moves into territory that brings a more friendly support to your Moon. For the remainder of the year, your sense of security is more likely to have a solid foundation, instead of having a basis that's less reliable.

If your Moon is from 0–6 degrees Libra, this is an excellent time to bring your artistic abilities to the forefront. Whether you decide to redecorate your home, change your personal appearance, or develop your talents more fully, the cycles of Uranus and Pluto move in helpful connections to your Moon. It's a great time to reshape your attitudes and open your consciousness.

If your Moon is from 7–12 degrees Libra, you'll feel prompted to develop your spirituality while Neptune transits in a powerful trine to your Moon. This cycle strengthens your connection to your inner self, although you have to put forth the effort to develop your inner awareness.

The downside of this cycle is that you feel a lack of motivation, since the impulse is to drift. Devoted meditation and some discipline toward your creative expression can help you avoid the lazy impulse from Neptune.

If your Moon is from 13–20 degrees Libra, you're ready to reshape your life so that your needs are better supported. Saturn travels in a supportive trine connection to your Moon from February through July, when you're most inclined to focus on creating stronger foundations. However, Pluto's sextile contact to your Moon prompts you to eliminate barriers and to let go of habits that stand in the way of your personal fulfillment. It's time to heal your relationships by redefining the way you interrelate.

If your Moon is from 21–29 degrees Libra, then this can be a banner year. Many of the things that you've been working toward are coming into fruition, and the satisfaction you feel can help you experience pure joy. Uranus' cycle brings an awakening and heightens your intuitive sensibilities. Then, in June, Saturn moves into a positive supporting trine to your Moon, helping you make healthy choices with your changes.

All individuals with Libra Moon will benefit from setting new goals this year. Saturn's self-discipline can be a real asset, but it's your ability to tune into what you feel, who you are, and what you need that makes all the difference.

Affirmation for the Year

I am responsible for my own happiness!

January

Even though others may not agree with your choices, you know your preferences. You may have to bide your time before their resistance subsides, though, and you may not be willing to compromise. A healthy debate can bring you closer to an understanding, as long as everybody understands the rules. If you're intimidated by another's influence or power, take a careful look at the situation after the New Moon on the 13th. It's time to discover real motives. Then, after the 18th, you'll be ready to deal with issues on a more equal footing. Resistance softens, and by the Full Moon on the 28th those sparks flying about can lead to a romantic entanglement. On the home front, employ the principles of feng shui to balance the energy in your personal environment.

February

Special touches at home from the 1st to 14th can alter things just enough to lighten your mood. Despite some friction in the air, you're generally amiable. You may simply need a positive outlet for your competitive drives while Mars travels in opposition to your Moon sign. Some of that friction could be sexual tension—particularly if there's an attraction that's not moving as quickly as you want. Send out signals from the 1st to 7th to let someone know that you're interested, and see what happens. You may lose interest, or decide that you'll take a more assertive approach during the New Moon on the 12th. Alert: some extra care may be necessary from the 21st to 28th if you are to avoid sending an indiscernible message.

March

You could have some trouble staying organized, since some things may take longer to accomplish than you anticipate. Despite your logical thoughts about the matter, you may feel more emotionally unsettled than you want to be. If you're out of sorts, pull away from the demands of your social calendar and indulge in a soothing massage. Or just curl up with a good book one weekend this month. Alone time during the New Moon on the 14th can help you reorder your priorities so that there's more time to take care of your needs. Selfish attitudes from others can get on your nerves, but will certainly bother you if you feel someone is being deceptive. The Libra Full Moon on the 28th can prompt extrasensitive emotions on your part, so keep that in mind if you sense that you've overreacted to a situation.

April

Whether it's you, or someone else, jumping to conclusions can land somebody in hot water. Circumstances beyond your control can leave you feeling emotionally spent from the 1st to 13th, and this can be complicated if your expectations have come crashing down around you. Your creativity comes to the rescue, and your ingenuity can inspire others to lend a helping hand. Despite the awkwardness of unfamiliar social situations, your grace helps you get through the experience unscathed. Still, if you feel hesitant about something, or do not really want to participate, your best interests might be best served by declining an invitation in the first place. Better options appear on the horizon after the 25th, when you finally venture into friendly territory.

May

Surrounded by power struggles, your fair-mindedness may lead to an invitation for you to arbitrate a dispute. Of course, you may have other things on your agenda, although if it's important to you, you'll make time to assure that a bridge to peace is shaped. Identifying those critical common links is easy for you right now, and your energy and actions can light the way for a harmonious agreement. Improvement in your intimate relationship looks promising, and time away from the daily grind can give you a chance to indulge in the delights of love after the 12th. The lunar eclipse on the 26th features fun and adventure, when travel, or a retreat, could be enchanting. A gathering at home can be a great way to renew old ties, especially if there are fences to be mended. Keep promises to a minimum after the 27th.

June

Those small differences in taste or preference can lead to a wide gap in understanding from the 1st to 6th. Trouble comes if you fail to clarify plans or if you leave too much to chance. It's all about expectations. You've heard it before: "Oh, I just assumed you'd be there." (Remember that time when you tried to be nice and duck away from a situation, and left someone to draw his or her own conclusion.) Fortunately, the energy of the solar eclipse on the 10th brings you back on point, and the elephant is definitely in the room. Humor helps you through the worst of it, but a genuine show of graceful generosity heals the hurt. Take your lead from others, while you reassure that they also know your feelings and thoughts on the matter. Forgiveness opens the way for renewal during the lunar eclipse on the 24th.

July

A hectic pace can leave you feeling frazzled from the 1st to 9th, even if things are in pretty good shape at home. It's difficult to stay in the moment, since you probably have something major in the works that leaves you wishing more people were on your team. Regain your sense of inner balance by allowing times through the day to stop, reflect, and regroup. Then, remember to pace yourself after the 13th, since you may have a lot at stake emotionally. Creative inspiration gives you a second wind from the 14th to 23rd. However, you're ready to invite something magical to lift you from the ordinary through the days and nights surrounding the Full Moon on the 24th. The planetary focus draws your attention to your unrealized hopes. Now is the time to listen to your dreams and see where they take you.

August

It's time for a change of pace. If you've been pushing beyond your capacities, then consider this the perfect month to slow down and take time to smell those prize-winning roses in your garden. The planets shift, and their heavenly tones inspire you to surrender to love. Venus shines through Libra, softening your heart, and you are ready to dance to the melody. Whether you're single or connected, your need to express what's in your heart brings new colors into your life. A different direction can alter or initiate a relationship during the New Moon on the 8th. But it's the power of the Full Moon on the 22nd that turns the tide. All you have to do is decide what you really want, or if your wants reflect your needs. From there, the rest is easy.

September

Express yourself! Mercury's two-month cycle in Libra gets rolling, encouraging you to make meaningful connections. From the 1st to 7th, you may feel more open to changes at home—like an innovative decor. Or, you may funnel this energy into your close relationships, breaking down barriers and getting into a more unconditional quality of love. Midmonth is a good time to evaluate your feelings, when you might also need to change your daily routine. Even your own hidden motivations can get in the way of your happiness during and after the Full Moon on the 21st. You may discover that there's some old resentment lurking in your heart. It's up to you to determine how to release it so you can move on and invite more joy to enter your life.

October

Rebirth can be a reason for celebration, but it's up to you. The Libra New Moon on the 6th can be like an open door that leads to greater personal satisfaction. Even though you may experience some disappointment with love, you can clean away the tarnish and bring the sparkle into your love life by relighting the flame in your own heart. Looking outside yourself for answers is likely to be a frustrating option now, since the wisdom you seek arises from your soul. Armed with insight, you'll feel ready to take the initiative where it counts. Mars marches into Libra on the 15th, and for the following six weeks, you're in command. Or at least you'll feel you're heading that direction. Your fears about your own inadequacy can emerge during the Full Moon on the 21st. Soliciting opinions is one thing, but you're the one who calls the shots.

November

Sorting through complex emotional issues can seem like trudging through the jungle without a machete. Fortunately, you've got one: Mars continues as your ally. What you have to do is assert yourself when it counts. In some situations, you'll need to cut through the illusions of control. Anger can arise, too, and you can be short on patience. Cooperation is usually your preferred way to do things, and now, more than ever, you're in no mood to paddle against the river. At home, you may simply have to deal with issues that refuse to stay beneath the surface. Think of this as a time when the cosmos is clearing all the drainpipes. A breakthrough during the lunar eclipse on the 20th opens the way for improvements. The solutions are right in front of you.

December

Laughter shared with your good friends raises your spirits. The playful elements of the solar eclipse on the 4th draw your attention to the way you respond to others whose values are different from your own. Somewhere in the midst of the funny part, wisdom emerges. Maybe that's what they mean by "rising above it all?" You may have to go out of your way to assure that others understand what you intend to communicate, since it's conceivable many people will simply operate within their own agendas. Your talent for locating common elements works to your benefit, and to the benefit of situations where others come together during the Full Moon on the 19th. (Family gatherings come to mind.) Take a break from the action after the 22nd, when your enjoyment comes from the sweet things in life.

SCORPIO MOON

You're in life for the total experience, and your taste for mystery and intrigue is only one dimension of your emotionally intense Scorpio Moon. While your enigmatic nature can baffle others, you can also be quite charismatic. All anyone has to do is exchange a look into your eyes, since your penetrating gaze can be unforgettable. It is your capacity to explore the elements of life that are unfathomable to many, and that sets you apart. Those very things can be the source of your creativity.

For you, home is a place that is tucked away from prying eyes, where you can enjoy periods of introspection, and where you can develop your talents away from the hassles of everyday life. You can create this sanctuary in the middle of a city, but you might also enjoy living in a remote area. You can project that same remote feeling to others when you do not want to get involved. After all, you do have your secrets—and probably want to keep it that way. However, once you're involved in a relationship, you prefer to delve into a wellspring of emotion and passion that will lead to a powerful bond. To trust another with your heart, you'll test their honesty. Only then can someone get past the layers that protect your vulnerability. You may absorb or repress more emotions than you express—especially negative feelings like shame, self-doubt, guilt or unresolved anger. Left unattended, these feelings can drain your capacity for love and joy. However, you also possess the capacity to release and transform these emotions, and then you can heal your life. You may find that it is through helping others change their lives that you connect with your own sense of self, and for this reason work in fields like counseling, medicine, or teaching can be especially rewarding.

As you uncover the secrets of your soul, your wisdom and artistry also grow. It is then that you emerge as a true healer, since the essence of life itself becomes food for your soul. The transformations carry you through a labyrinth of experiences that a continually reshape the course of your life. You grow closer to unity with the Source. It is the resulting power that kindles unmatched joy.

Famous Individuals with Scorpio Moon

Whoopi Goldberg, Nostradamus, Georgia O'Keefe

The Year at a Glance for Scorpio Moon

A feeling of hope fills your soul as you begin your journey into 2002, and the vision and insight you hold in your heart help guide your choices. Change definitely surrounds you, and the impulse to make major alterations in your life can prompt you to move, redefine your career, and revitalize your closest relationships. In some situations, only a few adjustments will be required. However, every change starts from inside you, and the most profound alterations can come from the way you choose to embrace your connection to your inner self.

The feeling that things are working out okay comes from the support you experience from benevolent Jupiter. From January through July, Jupiter makes a friendly trine contact to your Moon sign, and your support system may be much more reliable. However, in August, Jupiter moves into territory that frustrates your Moon, and you can go overboard. It's more difficult to define limits, since situations can appear on the surface to be better than they are at the depths. Fortunately, your talent for making the most of things leads to progress under the influence of Venus cycle in Scorpio from September through December. This will be the time when you can be more emotionally satisfied, but only if you maintain a balance between your needs and wants.

If your Moon is from 0–6 degrees Scorpio, you're clearing repressed emotions to make room to express and fulfill your needs this year. Pluto's cycle makes a semisquare connection to your Moon, stimulating your ability to break through your own resistance to change.

If your Moon is 7–13 degrees Scorpio, illusory Neptune tests your ability to know what you need. While Neptune squares your Moon you can fall victim to deception from others, especially if you're in denial about the truth of your situation with them. A tendency to escape emotional pain at any cost can send you reeling into the feeling that you've been victimized, and for that reason, you'll need to work extra hard to be honest with yourself. Your intuitive sensibilities are still working. But others can influence you, too. It's time to learn about emotional boundaries.

If your Moon is 14–20 degrees, Scorpio, this is your year to make adjustments in your personal life that will strengthen your sense of emotional security. You may need to change some destructive habits, or it can be time to clear away the clutter from your life in order to make room for your self-expression. Anything or anyone threatening your personal power can test you while Pluto and Saturn each make connections to your Moon. However, your greatest test can come when you realize how you've blocked yourself from experiencing real happiness.

If your Moon is 21–29 degrees Scorpio, you're experiencing the unsettling energy of Uranus traveling in square to your Moon. In addition, Saturn makes a quincunx contact to your Moon, and for these reasons you may feel that your emotions are like a roller coaster with poorly functioning brakes. You're ready to break away, but remember not burn bridges until you've crossed them.

Affirmation for the Year

Love heals my life.

January

Those who would pose intellectual arguments about certain feelings being illogical may deserve your compassion, since you're going for a more penetrating experience. Your creative drives are empowered by Venus, Mars, and Jupiter. Funneling this energy into your family, or your home, can bring delightful results. You're ready to make a statement with impact, and with most of the obstacles out of the way, the New Moon on the 13th is a great time to show others what you mean. Your momentum continues to carry you until the 20th. After that, resistance can arrive in the form of lacking commitment. Watch your vulnerable side, since another's failure to respond can signal that they may not be as dedicated as you are. In relationships, you may want to ask the hard questions, but let your intuition tell you when and how you can be most effective with your inquiry.

February

Disruptions can wreck your focus, and until after the New Moon on the 12th you'll have to put more energy and effort into caring for your own needs. The support you would like to have may not be there when you need it most, since circumstances beyond your control can get in your way. But take heart. After the 11th, Venusian tenderness adds a cushion of emotional care and comfort. It's easier to make needed improvements at home, and—as an added bonus—a love relationship can flourish. Smooth over disagreements by staying in the moment, since bringing up past hurts is not likely to accomplish much. The contrast between then and now may even help you embrace the things you like most. Make room for pleasure and expressions from the heart during the Full Moon on the 27th. After all, you're worth it!

March

Even with people you adore you can feel a tiny bit competitive. It's the friction from Mars in a challenging opposition to your Moon sign that brings out your feisty qualities. Any sexual tension can be amplified, and might actually work in your favor if you use it right. (If anybody knows how to do that, it would be you!) Improvements on the home front fare best from the 1st until the New Moon on the 14th. Then, confusion can cause trouble until the 17th, when you may find yourself worrying about things you cannot control. Return to renovation, or the tasks of a move, on the 22nd, but try to finish before the Full Moon on the 28th. By that time, dividing your attention between work and home can be too much of a drain.

April

Balance is the key to handling the demands on your time, since you can exhaust yourself emotionally if you spend too much energy taking care of everybody else while ignoring your own needs. Before you sacrifice yourself, ask the vital question: can the other person handle some of these responsibilities? This can also be a test of how far you've come in dealing with any codependent tendencies. After all, you probably have a remarkable capacity for self-abuse when you get right down to it—but does that do you (or the other person) any real good? Such situations can lead to a deepening feeling of resentment, and you may find yourself wondering when (or if) it will be your turn. It starts with small things. Make time for yourself each day, just to regroup and relax. These releases will help diffuse a buildup of tension that can peak during the Scorpio Full Moon on the 27th.

May

Too much chatter from others who talk around the issues can be as irritating as gnats. You may decide that the best remedy is to keep to yourself, at least when you can. Communication is one thing, but a barrage of words with little substance behind them can leave you feeling out of sorts. You may also have several things in the air at once, only to discover that you have not yet mastered the art of juggling. Reinforcements may arrive in the nick of time. Before you decide this means you are admitting to some sort of defeat, reconsider. It all depends on how you ask. Some ease in the situation arises after the 19th, when you begin to feel more appreciative of yourself, and others. The lunar eclipse on the 26th reminds you that a pleasurable indulgence can be a lot of fun.

June

The skyscape shifts, and tension begins to dissolve. While tests of your patience may continue, you're getting more valuable rewards for all your efforts. Mars moves into friendly territory, and your emotional resilience returns. The magic happens when you concentrate on doing the things that make your heart happy. The sparkle returns to your smile, and from the 1st to 14th you attract support and understanding in your close relationships as a result. Others demand their share of the celebrations from the 15th to 21st, but by the time the lunar eclipse occurs on the 24th there seems to be something for everyone. That makes it much easier to plan family gatherings, friendly dinner parties, or a great weekend enjoying the beauty of life.

July

Home is definitely where the heart is, and you see evidence of that truth when you tune in to the increasing joy in your life now. Show your appreciation during the New Moon on the 10th, when your creative desires grow strong and open the way for a feeling of success on multiple levels. Travel can lead you homeward, too, when you connect with those whose interests and ideals support your own. While time spent with friends will fill the coffers of your heart, you may also feel inspired to make alterations in your life that makes it easier to be with those you love. Find ways to enhance the beauty of your personal surroundings. A move fares very nicely from the 9th to 21st. Watch for complications from family during the Full Moon on the 24th. Vague won't do: you'll need details in order to be effective.

August

The answer to dilemmas arising from the 1st to 6th rests in practical choices. There's a tendency for emotions to explode during the New Moon on the 8th. Your reserved reaction can bring calm, even if you do feel a bit out of control in your heart of hearts. Talk about your concerns with someone you trust, since sorting through the problem will help you diffuse negative feelings. Defining the limits of what's expected from you can make a huge difference in the way you handle changes in your life now. Some unexpected changes can be unsettling during the Full Moon on the 22nd, but after the storm, you can see everything more clearly. It's just a little cosmic reminder that a day does make a difference.

September

The universe provides a gift for you. From now through the end of the year, Venus lends her loving elegance to your life. This long cycle provides an opportunity for you to kindle love in your life, and that light illuminates your values and needs. Bring more natural beauty into your life, and seek ways to express your tender side. Even if some things fall apart, what you discover in the remains may be a jewel you had previously overlooked. The New Moon on the 7th exposes the areas in your life in need of repair—especially at home. A quick fix might not suffice, since surface repairs are likely to fail. The same is true emotionally. You're ready to heal your relationships, and may have little patience for anyone who is unwilling to invest the required commitment. Strike an agreement during the Full Moon on the 21st—if you're ready.

October

Solving problems when others cannot see their way past them brings a smile to your face. Intuitive insight gives you an advantage, particularly if the details seem to mask the core problem. An old issue rises to the surface from the 1st to 12th, and you have a chance to release its burden on your heart. Honesty works best, even if the truth is unflattering to someone. Plus, you simply cannot hide from yourself any longer. Once Venus turns retrograde on the 10th, you may reconsider your commitments. This cycle brings you in touch with your values, and those who do not honor what you hold dear may no longer fit into your life. Immediate action may not be required, but sorting through the situation will help you determine the most productive course to follow.

November

The Scorpio New Moon on the 4th marks a period of spiritual rebirth, when you can release the things from your past that no longer fit into your life. You may feel more emotional, but in a good way. Of course, the cosmos provides a little test. Just as the puzzle of your needs starts to come together, unfulfilled expectations can dismantle your objectivity—temporarily. You're learning the limits of your emotional capacity. (Where your needs end and another person's begin.) This cycle of enlightened insight helps you make significant life choices. You may decide to move, alter a relationship in some way, shift your career path—but it's all done in the name of personal evolution. The lunar eclipse on the 20th brings everything into focus. From there, it's all a matter of one step at a time.

December

The solar eclipse on the 4th may rekindle memories from your childhood. In many respects, your inner child is begging you to play. Your creative vitality sings, and the more involved you can be in an artistic or creative project, the more alive you'll feel. Your most soulful needs are given room to be answered while Venus and Mars move together in Scorpio through the entire month. Expressions of love revitalize your life. In addition, look for opportunities to beautify your home. Feng shui balancing can bring an amazing flow of energy into your life, and you may be ready to give it a try. It's easy to be carried away or to overdo it in the realm of indulgence after the 22nd, so try to keep a watch on your budget, and your diet, to avoid actions you'll later regret. Otherwise, this is your month to enjoy the pleasures of life.

SAGITTARIUS MOON

You think in terms of possibilities. The adventure of exploring places, people and ideas fills the yearning of your Sagittarius Moon. Your soul is driven by a quest—always inquiring, "Why?" Far horizons can prompt you to travel, but you may also decide it's best to journey into a world where philosophical ideals and spiritual truth take you far away from the heaviness of daily life. Your independence is a reflection of your boundless soul, and anyone who attempts to restrain your need to express your idealism or to adventure into new territory is likely to be left in the dust when you make your exit.

While you may bristle when others hold close-minded ideas, you usually appreciate a heated debate, and enjoy philosophical conversation even when you disagree. The inspiration to travel along the freeway of wisdom and truth drives you to invent great excuses to get away or to take a journey off the beaten path. For that reason, you need a partner who appreciates your occasional wanderlust, since you can be exhausted by situations which require your constant attention. Passionate and demonstrative, you'll share the secrets of your heart when you know that you can be trusted to return when the time is right. However, you might also avoid commitment because you fear you might miss something (and sometimes, it's right in front of you).

You can feel at home almost anywhere, and may even live in different places around the globe. For you, home is an uplifting feeling. It's the inspiration you feel when you're one with nature. It's the experience of harmony between your spirit and heart. When you surrender to the embrace of divine truth, you're at home. Your ultimate home space may be a nest on a mountaintop, or in a beautiful valley, where the beauty of nature greets you in the morning and sings you to sleep at night. Then, when you dream, you go further in your quest, wondering about vast possibilities and reasons. It's sufficient fuel to get you through the next day—when your sense of wonder inspires others to believe in tomorrow.

Famous Individuals with Sagittarius Moon

Larry King, Tiger Woods, Oprah Winfrey

The Year Ahead for Sagittarius Moon

These are definitely interesting times for you, since the cycles for the year bring focus, surprise, and regeneration. That's a lot to swallow in one year, and you are assured that you will not be bored. With a head full of inspiring ideas, a helpful network of friends, and the opportunity to move toward unexplored horizons, you're eager to experience fresh insights. Shouldering your responsibilities may actually be easier, since they can ground you and may be the source of the foundation from which you launch your aims.

Jupiter's cycle during 2002 begins in an irritating connection to your Moon. From January through July, you may feel an underlying sense of dissatisfaction, since your list of wants seems never to be fulfilled. You have to ask yourself if you actually need what you think you want. That could eliminate a lot of things in short order! However, in August, Jupiter moves into friendly territory for your Sagittarius Moon. Your self-confidence grows stronger, and the emotional supports that make your life more enjoyable are easier to attract.

If your Moon is 0–5 degrees Sagittarius, you're building on the foundations you established last year. There is a test of your priorities and choices during the lunar eclipse on May 26th, when a crisis at home can prompt you to evaluate your situation and determine what you need to change. From that point, you feel a sense of renewal.

If your Moon is 6–12 degrees Sagittarius, your spiritual ideals and needs enhance your life experience this year while Neptune travels in a supportive contact to your Moon. You may feel a deep desire to nestle into a quiet space where you can reflect on the meaning of life, or you may feel that this is the perfect year for a sabbatical.

If your Moon is 13–20 degrees Sagittarius, you're feeling the impact of Pluto's transit conjuncting your Moon. It's time for a makeover—from the inside out. However, external changes can also happen, in the form of a move, renovation, or alteration in your life path. This cycle lasts about two years, but the effects of your choices and changes can last a lifetime. From February through June, Saturn is also affecting your Moon while it transits in opposition, challenging you to let go of the things you no longer need. These two cycles together can leave you with the feeling that you are not in control—but you are always in control of your responses.

If your Moon is 21–29 degrees Sagittarius, it's time to free yourself of situations and attitudes that inhibit your ability to fulfill your needs. Uranus transits in a helpful sextile contact to your Moon, stimulating your independence and desire to try something different. Innovations at home can range from a move to incorporating technological advances into your personal environment. From July through December, Saturn will travel in opposition to your Moon, and the unfettered feeling you had earlier in the year may be more difficult to duplicate. However, you'll be better able to focus your attention on your responsibilities.

All individuals with Sagittarius Moon must contend with Saturn's continuing trek in opposition to your Moon during 2002. The essence of this cycle is clarification of what is really important. You learn to let go of unnecessary burdens, but you also discover that you have strength to meet the obligations necessary to get you where you're going.

Affirmation for the Year

I am aware of the impact of my words and actions upon others.

January

Maintaining a cool head can be a real feat from the 1st–17th, since friction from Mars can stir angry feelings, or lead you into hostile situations. You may not even see it coming, and that can be the worst blow of all. There are plenty of things and people to distract you, and your salvation comes from taking extra time to ground your energy whenever possible. Fortunately, your awareness of your immediate surroundings improves after the 20th, when your emotional sensibilities are supported by friendlier contact from the cosmic vibrations. The magic of an intimate relationship can be purely delicious, although this can be an excellent period to improve family harmony, too. Discovering shared ideals brings you closer during the Full Moon on the 28th, when it's time to dance for joy!

February

Projects move along quite nicely, although you'll enjoy a break in the action to explore your creative impulses. A change in your daily routine can actually streamline your work schedule and make room to enjoy spontaneity. Travel fares best from the 1st to 10th, since after that time you may be needed close to home. The home fires burn warmly, though, and instead of going out to discover adventure, it's quite likely to come to you during the New Moon on the 12th. (You may want to issue an invitation!) After then, you may run into a difference of opinion that stems from style or taste variations, and this can put a damper on your enthusiasm. However, deeper issues that stem from a need for greater appreciation and understanding may surface near the time of the Full Moon on the 27th. Talk about them.

March

A breakthrough in understanding helps you get past the discomfort zone in your relationship from the 1st–9th, when humor helps immensely. After all, some of the most awkward circumstances lead to marvelous belly laughs! However, sensitive spots need extra care, since a cavalier approach could be unnecessarily hurtful. Improvements or changes at home move along quite nicely after the 7th, when Venusian good taste enhances the expression of your Moon energy. That same influence softens the edges in a close relationship, but still heats up sufficient interest to keep things moving along. Romantic moments during the Full Moon on the 28th can initiate a significant chance in the way you relate to your partner. Yes, that sense of humor may still come in handy!

April

You can stumble over the obvious if you get into a hurry, so curb your enthusiasm from the 1st to 12th if you're in unfamiliar territory. However, most of the resistance you experience will be virtually impossible to miss, and it is definitely important to deal with it instead of trying to just work your way around it. Creative solutions are right at your fingertips, and this is one time when you'll be glad you put effort to make amends. Try a fresh approach during the New Moon on the 12th if you feel stuck. There's an opening for innovation. Then, for the remainder of the month, concentrate on your responsibilities. Keep in mind that asking for help is not only allowed, but it's a sign of personal commitment. Address the temptation to skip out by identifying the things you enjoy about your responsibilities, or the benefit you gain from them.

May

Do you remember that line on your report card, "Works well with others"? The planetary cycles test you on this ability, since dealing with others and their needs can push your own needs completely out of the picture. It can feel that way. Distractions can also be a problem, and keeping your priorities in order can be quite a challenge. However, open communication makes a huge difference, and although you may have to continually alter your schedule to accommodate changes, work with others will bring significant rewards. Renovations at home can be a big mess once Mercury turns retrograde on the 15th, so try to complete what you can early in the month. The stimulus of the Sagittarius Lunar eclipse on the 26th brings your most significant issues to the table, it's also a great time to establish a powerful link in a relationship.

June

The solar eclipse on the 10th can mark a time of resolution in a relationship. Whether you stay or go, your awareness of your needs intensifies, and your ability to discern how well your situations fits those needs is part of your decision. When it comes to personal honesty, your relationship can be like a mirror—it allows you to see yourself more clearly. You do have to open your eyes and take a look, though. If you like what you see, the adjustments you make can fine-tune your commitment and raise your love to a higher level. After the 13th, the song of Venus sings a melody that stirs your soul, and it's easier to express how you feel. By the time the lunar eclipse occurs on the 24th, the landscape of your life can be greatly improved.

July

Love blossoms from the 1st–9th, although mushy displays of affection may not be your style. For you, something grand and inspirational makes a more significant impact. Still, the comforting types will be out in droves during the New Moon on the 10th, and while you may not understand the reason for that potluck dinner, you can certainly enjoy the bounty of the buffet. On the home front, it's a mixed bag this month, since you're fired up and ready to go after the 14th. Mars sparks your enthusiasm, and funneling your energy into a project that enhances your quality of life can be an elixir for your soul. You simply have to be discriminating about inviting others to peek in on your progress, since unless they understand your motivation they may find fault with it. Fortunately, the Full Moon on the 24th ushers in a period of vision and hope.

August

You may feel as though the clouds have lifted and the Sun is shining into your heart! Jupiter's trek through fiery Leo feels good to your Sagittarius Moon, and for the next twelve months, your optimism grows. The New Moon on the 8th marks an excellent time to initiate significant changes at home, or to embark on the grand adventures of a relationship. A move can be the answer to long-standing dreams, although some of the details can be unnecessarily complex midmonth. If you decide to funnel your increased energy into travel, set out for places that you've yearned to explore, and give yourself plenty of time for spontaneous side trips. Pure excitement accompanies the Full Moon on the 22nd, when you can be inspired to open your heart and let the love light shine.

September

Tension slips into the picture at home. It may be due to the fact that there's more going on there this month. Talk over expectations from the 1st to 7th, when it's easier to clarify who wants what. But steer clear of taking the lead during the New Moon on the 7th, since somebody else probably expects to be in the driver's seat. It's one of those times when nodding your head affirmatively might work to your advantage. A breakdown can escalate problems after the 14th, and expect that Murphy's Law will be operating in full force. Not only is Mercury in retrograde, but you may be caught in the middle of problems that clearly belong to someone else. If you wonder how you get off this particular movie set, remind yourself that sometimes a quiet exit is your best bet.

October

If you've ever pondered how to discover your emotional limits, pay attention to what's happening from the 1st–15th. All the promises you've halfway uttered seem to come due at once, and your schedule of appointments can be a mess. You prefer an unencumbered day-planner that gives you time for a long lunch—just in case. The overriding emotion you feel is likely to be anger, even if it is in the form of agitation. It's easy to blurt out the wrong words at the wrong time, too, and that just makes everything worse. A little self-knowledge goes a long way, and if you watch for the triggers, you can avoid shooting out angry words on impulse. After the 15th, a calming breeze cools the overheated situations, and you can get down to the things that really matter. Or you may spend time mending fences.

November

Grab the tissues. Somebody may need to cry on your shoulder. Of course, they have to catch you on a break, although you'll make time if you know it's important. Since your preference is to live a life with few regrets, you may wonder about those who seem to collect guilt like a sponge absorbs water. Your insights can help, and you'll quickly discover who needs you because you have a knack for opening the windows to their soul. After the 19th, there's a big change, since Mercury moves into Sagittarius and you'll feel that you finally have a chance to express the things in your own heart. However, it's the impact of the Lunar eclipse on the 19th/20th that brings unresolved issues from your past home to roost. Just in time for a serving of turkey, too!

December

Gathering with friends to celebrate can be lots of fun early in the month, although spreading good cheer may be on your agenda until the clock chimes the last hour of this year. The Sagittarius solar eclipse on the 4th heralds a time of personal renewal for you. This is your cycle to listen to the voice of your soul, and to bring your deepest needs into the light. Outreach to those who share the love in your life can be especially gratifying and may lead toward a more profound connection, but you may have to take the initiative. Watch for signals that indicate that someone has misread your actions or intentions, since some emotionally charged situations can be like walking through land mines after the 15th. Expressing your gratitude during the Full Moon on the 19th opens the way for all sorts of possibilities.

CAPRICORN MOON

The sweetness of successfully accomplishing your aims feeds your Capricorn Moon. You thrive on challenges, and may feel most alive when you're climbing toward your goals. Hard work keeps your self-respect intact, and you admire others whose integrity and determination have given them a place of honor. Responsibilities are serious business for you, and you do not make commitments without sober consideration of their obligation. Yet it is the process of living a productive life that steadies you through the ups and downs, and enriches your ability to guide and support those who trust you.

At home, you prefer surroundings that reflect simplicity and quality, and might especially enjoy a natural setting. Family heirlooms may require a place of honor in your home, although you'll appreciate those that still have a practical function. Dedication to home and family drives your hard-working ability, and you have a strong desire to assure that your children learn lessons of self-respect above all things. While you might feel that you have to do all the work to assure that those you love have their needs fulfilled, calling on others to share the load will help you avoid resentment. Fortunately, you also know how to make your work enjoyable, and you can be endlessly creative.

You're a natural teacher whose guidance may be cherished by your family, friends, and coworkers. Those who know you have learned about your wicked wit, since you can find humor when it's most needed. Plus, you do love to play—but only when you feel that everything is under control so that you can finally let your hair down. You can get in trouble emotionally if you try too hard to be appropriate all the time, since moments which require an outpouring of tenderness can be difficult if you feel exposed (like in public). Opening to the flow of love in relationships involves giving and receiving—and it's the receiving part that can make you feel vulnerable. Accepting your vulnerability is not easy, but it is the key to inviting joy to fill your soul. Besides, shutting out joy diminishes the returns on your hard work—and that's not very practical, is it?

Famous Individuals with Capricorn Moon

John Glenn, Magic Johnson, Susan Sarandon

The Year at a Glance for Capricorn Moon

Your organizational skills will come in handy this year, since you have a number of priorities. You may feel that you're bidding goodbye and saying hello at the same time. This is a good thing. You can feel that when one door closes, another opens. Your self-confidence is strongly supported by Jupiter's protective benevolence during most of the year, and other cycles suggest that emotional healing brings everything into focus. It's time to listen to the song of your soul, and to reshape your life so that you are fulfilled on a deep level.

With Jupiter transiting in opposition to your Moon from January through July, you feel a challenge to improve the overall condition of your life. Your needs for laughter, adventure, and optimism are stimulated by this cycle, and opening your heart to joy becomes a positive quest. The only downfall of this cycle is determining limits, although you've always been pretty good at this. In August, Jupiter moves into different territory, and you may find that others are more willing to lend a helping hand. All you need to define is what they want in return!

If your Moon is from 0–10 degrees Capricorn, you're feeling the power of Chiron transiting in conjunction to your Moon. This cycle helps you open to a true sense of purpose, and identifying the areas of your life that need to be healed is part of that process. You may also have a chance to play a significant role in the evolution of others, discovering many things about yourself in the process!

If your Moon is 7–12 degrees Capricorn, you're feeling drawn to reach into a different level of consciousness, refreshing your spirituality, while Neptune transits in semisextile. (You're undergoing the Chiron cycle described above if you have a 7–10 degree Capricorn Moon.) Neptune's influence beckons you to explore your inner self, and to let go of your resistance to your emotional sensitivity.

If your Moon is 13–20 degrees Capricorn, you're feeling a pull from two cycles. Pluto transits in semisextile contact to your Moon, helping you eliminate emotional burdens of shame and guilt. However, Saturn is also traveling in an irritating quincunx aspect to your Moon, and that cycle will test whether or not you are successful at eliminating negative emotions and self-destructive habits. The influence from Saturn will begin to dissolve in late summer, although you'll continue to transform your life throughout the year. Renovations at home are also part of this.

If your Moon is 21–29 degrees Capricorn, you are experiencing a combination of two cycles. First, Uranus transits in semisextile to your Moon, bringing an impulse to break away from the things you do not need or like. This cycle lasts all year, and may stimulate feelings of rebellion if other people are pushing you too hard. You might also decide it's time to move. However, beginning in July you're also experiencing pressure from Saturn in an itchy quincunx to your Moon. From this influence you can run into unfinished obligations, old habits, and situations which test your ability to know what you do and do not need.

All individuals with Capricorn Moon are exercising a need to rebuild your life. As a result, you may be making improvements at home, mending fences in relationships, and refining your life work.

Affirmation for the Year

Abundance flows into my life from every direction, and I am grateful.

January

Inspired to put your most creative efforts into your personal life, you can make tremendous headway breaking through an old emotional block. Venusian vibrations soften your heart, and while she moves gently through Capricorn until the 20th you'll find it easier to show how you feel. Bring beautiful things into your home that add comfort where you need it most. The Capricorn New Moon on the 13th ushers in your cycle of soulful rebirth, and it is during and after this time that you'll feel most in touch with your desire to fulfill your most profound needs. Allow extra time to enjoy the people, places, and things that confirm your values. Relationships fare best until the 20th, but after that time you may feel more competitive and driven, and a focus beyond the personal may seem more appropriate.

February

Disruptions can frustrate your progress on a project at work, or at home, and your attitudes may reflect your discontent. Fortunately, you can probably put everything into sensible order from the 4th–11th, when explaining your priorities and needs works to your advantage. An undercurrent of anger may be present throughout the month, and unless you make a conscious effort to be aware of how you're handling these feelings, you can appear grumpier than you intend to be. Much of the tension in your life can dissolve if you have a creative outlet for your energy after the New Moon on the 12th. Special touches, repairs, or interesting projects around the house can be especially gratifying. Invite someone special to share dinner the night before the Full Moon on the 27th, when sharing your common hopes can be truly inspirational.

March

You may feel a deep sense of satisfaction this month, since your productivity improves day by day. Mars travels in earthy Taurus, lending energy to your ability to fulfill and express your needs. Practical matters move along quite nicely, repairs are working like a charm, and asserting your need to be in control meets with little resistance—except midmonth. Then, others may appear to be more cooperative than they are, or they may be deceptive because they've not accomplished what you expect. This is the time to double-check everything, and to extend grace when you can. The less disciplined types can get on your nerves during the Full Moon on the 28th. Whether they're children or just kids at heart, you may still ask them to play outside!

April

Strengthen the foundations in your life this month. You can attract the right support at the right time, but must identify precisely what you want or you could get factory seconds! Unexpected changes can leave you wondering if you've made the right choices from the 5th to 11th, but most things are clarified just in time for the New Moon on the 12th. Since you know there might be disruptions, leave extra room with deadlines, and allow space to enjoy a good laugh. The awkward moments later in the month arise when you try to second-guess an evolving situation in a relationship. The universe sets up a challenge that illustrates which things you can control and which things you cannot. Sounds simple. Once again, that sense of humor will come in handy. Sensual moments warm your heart before and during the Full Moon on the 27th, and that, of course, puts a sparkle in your smile.

May

You may actually welcome a few of the distractions that arise, but only if they don't get in your way. Prioritizing helps immensely, since during the New Moon on the 12th you can bring order into the chaos, at least to some extent. The most irritating element can be changes in the cost of a project, or the news that one of your kids needs platinum inlaid braces. Before you figure you're going to have to sell a pound of flesh to make ends meet, take another look. There may be untapped resources, and it's a great time to barter. The same is true emotionally: you do have something to offer another person in exchange for a true level of support. Partnership ventures prove their merit after the 20th, and by the time the changes happen during the lunar eclipse on the 26th, you'll be ready for them.

June

Accepting diversity probably works for you on a practical level, since you can appreciate the multiple dimensions of the way things work in nature. The solar eclipse on the 10th helps unlock your own ability to do more than one thing at a time, and to invite different kinds of people into your inner circle. Cooperative ventures that involve partnering with others whose talents compliment your own can be rewarding on practical and emotional levels this month. In fact, even a competitive situation can spark a level of excellence that you rather enjoy. The Capricorn lunar eclipse on the 24th is significant for you, since you're ready to strike a balance, and you may find it's wise to allow someone else to take the lead. It's a great time to applaud the success of children, partners, or good friends. Stay open. A lot of good things are coming your way.

July

Supportive cooperation is one thing, but if someone steals your thunder in the guise of cooperative effort, you're likely to take offense. While partnership can work to your advantage during the New Moon on the 10th, a lopsided agreement will never do. For this reason, it's crucial that you define expectations. With a balance of power in place, everyone wins. With so much energy coming from your connections to others, you may also feel that your needs have suddenly taken a back seat. That might be okay if you want it that way, but once again, there's the question of expectation. Improvements around the house go smoothly from the 9th to 20th. Home and family matters can be filled with fun and celebration, although you'll appreciate some quiet time near the Full Moon on the 24th.

August

Differences in style and self-expression certainly define the texture of your close relationships, and the contrasts may stand out more than the points of agreement. It's like color preference—one of you may like Day-Glo colors while the other prefers black. There are stark differences, but they look good together. Your commonsense approach may be sought after from the 4th–26th, when others are trying to handle and unexpected turn of events. You may be most comfortable maintaining a low profile when you can, since you're still observing which way the wind is blowing before you set sail. After the zany antics surrounding you during the Full Moon on the 22nd, you'll be happy to make a quiet exit to a place where you can let your hair down and just be yourself.

September

This is a productive month, when you can make headway on changes, repairs, or renovations at home. Relationships improve through simple, open communication, although you may have to go out of your way to clarify what you mean. However, you may also be busy with political or cultural activities that help to add a sense of meaning to your life. Your life work itself takes on a more significant focus, and instead of thinking in terms of career or job, you may realize that you've begun to think in a more comprehensive way. After all, you like to put significant effort into anything (or anyone) meaning a lot to you. From the New Moon on the 7th until the Full Moon on the 21st, you can forge your way through most obstacles and make tremendous headway when it comes to reorganizing your life around your deeper needs. Areas of resistance show you what you may need to leave behind in the process.

October

It's time to restore something of value. You might also decide that means you! In the process, you may have to tear down an external wall, rip off an old covering, or replace a few outworn parts. The emotional and physical renovations may arise from a chronic problem becoming too bothersome. Although progress may go more smoothly from the 2nd to 14th, you can make significant headway almost any time this month. It's just that you can run into conflicts with others or can feel more easily frustrated after the 15th—when Mars moves into an expression that irritates your Moon. It's like wearing itchy wool when the weather's too warm. Watch your emotional triggers, since others can push your buttons near the Full Moon on the 21st, and you can overreact before you know it.

November

Your motivation to change things can feel like a fire in your belly, and a lot of things can be stirred up in the process. The healing energy in your life during the New Moon on the 4th helps you release what you no longer need, and as a result you may feel driven to clean out closets, attics, and drawers in an effort to eliminate clutter. You're doing the same thing emotionally—clearing out negative emotions, opening to the pure power of love and joy. Unresolved anger can still take its toll and repressed emotions can beg for liberation. It's up to you to find healthy ways to direct these needs. By the time the lunar eclipse occurs on the 19th/20th, you may feel that you've come full circle yourself. Think of this as a time to transplant yourself into more fertile soil.

December

Don't you just love it when everything falls into place? If you are clear about your priorities, you can do a lot to assure that you fulfill each and every one of them. Or at least, you can get things moving along in the right direction. The solar eclipse on the 4th can stir your dreams, helping you see the things from your past that need some extra attention right now. After that, you're focused on the present moment, and can bring a real sense of unity in to your family. While some may distract you from the deeper meaning of what you intend to do, you can see through their motivations and may surprise them with your insightful way of handling things. For you, this is a time to be genuine, and you'll appreciate others who can see that. Open your heart. From there, the embrace of what's important is second nature.

AQUARIUS MOON

The glint in your eye is sparked by your awareness of the common spirit all humanity shares. Through your Aquarius Moon, you are connected to the spirit of good will for all. The paradox is that you also like being different, since you realize that uniqueness that ignites human evolution. You're likely to react personally to abuses of human liberty, or to indignities that demean the spirit of life itself. However, then you're on the leading edge of evolutionary change, your heart is filled with joy. You're the visionary, and following that soulful vision calls forth the most extraordinary elements of your being.

Logic is the bread of life for you. When you're upset, finding the logic behind a situation, or discovering a logical solution, helps you cope. Another paradox: your intuitive insights are powerful, and often fly in the face of logic. When you're in that deep inner space where logic and intuition flow together, you can seem remote. Yet, it is from that space that your powerful artistry and genius emerge. Since emotions are not always logical, this need can impair your ability to understand those who seem too emotional, although your desire to accept them helps. In relationships, others need to learn that you can be aloof at times. However, when you're sharing time, energy, and love, your spirit inspires hope. Your friends understand that about you and may be willing to give you the unconditional love you crave. With family, you can seem like the misfit until they learn how your difference brings a complimentary tone to their song. Those at ease with your eccentricities and independent manner of doing things will be able to handle getting close. Others may simply watch from the sidelines.

You need a home space that gives you room to express your individuality. Gadgets and innovations make a place feel like home, although you may have some unique artifacts from past times in your personal space. You love extraordinary people, places, and things. After all, it is through welcoming the expressions that shatter the boundaries of the ordinary that you feed your soul and merge with the ultimate intelligence of the Source and express the paradox of unity through diversity.

Famous Individuals with Aquarius Moon

David Copperfield, Princess Diana, Carl Lewis

The Year at a Glance for Aquarius Moon

This new millennium has been pretty amazing for you so far, and this year brings a series of positive challenges and clear opportunities to develop the security you need to express your ingenuity. With most obstacles behind you for a while, you're ready to initiate changes that support your needs more fully. Relationships improve, your life path seems clearer, and your connection to your soul is strengthened.

Jupiter's cycles provide the most unusual challenges, since identifying your limitations can be a problem. Jupiter stimulates expansion and growth, and when it makes a frustrating contact to your Moon, you're more tempted to indulge in things you do not need. Or, you may be overindulgent in the good things of life. You know—it's like knowing when to leave a great party. With awareness that you may be unnecessarily self-absorbed, or that you can overcommit and get in over your head, you can use better judgment when you make those promises.

If your Moon is 0– 5 degrees Aquarius, it's time to reshape your habits while Pluto cycles in semisquare contact to your Moon. This is a period of breakthrough, when old attitudes simply do not fit the renewed version of you. However, you can feel awkward as you abandon these attitudes or automatic responses, and may grieve more than you thought you would. You'll even miss a destructive habit—but at least you're breaking it.

If your Moon is 6–12 degrees Aquarius, you're feeling a heightened emotional sensitivity this year while Neptune travels in unity with your Moon. This significant cycle can encourage you to develop your intuitive and psychic abilities, although your sense of compassion is also intensified. Defining your personal boundaries can be tricky, so before you decide to give away your heart (or your worldly goods), seek objective feedback to reassure that you're seeing things as they are, instead of just as you want them to be.

If your Moon is 13–20 degrees Aquarius, you're experiencing the benefits of Saturn and Pluto both bringing clarity and transformation into your life. You may decide that it's time to move, build your dream home, establish a family, or step onto a life path that fulfills your destiny. It's a time to focus on your real needs, and to exercise your talents and abilities.

If your Moon is 21–29 degrees Aquarius, you're in for the ride of a lifetime! Uranus transits in conjunction to your Moon, and you may feel more alive, free, and clear than you've ever felt. This is definitely your year to break away from inhibitions—whether they're in the form of fear, relationships, jobs, or outworn obligations. Since Saturn moves into a supportive trine contact to your Moon starting in July, your ability to determine the most effective choices is enhanced. It's like having a special lens through which you can see all the details and possibilities with greater clarity.

All individuals with Aquarius Moon are feeling some support from Saturn—one way or another. That means you may feel that you finally fit into the world, and your unique expressions, feelings, and needs seem to be welcome. On a fundamental level, it's time to live according to your highest needs.

Affirmation for the Year

I can see my life path and I follow it with joy in my heart!

January

Imaginative ideas heighten your sense of excitement, although you may not feel that you have time to do much with them until after the New Moon on the 13th. Even then, ongoing projects or situations that require your involvement may require more of your time and energy than you like. With Mercury turning retrograde on the 18th, you may feel pulled into circumstances where you feel that you're repeating yourself. The good news is that you're making significant connections, and others are seeking your insights or advice. Your artistry flows more freely from the 18th–31st, when Venus travels through Aquarius and invites you to share your talents with the world. This same energy brings grace into your closest relationships, and you may even attract someone new and fascinating. Either way, make room for love to flow during the Full Moon on the 28th, when your shared dreams carry you into true ecstasy.

February

Your passion is sparked by feisty Mars, but it's the alluring power of Venus coupled with Uranus in Aquarius that stirs the magic. These energies pull on your heartstrings, and as you surrender to the feelings, all sorts of things can change. At home, you're innovative and bold. In your relationships, you're absolutely yourself. At work, your talents speak for themselves. Your soulful emotional rebirth arrives during the Aquarius New Moon on the 12th, when it's time to listen to your inner voice and change your life so you can dance to its song. After the 18th, you're likely to run into jealousy from others who can try to trip you because they're insecure. However, your awareness helps you step carefully away from the trap, and allows you to either offer a tender response. It's one time when your kind-heartedness is definitely to your advantage.

March

Even if you don't want to slow down, you may have to. There's some resistance out there, and it comes from the "prove it to me" types. While you can be practical-minded, you may be frustrated if you have to put together a model, when you can see how things can work just by imagining them! It's friction from Mars that's the trouble, and it may come from your family first. At home, repairs can take longer than you like, or you may have to interrupt your plans to repair something that's broken down after heavy use. Reach out to your network of friends or experts after the 8th, when help can arrive just in time. After the 20th there's more light shining through your daily life, and you can feel revitalized by spending time in an exchange of ideas. The Full Moon on the 28th draws your attention to spiritual concerns, when the soul-ties in a relationship are likely to bring you closer.

April

Getting something right might require more effort than it's worth. Experiment with possibilities, but give yourself permission to start over, or to try something different, if you don't like what you see or feel. Projects around the house are top contenders for "it looked good in the drawing—but. . . ." This "good in theory" quality also invades your relationships. In personal situations, you can feel clumsy or out of step with others, and if you find yourself in unfamiliar circumstances you can be particularly uncomfortable. Perhaps you can convince a trusted friend to join you for support? After the 14th, staying active helps you vent some emotional tension. However, the Full Moon on the 27th may bring family issues to the table. What's the good news? Your sense of humor works like a charm!

May

Fasten your seat belt! After testing your ideas and consulting with the experts, you're ready to turn your plans into something tangible. With friendly assistance from the cosmos, the way is clear to move forward. A cautious beginning works best from the 1st to 5th, and then you're feeling momentum. Relationships can blossom, but your creativity simply soars! Despite Mercury's retrograde cycle, which begins on the 15th, you can still make headway. In fact, going back to the drawing board may actually speed your progress. Travel can take you to places that stir the memories of your soul this month. You may meet others who have that feeling, too. Reflect on your deepest yearnings during the Lunar eclipse on the 26th, and ask the question of your inner self. Answers are sure to follow.

June

Watch out for those who seem overly needy, since you can feel trapped before you know it! Your actions can stir a powerful response from others, and while you may simply be exploring possibilities, someone else may have made pretty big plans already! The solar eclipse on the 10th is like a wake-up call, and you'll do yourself a favor if you open your eyes right away, instead of waiting for the coffee to kick in. While you can create a bridge of understanding by talking, it's the words between the lines that can be more troublesome. Social gatherings at home, or class reunions elsewhere, may leave you with some good pictures. However, you may discover that you are less connected than you thought. The purpose is to get confirmation of who you are now.

July

Day-to-day duties can require more of your attention, and you may end up doing things you normally rely on others to handle for you. Indirect aggression from others can create an undercurrent of mistrust, and it's more likely to be due to a failure of unrealistic expectations. If you wonder why somebody's upset with you, you may just discover that they expected you to magically transform their world. You can be undone if you try to fulfill such dreams. Deep in your heart of hearts, you may suffer a few disappointments of your own. Creative outlets help you vent your sadness, although there's nothing like a hug at the right time to help your doldrums to melt away. Reach out to someone you trust during the Aquarius Full Moon on the 24th. Or, if you prefer, make this a time to do something special for your best friend.

August

Inspired to follow your most powerful hopes, you can feel that you're ready for just about anything. Of course, it could be an illusion, especially if you have not yet received confirmation from those who are supposed to blast off into space with you! Safeguard your hopes by keeping a careful eye on the paperwork from the 1st–7th. The New Moon on the 8th opens the way for you to move ahead. Help arrives, and you may even get more than you expected. There is another Aquarius Full Moon this month, and when it occurs on the 22nd you may feel that you've reached a significant plateau. Relationships are definitely up for review. From the 8th–22nd, developments on the home front can include renovations, repairs, or a move. However, the arrival of different people on the scene can change the picture dramatically. It's up to you to decide how you'll incorporate them into your life.

September

Stay in touch with people who understand you, since you'll appreciate their feedback and support. This is not a time to go it alone, and if you are making major alterations in your living space or relationship, an advisor can become your best friend for a while. Old resentment can surface during the New Moon on the 7th, although it may be triggered by a happy event. This strange juxtaposition exists to test your ability to stay in the moment. This will come in handy when you are defining what you expect from any situation, since assumptions can be truly problematic after the 14th. After the 22nd, the flow of communication lifts your spirits, although you may still see signs that there's another hurdle down the road.

October

Emotionally charged situations can be quite a tangle, and part of the problem may be poor communication. Although Mercury's retrograde ends on the 6th, other factors indicate that unfinished issues are likely to stir up trouble. It's the Venus retrograde cycle that stimulates all the questions about your real feelings. The communication trouble is likely to involve your connection with your inner self. Pressures from others, or from the outside world itself, can be a distraction from this personal dialogue. A retreat from your daily routine during the New Moon on the 6th provides fresh perspective. Then, after the 16th, the stimulus from Mars helps you translate what's going on inside to the people around you. A gathering of special friends brightens your sense of home. Then, to top it off, true affection can turn the tide during the Full Moon on the 21st.

November

It would never be like you to try to change your spots so you could fit in, but right now, those polka dots may make a bigger statement than you intended. With Mercury and Venus undulating through Scorpio's territory, there's a lot of emotional intensity surrounding you. Trouble is, deciphering what people really need from you can be like solving a mystery in the dark. You'll feel most comfortable with an evenhanded approach based on logic, but may have to give others room to operate from their hearts, too. Focus on creative projects when you can, and look for ways to incorporate improvements into your personal space. Then, when the smoke starts to clear following the lunar eclipse on the 19th/20th you can gather a few more clues about where to go next.

December

You may be thinking that it's just the time of year, and you could be right. But the planets tell the story of an unresolved need to please someone. During the solar eclipse on the 4th, a flash of insight can reveal that your silent hopes and dreams may still be in a category labeled "postponed." Some of your priorities do involve a desire to assure that those you love are happy, and that's a good thing when you feel good about it. What needs to be eliminated is resentment, since it tends to keep those delayed gratification elements in place for far too long. Where's the good news? From the 1st to 8th, the time you spend with friends simply lights up your life. That's what reminds you of those dreams. Where you go from there is up to you. See what's up when the Full Moon rises on the 19th. And who's there with you.

PISCES MOON

Your Pisces Moon brings a quality of enchantment to your sense of the world. While some may see only what is, you see what can be. Your ability to rise above the ordinary into the spiritual essence of life endows you with an embrace of faith. Yet, you are extremely sensitive emotionally, and you can tap into the entire breadth of human emotion—from pain to pure joy. While some may wonder if intuition really works, your perception of life incorporates this profound level of insight. You know it's real. You can reach into the intangible realms, where your imagination grabs the spark you turn into a love for music, art, drama, and creativity. You have the magic touch.

With all your sensibilities, you can become truly compassionate. However, it's tough to know when to hold on and when to let go, since you can lose track of your emotional boundaries. That sensitivity can prompt you to reach out to make a difference, and may go too far and sacrifice your own needs in favor of the demands you feel from others. Your creative expression is another story. When you surrender yourself to your creativity, you become that which you are creating. This can bring healing and inspiration into your life. What you could use, though, is a kind of emotional filter—something that helps you stay open to the creative, compassionate flow of energy, but which blocks you from being victimized or emotionally drained. That filter resides in your inner self, and is one reason why spirituality is such an important element of your life.

At home, a place that gives you a chance to drop your cares and nourish your dreams will feel best. In the world, learning to make healthy choices and keep yourself safe from deceitful people requires you to be clear about your needs. Balancing tools like dance, yoga, meditation, and music can help you keep your emotional wholeness intact. Then, in your relationships, you can allow the flow of love to move you toward the connection you hope to find with your soul mate. Ultimately, the transcendence you crave will unify you with the Source, and from there, pure love can flow through you and into the world.

Famous Individuals with Pisces Moon

Joe DiMaggio, Betty Ford, Dorothy Hamill

The Year Ahead for Pisces Moon

Your hopes for the future are bright this year, and it's a time when many of your dreams can become reality. Maintaining a healthy balance between your inner life and the demands of the world is a strong priority for you during 2002. Your responsibilities can weigh heavily on your heart, and that means it's crucial to know how much of the burden is yours to carry. Support is there, but you may have to ask before someone realizes you could use a helping hand.

Jupiter's good fortune smiles in your direction from January through the end of July, when your abilities and talents may also garner the recognition they deserve. Your job is to make the most of the abundance in your life, since the trine connection from Jupiter to your Moon can also leave you feeling a bit lazy. To benefit from this cycle, put your energy into the opportunities that come your way. In August, Jupiter changes signs, and your productivity can increase, although you'll need to be attentive to a tendency to go beyond your emotional and physical limits.

If your Moon is 0–7 degrees Pisces, you have moved past a major milestone in your life during the past year. This year, you can build on what you've learned, and with Chiron in a positive sextile connection to your Moon, you can concentrate on elements which help you fulfill your life purpose.

If your Moon is 7–12 degrees Pisces, you may experience a heightened intuitive and emotional sensibility. Neptune's cycle in semisextile contact to your Moon stimulates a kind of spiritual initiation, when you're ready to surrender to your most soulful needs as part of your spiritual evolution. In addition, from January through April, you're experiencing the final four months of Saturn's cycle in a frustrating square aspect to your Moon. The beginning of the year is the most trying, and after that it will be easier to devote more time to your creative and spiritual pursuits.

If your Moon is 13–20 degrees Pisces, you're feeling an exceptional challenge. Two cycles bring friction into your life. First, Pluto's transformational energy stimulates your need to eliminate habits and attitudes which are counterproductive. Then, from April to June, Saturn also transits in square to your Moon, testing your resolve to continue your evolutionary growth. You may leave behind people and situations as you move into a different stage of your life. However, more important, you are clearing the way for unparalleled personal growth.

If your Moon is 21–29 degrees Pisces, you're feeling a need to break free and to rise above your current life circumstances. Uranus transits in semisextile to your Moon, and what once may have satisfied your needs may no longer suffice. You're ready to move forward, and can take steps to elevate your consciousness and improve yourself in the process. In July, Saturn moves into a tense square to your Moon, and for the remainder of the year, you'll be working to establish different, more solid, foundations.

All individuals with Pisces Moon can feel a bit melancholy this year since Saturn travels through territory which shakes your old foundations. You'll see a change of the guard, and may feel challenged to take more responsibility for fulfilling your needs. This is definitely a milestone year!

Affirmation for the Year

I am safe and secure in the face of change.

January

Fueled by your creative passions, you're eager to make headway with changes in your close relationships. Mars recharges your ability to assert your needs while it travels in Pisces through the 18th. You can also feel impatient and may be more edgy than usual, too. On the home front, renovations and repairs fare best from the 1st to 17th, when you'll prefer to direct the action to assure it's done the way you want it. Start the process of a new routine, changes in diet or other self-improvement options during the New Moon on the 13th. After the 21st, your objectivity can fall by the wayside. You may be swayed by actions or ideas from well-intentioned people, who are, unfortunately, mislead. You'll do yourself a favor by pretending you're part of the audience, where you can observe the situation from a safe zone.

February

Your objectivity returns after the 4th, although a cautious approach helps protect your emotional vulnerability. Surprising changes alter the picture after the 6th, and while everyone around you may be responding with knee-jerk responses, you may want to wait for the dust to settle. On the 12th, Venus graces your Moon while she travels in Pisces for the following four weeks. During this time, you'll feel more comfortable about fulfilling your needs and signaling that special someone that you're ready for love. Within the focus of the present moment, you're fine. But it's when you start making future plans that you can run into trouble. You may feel the same way about a project at home or a creative endeavor, and decide to scrap your plans and go back to the drawing board after the Full Moon on the 27th.

March

Start from an inner focus, and reach deep into yourself to find the essence of pure love. From this connection, you can feel the stirring of a bountiful hope. The Pisces New Moon on the 14th marks your time of emotional rebirth. Conscious awareness of your most profound needs launches you on a course where personal fulfillment becomes reality. In many respects, you can move directly into the flow—just the way you like it. Mars' cycle helps you focus your efforts, helping you build a foundation for your dreams. A move or other changes in your home space can be a real exercise in creativity, and you'll benefit by having the comfort zone you require. Extra efforts to connect with others pay off from the 12th–28th when an exchange of ideas leads to clear understanding.

April

Even the distractions from all those people who are in a big hurry are not likely to bother you, since you have your eye on the prize. Grounded in a secure feeling of love, you're ready to take on whatever is necessary. You may even surprise yourself with your resourcefulness, but that should not stop you from calling in the experts when you need them. On a personal level, your relationships blossom, and the hard work you've done to reach out and heal old wounds makes a difference. A breakthrough before the 10th can create a change of plans, since you may decide that you're ready for something (or someone) different. Maybe it's time for a fantasy, or two. You can create the perfect ambience, and share memorable pleasures during the Full Moon on the 27th.

May

Everybody seems to need a piece of you. Family demands can scatter your energy, but work itself can be filled with disruptions and changes which make it difficult to keep a steady course. If you feel like a sailboat in a storm, don't be surprised. There's a lot of wind blowing around, and some of the unkind words or ill-considered actions can hurt your feelings. Locating a safe harbor might require you to look within yourself, since relying too much on others can lead to trouble. Knowing that you're more vulnerable now, you can pull back just a bit and concentrate on your top priorities. Love provides comfort and care after the 19th, when you can enjoy quiet moments at home with your sweetie. The lunar eclipse on the 26th brings things into focus: Sometimes it's important to say "no" when an unwanted invitation arrives.

June

Family issues come into focus during the solar eclipse on the 10th, when power plays may be fairly obvious. You may be able to stay out of the line of fire, since your focus takes you away to things that are higher on your priority list. Oh, it's not that you don't care; there are simply some situations where you're not supposed to be a player. A creative project close to home will bring gratifying results, although you might blow your budget if you're not careful. Wherever your creative passions take you, you can accomplish amazing things now, and may even inspire others to follow your lead. After the 22nd, the landscape changes, and your self-confidence grows. Celebrate whenever possible, since you're ready to fill your heart with joy.

July

Cooperation from others may lead you to wonder exactly what you've done right. Just accept the help and say "thanks." You deserve good things, and your kind heart and desire to make a difference have always been to your advantage. You're just getting some positive payback, that's all. The New Moon on the 10th marks a fabulous time to get things moving in a relationship, make changes at home, or enjoy all the marvelous things life has to offer. Before you munch into that third piece of pie, you might want to reconsider, though—since it's easy to overdo it, too. Practical matters bring you back to planet earth after the 12th, when a relationship may need extra time or energy. It could be that you need different things from one another now, and if you address those concerns now, you'll save yourself a lot of heartache later.

August

Jupiter's change of residence can leave you feeling that you're missing something. It's time to adjust your priorities and reconsider your needs. Old ways of doing things may simply be unsatisfactory, and the New Moon on the 8th can motivate you to change a few habits. If you need more objectivity, consider consulting with someone you trust from the 6th–26th. Since feelings of guilt can motivate you to take on things you'd rather not do, it might help to have that shoulder to lean on when you ultimately have to make the hard choice. A disagreeable situation can leave you feeling emotionally drained, particularly if you feel overwhelmed by those who have taken unfair advantage of you. Maybe it's time to review your commitments and contracts. At the least, you'll want to define your role—make room for your needs when you do.

September

Challenges give you a sense of direction. However, you can feel emotionally vulnerable if somebody's attacking you. Before you buy into the turmoil, try to peer beneath the surface to determine how to play the game. You can turn the tide during the New Moon on the 7th by defining the rules on your own terms. Now, that'll surprise them! You may have the protection of honorable motivation on your side, especially if you're allowing love to guide your actions. After the 7th, the Venusian flow of energy adds emotional resilience and support. The great news is that this cycle lasts through the end of the year. You can take your time to create healthy changes in your relationship. Then, during the Pisces Full Moon on the 21st, you'll feel more self-assured about exploring honest issues about intimacy.

October

Stubborn resistance from others can be a real pain from the 1st to 15th. Your resilience and tolerance definitely work to your benefit, particularly if someone brings up issues you thought were long since resolved. It's just another chance to see how deep resentment can be buried. Venus moves into her retrograde cycle on the 10th, and for the following six weeks everyone may complain about their relationships. To drown out the whines, try the music that makes your heart sing. If you're unhappy about one thing, you can turn to another that feels better. Extra effort spent on creative or artistic pursuits is definitely rewarding, although you may not feel ready to show your masterpiece to the world just yet. Fine-tune after the 24th, when a limited audience can encourage you to keep going.

November

Eliminate old habits that drain your energy. It's time to revitalize your diet, alter your routine, and restore your emotional balance. Meditation can work wonders, but you might also decide that a different physical fitness routine brings mind, sou,l and body into harmony more completely. Get started during the New Moon on the 4th, when a scrumptious, but healthy, meal shared with someone you adore can be completely satisfying. After dinner might not be too bad, either, since you're eager to determine your honest feelings about a relationship. Alterations at home, including a move, can motivate you to eliminate clutter and open your personal space so that you feel more peaceful. Feng shui applications may be just what you've needed to shift the flow of energy during the lunar eclipse on the 20th.

December

Venus and Mars travel in tandem, playing a soulful tune you love to sing to. Take a personal inventory during the solar eclipse on the 4th to determine how far you've come since summer in releasing some of your old emotional attachments. You may feel eager to open to pure love, but if there's an old wound, the flow of energy can be uncomfortable. Listen to your heart, and allow your intuitive self to light your way. This is one time when you'll be happy that you know what it means to surrender. After all, love may have wisdom beyond your own. Open the way for others to be straightforward about their feelings and needs, since it's time to alter the course of existing relationships. Even a few awkward moments after the 22nd are not likely to dampen your enthusiasm. It's a pretty nice way to end a year!

About the Author

Your personal Moon sign descriptions and forecasts for this book were written by internationally renowned astrologer, author, and teacher, Gloria Star. She has written written the *Sun Sign Book* for Llewellyn since 1989, and has been a contributing author of the *Moon Sign Book* since 1995. Her most recent work, *Astrology & Your Child*, was released by Llewellyn in December 2000. Her book, *Astrology: Woman to Woman* (Llewellyn, April 1999) was released to rave reviews. She also edited and coauthored the book *Astrology for Women: Roles and Relationships* (Llewellyn 1997). Her astrological computer software, "Woman to Woman," was released by Matrix Software in 1997. Her column, "Astrology News," is a feature in *The Mountain Astrologer Magazine*. She has also written online for several large websites.

Listed in *Who's Who of American Women*, and *Who's Who in the East*, Gloria is active within the astrological community, where she has been honored as a nominee for the prestigious Regulus Award. She has served on the faculty of the United Astrology Congress (UAC) since its inception in 1986, and has lectured for groups and conferences throughout the U.S.A. and abroad. She has served on the Board of the United Astrology Conference (UAC), and is a member of the Advisory Board for the National Council for Geocosmic Research (NCGR). She also served on the Steering Committee for the Association for Astrological Networking (AFAN), was editor of the AFAN newsletter from 1992–1997, and is now on the AFAN Advisory Board. She currently resides in the shoreline township of Clinton, Connecticut.

Moon Sign Book Contributors

Kevin Burk

Kevin Burk has been practicing astrology since 1993 in San Diego, California. He holds a Level IV Certification in astrological counseling from the National Council for Geocosmic Research, and has been counseling professionally since 1996. Astrological Horoscopes & Forecasts, Kevin's astrology website at http://www.astro-horoscopes.com is one of the most extensive astrological resources on the Internet, providing a wealth of astrological information. Kevin's first book, *Astrology: Understanding the Birth Chart* (Llewellyn 2001), is available from your local bookseller. Kevin is currently working on several astrology projects, including a book on the Moon's Nodes, and a book and workshop on relationship astrology. Kevin has a Scorpio Sun, Cancer Moon, and Gemini Rising.

Robin Antepara, M.A.

Robin Antepara, is an astrologer who divides her time between Tokyo, Los Angeles, and Brattleboro, Vermont. She is currently working on a Ph.D. in depth psychology at Pacifica Graduate Institute.

Kris Brandt Riske

Kris Brandt Riske holds professional certification from the American Federation of Astrologers and serves on the national Board of Directors of the National Council for Geocosmic Research. She has had numerous articles published in popular astrology magazines, writes for AMI astrological publications and allpets.com. She is the author of *Astrometeorology: Planetary Power in Weather Forecasting*. Kris has a masters degree in journalism.

Nina Lee Braden

Nina Lee Braden, webmaster of the award-winning website, Moonstruck, is a Scorpio with a Cancer Ascendant and Leo Moon. Astrology opened fascinating new doors for Nina Lee, and she doesn't know how she managed her life before she began the study of astrology. She is a life-long resident of Tennessee.

Stephanie Clement, Ph.D.

Stephanie Clement is an accomplished astrologer and author, with twenty-five years of professional experience. She is on the board of the American

Federation of Astrology (AFA) and has degrees in english literature, humanistic psychology, and transpersonal psychology. she has had numerous articles published in astrological magazines, and has written several books: *Planets and Planet-Centered Astrology*, *Counseling Techniques in Astrology*, *Decanates and Dwads*, *What Astrology Can Do for You* (Llewellyn 2000), *Charting Your Career* (Llewellyn 2000), and *Power of the Midheaven* (Llewellyn 2001) and *Dreams: Working Interactive* (Llewellyn 2001). She also writes a monthly astrological column for a financial institution, and serves on the faculty of Kepler College.

Alice DeVille

Alice DeVille, an internationally known astrologer and writer, has a busy consulting practice in northern Virginia. She specializes in relationships, career and change management, real estate, and business advice. She has developed nearly seventy workshops related to astrological, metaphysical, and business themes. Alice also writes astrology articles for the Star IQ.com website. Contact Alice at DeVilleAA@aol.com for further information.

Phyllis Firak-Mitz, M.A.

Phyllis Firak-Mitz is a professional astrologer for over eighteen years experience. She has published, lectured, and made numerous radio and television appearances teaching about her favorite subject: the ways astrology helps us maximize our psychological well-being and spiritual growth.

Lisa Finander

Lisa Finander is an astrologer, tarot reader, and dreamworker. She writes, lectures, teaches, and conducts workshops on all these subjects. Lisa has a B.A. in psychology and symbolism from Metropolitan State University, St. Paul, Minnesota. She has studied storytelling, art threrapy, poetry, collage, and many other creative pursuits. She uses the symbols of astrology, dreamwork, and tarot to assist people in creating their lives consciously. She lives in Minnesota with her husband Brian and their three cats— Jampers, Sparky, and Toby.

Kenneth Johnson

Kenneth Johnson holds a degree in comparative religions with an emphasis in the study of mythology. He has been a practitioner of astrology since 1974, and is the coauthor of *Mythic Astrology: Archetypal Powers in the Horoscope* (Llewellyn 1993), as well as the author of five other books on myth, legend, and magical lore. He lives for part of each year on the southern edge of the Big Sur Coast, and also on the island of Kauai. He divides his time between writing, teaching, and traveling.

Penny Kelly

Penny Kelly has earned a degree in naturopathic medicine and is working toward a Ph.D. in nutrition. She and her husband Jim own a fifty-seven-acre farm with two vineyards, which they are in the process of restoring using organic farming methods. Penny is the author of the book *The Elves of Lily Hill Farm* (Llewellyn 1997).

Terry Lamb

Terry Lamb, M.A., C.A., is a counselor, instructor, and healer specializing in spiritually oriented growth through astrology and subtle-body healing. She is author of *Born To Be Together: Love Relationships*, and *Astrology and the Soul*. She is the director of the Astrological Certification Program, and is fourth-level certified by the National Council for Geocosmic Research (NCGR). She is NCGR's treasurer and serves on their board of examiners. She is published in magazines and websites, including her own (www.flash.net/~tlamb).

Carol LaVoie

Carol LaVoie is a full-time professional certified astrologer, NCGR Level IV, with over twenty-two years of astrological expertise. At the Astrological Institute of Research Carol, offers her clients a full line of professional astrological services including natal & predictive charts, horary, electional, relationship and parent/child counseling, and chart rectification. Her approach to a session blends practicality with self-realization to offer clients direction, awareness and fulfillment. She writes for numerous astrology magazines, lectured to many organizations, is involved extensively with the media, and has a book on the way. She also works closely with the development and marketing of Air Software. Carol can be reached at: http://www.alphee.com

Harry MacCorrmack

Harry MacCormack is an adjunct assistant professor of theater arts (play writing, screen writing, and technical theatre), and owner/operator of Sunbow Farm, which is celebrating a quarter-century of organic farming.

Dorothy Oja

Dorothy Oja is a passionate career astrologer with thirty years of study and practice through MINDWORKS. She has served the astrological community in various positions. Most notably, she served four years as Chair of AFAN's Legal Information Committee. Her specialties include analysis/research of social and cultural trends, relationships, and electional astrology. Her interpretive relationship computer report, "Compatibility & Conflict," is available through Cosmic Patterns, Inc. Dorothy lectures, teaches, and writes.

Leeda Alleyn Pacotti

Leeda Alleyn Pacotti embarked on metaphysical self-studies in astrology and numerology at age fourteen, after a childhood of startling mystical experiences. After careers in antitrust law, international treaties, the humanities, and government management in legislation and budgeting, she now plies a gentle practice as a naturopathic physician, master herbalist, and certified nutritional counselor.

Sheri Ann Richerson

Sheri Ann Richerson has over seventeen years experience in newspaper, magazine, and creative writing styles. She is the editor for the on-line newsletter *S & J Bargain Bin Metaphysical Tidbits*, and also an on-line free-lance writer for *Beyond Infinity*, where she writes about herbs, aromatherapy, and astrology. She also writes for *Information Partners*, *Terra Viva Organics*, and is a contributing editor for Suite101.com. Sheri is a lifetime member of the International Thespian Society. Her favorite pastimes are riding her motorcycle, horseback riding, and gardening. She enjoys growing herbs and tropical plants the most, and lives in Huntington, Indiana.

Bruce Scofield

Bruce Scofield currently maintains a private practice as a full-time astrologer in Amherst, Massachusetts. He works with clients by telephone and mail. He has a masters degree in history, is the author of twelve books, and has researched the mysterious astrology of the Aztecs and Maya. His website, www.onereed.com, contains articles and information about his services.

Maria Kay Simms

Maria Kay Simms, author of *A Time for Magick* (Llewellyn 2001), is a Wiccan high priestess, credentialed as Elder Priestess by Covenant of the

Goddess. She has also authored several astrology books, including *Your Magical Child* (Llewellyn 1994). Maria has been an astrologer for twenty-seven years. She holds professional certification from National Council for Geocosmic Research (NCGR). and American Federation of Astrologers (AFA). She is currently the elected Chair of NCGR.

Kaye Shinker

Kaye Shinker teaches financial astrology at the Online College of Astrology (www.astrocollege.com). She serves on the National Council of Geocosmic Research (NCGR) board of examiners and is active in the Chicago and New Orleans chapters. A former teacher, she and her husband own race horses and travel around the U.S. in a RV.

Kathleen Spitzer

Kathleen Spitzer is an accomplished astrologer and tarot reader. She teaches, consults, and writes about the planets and the Moon, contributing articles to various magazines. She gardens, cooks, and cuts her hair by the Moon, which hangs in the clear sky over the seacoast of New Hampshire.

Lynne Sturtevant

Lynne Sturtevant has had a life-long fascination with ancient cultures, mystery cults, myths, fairy tales, and folk traditions. She is a freelance writer who lives in Arlington, Virginia, with her husband and pets.

Valerie Vaughan

Valerie Vaughan is a professional science research librarian and certified astrologer Level IV at the National Council of Geocosmic Research. She has published numerous books and articles on the scientific basis of astrology and the astrological roots of science.

Christopher Warnock, Esq.

Christopher Warnock practices as an attorney and traditional astrologer in Washington, D.C. He received an M.A. (Hons.) concentrating in Renaissance history from the University of St. Andrews (Scotland) and a J.D. from the University of Michigan. He has published in the *Horary Practitioner*, *Pathways,* and the *Mountain Astrologer*. His Renaissance astrology website is located at http://www.renaissanceastrology.com.